Africa since 1800

Africa since 1800

ROLAND OLIVER
ANTHONY ATMORE

Third edition

CAMBRIDGE UNIVERSITY PRESS

CAMBRIDGE
LONDON   NEW YORK   NEW ROCHELLE
MELBOURNE   SYDNEY

Published by the Press Syndicate of the University of Cambridge
The Pitt Building, Trumpington Street, Cambridge CB2 1RP
32 East 57th Street, New York, NY 10022, USA
296 Beaconsfield Parade, Middle Park, Melbourne 3206, Australia

First published 1967
Reprinted 1969
Second edition 1972
Reprinted with corrections 1974
First paperback edition 1977
Third edition 1981

Printed in the United States of America

Phototypeset in V.I.P. Plantin by
Western Printing Services Ltd, Bristol
Printed and bound by Vail-Ballou Press, Inc.
Binghamton, New York

British Library cataloguing in publication data

Oliver, Roland
Africa since 1800. – 3rd ed.
1. Africa – History
I. Title   II. Atmore, Anthony
960'.2   DT20   80-49957

ISBN 0 521 23485 9 hard covers
ISBN 0 521 29975 6 paperback

(2nd edition ISBN 0 521 08552 5 hard covers
                ISBN 0 521 29240 9 paperback)

Contents

Contents

List of maps

Preface to the third edition

This third edition of *Africa since 1800* has been prepared to coincide with the publication of our new book, *The African Middle Ages 1400–1800*. *Africa in the the Iron Age*, by Roland Oliver and Brian Fagan, appeared in 1975, so that the trilogy originally proposed by Philip Harris when he was at the Cambridge University Press is now complete.

This edition carries the story to April 1979. In fact, as we write, the news bulletins are reporting the occupation of Kampala by Tanzanian and free Ugandan forces, while the elections intended to produce the first black majority government in Zimbabwe (Rhodesia) are due to start in two days' time. As we remarked in the preface to the second edition, Africa is at present passing through a period of very rapid change, which makes the interpretation of recent events exceptionally difficult. Nevertheless, the situation in the continent as a whole seems more stable than in 1971. Despite sudden and radical changes of government in several countries, the frontiers of Africa have still held firm. And there have been some significant changes from military to civilian rule, as well as others in the reverse direction. While the level of foreign intervention in Africa has grown, it has been demonstrated by several African countries that they retain the power to change their allies in the world outside. All this gives some ground for confidence that the perspective in which we have examined the African past may hold its general validity for some time to come.

In this third edition Chapters 21, 23 and 24 are completely new, while Chapters 19, 20 and 22 have been fundamentally revised. Elsewhere, we have taken this opportunity to modernise the forms of African country- and place-names, so that in general colonial forms are used only in relation to the colonial period. We have attempted not only to present a critical and chronological treatment of the post-independence period, but also to relate it firmly to the unfolding historical processes which have preceded it and to break it down into fairly distinctive periods. Finally, although scholarly publication on African history has grown significantly during this past eight years, we have drastically abbreviated our Suggestions for Further Reading, so as to adapt them to the needs of students rather than teachers. Those who require more detailed information can now consult the bibliographical sections of the *Cambridge History of Africa*, the relevant volumes of which should be available within a short time after the publication of this edition.

Roland Oliver
Anthony Atmore

1 Africa north of the equator

THE SAHARA AND ISLAM: THE BONDS UNIFYING NORTHERN
AFRICA

The geography of the northern half of Africa is dominated by the
Sahara desert. Throughout its vast area, 2,800 kilometres from north
to south and nearly 8,000 from east to west, rainfall is less than 13
centimetres a year. Except round a few oases, where underground
supplies of water reach the surface, the only people living there until
modern times have been nomadic herdsmen. Only in the last few
years have oil and natural-gas fields been found under the desert.
Nomads have become technicians and workers, living in the oil towns
which draw their essential water supplies from far underground by
deeply bored artesian wells. To the north of the desert lies the temper-
ate Mediterranean coastland, its rainfall concentrated mostly between
January and March. Southward are the tropics, the land of the summer rains. Racially as well as geographically, the Sahara marks a
frontier. In the desert and north of it live Berbers and Arabs,
fair-skinned peoples of Caucasian stock. South of the desert is the
'land of the blacks' – to the Greeks 'Ethiopia', to the Berbers 'Akal
n'Iguinawen' (Guinea), to the Arabs 'Bilad as-Sudan'.

The Sahara, therefore, has been a barrier against large-scale migrations. But it has not stopped the movement of small numbers of men
carrying their ideas and skills from one side to the other. The desert
has always been a formidable obstacle to human communications, but
for two thousand years at least, since the introduction of the horse and
the camel made travel easier, men have persevered in overcoming its
difficulties. Before the days of the motor-car and the aeroplane it took
two months or more to cross. Nevertheless people did cross it, not
merely in the course of isolated journeys of exploration, but regularly,
year after year, in the course of trade, education and pilgrimage. Long
before any sailing-ship from Europe reached the Atlantic coast of
West Africa, the Sudanic lands immediately to the south of the desert
were in touch with the lands to the north. Between the eleventh
century and the sixteenth, at least the townsfolk of the Sudanic
countries began to be Muslims, like the Arabs and Berbers to the
north. Their learned and pious men studied Arabic, the language of

the Koran, the Holy Book of Islam, and made the pilgrimage to the holy cities of Mecca and Medina. Above all, the merchant caravans kept touch with developments in the outside world. The rulers and the rich men on both sides of the desert worshipped the One God, read the same books, shared the same luxuries, discussed the same things.

It is debatable just where the southern frontier of northern Africa lay at different times in its past history. Until the twelfth and thirteenth centuries it probably included little more than the open grasslands, forming a belt 500 or 600 kilometres wide to the south of the desert margin, from the Senegal to Lake Chad, and eastward through Darfur and Kordofan to the Ethiopian highlands. Throughout this region beasts of burden could circulate, and troops of armed horsemen could control and levy tribute upon the populations of quite large states. To the south again lay the woodland belt, thickening progressively into dense equatorial rain-forest. Here, because of tsetse-fly in the woodlands and lack of fodder in the forest, all goods had to be carried by porters, and soldiers fought on foot. Markets and states were smaller, and there were no towns where Islamic religion and learning could gain a foothold. Nevertheless, by the fourteenth and fifteenth centuries at least, some northern influences were beginning to penetrate even these southern lands. When the Portuguese discovered the West African coast they found that the trading frontier of the Sudanic kingdoms had already reached the sea. During the three following centuries the European traders, operating from the Atlantic coastline, pushed the economic frontier northwards again, but only by a matter of 300 to 500 kilometres. By 1800 there was still far more of West Africa south of the Sahara which looked northwards for its contacts with the outside world than southwards to the Atlantic coast and the trade of Europe. And, of course, through the whole vast region to the east of Lake Chad there remained no other source of outside contacts but the northern one. The civilisation of the Sudanic belt exercised some influence as far south as the equatorial forests and the Nile swamps.

At the beginning of our period, therefore, the whole of Africa north of the equator can be considered together. All this part of the continent was in some sense within the range of Muslim civilisation. All but a fraction of it looked northwards and eastwards for its outside contacts, and in this it differed from most of the southern part of the continent.

2

1   Northern Africa: geographical features and vegetation

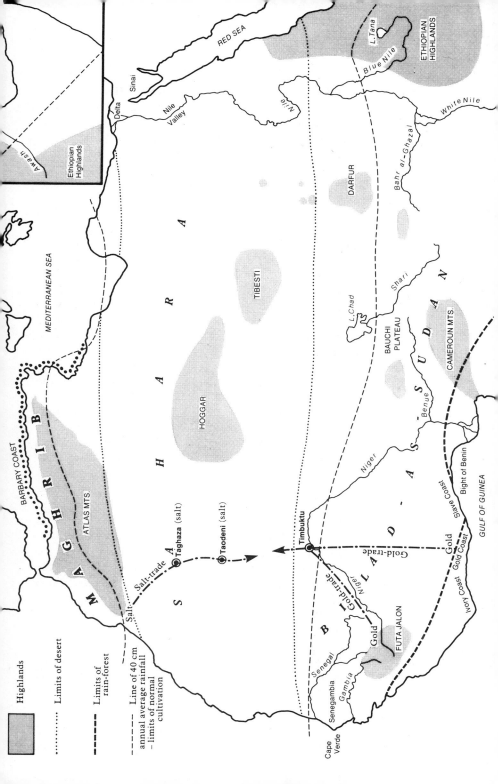

Highlands

•••••••• Limits of desert

▬ ▬ ▬ Limits of rain-forest

– – – – – Line of 40 cm annual average rainfall
– limits of normal cultivation

MEDITERRANEAN SEA

BARBARY COAST

ATLAS MTS.

M A G H R I B

RED SEA

Sinai

Delta

Nile Valley

Nile

Blue Nile

L. Tana

ETHIOPIAN HIGHLANDS

White Nile

Bahr al–Ghazal

DARFUR

S A H A R A

TIBESTI

HOGGAR

Shari

L. Chad

BAUCHI PLATEAU

Benue

CAMEROUN MTS.

S U D A N

Salt-trade

Taghaza (salt)

Taodeni (salt)

Timbuktu

Gold-trade

Gold-trade

Gold

Gold

Niger

Niger

B I L A D – A S –

FUTA JALON

Senegal

Gambia

Senegambia

Cape Verde

GULF OF GUINEA

Bight of Benin

Slave Coast

Gold Coast

Ivory Coast

Gold

Aswan

Ethiopian Highlands

COUNTRIES OF THE MEDITERRANEAN COAST

By the end of the eighteenth century men in the Muslim world as a whole had lost much of the energy and sense of purpose that had driven them to produce such a brilliant culture in the early centuries of Islam. They had failed to keep abreast of the new inventions and techniques being discovered in western Europe, particularly in military affairs and transport (such as the improvements made to sailing-ships). This failure to make progress affected all parts of Africa considered in this chapter in one way or another. It applied in particular to the lands north of the Sahara from Egypt in the east to Mauritania in the west. All these countries except Morocco had formed since the sixteenth century a part of the Turkish Ottoman empire (so-called after Othman, the founder of the ruling dynasty), with its capital at Istanbul. (Istanbul had earlier been called Byzantium when it was the capital of the eastern Roman empire.) By the eighteenth century Ottoman power had declined considerably from the peak reached two centuries earlier. Provincial rulers now acted almost independently of the Sultan at Istanbul. ('Sultan' is an Arabic word for the secular authority of a ruler. There were many sultanates in the Muslim world; the Ottoman was the greatest.)

Egypt at this time was ruled by the *amirs* (commanders) of the *mamluks*. These were slaves who had been captured as boys from the lands on the fringes of the Muslim world, from the Christian lands around the Caucasus. Unlike slaves in most other societies, however, they enjoyed a highly privileged position. They were given a special education as Muslims and as cavalry soldiers. At the end of their military service they were freed, and could reach the highest positions as amirs in the Ottoman military and civil service in Egypt. These amirs themselves recruited fresh slave troops to form their own armed supporters, and so, generation after generation, new mamluks were brought to Egypt. They had governed the country since 1260, and the Ottoman conquest in 1517 had done little to reduce their power. To the peasant millions of Egypt who toiled and were taxed, Mamluk rule was a harsh one. But it supported a leisured and educated class which made Cairo, at least, one of the greatest centres of luxury and learning in the whole of the Muslim world.

West of Egypt, the countries of Tripoli, Tunis, Algeria and Morocco were known to the Arabs collectively as *al-Maghrib* (the West). Here, in contrast with Egypt, the authority of governments rarely extended far beyond the main cities. In the hinterland of all these countries lived fierce nomadic tribes, both Berbers and bedouin

(Arabic *bedawi*, tent-dwellers) Arabs. These could only be rather loosely controlled by playing off one against another. In Tripoli the Ottoman government had been represented since 1711 by the local Karamanli family, which had concentrated its efforts mainly on developing the trans-Saharan trade from Bornu and the Hausa states. By this route came a steady supply of Negro slaves, who were distributed by the merchants of Tripoli to Istanbul, Damascus, Cairo and all over the western part of the Muslim world. Tripoli was likewise a distributing centre for the splendid leatherwork of the Hausa cities, already well known in western Europe as 'Morocco', and for the kola-nuts brought by the Hausa merchants all the way from the Asante forests. These were one of the few stimulants permitted by Islam, and were served as a luxury throughout northern Africa.

Tripoli, however, had no monopoly of the trans-Saharan trade. Perhaps the greatest centre of the desert trade was at the oasis of Ghadames, where Tunisia, Algeria and Libya now meet. The town stood where caravan routes from the central and the western Sudan converged, and Ghadames merchants were well known in Hausaland and Timbuktu alike. From Ghadames some of the Sudan trade was carried to Tunis and Algiers. These were busy ports from which merchants could more easily reach the markets of western Europe than from Tripoli. The *beys* (rulers) of Tunis had been drawn since 1705 from the local Hussainid family, whose armed forces protected a large settled population from the attacks of the nomadic Berbers of the eastern Atlas. These peasant farmers of the Tunisian plain were some of the greatest wheat-producers of the whole Mediterranean area. In the coastal towns a sophisticated middle class of merchants and administrators, enjoying a long tradition of Islamic civilisation and learning, ran a more orderly system of government than was possible in any other Maghrib country.

The Ottoman rulers of Algiers were known as the *deys*. Unlike the rulership of Tunis, this office had not fallen into the hands of a single family, to be passed down from father to son. It was filled on the death of the reigning dey by election from among a group of merchants and soldiers who were the most influential men in the city. The merchants, called *corsairs* by Europeans (from an Italian word meaning to chase), traded by sea with the European countries. Occasionally they committed acts of piracy against European shipping, for which they became famous. During the seventeenth century Algiers had been one of the richest and most attractive cities of the Mediterranean. Dr Shaw, an English traveller early in the eighteenth century, commented favourably on the surroundings of the city:

The hills and vallies round about Algiers are all over beautified with gardens and country-seats, whither the inhabitants of better fashion retire, during the heats of the summer season. They are little white houses, shaded with a variety of fruit-trees and ever-greens; which, besides the shade and retirement, afford a gay and delightful prospect towards the sea. The gardens are all of them well stocked with melons, fruit, and pot-herbs of all kinds. The natives of Algiers live extremely happy, for though the government is despotic it is not so in reality.[1]

Even at the time of its surrender to the French in 1830, it was described as 'perhaps the best regulated city in the world'. The French conquerors found that the majority of the Algerines were better educated than the majority of the local Frenchmen. This was after half a century of grave political disorders due to revolts among the Arab and Berber tribes who roamed over the high plateaux of the interior behind the coastal plains. These tribes were led by *marabouts*, the Muslim holy men, and they carried their attacks to the very outskirts of the cities on the Mediterranean shore.

In Morocco the extent of territory paying tribute into the sultan's treasury had greatly declined since the late sixteenth and early seventeenth centuries. Then, for a few years, the kingdom had stretched right across the desert to Timbuktu. Increasingly, as in Algeria, tribal groups from the high Atlas and the desert fringes penetrated the settled areas and extorted tribute from the peasants of the plains. The inefficient armies of the sultan could do little to prevent them. Nevertheless Morocco was still the terminus of a considerable trade to the south. Morocco continued to control the production of most of the salt consumed in the western Sudan, and it was the need for salt which kept the gold of the upper Senegal–Niger region flowing northwards across the desert rather than westwards to the Atlantic, where the French at St Louis, on the mouth of the Senegal river, were so anxious to receive it. (The exchange of gold and salt had been a major item of trade since the early Middle Ages.) Slaves from Timbuktu still went northwards to Morocco in great numbers. Despite the direct sea routes, a great many European manufactures, especially English cotton goods, were distributed over West Africa by Moroccan merchants who bought them at the port of Mogador. Commercially and culturally, if not politically, Mauritania belonged to Morocco. Arabic-speaking Moors lived all over the western edge of the Sahara as far south as the banks of the Senegal. Their holy men practised the characteristic Maghribi forms of the *marabouts*, becoming followers of

---

[1] T. Shaw, *Travels and Observations Relating to the Several Parts of Barbary and the Levant* (Oxford, 1738), p. 71.

such Muslim religious orders as the Ramaniyya, which was founded in 1770 in Kabylia (Algeria), and the Tijaniyya. This was established in 1781 by Sidi Ahmad Tijani at Ain Mahdi, near Laghouat on the edge of the desert in southern Algeria. Tijani's teaching was accepted by the great Moroccan university at Fez, and his order prospered in Mauritania, and among the Tuareg tribesmen of the central Sahara.

STATES OF THE SUDAN REGION

Most of the states to the south of the Sahara were affected in some degree by the stagnation of the Islamic world as a whole. Generally there was less security for traders and pilgrims than there had been, and, in consequence, less wealth, less learning and less religion. Among the states most affected was Ethiopia, which, though Christian in religion, lay close to the Arabian heartlands of Islam and suffered severely from the decline in Red Sea trade. Ethiopia was still at the end of the eighteenth century disturbed on its southern frontier by the invasions of pagan Galla (Oromo) which had been going on since the early sixteenth century. The Galla were a people whose language and origins were similar to the Somalis. The capital of Ethiopia had been fixed, in the seventeenth century, at Gondar, but this attempt at centralisation had not been successful. When emperors moved about their whole kingdom, they could keep an eye on what was going on. But afterwards, the authority of the monarch was acknowledged only locally around Gondar. Governors of the outlying provinces were able to rule independently of his control. Since the expulsion of the Jesuit missionaries in 1632, virtually the only foreigners to be permitted entry had been the handful of skilled artisans from eastern Europe who were always employed about the court. The country had turned in upon itself, and the result had been nearly ruinous. Jesus II (1730–55) was the last of the eighteenth-century emperors to exercise any real authority. After that, rival emperors became a regular feature; and by the early nineteenth century one of them had fallen into such abject poverty that, when he died, there was not enough money in the treasury to pay for a coffin.

West of Ethiopia lay the Funj sultanate, with its capital at Sennar on the Blue Nile, which during the sixteenth and seventeenth centuries had been a considerable centre of trade and learning. When the Scotsman James Bruce, who wrote a marvellous description of his dangerous travels in Ethiopia, passed through the country on his way down the Blue Nile in 1770, there was still a standing army of 1,800 horse and 14,000 infantry. The sultans had by then lost control of

7

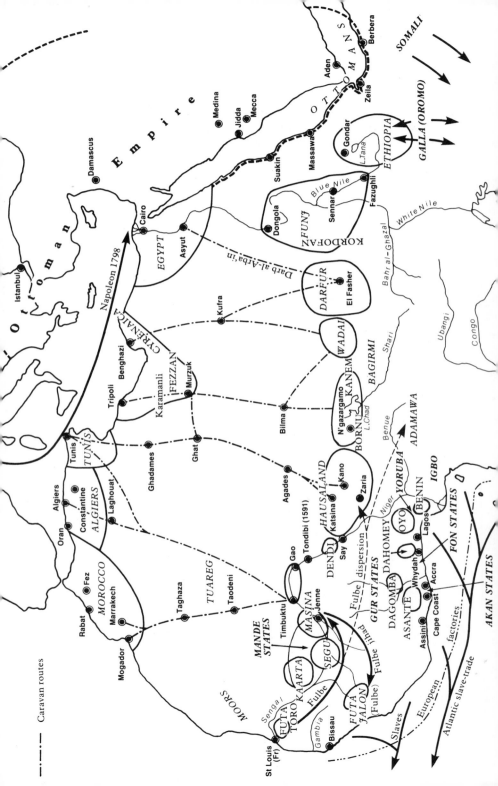

Caravan routes

Istanbul

O t t o m a n   E m p i r e

Damascus

Medina
Jidda
Mecca

Cairo
EGYPT
Asyut

Napoleon 1798

Suakin
Massawa

Aden
Zeila
Berbera

SOMALI

Gondar
L.Tana
ETHIOPIA

GALLA (OROMO)

Blue Nile
Sennar
Dongola
FUNJ
KORDOFAN
Fazughli
White Nile

Darb al-Arba'in

DARFUR
El Fasher
Kufra

Bahr al-Ghazal

Ubangi
Congo

CYRENAICA

Benghazi
FEZZAN
Tripoli
Murzuk

Karamanli

WADAI
KANEM
BAGIRMI
Shari

Tunis
TUNIS

Bilma

N'gazargamo
L.Chad
BORNU

Benue
ADAMAWA

Ghadames
Ghat

Agades

HAUSALAND
Kano
Katsina
Zaria

Algiers
Oran
Constantine
ALGIERS
Laghouat

Tondibi (1591)
Gao
Say
DENDI

Niger
YORUBA
OYO
BENIN
IGBO

Fulbe dispersion

Fez
MOROCCO
Rabat
Marrakech

Taghaza
TUAREG
Taodeni

Timbuktu
MASINA
Jenne
MANDE
STATES

GUR STATES
DAHOMEY
DAGOMBA
ASANTE
FON STATES

Lagos
Whydah
Accra
Cape Coast
Assini

AKAN STATES

Mogador

MOORS

KAARTA
SEGU

Fulbe

FUTA
JALON
(Fulbe)

factories

Senegal
FUTA
TORO
Fulbe
Gambia
Bissau
St Louis
(Fr)

Fulbe jihad

Fulbe (Fulbe)

European
Atlantic slave-trade
Slaves

Nubia and of Kordofan, and the rich trade in ivory, which had formerly been exchanged for Indian cottons at Jidda, on the Arabian side of the Red Sea, had now shrunk to a trickle. Bruce was not impressed by what he saw there. 'War and treason', he wrote, 'appear to be the only occupations of this horrid people, whom Heaven has separated by almost impassable deserts from the rest of mankind.'[2]

More prosperous than the Funj sultanate were now those of Darfur and Wadai, one on each side of the modern frontier between the Sudan Republic and Tchad. Though nominally Muslim, it is clear from the early nineteenth-century accounts of Muhammad al-Tunisi, one of the *ulama*, or religious dignitaries, of Cairo and a lecturer in the French medical school there, that here, as in many states of the western Sudan, the ancient pagan ideas of divine kingship still persisted. Al-Tunisi describes an annual ceremony of re-covering the royal drums, when a boy and a girl were sacrificed; and he also describes the sultans taking part in almost Pharaonic rituals of seed-time and harvest:

At the beginning of the planting season the Sultan rides out in great pomp, escorted by more than a hundred young women, by his slave boys and by a troop of flute-players. When he reaches the open fields, he dismounts from his horse, takes different kinds of seeds, and sows them, while a slave hoes the ground.[3]

The wealth of these two states consisted of slaves raided by their armies of horsemen from among the defenceless pagan tribes to the south, and also in the rich copper deposits of Hofrat an-Nahas accessible from both of them. The main trade route for the region was the *Darb al-Arba'in* (the Forty Days' Road) leading due northwards to reach the Nile at Asyut.

The ancient empire of Kanem–Bornu, with its wide territories to the east and west of Lake Chad, was probably, at the end of the eighteenth century, the most civilised of the Sudanic states. It was no longer as powerful as it had been at two earlier periods of its history; but its rulers were still at least pious and literate Muslims, and justice was administered according to Islamic law. The capital at this time was the brick-built town of N'gazargamo, some 95 kilometres west of Lake Chad, the ruins of which can still be seen, and which cover a circular area about 3 kilometres in diameter. Here the *mais* (kings) lived a dignified but secluded existence supported by the tribute

---

[2] James Bruce, *Travels to Discover the Source of the Blue Nile, 1768–1773* (London, 1790), vol. 4, p. 437.
[3] Muhammad bin 'Umar al-Tunisi, *Voyage au Ouadây*, tr. Dr Perron (Paris, 1851), p. 159.

9

2 Northern Africa in 1800

collected for them by their provincial governors from the peasantry of a kingdom measuring perhaps 1,000 by 500 kilometres.

Commercially, however, the most active part of the central Sudan was not Bornu but the city states of Hausaland lying along its western flank. Though never politically united, these Hausa cities were unique in the Sudan in possessing manufacturing industries on a really important scale. Weaving, dyeing, leatherwork, glass-making, smithing and metalwork of every description were carried out. At the end of the eighteenth century Katsina was still the leading city: soon it was to be Kano, already second, with Zaria a close third. It was from these cities rather than from N'gazargamo that the great caravan routes radiated out across the Sahara to Tripoli and Ghadames and on to Tunis. Bornu with its cavalry armies supplied most of the slaves exported northwards. The manufactures were from Hausaland and their distribution covered the whole of northern Africa.

South of the Sahara from the Maghrib, the powerful empires of the western Sudan of medieval times had broken up by the end of the eighteenth century into many weak kingdoms. (Medieval times or the Middle Ages is the period in Africa from roughly the fourteenth to the eighteenth century.) The great empire of the Songhay Askias, which had stretched in the sixteenth century from the upper Senegal to the frontiers of modern Nigeria, had come to an end with the Moroccan invasion of 1591. At the battle of Tondibi the Moroccans used fire-arms for the first time against Sudanese cavalry and foot-soldiers armed only with bows and spears. The conquerors settled down, and their descendants formed a new ruling class, the *arma* (shooters, gunmen), which soon became independent of the sultan of Morocco, the soldiers electing their own *pashas* at Timbuktu and their *kaids* in the garrison towns around the loop of the Niger bend from Jenne to Gao.

After the Moroccan conquest what remained of the ruling class of Songhay retreated down the Niger and set up an independent government in the southerly province of Dendi. Upstream from Jenne, on the western side of the Niger bend, the Mande subjects of the Songhay empire broke up into an immense number of little village states, although here and there in Mandeland families and clans of pagan war-lords, getting fire-arms in exchange for slaves, set up some larger kingdoms like those of Segu and Kaarta. However, the really vital region of the western Sudan during the seventeenth and eighteenth centuries was the far west. Here, in Futa Toro on the south bank of the lower Senegal, there had grown up in the medieval period an extraordinarily virile people of mixed Berber and Negro descent, known as the Fulbe (French: *Peul*; Hausa: *Fulani*). Unlike any other

10

negroid people of the western Sudan, the Fulbe were mainly specialised pastoralists. The constant need to find fresh grazing grounds for
their cattle caused many of them to leave their homelands. As early as
the fifteenth century they were spread out in small groups all over the
savanna belt of West Africa as far to the east as Hausaland. Until the
eighteenth century these scattered Fulbe were mostly pagan. However, those Fulbe who remained in their Futa Toro homelands were
converted to Islam by *marabouts* from Mauritania in the sixteenth and
seventeenth centuries and formed Muslim brotherhoods, full of zeal
for their new faith. One Fulbe clan, the Torodbe, became the
missionary and clerical leaders of the whole of the Fulbe people.
Wherever Fulbe were dispersed, there Torodbe preachers were to be
found, and with them the belief in conversion by jihad, or holy war. It
was, of course, but a short step from religious revival to political
revolution. The two bases of the Fulbe movement were Futa Toro and
Masina, a Fulbe-led state south-west of Timbuktu, once tributary to
Songhay, which became independent after the Moorish conquest.
From Masina in the eighteenth century Torodbe missionaries carried
the jihad to Futa Jallon, the mountain country on the borders of
Guinea and Sierra Leone, and eastwards across the Niger bend to Say.
From this background of missionary zeal and holy war, the great
Fulbe jihad of the early nineteenth century arose.

It is often said that the seventeenth and eighteenth centuries were a
period of decline in the western Sudan, and certainly this was a time of
great political disorder. But, thanks to the Torodbe and other clans of
religious leaders, much of the learning of the medieval Sudan was kept
alive. It is possible that by the end of the eighteenth century both
Islam and Arabic education were more widely spread than they had
been during the great days of the medieval empires. Despite the
political disorders, trade continued to flow. There seems to have been
a breakdown in communications between the western and the central
Sudan. This was because, after the defeat of Songhay, no other power
was able to control the fierce Tuareg nomads living to the north and
east of the Niger bend. But the routes running north-west from
Timbuktu and north from the Senegal remained open and active until
well into the nineteenth century – more active by far than the routes
from Timbuktu westwards to the Atlantic coast.

STATES OF THE WOODLAND AND THE FOREST

It was among the states of the woodland and forest zones to the south
of the savanna belt that the coming of the Europeans and the Atlantic   11

trade had made by the eighteenth century a crucial change. In origin these states were influenced by the kingdoms to the north of them. In all probability the Akan states of modern Ghana and the Ivory Coast were inspired by the Mande kingdoms in the region west of the Niger bend, while the states of the Edo- and Yoruba-speakers in southern Nigeria, the Fon-speakers of Dahomey (now Bénin), and of the Gur-speakers of northern Ghana, Upper Volta and western Niger, were all in some sense the offspring of pre-Islamic kingdoms in the Hausa region. These woodland and forest states were more backward than the Muslim kingdoms to the north. The dense tropical vegetation made them difficult to reach, and the tsetse-fly prevented the use of cattle and horses. They were rather isolated from outside influences until they were caught up in the Atlantic slave-trade. As Samuel Johnson, the historian of the Yorubas, pointed out:

It should be remembered that light and civilisation with the Yorubas came from the north . . . The centre of light and activity, of large populations and industry, was therefore in the interior, whilst the coast tribes were scanty in number, ignorant and degraded, not only from their distance from the centre of light, but also (later) through their demoralising intercourse with Europeans and the slave trade.[4]

It was the same in Ghana and the Ivory Coast as it was in Nigeria. The most important of the woodland and forest states had at first been those on the northern side. The smallest and the most backward, populated only by fishermen and salt-makers, had been the little states on the coast.

The Atlantic slave-trade, which was begun by the Portuguese early in the sixteenth century, when a trickle of Africans were shipped across the ocean to work in the Spanish and Portuguese colonies in South America and on the islands of the Caribbean, had developed by the end of the seventeenth century into a steady flood. Most of the European maritime countries took part in it, especially Britain and France. The brisk competition for slaves among the European powers meant that the states on and near the coast had easy access to firearms, which they exchanged for slaves from the Europeans. In the eighteenth century a typical payment for 'a man and a girl' was

> One roll tobacco, one string pipe coral,
> One gun, three cutlasses, one brass blunderbuss,
> Twenty-four linen handkerchiefs, five patches [of cloth],
> Three jugs rum, twelve pint mugs, one laced hat.[5]

[4] Samuel Johnson, *History of the Yorubas* (Lagos, 1921), p. 40.
[5] Logbook or journal of a slaving ship, cited in Basil Davidson, *Black Mother* (London, 1961), p. 95.

The fire-arms were used against the formerly more important states inland. Within the woodland and forest states there had been by the end of the eighteenth century a considerable change in the balance of power. The rising states were those based near the coast, especially Asante and Dahomey, which had grown by the use of fire-arms acquired through the Atlantic slave-trade. The most dramatic demonstration of this shift in power occurred in 1745 when the musketmen of Asante defeated the armoured cavalry of Dagomba, who in any earlier period would have chased them mercilessly out of any open country they had dared to enter. This process, begun in the seventeenth and eighteenth centuries, was to be carried much farther in the nineteenth.

THE ENCIRCLING POWER OF EUROPE

The only real colonial power operating in the northern half of Africa at the end of the eighteenth century was Ottoman Turkey. Its dependencies in Egypt, Tripoli, Tunis and Algiers were, admittedly, almost 'self-governing', but they did at least contribute revenue to the sultans at Istanbul. The European powers trading with North and West Africa had, in contrast, nothing but a few footholds, in the shape of fortified trading factories scattered along the West African coast from St Louis on the Senegal to Whydah in Bénin. These forts, whether British, Danish, Dutch, French or Portuguese, were designed mainly to protect the operations of one group of European traders from the competition of another group. Few of the castles could have withstood a determined attack by the local Africans, and their governors had to be cautious in exercising jurisdiction outside the walls. They carried on their trade with the help of middlemen living in the coastal towns. Though they were exporting by the end of the century around 100,000 slaves a year from West Africa alone, the Europeans seldom captured a single slave for themselves, and save for the French on the Senegal it was the rarest thing for any European to venture 20 kilometres inland. Nor did there seem to be at any time in the eighteenth century the slightest likelihood of a change in the pattern of these relationships, which were satisfactory to the Europeans and the Africans alike. It is true that by the end of the century the slave-trade was under attack in one or two European countries. A judge in an English court had declared in 1772 that there was no such thing as slavery on English soil. And fifteen years later a group of philanthropists in England – men who were inspired by the religious revival started by John Wesley to improve the condition of the poor and down-trodden – bought a few 13 square miles of the Sierra Leone peninsula for the purpose of settling Negro slaves freed in England and across the Atlantic in Canada. From this tiny beginning, the result of the stirring of the consciences of a few distinguished men, truly 'a cloud no bigger than a man's hand', sprang the ever-growing flood of European interference in tropical Africa during the century to come. But nobody at the time could have foreseen this.

To contemporaries the change in the balance of power in the Mediterranean must have seemed much more impressive than any growth of European power in tropical Africa. To Britain, and therefore to France, India and the routes to India were already a matter of the most serious strategic importance. When these two powers were locked in combat at the end of the century, it seemed a natural move that Britain should forestall the French by seizing the Cape of Good Hope from the Dutch. That Napoleon should reply by occupying Egypt was surprising only in that it finally showed the weakness of the Ottoman empire in relation to European military might. The Mamluk armies surrendered to the French in a single battle fought near the Pyramids in 1798. The French were removed three years later only through the powerful assistance of the British. It was all very well for al-Jabarti, a citizen of Cairo, and an eye-witness of these events and the last of the traditional Muslim chroniclers of Egypt, to write:

The presence of the French in Cairo was intolerable . . . Muslims died of shame when they saw their wives and daughters walking the streets unveiled, and appearing to be the property of the French . . . It was bad enough for them to see the taverns that had been established in all the bazaars and even in several mosques . . . The scum of the population was doing well, because it benefited from the new freedom. But the *élite* and the middle class experienced all sorts of vexation.[6]

What had happened once could happen again. It was only surprising that it did not happen for another eighty years.

[6] *Chronique d'Egypte, 1798–1804*, ed. and tr. Gaston Wiet (Cairo, 1950), p. 45.

2 Africa south of the equator

The geography and climate of Africa south of the equator is much less simple than that of the northern half of the continent. Very briefly, however, high and rather dry steppe country runs south from the Ethiopian highlands through East Africa. It then crosses over towards the western side of the subcontinent, ending up in the Kalahari Desert and the dry lands of the Orange Free State and Botswana on one side of it, and of Namibia on the other. On the other hand, low-lying and distinctly humid country extends from Cameroun right across the northern half of the Congo basin to Lakes Tanganyika and Malawi. From there it continues down the Zambezi valley to the Indian Ocean and round through southern Mozambique into Natal. In general the steppe country is too dry for agriculture, whilst the dense forests of the humid region make farming difficult. The best conditions for human occupation are found in the borderlands between the two zones, and therefore in the very middle of the subcontinent. This is where the dense populations still are; and this is where political institutions first developed and where at the end of the eighteenth century they were most flourishing.

There is one particularly striking fact about the peoples who live in Africa south of the equator, which is that nearly all of them speak very closely related languages belonging to a family known as Bantu (from the common word *muntu*, a man; plural *bantu*, people). The exceptions to this rule, the people who speak languages which do not belong to the Bantu family, are all found in the dry zones of the north-east (parts of Kenya and Tanzania) and the south-west, where the practice of agriculture is difficult. It looks therefore as though the Bantu-speakers were the first agriculturalists in this part of Africa. From the study of language relationships it seems as though the 'cradle-land' from which they dispersed was the woodland region immediately to the north of the equatorial forest. Starting perhaps 2,500 years ago, the early Bantu spread southwards from this general area. There were four main regions where dense populations grew up and powerful states arose: the light woodlands south of the Congo rain-forest, 15 including Katanga (Shaba) itself; the interlacustrine lands (or lands between the East African lakes); the hilly region on either side of the lower Congo river; and the Zimbabwean plateau.

(1) *The Luba–Lunda states.* In the light woodland region extending for 800 to 1,000 kilometres to the south of the Congo forest – that is to say, in the southern half of the Congo basin, up to and including the Congo–Zambezi watershed – conditions were almost ideal for human occupation. Rainfall was adequate, but not excessive. There was excellent fishing in the northward-flowing tributaries of the Congo river system, and hunting in the strips of forest which lined the river-banks, with plenty of open country suitable for agriculture in between the streams. The rich mineral deposits of Katanga were being extensively exploited by the thirteenth and fourteenth centuries, and metal-working in iron and copper had even then reached an advanced stage. The earliest large states in this region would appear to have been those of the Luba peoples in the northern half of Katanga. By the end of the eighteenth century, however, the two most important kingdoms were those of the Lunda, farther to the west and south. These were the kingdom of the Mwata Yamvo, which occupied the whole south-western corner of the modern state of Zaïre, and the kingdom of the Mwata Kazembe, astride the Luapula river in southern Katanga. These great states, however, were but the centre of a whole cluster of smaller ones, which filled up most of southern Zaïre, the interior of Angola and north-western and north-eastern Zambia.

The rulers of the two great Lunda kingdoms and of several of the more important outlying states were kings who were regarded as divine. These were very like those in Darfur and Wadai, described in Chapter 1. The courts of these kings, and the rituals connected with them, provided the centres for larger and more progressive societies than would have been possible without them. The capitals of the Lunda kings, though not as permanent as West African towns, were considerable centres of government and trade. The palace population was large because the kings took hundreds of wives and concubines drawn from all the main family groups in the country. The court officials were numerous. So also were the skilled craftsmen – potters, smiths, weavers, basket-makers, brewers, wood-carvers, huntsmen and traders – the majority of whom congregated round the capital and lived off the tribute paid in foodstuffs by all the surrounding countryside. Describing such towns as late as 1906, the German explorer Leo Frobenius wrote:

When I penetrated into the region of the Kasai and the Sankuru I found villages still existing whose principal streets were lined on both sides, and for

3   Africa south of the equator: geographical features and vegetation. Parts of central Tanzania and around Lake Turkana in Kenya have less than 40 cm annual average rainfall

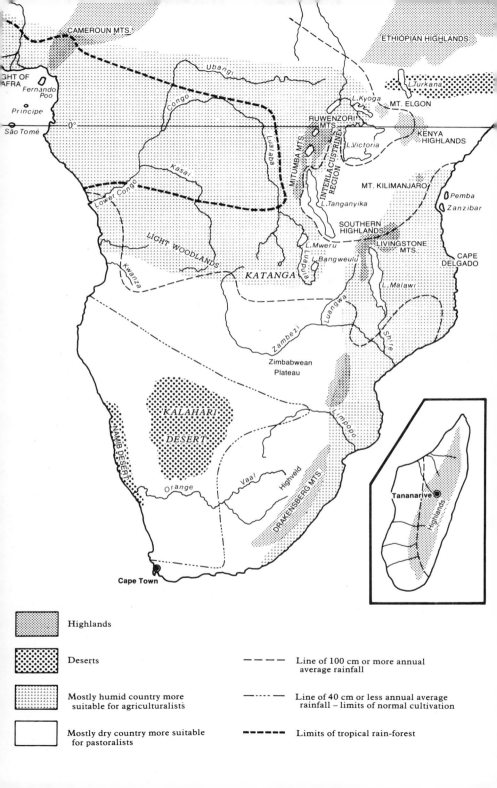

CAMEROUN MTS.
ETHIOPIAN HIGHLANDS
BIGHT OF BIAFRA
Fernando Poo
Príncipe
São Tomé
0°
Ubangi
Congo
L. Turkana
L. Kyoga
MT. ELGON
RUWENZORI MTS.
MITUMBA MTS.
L. Victoria
KENYA HIGHLANDS
Lualaba
Kasai
INTERLACUSTRINE REGION
L. Tanganyika
MT. KILIMANJARO
Pemba
Zanzibar
Lower Congo
LIGHT WOODLANDS
SOUTHERN HIGHLANDS
LIVINGSTONE MTS.
CAPE DELGADO
Kwanza
L. Mweru
Bangweulu
KATANGA
Luapula
L. Malawi
Luangwa
Shire
Zambezi
Zimbabwean Plateau
KALAHARI DESERT
Limpopo
NAMIB DESERT
Vaal
Orange
Highveld
DRAKENSBERG MTS.
Cape Town

Tananarive
Highlands

Highlands

Deserts

Mostly humid country more suitable for agriculturalists

Mostly dry country more suitable for pastoralists

– – – Line of 100 cm or more annual average rainfall

–·–·– Line of 40 cm or less annual average rainfall – limits of normal cultivation

▬ ▬ ▬ Limits of tropical rain-forest

miles on end, with four rows of palm-trees, and whose charmingly decorated houses were each of them a work of art. There was not a man who did not carry sumptuous weapons of iron or copper, with inlaid hilts and damascened blades. Everywhere there were velvets and silken stuffs. Every cup, every pipe, every spoon was a piece of artistry, fully worthy of comparison with the creations of Europe.[1]

(2) *The interlacustrine kingdoms.* 'Interlacustrine' means 'between the lakes' and is the region bordering upon the eastern edge of the great Congo forest and taking in all the country between Lake Albert, Lake Victoria and the northern part of Lake Tanganyika. This region today covers southern Uganda, north-west Tanzania, Rwanda, Burundi and adjacent parts of eastern Zaïre. All of it is pleasant, easy country to live in. The average rainfall is between 75 and 100 centimetres, and the rains are well distributed throughout the year. Not only has the population there grown by natural increase, but like all rich countries it has attracted waves of foreign conquerors. These came mostly from the Ethiopian borderlands and from the plains and swamps of the Nile and its tributaries in the southern Sudan. They were Nilotes and Paranilotes, physically and linguistically distinct from the Bantu. By the end of the eighteenth century six large neighbouring states had grown up here – Buganda, Bunyoro, Ankole, Karagwe, Rwanda and Burundi – which are shown on map 4. Though not as big as the great states of the Sudanic belt of the northern part of the continent, all of them probably had populations of half a million or more people. As with the pre-Islamic states of the Sudan, they were ruled by divine kings who governed through an elaborate hierarchy of court officials and provincial chiefs. As with the kingdoms of the Mwata Yamvo and the Mwata Kazembe, many smaller states clustered around these big ones, some of them paying tribute to one or other of the large kingdoms, but most in practice independent of all of them.

The first European travellers who came upon this region in the mid-nineteenth century felt that they were entering a new world. They had walked 1,200 or 1,300 kilometres from the east coast along tortuous footpaths never more than a few inches wide, through sparsely inhabited country where provisions were hard to come by and even drinking water was often a problem. Along most of their route every day's march had brought them into the territory of some new petty potentate with whom they had to negotiate permission to pass. And then suddenly they found themselves in a world of plenty and of order. Here a ruler's writ or authority could run for 150

[1] *Histoire de la civilisation africaine* (Paris, 1952), p. 15.

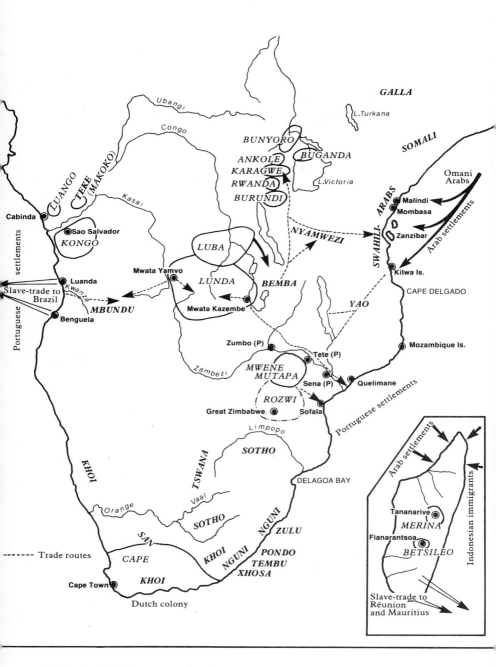

4 Africa south of the equator in 1800

kilometres from his capital. His messengers sped along wide, well-beaten roads to the provincial or district headquarters to which they were going. Speke and Grant in 1862 stayed with the 'ever-smiling' King Rumanika of Karagwe while runners were sent to announce their arrival to Kabaka Mutesa of Buganda. Once their passport was granted, they were accompanied for the rest of their journey by royal guides, and food and lodging were arranged at the end of each day's march.

(3) *The Kongo kingdom.* To the south of the estuary of the Congo river, in what is today northern Angola, lay the kingdom of Kongo, which, when discovered by the Portuguese at the very end of the fifteenth century, was at the height of its power. A sixteenth-century Roman Catholic priest described the authority of the Kongo monarchy in the following terms:

At the head of the Kongo kingdom is a king of kings who is the absolute lord of all his realm, and none may intervene in any of his affairs. He commands as he pleases. He is not subject to any law. The village chiefs have above all to take care to collect from their subjects the taxes which are due to the king, and which they each of them carry to the governor of their province. The governor presents himself twice in each year at the royal capital in order to pay in the tribute, and if the king is satisfied, he replies with the one word *wote*, which means 'you have done well'. In this case the governor esteems himself highly favoured and makes many clappings of his two hands. As a sign of his joy he throws himself on the ground, covering his body with dust. His servants do the same, and then take him on their shoulders, and go through all the city crying his praises. But if the king does not say this word *wote*, he retreats greatly discomfited, and another time he takes care to bring a larger tribute. The tribute is not fixed as to quantity: each brings as much as he can. But if the governor does not do better, the king addresses to him a strong reprimand, and takes away his post. Such a man then becomes as poor as the most miserable of all the blacks.[2]

By the end of the eighteenth century the kingdom was very weak compared to its previous magnificence. It had fallen apart into the provinces that had formerly owed allegiance to the king, who by then exercised little power even over the lands immediately surrounding his capital. The region as a whole was, however, a densely populated and even prosperous one. Inland from Kongo, on the north bank of Lake Malebo (Stanley Pool), there was the kingdom of the Teke, with its ruler who bore the title of Makoko. And to the north of the estuary, between the Teke and the sea, there were the kingdoms of the

---

[2] Vatican document, quoted in J. Cuvelier and L. Jadin, *L'ancien Congo d'après les archives romaines* (Brussels, 1954), pp. 33–4.

Loango coast, which had once paid tribute to Kongo, but had long since become independent. All this region was an exception to the general rule that the most important states were to be found in the interior of Bantu Africa, and the reason would seem to be largely geographical. To the west of the Congo forest, both north and south of the cataracts and falls of the lower Congo between its estuary and Lake Malebo, there is a belt of high grassland and light woodland. This really forms an extension of the geographical conditions of southern Zaïre. Possibly these kingdoms were founded by migrants from the east, who moved round the southern margins of the forest from Lubaland; but it is also possible that they had had connections with the states of West Africa from ancient times.

(4) *Mwene Mutapa*. The fourth and last region of Bantu Africa which had developed a dense population and a system of powerful states was the region of the Zimbabwean plateau and the neighbouring parts of the Zambezi valley and the lowlands of southern Mozambique. This was a region rich in gold and ivory, where at least from the fifteenth century onwards a series of Shona-speaking states had recognised the paramount authority of a great king called the Mwene Mutapa. This ruler had his capital on the southern edge of the Zambezi valley some one hundred kilometres north-east of modern Salisbury. When the Portuguese colonised the lower Zambezi valley from the late sixteenth century onwards, they gave protection to successive Mwene Mutapas who were their inland neighbours. Gradually the Mwene Mutapas became so dependent upon the Portuguese that outlying parts of their empire broke away and became independent. By the end of the eighteenth century, therefore, they were ruling only a small remnant of their former kingdom and this only with Portuguese support and protection. But other, formerly dependent, states were still in existence round about, including one, the Rozwi kingdom of the Changamires, which seems to have enjoyed considerable prosperity during the period of Portuguese trading contact. Although the medieval capital site of Great Zimbabwe lay within this state, it was no longer a place of any importance. The Rozwi capitals were built further to the west, in the region between Gwelo and Bulawayo, where ruins like those at Naletale and Dhlo-Dhlo have yielded objects datable to this period.

THE TRADE ROUTES OF BANTU AFRICA

With the exception of the lower Congo region, therefore, the most populous and politically advanced parts of Bantu Africa ran in a great crescent through the centre of the subcontinent. This belt ran from the interlacustrine region in the north through the southern Zaïre region to that of Zimbabwe and southern Mozambique. The most striking fact about these Bantu states was that, unlike their counterparts in the Sudanic belt of Africa, they were almost wholly cut off from the outside world. The great Bantu states completely lacked, until after the eighteenth century, the Islamic influence which was so important in the more powerful states of the Sudan. Trade links with the outside world were difficult to establish and slow to develop. So far as we know at present, the only trade route deep into any part of Bantu Africa during medieval times was up the Zambezi valley from the southern part of the east coast. Here the Arabs were trading cloth and beads for gold and ivory at least by the tenth century and possibly earlier. The Mwene Mutapa's state used this line of approach to the Indian Ocean. In the sixteenth century the Portuguese replaced the Arabs on the Zambezi, and henceforward this line of communication ran through their hands.

The more important part of the Portuguese contribution, however, was their opening of the Atlantic coast of Bantu Africa to sea-borne trade with Europe and South America. Their first venture in this direction was with the Kongo kingdom, where they made the Kongo kings their allies. They also supplied them with Christian missionaries and technical and military aid. In the course of a hundred years, however, their interests had shifted southwards to Luanda and Benguela, where they found it easier than in Kongo to obtain slaves, which were needed in ever-increasing numbers to work the sugar plantations of their colony of Brazil. The demand of the Portuguese for slaves was mainly supplied by the almost continuous wars which they fought against the Mbundu peoples of central Angola. They also sent African trading agents (*pombeiros*) to open commerce with the interior. The slave-trader James Barbot observed in 1700 that

These slaves have other slaves under them, sometimes a hundred, or a hundred and fifty, who carry the commodities on their heads up into the country. Sometimes these pombeiros stay out a whole year, and then bring back with them four, five, or six hundred slaves.[3]

In this way the Portuguese made indirect contact with the Lunda kingdom of Mwata Yamvo and its many satellites. By the end of the eighteenth century the main Lunda kingdoms and their related dynasties had acquired guns, cloth and other European luxuries, and

[3] In A. and J. Churchill, *Collections of Voyages and Travels* (London, 1732), vol. 5, p. 522.

their own industries had developed greatly by learning from European examples. Splendid axes and cutlasses were made by the Lunda smiths in the period following the European contact. Manioc (or cassava), the South American root-crop, was introduced by the Portuguese and rapidly became the staple food for the whole of the southern Zaïre region.

The important region which remained right out of touch with the outside world until late in the eighteenth century was the interlacustrine region. To the west of it lay the Congo forest; to the north lay the Nile swamps; to the east lay the Kenya highlands, inhabited mainly by nomadic and warlike pastoralists such as the Nandi and the Masai. The easiest line of approach, therefore, was from the south-east, but it was a long time before this was developed. It does not seem that the medieval Arab traders and settlers of the east coast had contact with any but the coastal peoples to the north of the Zambezi. Certainly the Portuguese, when they occupied this part of the coast during the sixteenth and seventeenth centuries, had no knowledge of any part of the interior that lay behind. It was in fact only when the Arabs of Oman (on the Persian Gulf) seized the northern part of the east coast from the Portuguese at the beginning of the eighteenth century that contacts with the interior began to develop; and even then the main agents of this contact appear to have been the Nyamwezi people, who inhabit most of the western part of modern Tanzania and who found their way down to the coast with ivory. Throughout the late eighteenth and early nineteenth centuries it was the Nyamwezi who organised and operated most of the carrying trade in East Africa. Their caravans covered the whole region from Katanga to the east coast, marching great distances with heavy loads and usually with very little to eat. The early travellers reported how the Nyamwezi boys used to prepare themselves for this way of life by carrying small tusks on their shoulders as they went about the villages. Traditional history relates that it was in the late eighteenth century that the first consignment of plates, cups, saucers, knives and cotton goods reached the kingdom of Buganda, at the heart of the interlacustrine region. From this time onwards the traditions tell of a steadily growing trade passing to the south of Lake Victoria and through the Nyamwezi country to the Zanzibar coast.

SOUTH AFRICA: BANTU AND BOER

Another part of Bantu Africa which had almost no contact with the outside world until late in the eighteenth century was the region south

23

of the Limpopo in what is now the Republic of South Africa. Two main groups of Bantu peoples lived here – the Sotho-Tswana (Basotho-Bechuana) on the highveld (*veld*, Dutch: plateau) to the west of the Drakensberg mountains, and the Nguni peoples (Zulu, Pondo, Tembu, Xhosa) in the fertile and well-watered coastal lowlands of Natal and the Transkei. Perhaps just because these Sotho and Nguni peoples were isolated from outside influence or interference, they did not create any large centralised states. Throughout most of Africa, powerful kingdoms developed in response to the threat of invasion, the desire to control trade routes, or as the result of the conquest of one group by another. None of these forces operated to any large extent in southern Africa until the beginning of the nineteenth century. Until then these peoples remained organised under a large number of ruling clans or families, who frequently quarrelled amongst themselves. In spite of this political instability, the South African Bantu lived fairly prosperously, especially after the introduction of maize, another South American food-crop, which spread there from the Portuguese trading stations in southern Mozambique. Such European visitors as passed through the land in the sixteenth and seventeenth centuries – mostly survivors of shipwrecks – commented on the large herds of sleek cattle. They noticed, however, that iron tools remained scarce except in the neighbourhood of Delagoa Bay. The governor of the Cape, Simon van der Stel, wrote a despatch to his superiors in Holland in 1689, telling them of the journey of the crew of a wrecked vessel, the *Stavenisse*. The country of the 'Magossebe' – Ama-Xhosa – is described as follows:

Their riches consist in cattle and assagais, also copper and iron. The country is exceedingly fertile and incredibly populous, and full of cattle, whence it is that lions and other ravenous animals are not very apt to attack men, as they find enough tame cattle to devour. They preserve their corn in cavities under ground, where it keeps good and free from weavels for years.

In their intercourse with each other they are very civil, polite and talkative, saluting each other, whether young or old, male or female, whenever they meet; asking whence they come, and whither they are going, what is their news; and whether they have learned any new songs or dances. The kings are much respected and beloved by their subjects; they wear the skins of buck and leopard. One need not be under any apprehension about meat and drink, as they have in every village a house of entertainment for travellers, where they are not only lodged but fed also.[4]

---

[4] D. Moodie, *The Record, or a series of official papers relative to the condition and treatment of the native tribes of South Africa, 1838–1842* (photo repr., Amsterdam, 1960), vol. 1, p. 431.

It was more than a century before the Dutch colony, planted at Cape Town in 1652, made any contact with these south-eastern Bantu peoples. Most of the western Cape province was still the country of the Khoi (Hottentots) and San (Bushmen) – the hunting and pastoral predecessors of the Bantu, now reduced to the south-western corner of a subcontinent of which they had once been the principal inhabitants. The Dutch settlers at the Cape expanded slowly into the interior, driving out the Bushmen. They made herdsmen and servants of the Khoi, whose tribal organisation was broken by the double attack of colonists and smallpox. This labour force was supplemented by slaves brought from both the west and east coasts of Africa and from the Dutch possessions in the East Indies. The Dutch settlers and their slaves increased at an almost equal pace – there were some 17,000 of each at the end of the eighteenth century. Intermarriage between all the racial groups at the Cape – Europeans, Negroes, Khoisan and Malays – was beginning to produce the mixed Cape Coloured population. Not until about 1770 did Boer (Dutch, farmer) and Bantu face one another across the Fish River, thieving each other's cattle by night and arguing about its return by day. There were frequent armed conflicts. In 1795, when the British first seized the Cape from the Dutch at the time of the Napoleonic wars, the problems on the eastern frontier were threatening and dangerous, but might still have been satisfactorily solved, given understanding and good will on both sides and a firm decision to maintain a permanent frontier between the two races by the European government at the Cape. But by the time the British returned permanently in 1806, the situation on the frontier had passed beyond the hope of peaceful negotiation and control.

THE EAST COAST

At the end of the eighteenth century, therefore, Bantu Africa was still a very secluded region in comparison with most of Africa north of the equator. The only part of it which had been for any long period in contact with a literate civilisation and a universal faith was the coastal region of East Africa. Here trading settlements were known to Greek geographers as early as the first century A.D., and stone-built Muslim towns were beginning to be founded by the twelfth century. By the seventeenth and eighteenth centuries not only the Arab settlers, but most of the Bantu inhabitants of the coastal belt, were beginning to be Muslims. They also became conscious of belonging to a society much wider than that of a particular part of tropical Africa. Within East

Africa the influence of this Swahili–Arab civilisation was very restricted indeed. Arab traders had preceded the Portuguese on the Zambezi, where both Sena and Tete had been built on the sites of earlier Arab settlements. Here also Arab traders resident at the Mwene Mutapa's court had instigated the murder of the first and most famous Roman Catholic missionary, Gonçalo de Silveira, in 1569. Silveira journeyed up the Zambezi and arrived, we are told, lean, haggard and fever-ridden at the court of the Mwene Mutapa. After a month's instruction, the Great King, his favourite wife and sister, and three hundred relatives and counsellors were baptised. But this success aroused the jealousy of the Arab traders (called in the Portuguese chronicles 'Moors'). They denounced Silveira as a spy and an evil magician, and the Mwene Mutapa had him strangled in his sleep. Elsewhere, however, until late in the eighteenth century, there is scarcely a reference to Arab or Swahili activities more than a few kilometres from the Indian Ocean coast.

THE PORTUGUESE IN AFRICA

After the Arabs came the Portuguese, whose direct influence was confined to the Kongo kingdom, the Kwanza and Zambezi valleys, and to a few offshore islands, including Luanda, Mozambique, Kilwa and Mombasa. In Kongo some thousands of people, including the royal family, became Christians. The Portuguese king corresponded with the king of Kongo as an equal, addressing him as 'Most high and powerful prince and king my brother'. Many of the Kongo people remained Christians for eight or nine generations, until the last links with Europe were cut by the quarrelling and fighting which broke out inside the country from the end of the seventeenth century onwards. On the Kwanza, and again on the Zambezi, some tens of thousands of Africans came to regard themselves as the subjects of the Portuguese rather than of any indigenous African state. Of these perhaps the majority became in some sense Christians, but only a tiny handful acquired any literary education or became assimilated to the Portuguese way of life and culture. In any case, the example of Portuguese manners and culture in such isolated settlements in Angola and Mozambique was not very inspiring. In one way or another, by conquest or by taking a people under their protection, the Portuguese destroyed most of the African states with which they came into direct contact. Much more important were the indirect effects of their presence. Undoubtedly the opening of the Atlantic slave-trade encouraged the building up of African states in the hinterland of

Portuguese Angola and Mozambique, as it had done also in West Africa. It was late in the nineteenth century before any Mwata Yamvo set eyes upon a live Portuguese, and yet the Mwata Yamvo's state, no less than that of Asante in West Africa, had grown up as a response to the trade brought to Africa by the Europeans. Whoever had guns had power. Whoever had cloth had prestige. These things were bartered for ivory, which was only obtained in sufficient quantities by properly organised elephant hunting, and which had to be transported safely to the Portuguese frontier markets. These activities could only be performed successfully by the ruler of an organised state who could command obedience over a wide area. Such states could be, and usually were, established and run on completely African lines. The Mwata Yamvo and the Mwata Kazembe, like the Makoko and the Mwene Mutapa, were, as we have seen, divine kings, and their political institutions were of a fully African kind. But the Lunda states would not have flourished where they did, or when they did, but for the Portuguese presence in Luanda and on the Zambezi.

After the Portuguese came the Dutch. But the Dutch settled beyond the Bantu sphere. Only after their colony had been growing for 120 years did it begin to affect the south-eastern Bantu. That was only shortly before the situation had been further complicated by the British annexation of the Cape.

MADAGASCAR

The island of Madagascar, one of the largest in the world, formed a kind of stepping-stone between Asia and Africa. From at least as early as the fifth century A.D. immigrants from South-East Asia had settled on the island, bringing with them Asian food-crops, such as rice and taro, and their distinctive Malagasy language and culture. Swahili–Arab merchant communities had made contact with Madagascar by the eleventh century, and African peoples, more or less Arabised, settled in the western and southern parts in large numbers. By the thirteenth century the Comoro Islands and some of the coastal regions of Madagascar had become part of the Muslim culture that had developed all round the shores of the Indian Ocean. The island probably supplied the East African coastal region with foodstuffs – otherwise it offered little of value to traders. The Portuguese and the Dutch called there for supplies on their voyages to the Far East. Only after coffee from Arabia had been introduced on to the French islands of Réunion and Mauritius in 1720 did Madagascar become of more commercial importance as a supplier of slaves to work   27 on the coffee estates. These naturally came mainly from the eastern side of the island, which faced Réunion and Mauritius.

At the same time, in the eighteenth century, the western part of Madagascar was being exploited by European and Arab settlers on the east and south-east coasts of Africa, for slaves, cattle and food-crops. The response of the Malagasy to this trade was similar to that of African peoples on the mainland. With the aid of European fire-arms, powerful states grew up. The greatest of these was the Merina kingdom of the Hova people, which in the nineteenth century conquered two-thirds of the island. The Hova were a group of almost pure Indonesians – the original settlers perhaps added to by much later arrivals. The Merina state was very small in the eighteenth century, stretching just a few kilometres around Tananarive. In 1787 King Nampoina came to the throne and embarked upon a career of expansion. By the time of his death in 1810 the Merina kingdom controlled much of the central plateau and had conquered many of its rivals. Nampoina had built the foundations of a powerful, centrally administered state.

3 West Africa before the colonial period, 1800–1875

THE FULBE JIHADS

Historians have often written of the nineteenth century in Africa mainly as a period in which Europeans were increasing their influence and power. So far as the first half of the nineteenth century is concerned, however, this is not really the correct way of looking at the history of Africa. In West Africa during this time the most significant happenings were the holy wars or jihads of the Fulbe. These events had nothing to do with direct European intervention in the region, and yet they affected the whole of the western Sudan.

As we mentioned in Chapter 1, these jihads had their origin in the revival of Islam in the western Sudan, which was brought about by the Arabic-speaking Moors who came into Mauritania from across the Sahara in the fifteenth and sixteenth centuries. The leaders of this revival retired from the hustle and bustle of politics and trade, and went to live in remote places. They trained small bands of devoted disciples both in the study of the Islamic scriptures and legal scriptures and legal traditions and in their own methods of prayer and devotion. The disciples were formed into brotherhoods (*tariqa*) called after the name of the founding teacher (for example, the Tijaniyya brotherhood named after Ahmad Tijani). The eighteenth-century jihads waged in Futa Toro and Futa Jallon were organised by Fulbe teachers, most of whom belonged to the ancient brotherhood called the Qadiriyya. Usuman dan Fodio, the leader of the great nineteenth-century jihad in northern Nigeria and Niger, was a member of this brotherhood.

Usuman dan Fodio was born into the Torodbe clan in 1754, in Gobir, the northernmost of the Hausa states. He studied under a famous teacher at Agades, the capital of the Tuareg state of Aïr in the Sahara north of his home. Here he came in touch with the reformist ideas then stirring throughout the Muslim world. These were a part of the great reaction of Islam as a whole to the advance of the Christian West. It had begun in Arabia with the Wahhabi movement in the eighteenth century, and led to the reform of old brotherhoods like the Qadiriyya and to the foundation of new ones. Typical of these new

brotherhoods were the Tijaniyya, which became particularly powerful in the western Sudan, and the Sanusiyya in Cyrenaica and the
eastern Sahara. There was of course no European menace on the spot
to react to in West Africa at this time. However, it does seem that,
along with the desire to reform the practice of Islam in the Sudan, the
religious leaders did have the sense of a threat to the Islamic world in
general from expanding European Christendom. Early European
explorers of the Sahara region, for example, encountered Muslim
teachers who asked them why the British had conquered India (which
had a large number of Muslims amongst its population).

This, then, was dan Fodio's background when he returned from
Agades to become tutor to the son and heir of the Hausa *sarki* (ruler) of
Gobir. In this position he gained a considerable influence in the
councils of the state, which he used to spread his zeal for religious
reform. In 1802 dan Fodio's pupil Yunfa became *sarki* on the death of
his father. Yunfa proved a bitter disappointment to his former tutor,
who now retreated from the court to his native village, where he was
soon joined by members of the reforming party. These became so
numerous that Yunfa threatened him with military action. Dan
Fodio, pointing to the historical parallel of the Prophet Muhammad's
flight (*hijra*) from Mecca, then retired to the remote district of Gudu
(21 February 1804). At Gudu his supporters rallied round him in such
numbers that he found himself at the head of a really formidable army
of warriors (Arabic *mujahidun*, from 'jihad'), all burning with religious fervour and intent on jihad. Dan Fodio was unanimously proclaimed *Amir al-Mu'minin* (in Hausa *Sarkin Musulmi*, Commander of
the Faithful), which was the traditional title of the caliphs, or successors, of the Prophet. (The caliphs were the rulers of the Arab empire
in the early, glorious days of the Muslim era.) After being proclaimed
Commander of the Faithful, dan Fodio swore to the disinterestedness
of his intentions, saying, 'If I fight this battle that I may become
greater than my fellow, or that my son may become greater than his
son, or that my slave may lord it over his slave, may the Kaffir [infidel]
wipe us from the land.'

After the declaration of jihad, dissatisfied men came from all the
Hausa states to swear allegiance to the *Amir al-Mu'minin* and to
receive in exchange the green banner of the True Believers. The
puritanical motives of the leaders of the jihad are well described by
Muhammad al-Tunisi (see Chapter 1), who was in Wadai in 1810 and
heard news of its success:

30 The Falata [Fulbe] accuse all other Sudanese of impiety and of heresy,

maintaining that only by force of arms can they be brought to repentance. They assert that the other Sudanese have altered and adulterated the principles of Islam, that they have broken the criminal code by allowing compensations of money for criminals, which is illegal and proscribed by the Holy Book. They claim that they have undermined the foundations of religion by proclaiming illegal and criminal innovations to be legitimate, by shameful customs such as adultery, the use of fermented drinks, passion for amusement, song and dance, neglect of the daily prayers, and refusal to offer alms for the poor. Each of these crimes and shameful deeds deserves vengeance and calls for a *jihad*. These ideas kindled the minds of the Fula for years, until suddenly there arose amongst them one renowned for his piety and godliness; the *Zaki* [Hausa, lion] who became a reformer and proclaimed the holy war.[1]

Not all the *mujahidun* were animated by such purely religious enthusiasm. The leaders were drawn for the most part from the educated Muslim Fulbe of the towns (Hausa, *Fulanin gidda*), who had come to despise, as al-Tunisi shows, the corrupt, half-pagan conduct of the old Hausa ruling families, known collectively as Habe. They were supported by many of the town Hausa, who treated the movement as an opportunity to free themselves from the Habe rulers and to fight among themselves. The jihad was also supported by virtually all of the pastoral Fulbe (Hausa, *boroje*) of the countryside. These were mostly still pagan but they felt a racial affinity with the town Fulbe and even belonged to the same clans. The main motive of most *boroje* was doubtless the hope of being able to loot the wealth of the Hausa towns.

The revolt swept all over Hausaland, the leading towns of Katsina yielding to dan Fodio's *mujahidun* in 1807, and Kano in 1809. The Habe dynasties were replaced by Fulbe *amirs*, most of whom had been appointed by dan Fodio in 1804 and 1805. Beyond Hausaland to the east, Adamawa, which had long been penetrated by pastoral Fulbe, became part of the new empire after a struggle lasting nearly thirty years. The political intrigues of the Fulbe religious teachers paved the way for the penetration of the *mujahidun* into Nupe and Yorubaland. They occupied the northern provinces of the old Oyo empire (see below, p. 37) which, as the emirate of Ilorin, became a base for the spread of Islam among the Yoruba. To the north-east the jihad was halted only in Bornu, where Muhammed al-Kanemi, a warrior and cleric from east of Lake Chad, successfully drove out the invaders. Al-Kanemi took over control of the affairs of Bornu, but the *mai* of the ancient dynasty was allowed to retain his court ceremonial although

---

[1] *Voyage au Ouadây*, tr. Dr Perron (Paris, 1851), p. 163.

deprived of all real power. The Scottish traveller Clapperton, who visited Bornu in 1821, remarked on the position of the *mai*:

The Sultanship of Bornu is but a name; the court still keeps up considerable state, and adheres strictly to its ancient customs, and this is the only privilege left them. When the sultan gives audience to strangers, he sits in a kind of cage, made of bamboo, through the bars of which he looks on his visitors, who are not allowed to approach within seventy or eighty yards of his person.[2]

The conquest period over, Usuman dan Fodio, always more of a scholar than a ruler, returned to his books. His empire was divided into two, his son Muhammad Bello ruling the eastern part from the newly founded city of Sokoto, and his brother Abdallah the western part from Gwandu. After Usuman's death in 1817, Bello was recognised by Abdallah as sultan of Sokoto, and he ruled there until his death in 1837. By this time the religious fervour of the movement was largely spent. The Fulbe had turned from religious reformers into a ruling class. Nevertheless it was under Fulbe rule that Islam first spread outside the towns into the country districts. Their rule was in general more progressive and more effective than that of their Habe predecessors, and their importance was by no means ended when Britain and France began to impose their power.

THE JIHAD IN THE WESTERN SUDAN

The successes of the Fulbe in Hausaland had important effects farther to the west. In 1810 Hamadu Bari (also known as Ahmadu Lobo), one of Usuman's early followers, led an army westwards across the Niger bend and drove out the Bambara overlords from his homeland, the Fulbe state of Masina. Here, as in Futa Toro and in Futa Jallon, the ground for reform had been prepared by the jihads of the previous century. The whole of this area was now undergoing a further period of revival as a result of the spread of the new and powerful brotherhood of the Tijaniyya. In 1826 a young cleric called Umar from Futa Toro made the pilgrimage to Mecca. He was initiated into the Tijaniyya in the holy city and then returned slowly homewards through the Bornu of al-Kanemi, the Sokoto of Muhammad Bello (whose sister he married), and the Masina of Hamadu Bari. Known now as al-Hajj Umar (the pilgrim), he settled in Futa Jallon and began to prepare the fiercest jihad of them all. He equipped his force with

[2] D. Denham, H. Clapperton and W. Oudney, *Narrative of Travels and Discoveries in Northern and Central Africa, in the Years 1822, 1823 and 1824* (London, 1826), cited in Thomas Hodgkin, *Nigerian Perspectives: an historical anthology* (London, 1973), p. 205.

fire-arms obtained from the Europeans at the coast, and at last in 1850 he launched them on the Bambara kingdoms of Segu and Kaarta and then on Masina. Had he not been checked by the French (see below, p. 39), he would have made for Futa Toro also. As it was, when he captured Timbuktu in 1863, his empire, based now at Hamdillahi near the old Bambara capital of Segu, stretched over the whole of the country from the Niger bend to the upper Senegal.

The empire of al-Hajj Umar did not last as long as that of Usuman dan Fodio. Umar himself was killed in 1864, and it took his son Ahmadu Sefu nearly ten years to establish his right to rule throughout his father's dominions. Even then, his rule lasted only until 1884. Nevertheless, the active survival of Islam under French colonisation throughout most of the region occupied by the Mande-speaking peoples was largely due to the revivalist movements carried forcefully into the whole of this region by al-Hajj Umar.

THE FOREST STATES AND THE OUTSIDE WORLD

Unlike the situation in the Sudanic region, the changes in the woodland and forest belt of West Africa came about only slowly and sporadically during the first sixty years or so of the nineteenth century. It is true that the whole attitude of the main trading nations towards West Africa underwent a complete change during the last years of the eighteenth century and the earliest years of the nineteenth. Denmark made the slave-trade illegal for her own nationals in 1805, Britain in 1807, Holland in 1814 and France in 1818. In 1815 and 1817 Spain and Portugal restricted their slave-traders to the seas south of the equator (as far as Portugal was concerned, this meant the trade between Angola and Brazil). Britain even carried this new anti-slavery policy so far as to establish a naval patrol in West African waters and to declare the freed-slave settlement on the Sierra Leone peninsula a Crown Colony (1808).

If they intended to continue trading in West Africa, all these nations had to seek a new basis for their commerce. This search for trade was one of the main reasons why so many European explorers undertook dangerous and arduous expeditions in West Africa during the first half of the nineteenth century. The first were the journeys of Mungo Park to the upper Niger in 1795 and 1805. The greatest was the journey of the German, Heinrich Barth, made between 1850 and 1856, as a result of which he wrote a magnificent description of the central and western Sudanic region. Here, as an example of his penetrating eye for detail, is a little of his description of the Tasawa

33

region of northern Hausaland (not far from Usuman dan Fodio's Gobir), which he entered by the desert route from Agades:

Tasawa was the first large place of Negroland proper which I had seen, and it made the most cheerful impression upon me, as manifesting everywhere the unmistakable marks of the comfortable, pleasant sort of life led by the natives: the courtyard fenced with a 'derne' of tall reeds, excluding to a certain degree the eyes of the passer-by; then near the entrance the cool shady place of the 'runfa' for ordinary business and for the reception of strangers . . . the whole dwelling shaded with spreading trees, and enlivened with groups of children, goats, fowls, pigeons and a horse or a pack-ox. With this character of the dwellings, that of the inhabitants themselves is in entire harmony, its most constant element being a cheerful temperament, bent upon enjoying life, rather given to women, dance, and song, but without any disgusting excess. Drinking fermented liquor cannot be strictly reckoned a sin in a place where a great many of the inhabitants are pagans; but a drunken person, nevertheless, is scarcely ever seen; those who are not Mohammedans only indulge in their 'giya', made of sorghum, just enough to make them merry and enjoy life with more light-heartedness.[3]

This was a state of affairs very similar to that about which the Fulbe reformers had complained some fifty years previously, apparently with little effect.

Side by side with the search by Europeans for trade routes and for objects of a new and legitimate commerce, there was the beginning of the first really unselfish Christian activity in Africa. Some Christians in Europe were deeply concerned for Africans as people with a right to share in the benefits of Christianity as well as the useful skills and knowledge built up by Christian civilisation in western Europe. Earlier Roman Catholic missionary efforts had only touched West Africa briefly and at one or two scattered points. The beginning of the nineteenth century, however, saw the establishment of flourishing Church of England (Anglican) and Methodist missions in Sierra Leone. Their converts were to play a most important part in the later history of the whole of the southern part of West Africa. The 1820s saw the coming of the Presbyterian Basel missionaries to the Gold Coast, and by the 1840s all the main Protestant denominations were represented in the Gold Coast, Dahomey, and in western and eastern Nigeria. Roman Catholic missions followed between the 1840s and 1880s.

Still, all these exploring and missionary activities were only the first stages in the development of European influence. The first half of the nineteenth century, from the point of view of African history as

[3] *Travels in Africa* (Centenary edn, London, 1965), vol. I, pp. 439–40.

opposed to colonial, saw little more than a continuation, and even a strengthening, of the eighteenth-century pattern amongst the woodland and forest peoples of West Africa. Despite the anti-slavery legislation in European countries, and despite the constant patrolling of the British navy, the slave-trade not only continued, but actually increased in scale. Whereas most authorities have estimated the export of slaves from the whole of West Africa at about 100,000 a year at the end of the eighteenth century, by the 1830s it had risen to about 135,000. Slavery, as distinct from the slave-trade, continued to be legal in the southern states of America until 1863, and throughout this period the illicit trade yielded great profits. The trade to Brazil and Cuba continued, though on a decreasing scale, until the 1880s, and as European and American merchants dropped out of the trade for fear of the punishments involved, their places were taken by Brazilian Negroes (Afro-Brazilians), whose operations were much more difficult to detect and prevent.

It would be wrong, however, to draw from these figures the simple conclusion that all the states of the Guinea forest were irretrievably committed to a continuation of the slave-trade. Asante, at least, had long outgrown its period of active expansion, during which the disposal of war captives had temporarily eclipsed the export of gold-dust and ivory. By the nineteenth century it was concerned mainly to hold its wide dominions. It was the sheer military power of Asante, fed by regular exchange of gold-dust for fire-arms with the Dutch at Elmina, which kept the British and their Fante allies along the central stretch of the Gold Coast in a state of constant alarm. The forts were expensive to maintain. They could pay their way only by the levying of customs dues on legitimate trade. Yet the trade routes were constantly subject to closure through the military operations of the Asante against their tributary states in the interior. Even the Fante were discouraged from agricultural production for export by threats of Asante invasion. Officially, British jurisdiction, whether vested in an unofficial Council of Merchants, as it was for most of the time up till 1842, or in a Colonial Office governor, as it was thereafter, was limited until 1874 to the coastal forts. Such informal influence as was exercised upon the coastal states was largely concerned with resistance to Asante pressure.

If a militaristic and still partially slave-trading Asante continued to dominate the affairs of the Gold Coast, the situation on the Slave Coast to the east of it was even more similar to what it had been in the eighteenth century. Here, as the modern air traveller so clearly sees, the coast is nothing but a narrow surf-hammered beach, behind which a vast system of interconnected lagoons provides secure access for canoes to all the rivers of Togo, Dahomey (Bénin) and western Nigeria. The methods of the slave-traders of the 1830s along this stretch of coast were described by Richard Lander:

As soon as a vessel arrives at her place of destination, the crew discharge her light cargoe, with the manacles intended for the slaves, and land the captain at the same time. The vessel then cruises along the coast to take in country cloth, ivory, a little gold dust, etc., and if a British man-of-war be near, the crew having nothing on board to excite suspicion, in most cases contrive to get their vessel searched whilst trading with the natives. They return to the place where the cargoe had been loaded, and communicate with the captain on shore who then takes the opportunity of acquainting his crew with the exact time in which he will be in readiness to embark. The vessel then cruises a second time up and down the coast, till the appointed day approaches, when she proceeds to take in her living cargoe.[4]

Dahomey, like Asante, had by the nineteenth century reached its full territorial extension. Unlike Asante, however, it had no export with which to procure the guns which it needed to maintain its military power. So long as the demand for slaves continued, therefore, the kings of Dahomey continued, however unwillingly, to supply it.

The bulk of Slave Coast slaves did not, however, in the nineteenth century at least, come from Dahomey. They came from Yorubaland and were exported through Porto Novo, Badagry and Lagos. All these ports were to the east of Whydah on the same lagoon system. Although there was a thriving Afro-Brazilian stronghold at Lagos, the main reason for this was the decline and disintegration of the ancient Oyo empire. This was the result of tensions from both north and south. On the one hand the southern Yoruba states – Egba, Ijebu and Ondo – had been growing steadily in power through access to the coastal trade. On the other hand Ilorin and other northern districts of the empire had been penetrated, as had the Hausa states, by the Fulbe, and were therefore involved in the jihad. The beginning of the end came in 1817, when the great chiefs of Oyo, led by Afonja of Ilorin, sent an empty calabash to the *alafin* (king), Aole, thus signifying that they no longer acknowledged his authority. Aole accepted the hint in the traditional fashion by committing suicide, but not before he had uttered his famous curse. From the palace forecourt he shot three arrows, one to the north, one to the south, and one to the west, saying,

[4] *Records of Captain Clapperton's Last Expedition to Africa* (London, 1830), vol. 2, p. 238.

'My curse be on you for your disloyalty and disobedience, so let your children disobey you. If you send them on an errand, let them never return to bring you word again. To all the points I shot my arrows will you be carried as slaves. My curse will carry you to the sea and beyond the seas, slaves will rule over you, and you, their masters, will become slaves.' Then, smashing an earthenware dish, he shouted, 'Broken calabash can be mended, but not a broken dish; so let my words be irrevocable.'[5]

The curse seemed to take immediate effect, for shortly afterwards Oyo was abandoned by its inhabitants, and those who stayed in that area became subjects of the Fulbe emirate of Ilorin. The majority of the people moved away, however, some founding a new town of Oyo about 150 kilometres to the south on the edge of the forest, while others settled at Ibadan, which grew to be the greatest Yoruba city within the forest belt. The states and provinces of the Oyo empire became independent of central control and started to fight each other both for extended frontiers and for control of the trade routes. The principal gainers from these wars were the Egba, who founded a new capital city at Abeokuta in 1830, controlling the routes to Porto Novo and Badagry, and the Ijebu, whose territory controlled the main route from Ibadan to Lagos. One result of these destructive, inter-necine struggles among the Yoruba was that vast numbers of captives were taken as slaves, so that by the 1840s Lagos and Badagry had become the greatest slaving ports in West Africa.

The Yoruba wars were a tragedy, for much of southern Yorubaland lies within that part of the forest belt where the oil-palm grows wild, and where, therefore, there was an easily marketable alternative to the slave-trade. Because of these wars, the oil-palm in southern Yoruba-land was not commercially exploited. It is indeed one of the curious facts of West African history that the one region where a peaceful changeover to legitimate commerce took place was the region where in the past the slave-trade had been most active. This was the region roughly corresponding to the eastern region of Nigeria, which at the end of the eighteenth century had supplied 20,000 slaves a year. Here the Efik and Ijaw villagers of the lagoon area used to take their great war-canoes up the rivers to the Igbo slave markets, and now they showed an equal enterprise in converting the Igbo to the collection of palm-nuts which were taken down the rivers to be sold to the Euro-peans. By the 1820s the region was beginning to be known as the Oil Rivers.

The European traders realised that if they could take steam-driven

[5] Samuel Johnson, *History of the Yorubas* (Lagos, 1921), p. 192.

ships (which were starting to be available in the 1820s, though it was not until much later that they replaced sailing-ships on the open seas) up the larger rivers into the forest region where the oil-palms grew, they could buy the produce cheaper and eliminate the coastal middlemen. This was the real significance of the discovery of the Niger mouth by John and Richard Lander in 1830, as the result of a journey down the river by canoe from Bussa to the delta. Eleven years later the British government was persuaded by philanthropists and traders alike to send an ambitious expedition to penetrate the interior using the new water route. But the west coast was extremely un-healthy for Europeans – it was known as 'the white man's grave'. The reign of the malarial mosquito had still another fifteen years to run before the use of quinine helped Europeans to overcome the fever that was so deadly for them. The Niger expedition of 1841–2 was a failure, over one-sixth of its European members dying in the space of two months. The commercial navigation of the Niger was delayed until the 1860s.

THE BEGINNINGS OF EUROPEAN INTERVENTION

Halfway through the century, therefore, the main characteristics of the societies of the southern, forested part of West Africa had changed very little except in the Oil Rivers district. This was in spite of the legal abolition of the slave-trade by the European powers, in spite of the British navy, and in spite of the small and scattered possessions of the French and the British, the Danes and the Dutch. In general, the slave-trade was still flourishing, and the main military states, Asante and Dahomey, were still increasing their strength. The only signifi-cant increase of European power, even during the third quarter of the century, was along the coast itself. Here, on the eastern sector of the Gold Coast, Britain in 1850 bought the Danish forts, in order to be able to impose customs duties along a sufficient stretch of coast to pay the expenses of her occupation. In 1872 the Dutch, finding their forts along the western sector of the coast no longer profitable, ceded them freely to the British. Another factor was Britain's intervention in the affairs of Lagos. The British supported the claims of Akitoye to the title of *Ologun* (the ruler of Lagos, at one time appointed by the Oba of Benin), and in 1851 helped him drive out his nephew and rival Kosoko. In return for British help, Akitoye promised to end the slave-trade from Lagos, but he could not keep his hold over the island city without further British support. When in 1861 Dahomey again threatened to attack Abeokuta, Britain rid herself of the

Akitoye–Kosoko dispute by annexing Lagos as a colony. From this point an almost inevitable path led forward to further intervention – on the one hand the punitive expedition against Asante in 1873 and the incorporation of the coastal states into the Gold Coast colony in 1874; on the other hand the gradual expansion of Lagos along the coast to the east and the west and the increasing interference of the British consuls in the affairs of the Oil Rivers states.

In the French colony on the Senegal a new phase of active intervention began with the appointment as governor of Louis Faidherbe in 1854. Since its reoccupation by the French in 1817 (it had been in British hands during the Napoleonic Wars) the colony had consisted of nothing more than a circle of agricultural villages around the port of St Louis. The only active trade was that in gum arabic with the Moorish tribes living in the desert to the north of the river. Trade with the interior, which the French so much wanted to develop, was prevented by the powerful Fulbe state of Futa Toro higher up the river on the southern side. Convinced that the Senegal would prove the commercial highway for the trade of the whole of the western Sudan, the French had a clearer motive for interior conquests than the British at any of their coastal bases. Conquest of the lower Senegal valley was therefore Faidherbe's declared policy, and in ten years he had carried it out, encouraging economic crops – especially groundnuts – in the conquered lands, and establishing schools as well as administrative centres in each newly acquired district.

Any kind of European intervention on African soil was likely to lead to more. Britain's creeping protectorates along the Lagos and Gold Coast stretches of the West African shore were one example. Faidherbe's policy of military conquest inland was another. It was, however, more difficult to call a halt to this inland conquest than to the growth of Britain's coastal possessions. The farther the French advance went inland, the more sharply it came into conflict with the Muslim states of the interior of the western Sudan. Already by 1857 Faidherbe was involved with the forces of al-Hajj Umar. The Muslim leader of the jihad temporarily checked the French advance south-east up the Senegal but was unable to prevent their attacking Futa Toro to the south of the river. The French conquest of Futa Toro was a blow to the prestige of al-Hajj Umar. Most of his *mujahidun* were emigrants from Futa Toro, which had been the original Fulbe jihad state. Clearly this was a situation which could end only in the defeat of the French and their retreat to St Louis, or else in the defeat of the Muslims and the French advance to Timbuktu and beyond.

39

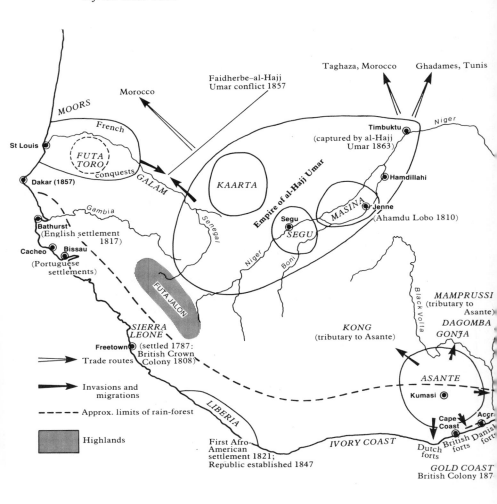

5a   West Africa, 1800–1875: western half

In West Africa, therefore, events were tending by the third quarter of the nineteenth century to increasing intervention by both France and Britain. There was still in 1875 nothing that could suggest the speed of events that were to follow in the next twenty-five years, however. Had France and Britain not been pushed by other European powers into a scramble for outright partition, their intervention

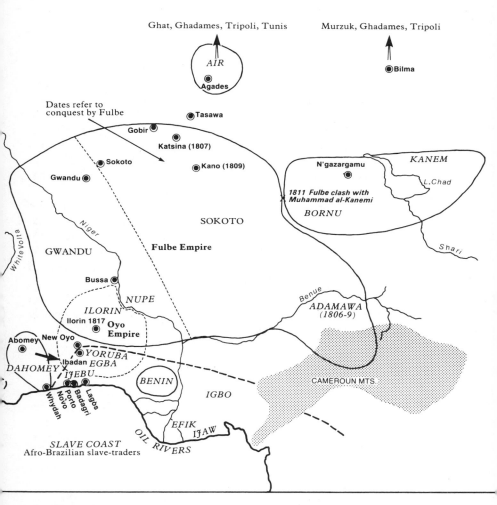

Ghat, Ghadames, Tripoli, Tunis

Murzuk, Ghadames, Tripoli

AIR

⊚Bilma

⊚
Agades

Dates refer to
conquest by Fulbe

⊚Tasawa

Gobir⊚

KANEM

⊚
Katsina (1807)

N'gazargamu
⊚

⊚Sokoto

⊚ Kano (1809)

L.Chad

Gwandu⊚

*1811 Fulbe clash with
Muhammad al-Kanemi*

SOKOTO

BORNU

Niger

Shari

GWANDU

Fulbe Empire

Bussa⊚

NUPE

Benue

ILORIN

ADAMAWA
(1806–9)

Ilorin 1817   **Oyo
Empire**

Abomey
⊚   New Oyo

YORUBA

Ibadan
X   EGBA

DAHOMEY X

IJEBU

BENIN

CAMEROUN MTS.

Whydah   Porto Novo   Badagri   Lagos

IGBO

SLAVE COAST
Afro-Brazilian slave-traders

EFIK   IJAW

OIL RIVERS

5*b*   West Africa, 1800–1875: eastern half

would undoubtedly have proceeded much more slowly than in fact it
did. Still, European armies – the outward sign of imperialism – had
already been in action against African states before 1875. In West
Africa at least the broad pattern that the partition was to follow had
been laid down and could lead only to an ever-growing area of colonial
occupation.

41

4 West-Central Africa, 1800–1880

The region we call 'West-Central Africa' is the region of the Congo forest and of the light woodland country to the south of it. Today this is the area occupied by Angola and the states of Zaïre, Gabon, the People's Republic of Congo and the Central African Republic. In terms of the older African states, it includes the area of the Luba–Lunda and the lower Congo kingdoms. The Portuguese were the most active external influence in this region, but were not the only one. During the first three-quarters of the nineteenth century the north-ernmost frontier of Angola was at the Loge river, and from here northwards to Mount Cameroun and up both sides of the Congo estuary, there was a kind of commercial no-man's-land, the shore dotted with the trading factories of English, Dutch, American, French and Spanish as well as Portuguese firms. During the second half of the nineteenth century, an even more important source of external influence was that of the Swahili–Arabs and Nyamwezi from East Africa. Only during the colonial period was the region as a whole reconnected with its natural ports of exit on the Atlantic coast.

THE POMBEIROS AND THE MWATA KAZEMBE

During the early part of the century Portuguese influence reached the interior by two main routes, one of which started in Luanda, the other in Benguela. The Luanda route was the older, and by the beginning of the nineteenth century it led in a sense right across the continent. Portuguese Luanda merchants themselves seldom left Luanda: indeed, the Portuguese government always did its best to prevent them from doing so. It knew that relations with the peoples of the interior went much more smoothly if trade was handled by the *pombeiros*. These, as we noted in Chapter 2, were African, or sometimes Mulatto, agents from the colony. They were employed by the Portuguese government or by private traders to lead caravans into the interior and to reside at the *feiras*, or garrisoned market-places. Peoples living beyond the Portuguese borders would bring their produce for sale to these markets. The most distant *feira* on the Luanda route was about 500 kilometres up-country at Kasanje. It had been founded in the seventeenth century at the capital of a tributary state, the inhabitants of which were a people called the Imbangala, who had originally formed a part of the Luba–Lunda dispersion. The *pombeiros* did not normally go beyond Kasanje. From there to the Mwata Yamvo's kingdom trade was organised by the Imbangala. The Mwata Yamvo sent his own caravans still further inland to the Mwata Kazembe's capital on the Luapula river. And by the end of the eighteenth century the Mwata Kazembe in his turn was in commercial contact with the Portuguese station at Tete on the Zambezi – the usual carriers on the last stretch of the route being the Bisa people of the north-eastern part of modern Zambia. At the end of the eighteenth century and several times during the early nineteenth century the Portuguese tried to survey this route. They hoped by this means to extend their own power and influence from coast to coast. In 1798 an expedition commanded by Lacerda reached the Kazembe's capital from Tete but had to turn back. In 1806, however, two *pombeiros* called Pedro João Baptista and Amaro José were sent out from Luanda and accomplished the double journey to Tete and back on foot with no greater hardship than that of being detained for nearly four years on the outward journey at the court of the Mwata Kazembe. Baptista wrote of the king in his journal:

The Kazembe is powerful in his capital, and rules over a great many people. His place is rather smaller than the Mwata Yamvo's. His orders are harsh, and he is feared by all the great chiefs, who are also lords in their own lands . . . When there are no travellers trading at his capital, he will order slaves and ivory to be collected, and will go with his ambassadors to chastise such chiefs as stop the way to traders coming from Tete to his country. The territory of Kazembe is supplied with provisions all the year round – manioc flour, millet, maize, beans, bananas, sugar-canes, potatoes, yams, gourds, ground-nuts, and much fish from the rivers Luapula and Mouva which are near. He owns three salt districts . . . He possesses victuals and oxen . . . which he sends and buys from the Huizas [Bisa] in exchange for slaves . . . King Kazembe has tea-pots, cups, silver spoons and forks . . . and gold money. He has a Christian courtesy: he doffs his hat and gives good day.[1]

The *pombeiros* noticed that the Kazembe, whose capital was almost in the middle of the continent, would normally export his slaves westwards via the Mwata Yamvo's kingdom to Luanda, while he sent his ivory eastwards to Tete. This was probably a just reflection of the market for slaves and ivory in the trade of the Atlantic and Indian Oceans at that time.

[1] *Lands of the Cazembe: Lacerda's Journey to Cazembe . . . also the Journey of the Pombeiros*, tr. R. F. Burton (London, 1873), p. 231.

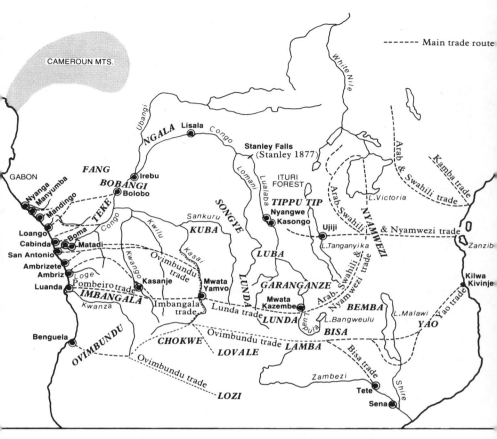

CAMEROUN MTS.

NGALA Lisala

Stanley Falls
(Stanley 1877)

FANG

GABON

BOBANGI Irebu
Bolobo

ITURI
FOREST

TIPPU TIP
Nyangwe
Kasongo

Arab & Swahili trade

Kamba trade

L.Victoria

Nyanga
Manyumba
Mandingo

TEKE

Sankuru

KUBA

SONGYE

LUBA

Ujiji

L.Tanganyika

& Nyamwezi trade

Zanzib

Loango
Cabinda
San Antonio
Ambrizete
Ambriz
Luanda

Boma
Matadi

Ovimbundu
trade

Kasanje

Mwata
Yamvo

GARANGANZE

Kilwa
Kivinje

Loge
Pombeiro trade
IMBANGALA
Kwanza

Imbangala
trade

Lunda trade

Mwata
Kazembe

BEMBA

L.Malawi

Yao trade

Benguela

OVIMBUNDU

CHOKWE

LOVALE

Ovimbundu trade

LAMBA

BISA

LUNDA

L.Bangweulu

YAO

Ovimbundu trade

Zambezi

Tete

Bisa trade

Shire

LOZI

Sena

------- Main trade route

6   West-Central Africa, 1800–1880: trade routes

THE OVIMBUNDU AND THE CHOKWE

By the middle of the nineteenth century great changes had taken place
along the old transcontinental route. On the one hand, as we shall see,
the trade eastwards from Kazembe had changed its direction from the
Portuguese on the Zambezi to the Swahili–Arabs of the Zanzibar
coast. On the other hand, the old Luanda route to the Mwata Yamvo,
using the Imbangala as intermediaries, had been superseded by a
more southerly route from Benguela. Trade on this route was in the
hands of the Ovimbundu of the Bihe plateau. The Ovimbundu, like
the Imbangala, were people who had been organised into small states
44   by conquering migrants from the Lunda area. From the eighteenth

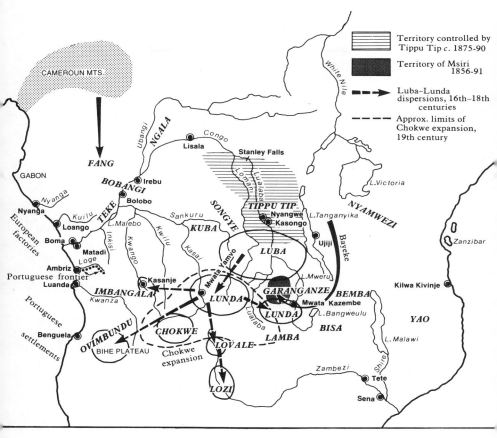

7   West-Central Africa, 1800–1880: tribal areas and migrations

century on they had been joined by considerable numbers of European refugees, some escaped convicts, some deserters from the Portuguese army. These people had passed on to their hosts their own skill with fire-arms and had thus helped to make them the greatest traders of the whole of the dry, upland region of the Congo–Zambezi watershed to the south of the Mwata Yamvo's kingdom. By 1850 their caravans, usually numbering two or three hundred porters, had penetrated south-eastwards into the Lovale and Lozi countries of the upper Zambezi valley, eastwards as far as the Lamba of the Zambian Copperbelt, and northwards right across the Mwata Yamvo's country and down the Kasai as far as the southern fringes of the Congo forest.   45

In part, the decline of the Luanda route and the rise of the Benguela one reflected a change in the commodities exported. The Luanda route had been above all a slaving route, and the Imbangala had for two and a half centuries been specialists in the supply of slaves. Luanda continued to export slaves openly and actively until 1838, when slavery was officially abolished in all the Portuguese possessions. Illegal shipments continued for another two decades, but of course from lesser ports and not from the capital of the colony. Hence the downfall of the Imbangala. And simultaneously with the abolition of the slave-trade the Portuguese lifted the government monopoly of the ivory-trade. This opened up new trading opportunities, which the Ovimbundu were better placed to exploit than the Imbangala. The Ovimbundu were traders rather than hunters. But their eastern neighbours, the Chokwe, were the great ivory-hunting specialists of the mid-nineteenth century. Their methods were ferocious in the extreme. They were well supplied with fire-arms, and were continuously on the warpath. They lived by pillage, taking slave-prisoners and incorporating them in their own war-bands, seizing stocks of dead ivory, and hunting out the elephants systematically in one region after another. The Ovimbundu traders, in fact, advanced behind a screen of Chokwe hunters and warriors, buying their ivory and supplying them with fire-arms in exchange. Thus the Chokwe, a small and almost unheard-of people in 1800, had by the end of the century conquered large areas between the upper Zambezi, the Kwango and the middle Kasai rivers and western Katanga, and it was they who in 1885 at last made an end of the great kingdom of the Mwata Yamvo.

THE NYAMWEZI AND THE ARABS

While the Ovimbundu and the Chokwe were displacing the Lunda and the Imbangala at the western end of the transcontinental route, the Mwata Kazembe, in the centre of it, was likewise being displaced by newcomers from East Africa. The story of the Nyamwezi and Swahili–Arab penetration of East Africa during the nineteenth century will be told in Chapter 6: here we are concerned only with that part of the movement which affected West-Central Africa. As early as 1832 the Kazembe rebuffed a Portuguese trade mission which visited him, saying that he was already getting all the foreign goods that he needed from the Zanzibar coast and that he no longer wished to trade with the Portuguese on the Zambezi. If he had foreseen the consequences of these new East African trading contacts, he might have been more cautious in rejecting the Portuguese proposals. For, about

1856, a Nyamwezi merchant, Msiri (the 'mosquito'), who had already made several trading expeditions to Katanga, settled down with an armed following at Bunkeya, on the northern edge of the Kazembe's kingdom. There he steadily built up his power and influence until he was strong enough to defy the Kazembe and to make himself the effective overlord of a large region which included the whole of the north and west of the Kazembe's kingdom. He also spread into the Luba kingdoms to the north of it. Msiri, with his Nyamwezi warriors, known in Katanga as the Bayeke, now added to his trading profits with regular tribute in ivory, salt and copper levied from the chiefs who had formerly paid it to the Kazembe or to the Luba kings. Like the Kazembes before him, he traded these products in many directions. The salt and copper (cast in small bars or crosses) went down the Kasai and the Lulua rivers to the peoples of the forest margin like the Kuba and the Songye, who traded it for ivory. The ivory Msiri exchanged for guns, obtained both from the Ovimbundu and the Portuguese in the west and from the Swahili–Arabs in the east. Msiri's empire, known to the early European explorers as Garanganze, lasted until the coming of the Belgians in 1891, when Msiri himself was shot in a scuffle with a Belgian officer. His Bayeke followers continued – even after independence – to form an important element in the politics of Shaba. Godfrey Munongo, for example, who was minister for the interior in Tshombe's Congolese government, was a Yeke – and a grandson of Msiri himself.

What Msiri was doing in southern Katanga was being done at the same time in northern Katanga and the Kivu region by other groups of East Africans, led in this case mostly by Swahili–Arabs from the Zanzibar coast. These had first crossed Lake Tanganyika about 1840 from their lakeside ferry-port of Ujiji. By about 1860 there was a regular Arab settlement at Nyangwe on the Lualaba (the upper Congo). Soon they were trading and raiding over the whole area between Lake Tanganyika and the Lomami river, where they met the sphere of the Chokwe raiders coming from the west. Like the Chokwe, they could penetrate where they wished, as the possession of fire-arms made them all-powerful and the ancient Luba and Songye kingdoms were even more defenceless than the Lunda kingdoms to the south. Like the Yeke invaders to the south of them and the Chokwe to the south-west, they were ruthless and rapid in their exploitation of the ivory resources of the country. They hunted elephants in armies, and the armies lived off the local populations and savaged them, levying tribute in foodstuffs and ivory, and burning and looting the villages at the slightest signs of resistance. 47

Nevertheless, behind the first line of advance of the elephant-hunters, the invaders of eastern Zaïre settled down to an organised way of life. Their townships, many of which still exist, were equipped with mosques, and the principal houses had all the little luxuries of urban life on the East African coast – beds, furniture, coffee-tables, even the beautifully carved doorways of Zanzibar. Around their settlements the Arabs developed thriving agricultural plantations. Europeans were much impressed by these Arab achievements, as can be seen from the following description of Kasongo, written by Sidney Hinde, the English medical officer of the Congo Free State forces that conquered the Arab lands of eastern Zaïre in 1893:

Kasongo was a much finer town than even the grand old slave capital Nyangwe. During the siege of Nyangwe, the taking of which was more or less expected, the inhabitants had time to carry off all valuables, and even furniture, to places of safety. At Kasongo, however, it was different. We rushed into the town so suddenly that everything was left in its place. Our whole force found new outfits, and even the common soldiers slept on silk and satin mattresses, in carved beds with silk mosquito curtains. The room I took possession of was eighty feet long and fifteen feet wide, with a door leading into an orange garden, beyond which was a view extending over five miles. We found many European luxuries, the use of which we had almost forgotten; candles, sugar, matches, silver and glass goblets and decanters were in profusion. The granaries throughout the town were stocked with enormous quantities of rice, coffee, maize and other food; the gardens were luxurious and well-planted; and oranges, both sweet and bitter, guavas, pomegranates, pineapples, mangoes and bananas abounded at every turn. The herd of cattle we found in Kasongo was composed of three distinct breeds . . .

I was constantly astonished by the splendid work which had been done in the neighbourhood by the Arabs. Kasongo was built in the corner of a virgin forest, and for miles round all the brushwood and the great majority of trees had been cleared away. In the forest-clearing fine crops of sugar-cane, rice, maize and fruits grew. I have ridden through a single rice-field for an hour and a half.[2]

TIPPU TIP

In the early days each of these Arab settlements was ruled by its founder and followers, who exercised a kind of loose political authority over the local African chiefs. The man who brought the Arabs of this region together, to recognise his own supremacy and, ultimately, that of the sultan of Zanzibar, was Muhammed bin Hamed, more generally known by his nickname of Tippu Tip. He was born in 1830

[2] S. L. Hinde, *The Fall of the Congo Arabs* (London, 1897), pp. 184, 187.

in Zanzibar, and his mother was a pure Muscat Arab of the ruling class. His father and his paternal grandfather were coastal Swahili who had taken part in the earliest trading expeditions to the interior. His paternal grandmother had been the daughter of a Nyamwezi chief, and Tippu's own earliest journeys were with Nyamwezi caravans travelling round the south end of Lake Tanganyika to Katanga. He was for a time associated with Msiri, but later left him and set up his own headquarters at Kasongo on the Lualaba, where he described himself as sultan of Utetera. This was in the late 1860s and the early 1870s. From then on, for twenty more years, Tippu Tip was the most powerful man in eastern Zaïre. He was loyal to the sultan of Zanzibar, yet, unlike most of the Arabs, he maintained excellent relations with the Nyamwezi. The Nyamwezi territory lay between him and the east coast, controlling his line of communications with Zanzibar. In 1877 he met the explorer Stanley at Nyangwe and accompanied him down the Lualaba to Stanley Falls (later Stanleyville), thus extending his ivory-hunting and other trading activities into the Ituri forest region. By the 1880s Tippu Tip was said to have 50,000 guns at his command. His territory touched that of the Chokwe in the south-west, while his station at Stanley Falls was only a fortnight's journey for the river-steamers which Stanley, by then in the employment of King Leopold of the Belgians, had launched at Lake Malebo. Tippu Tip realised that the European powers were closing in on tropical Africa. From 1883 to 1886, therefore, he made a great effort to rally the Arabs of eastern Zaïre to acknowledge the political authority of the sultan of Zanzibar, in the hope that the sultan's dominion over East Africa would be recognised by the Europeans. In this way Tippu Tip hoped that his rule in eastern Zaïre would become more permanent. But his efforts were in vain: the European powers at the Berlin Conference (see Chapter 9) did not uphold the sultan's claims over the interior of East Africa. Tippu Tip's last years in Zaïre (1877–92) were spent in the improbable role of King Leopold's 'governor' at Stanley Falls. After his eventual retirement to Zanzibar, his former lands had to be conquered, as we have seen, by European forces. However, as with Msiri's Katanga, the Belgians took over many of the institutions of Arab rule in eastern Zaïre and employed many Swahili in positions of subordinate authority. In fact, the Swahili language, known locally as Kingwana, remains the common language of this part of Zaïre to this day.

THE LOWER CONGO REGION AND THE CONGO RIVER ROUTE

The part of West-Central Africa least known to Europeans at the beginning of the nineteenth century was the region north and south of the lower Congo, which at the end of the century was to be the main centre of interest and of the struggle for political control. The most important factor in this region was the geographical one. The Congo river and its tributaries that converge upon Lake Malebo provide something like 6,500 kilometres of waterways which are navigable without interruption. But the 400 kilometres of river between Lake Malebo and the Atlantic Ocean passes through a district of steep and broken hill country in a series of cataracts and waterfalls. This country is as hard to travel through as any in the world. Only with immense difficulty did Stanley and other officials of the Congo Free State have a road cut across the stony hills and forested valleys to transport parts of steamships up to Lake Malebo to be reassembled for use on the navigable waterways. But previous to this, so long as water transport on the upper river was by canoe and so long as head porterage was the only means of transport over the cataract region, the economic possibilities of the Congo river system were limited. At the beginning of the century, when the Portuguese government maintained its monopoly of the ivory-trade, a certain amount of ivory and other traffic used the northward-flowing tributaries of the Congo in order to by-pass Portuguese territory. This trade did not come together at Lake Malebo, which was not yet, as it later became, a commercial bottle-neck. Instead it passed from the rivers to the scores of European trading factories scattered along the coast to the north of the Portuguese possessions in Angola, along numerous side routes through the forest and down the streams that flowed directly into the Atlantic. The staple or main product of this trade was ivory, but, as the nineteenth century went on, it came to include also palm-oil and palm-kernels, beeswax, coffee, raw cotton, and rubber. By the 1870s the volume of British trade alone from the West-Central African coast rivalled that from the Oil Rivers district of southern Nigeria.

It was ivory, however, which formed the backbone of the trade. It was ivory which had the highest value and which did not deteriorate in transport. It was ivory therefore which came from farthest afield – from the Lunda-dominated countries of the Kwango and the Kasai, and from the forest peoples of the main river. Among these, the Teke from the northern shores of Lake Malebo acted as the main traders and carriers for the whole region below Bolobo. Above Bolobo the Bobangi took their place as far as Irebu, and beyond that the Ngala, who traded as far as Lisala, 1,600 kilometres from the sea. This was the farthest point from the west coast where Stanley found European merchandise during his journey down the Congo in 1877. The European guns and cloth which he saw here had taken five years to reach their destination. North of the main river, in the region between the Ubangi and the coast, the part taken by the Chokwe farther south was played by the Fang (French, Pahuin) people. These were immigrants into West-Central Africa from the interior of Cameroun. They had moved southwards from the savanna into the rain-forest and had become the pre-eminent ivory-hunters, exchanging their ivory, generally through African middlemen, for European goods, especially guns, at the factories on the Gabon coast. The Fang at this time were very fierce and were widely reputed as cannibals, and Mary Kingsley, a courageous Englishwoman who travelled through their country in 1894, described how the inhabitants of a Fang village started to sell her their store of elephant tusks and india-rubber:

I did not want these things then, but still felt too nervous of the Fangs to point this out firmly, and so had to buy . . . I found myself the owner of balls of rubber and some tusks, and alas, my little stock of cloth and tobacco all going fast . . . To be short of money in a Fang village is extremely bad, because these Fangs, when a trader has no more goods to sell them, are liable to start trade all over again by killing him and taking back their ivory and rubber and keeping it until another trader comes along.[3]

The whole of this pattern of trade which found its way by lateral or side routes to European trading factories scattered along the coast from Mount Cameroun to Angola was, however, placed in danger by Stanley's journey down the Congo in 1877 and by his demonstration that above the lower Congo cataracts there were thousands of kilometres of smoothly flowing waterways, easily navigable by steamers. The British government was satisfied with the old pattern of trade and took no action when Stanley returned to England and told of his discoveries. However, King Leopold of the Belgians, who had by this time spent nearly twenty years studying the colonial activities of other nations and looking for an opportunity to establish an empire of his own, listened with interest to Stanley's stories. Already Leopold's eyes were fixed upon the Congo basin, though he was planning to approach it from the east, using the Swahili–Arab routes. With Stanley's report before him, he completely changed his plans: he would by-pass the cataracts on the lower river with a railway and launch steamers on the upper river. At once the Congo would become a bottleneck, funnelling the trade of the whole vast river basin into his net. The Arab and Nyamwezi empires would be rolled back. The Chokwe would cease to be of any commercial importance. Under a European

---

[3] 'Some Unpublished Travels', cited in Stephen Gwynn, *The Life of Mary Kingsley* (London, 1933), pp. 109–10.

reorganisation of its trade, the region as a whole would resume its natural unity.

King Leopold's design, as we shall see, did more than anything else to spark off the European scramble for Africa. It brought to an end an old chapter of African history. When the Portuguese first came to West-Central Africa in the fifteenth century, they had opened its trade to the westwards – to the coast and to the lands across the Atlantic Ocean. Through their subsequent concentration on the slave-trade, however, and through their unenlightened attempt to hold down the price of ivory by a royal monopoly, they allowed the East Africans during the first three-quarters of the nineteenth century to divert most of the ivory-trade away from its natural Atlantic outlets into the trading system of the Indian Ocean. From the point of view of geography this was all wrong. Stanley Falls and Bunkeya (Msiri's capital) were both much nearer to the west coast than to the east. But it took Stanley's journey and King Leopold's commercial vision to reverse the swing of the pendulum, which otherwise would have left West-Central Africa a dependency of East-Central Africa and a part of the Muslim world.

5 Southern Africa, 1800–1885

In tropical Africa the basis for the early meetings between Africans and people from the rest of the world was trade. In South Africa such encounters were usually over land. In tropical Africa European and African merchants, even those engaged in the wretched slave-trade, met on an essentially equal footing. They treated each other with a mixture of suspicion and respect. Europeans and Arabs were careful to acknowledge the authority of African rulers and to pay attention to the manners and customs of African peoples. In South Africa the Europeans were present from the beginning not as traders but as settlers. As their numbers grew and as they pushed inland from their first foothold on the Cape peninsula, they cast envious eyes upon the land of the local people. During the seventeenth and most of the eighteenth centuries this land was that occupied by the San hunters and by the Khoi herdsmen. Thereafter, it was the much more densely settled land of the Bantu, who were agriculturalists as well as pastoralists. The only way the Boers could gain possession of the fertile land of the eastern Cape province was by conquest. Such a conquest might take the form of a party of frontier farmers, on horseback and armed with their hunting rifles, driving out the inhabitants of a nearby San or Khoi encampment or Bantu village. Or it might be carried out by the official forces of the colony, involved in a frontier war which was the consequence of the raids and counter-raids of Dutch and African farmers. Naturally the conquerors felt superior to the conquered, and justified their actions on the grounds of their superiority.

The Boers' feeling of superiority is illustrated in an English traveller's account of a frontier farmer who was flogged and imprisoned by the British military authorities in 1798 for ill-treating a Khoi servant:

For the whole of the first night his lamentations were incessant; with a loud voice he cried, 'Myn God! is dat een maniere om Christian mensch te handelen'. (My God, is this the way to treat a Christian man.) His, however, were not the agonies of bodily pain, but the burst of rage and resentment on being put on a level with one of the Zwarte Natie [Black Natives], between

53

whom and themselves the Boers conceive the differences to be fully as great as between themselves and their cattle.[1]

Here we have the origins of the race attitudes characteristic of South Africa.

We have seen (Chapter 2, p. 25) that during the first thirty or so years after the Boers and Bantu met on what came to be known as the Eastern Frontier of the Cape Colony in the 1770s a solution to the conflicts arising out of cattle-stealing and demands for more land might have been found if the two groups had been kept apart. An agreement to halt further expansion and the creation of a frontier properly defended by soldiers, like those which exist between modern states, might still have been possible. After the first or second decade of the nineteenth century no solution along these lines had any real chance of success. The demands of people on both sides of the frontier for land could not be satisfied. The struggle for control of the land of southern Africa had to be fought out until one side or the other emerged as victor.

SHAKA AND THE ZULU NATION

When the first clashes between white and black people took place along the Fish river, the population of the Nguni-speaking Bantu was increasing like that of the Boers. On the Bantu side of the frontier there was less and less available land on which people could live and graze their cattle. Cattle, which required a large area of pasture, were an essential feature in the lives of the South African Bantu; they were the outward sign of their wealth and power, and no man could marry without handing over cattle to his bride's family. In earlier times this pressure of man and beast upon the land would have been met by further expansion along the coast in a south-westerly direction, at the expense of the more thinly settled Khoi of the western Cape. This line of expansion was now blocked by the Boer farmers, who, as we have seen, were also hungry for fresh land. Thus any Bantu people seeking to enlarge its territory could do so only at the expense of its neighbours. In the early years of the nineteenth century one Nguni group expanded in this way, with the result that most of South Africa was plunged into a period of destruction and violence known to Africans as the Time of Troubles (Sotho, *difaqane*; Zulu, *mfecane*).

The Zulu were originally a small clan living in the territory of one of

---

[1] Sir J. Barrow, *An Account of Travels into the Interior of Southern Africa in the Years 1797 and 1798* (London, 1801), vol. 1, p. 398.

the Nguni rulers in Natal, Dingiswayo. Shaka, who was born in 1787, was one of the sons of the Zulu clan-chief. He quarrelled with his father and took refuge at the court of Dingiswayo, where he grew up to become a regimental commander. In 1816, after the death of his father, he was made chief of the Zulu clan by Dingiswayo. Two years later Dingiswayo was murdered and Shaka took over the military empire that he had started to build up. Shaka proved to be a military leader of outstanding genius. He reformed the organisation, weapons and tactics of Dingiswayo's *impi* (Zulu, regiments). The young warriors were formed into a regular army, and were not allowed to marry until they had completed their military service. Adolphe Delegorgue, a French traveller in the 1830s, wrote of the transformation brought about by Shaka (the older spelling of his name was with 'Ch'):

Before Chaka the Zulus wore sandals, and in their battles they hurled the *assagai* [Zulu, spear], as the Amakosa [Xhosa] still do. Above all, they charged in a mass, and without observing any orderly arrangement. Chaka formed regiments of a thousand men each. He did away with the sandal, in spite of the thorny nature of the vegetation, and ordered every warrior to take but one assagai, which was to be exhibited after a fight, stained by the blood of an enemy. The struggle could only be hand to hand. This new way of fighting, unknown to the neighbouring nations, greatly facilitated Chaka's conquests.[2]

Shaka experimented with the new *assagai* before making it the standard weapon of his *impis*; a trader, Henry Fynn, who first visited the great king in 1824, heard of the 'sham-combat' and recounted it in his diary, as an example of Shaka's thoroughness and of his ruthlessness:

Chaka disapproved of the custom of throwing the assagai. To substitute a different mode of attack, he assembled two divisions of his followers, who were ordered to supply themselves with a reed each from the river-bank, that he might be convinced of the effect which only one weapon would produce when used at close quarters. The two divisions then opposed each other, the one throwing their reeds, the other rushing on and stabbing their opponents. The result of this collision met with Chaka's entire satisfaction; few in the first division escaped being wounded, and several severely. Chaka then ordered six oxen to be slaughtered, and collecting the assagais of his followers, he ordered the shafts to be broken and used in cooking the meat. The prime parts were given, hot, to those who had been conspicuous for courage: the inferior parts, after being soaked in cold water, were given to those who had been seen to shrink in the combat.[3]

[2] *Voyage dans l'Afrique australe* (Paris, 1847), vol. 2, p. 218.
[3] *The Diary of Henry Francis Fynn*, ed. J. Stuart and D. McK. Malcolm (Pietermaritzburg, 1950), p. 283.

Shaka's *impi*, which in battle encircled the enemy like the horns of a buffalo, were so effective and so highly disciplined that they proved almost irresistible. The neighbouring Nguni chiefs were defeated and their lands used by the Zulu for grazing cattle. Many of the young men and women, however, were incorporated into the Zulu nation, which under Shaka and his successor Dingane, who murdered his royal brother in 1828, came to dominate most of the area of modern Natal. As we shall see (p. 60), it was the existence of this aggressive and rapidly expanding kingdom in the rear of the Cape Colony's eastern frontier which made the policy of separation along the line of an agreed and stabilised frontier impossible to carry out.

THE TIME OF TROUBLES: MOSHESH AND THE BASUTO

The effects of the Zulu expansion were felt throughout southern Africa. In the hope of escaping from Shaka and his *impi*, fugitives from Natal streamed across the Drakensberg mountains. Under their impact the Sotho-Tswana peoples of the highveld clashed upon one another like an avalanche of stones rolling down a hillside. Thousands of displaced people wandered over the veld or sought refuge in the mountains. Some were driven by famine to live by violence and pillage, and set out like the Zulu on campaigns of conquest. The brunt of the invaders' onset was borne by the Batlokwa, who were ruled by a redoubtable chieftainess called Mantatisi and later by her son, Sikonyela. Assimilating many of the refugees from Natal, Sotho peoples struck out against the Sotho-Tswana peoples of the western Transvaal and Botswana and threw them into utter disorder. Only after the middle of the century did the various Tswana peoples, such as the Bakhatla and the Bamangwato, re-emerge as stable chiefdoms. One Sotho group, the Bafokeng or Makololo, were driven northwards by Mantatisi. Their leader, Sebetwane, is said to have appealed to his people in 1823 in the following words:

My masters, you see that the world is tumbling about our ears. We and other peoples have been driven from our ancestral homes, our cattle seized, our brothers and sons killed, our wives and daughters ravished, our children starved. War has been forced upon us, tribe against tribe. We shall be eaten up one by one. Our fathers taught us *Khotso ke nala* – peace is prosperity – but today there is no peace, no prosperity! What are we to do? My masters, this is my word: Let us march! Let us take our wives and children and cattle, and go forth to seek some land where we may dwell in tranquillity.[4]

---

[4] Quoted in Edwin W. Smith, *Great Lion of Bechuanaland: the life and times of Roger Price* (London, 1957), p. 367.

Thereupon he led the Makololo northwards, in a running struggle with their great enemies, the Ndebele, to the east of them. Finally, about 1840, they settled on the upper Zambezi, after having overcome the Lozi people of the Barotse kingdom and made them their subjects. Their rule over the Barotse only lasted some twenty years, but this was time enough for their Sotho language to become the language of Barotseland.

In two other areas refugees from the Mfecane were gathered together by very able chiefs who merged them into new nations strong enough to withstand pressure from the Zulu and, later on, even from the Europeans. One of these was the Swazi kingdom, created by Sobhuza and his successor Mswazi. The other was Lesotho. The creation of this kingdom was the life's work of Moshesh, one of the greatest leaders southern Africa has known. His character and the steps he took to build Lesotho were described by Eugène Casalis, the French missionary who first entered the country in 1833 and who spent many years as Moshesh's adviser on 'foreign affairs'. Casalis wrote of Moshesh in the rather pompous language characteristic of many Europeans at that time: 'Moshesh has an agreeable and interesting countenance, his deportment is noble and dignified, his features bespeak habits of reflection and of command, and a benevolent smile plays upon his lips.' Casalis was told of the peaceful times before the Mfecane:

At the time of Moshesh's birth (about 1790) the country of the Basutos was extremely populous. Disputes arose from time to time between the various communities, but generally little blood was shed. The green pastures of Butobute, Moshesh's home, and the steep hills where he and his companions hunted, are still celebrated in the national songs of the Basuto. At the moment when it was least expected, these favourite sports were suddenly interrupted by disastrous invasions from Natal. Desolation was carried into the peaceful valleys of Lesuto, fields remained uncultivated, and the horrors of famine were added to those of war. Nearly all the influential men in the country were swept away by the tide of war. Moshesh breasted the stream. Being of a very observant disposition, he knew how to resist and how to yield at the right moment; procured himself allies, even among the invaders of his territory; set his enemies at variance with each other, and by various acts of kindness secured the respect of those even who had sworn his ruin.[5]

In their struggles against both Zulu and Boers the Basuto were aided by the mountains of their country, which provided them with defensive positions almost impregnable even by troops armed with rifles. Moshesh's great tactical and diplomatic skill, which enabled the

---

[5] Eugène Casalis, *The Basutos* (1861) (Cape Town, 1965), pp. 15–16.

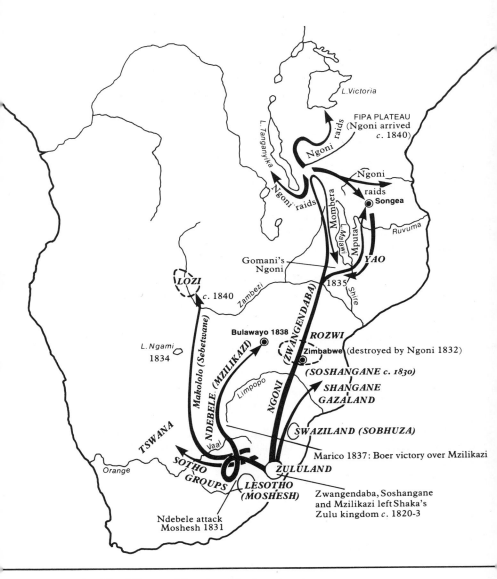

L.Victoria

FIPA PLATEAU
(Ngoni arrived
c. 1840)

L.Tanganyika

Ngoni

raids

Ngoni

Ngoni raids

raids

Songea

Ngoni raids

Mombera

Ruvuma

Malawi

Mputanga

YAO

Gomani's
Ngoni

1835

Shire

LOZI

c. 1840

Zambezi

ROZWI

Makololo (Sebetwane)

Bulawayo 1838

(ZWANGENDABA)

L.Ngami
1834

NDEBELE (MZILIKAZI)

Zimbabwe (destroyed by Ngoni 1832)

(SOSHANGANE c. 1830)

*SHANGANE
GAZALAND*

Limpopo

NGONI

SWAZILAND (SOBHUZA)

Marico 1837: Boer victory over Mzilikazi

TSWANA

Vaal

*SOTHO
GROUPS*

ZULULAND

*LESOTHO
(MOSHESH)*

Zwangendaba, Soshangane
and Mzilikazi left Shaka's
Zulu kingdom c. 1820-3

Orange

Ndebele attack
Moshesh 1831

8   The Mfecane: Nguni and Sotho migrations

Basuto to exercise an influence quite out of proportion to their num-
bers and military strength, is shown in the way he treated Mzilikazi's
Ndebele after they had failed to capture his mountain fortress of
Thaba Bosiu in 1831:

Accustomed to victory, the Zulus advanced in serried ranks, not appearing to notice the masses of basalt which came rolling down with a tremendous noise from the top of the mountain. But soon there was a general crush – an avalanche of stones and a shower of spears, which sent back the assailants with more rapidity than they had advanced. The chiefs who were seen rallying the fugitives, and snatching away the plumes with which their heads were decorated, and trampling them under foot in a rage, led their men again towards the formidable rampart. But in vain. The next day the Zulus retired. At the moment of their departure a Mosuto, driving some fat oxen, stopped before the first ranks, and gave this message. 'Moshesh salutes you. Supposing that hunger had brought you into this country, he sends you these cattle, that you may eat them on your way home.' Moshesh was never troubled by these people again.[6]

Some Zulu groups, whose leaders had quarrelled with Shaka, left Zululand to make their own conquests elsewhere. Soshangane took his people, the Shangane, into Gazaland in southern Mozambique, where they conquered and largely absorbed the Tsonga, who were the earlier inhabitants of that region. Next, Zwangendaba and his warriors swept northwards across the Limpopo and on to the Zimbabwean plateau, where they destroyed the old Rozwi kingdom of the Changamires, the rulers of the western plateau. Before long, however, Zwangendaba and his 'Ngoni' moved on, to settle finally in the highlands east and west of Lake Malawi. Some of the farthest-flung of these Ngoni *impi*, always gathering fresh recruits from the peoples they defeated, campaigned as far north as the southern shores of Lake Victoria and as far east as the Indian Ocean. As we shall see in Chapter 6, they had a considerable effect on events in East Africa. Lastly, Mzilikazi led his Ndebele (Sotho, *Matebele*) Zulu across the Drakensberg and on to the highveld, in the wake of Mantatisi and Sebetwane's Sotho groups, until they were defeated near modern Pretoria by the invading Boers in 1837. The Ndebele then retreated north across the Limpopo and settled on the western part of the Zimbabwean plateau (Matabeleland), making many of the local Shona people, the former subjects of the Rozwi kingdom, into their tribute-paying subjects.

THE EXPANSION OF THE BOERS: THE GREAT TREK

Refugees also fled from the Zulu armies into the eastern Cape Colony, increasing the frontier conflicts with the Dutch farmers, whose numbers were increased by 5,000 British settlers in 1820. The lawlessness on the frontier and the rough treatment by the Boers of their

[6] Ibid. p. 63.

semi-servile labourers shocked the humanitarians and missionary societies in Britain. These, during the early years of the nineteenth century, forced the British government to adopt a more responsible concern for the non-white peoples of the British empire. The most outspoken of the Christian missionaries in South Africa was John Philip of the London Missionary Society. Mainly through his efforts, the Khoisan of the Cape Colony were brought under the protection of the law in 1828. Later, after the abolition of slavery in 1833, he extended his campaign to include the former slaves. In the eyes of the Boers the British government was more concerned with giving legal protection to their servants than with helping them to expand at the expense of the Nguni tribes. Every Dutch farmer's son considered it his birthright to possess a 6,000-acre ranch when he got married, and in this wasteful way the available land within the colony's borders was soon exhausted. In 1836 a large area of land on the eastern frontier which had previously been annexed to the colony was returned to the Africans, because the British government was not prepared to meet the expense of administering it. This was more than the Boers would endure, and many trekked (*trek*, Dutch: a journey, a migration) out of British territory and across the Orange river to the north. Anna Steenkamp, the sister of one of the leaders of the Great Trek, gave as one of their reasons for leaving the Cape

> The shameful and unjust proceedings with reference to the freedom of our slaves: and yet it is not so much their freedom that drove us to such lengths as their being placed on an equal footing with Christians, contrary to the laws of God and the natural distinction of race and religion, so that it was intolerable for any decent Christian to bow down beneath such a yoke; wherefore we rather withdrew in order thus to preserve our doctrines in purity.[7]

Livingstone later commented: 'The Boers determined to erect themselves into a republic, in which they might pursue without molestation the "proper treatment of the blacks". This "proper treatment" has always contained the element of compulsory unpaid labour.'[8]

The Trekkers had learned from hunters and traders that fertile parts of Natal had been virtually depopulated by the Zulu and turned into grazing lands. They planned to infiltrate the Zulu lands by moving across the Transvaal and descending through the Drakensburg passes into Natal. By this means they hoped to outflank the densely settled Nguni between the Fish river and Natal. At first the Zulu king Dingane successfully resisted this encroachment. By 1839,

[7] Quoted in John Bird, *Annals of Natal* (Pietermaritzburg, 1888), vol. 1, p. 459.
[8] *Missionary Travels and Researches in South Africa* (London, 1857), p. 29.

however, the Boers under Pretorius had defeated them and had set up a republic in Natal. This action brought them into conflict once again with the British government, which would not allow the existence of a rival European state on the shores of the Indian Ocean. It also rightly feared the effects of Boer penetration into Natal on the encircled Nguni of the eastern Cape. Natal was therefore annexed by Britain in 1845. Frustrated in this way, most of the Natal Boers returned to the highveld, where other groups of farmers had already driven the Ndebele across the Limpopo. The British government half-heartedly followed the Boers north of the Orange river, but in 1852 and 1854 recognised the independence of, respectively, the Boer republics of the Transvaal and the Orange Free State.

In the middle years of the nineteenth century, therefore, South Africa consisted of two British colonies, the Cape and Natal, the two Boer republics, and many independent African kingdoms and chiefdoms, of which the Basuto and Zulu kingdoms were the largest. The total white population was little more than 300,000; the African population was between one and two million. In 1853 the Cape Colony was granted a constitution with an elected parliament, and in 1872 full internal self-government, with ministers responsible to parliament. The franchise was non-racial; that is, representatives were elected by people of all races, provided they owned property of a certain value or received a certain amount in wages. This liberal political attitude of the Cape was not shared by the other Europeans in South Africa. In the Boer republics only white people were recognised as citizens, and only white males exercised the vote.

THE END OF THE INDEPENDENT AFRICAN STATES

The discovery of great diamond deposits near the junction of the Orange and the Vaal rivers in 1868 hastened the inevitable process whereby the self-governing African peoples and states lost their independence and were brought under European rule. Already in 1856–7 the situation had seemed so desperate to the Xhosa and Tembu living immediately to the east of the Cape Colony that they followed the prophecy of a girl, Nongquase. She stated that if, on a certain day, the cattle were killed and the grain destroyed, the tribal ancestors would drive the Europeans into the sea. The result, of course, was a disastrous famine, in which thousands died, while thousands more abandoned their land and went to seek work and food in the Cape. The opening of the diamond mines greatly increased the demand for labour, and Africans converged upon Kimberley from all over 61

9 Southern Africa, 1880–1885: African migrations

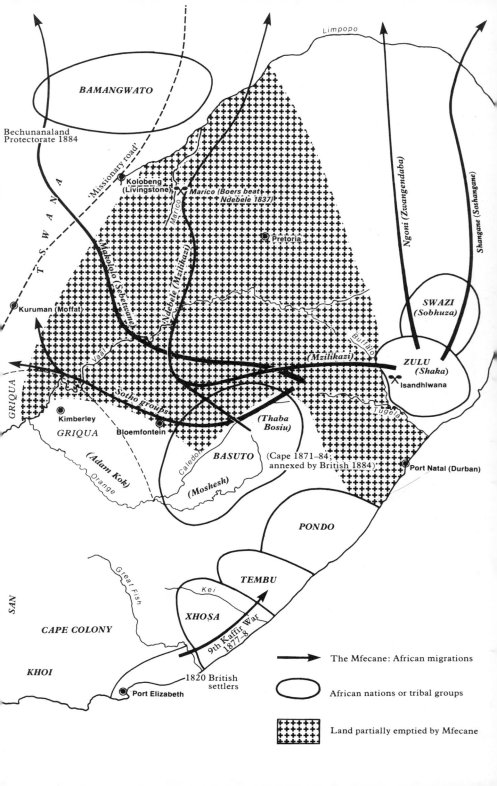

BAMANGWATO

Bechunanaland
Protectorate 1884

'Missionary road'

T·S·W·A·N·A

Kolobeng
(Livingstone)

Marico (Boers beat
Ndebele 1837)

Marico

Pretoria

Makololo (Sebetwane)

Ndebele (Mzilikazi)

Kuruman (Moffat)

GRIQUA

Vaal

Sotho groups

Kimberley

GRIQUA

Bloemfontein

(Adam Kok)

Orange

Caledon

(Thaba Bosiu)

BASUTO

(Mzilikazi)

Limpopo

Ngoni (Zwangendaba)

Shangane (Soshangane)

SWAZI (Sobhuza)

ZULU (Shaka)

Isandhlwana

Buffalo

Tugela

(Mzilikazi)

(Cape 1871–84;
annexed by British 1884)

(Moshesh)

Port Natal (Durban)

PONDO

Great Fish

TEMBU

Kei

SAN

XHOSA

9th Kaffir War 1877–8

CAPE COLONY

KHOI

1820 British
settlers

Port Elizabeth

➤ The Mfecane: African migrations

⬭ African nations or tribal groups

▦ Land partially emptied by Mfecane

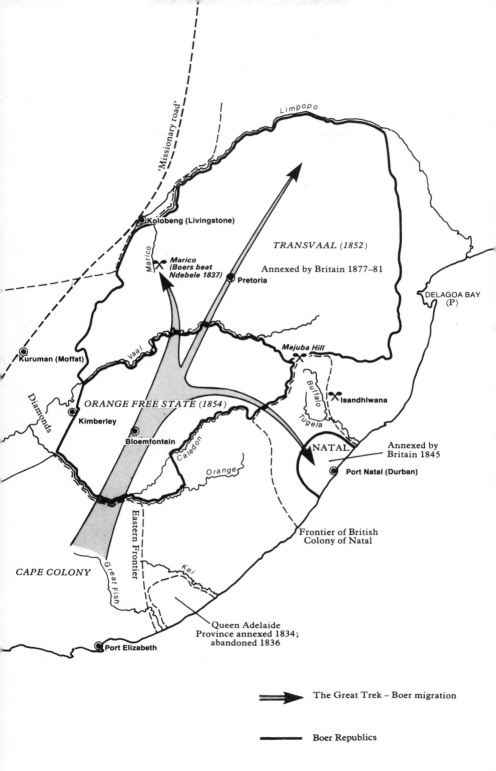

'Missionary road'

Limpopo

Kolobeng (Livingstone)

Marico

*Marico
(Boers beat
Ndebele 1837)*

Pretoria

TRANSVAAL (1852)

Annexed by Britain 1877–81

DELAGOA BAY
(P)

Kuruman (Moffat)

Vaal

Majuba Hill

Buffalo

Isandhlwana

Tugela

ORANGE FREE STATE (1854)

Diamonds

Kimberley

Bloemfontein

Caledon

Orange

NATAL

Annexed by
Britain 1845

Port Natal (Durban)

Eastern Frontier

Frontier of British
Colony of Natal

CAPE COLONY

Great Fish

Kei

Queen Adelaide
Province annexed 1834;
abandoned 1836

Port Elizabeth

The Great Trek – Boer migration

Boer Republics

southern Africa. In the early days of the mining the companies regularly paid these workers in guns and ammunition, and so thousands of Africans returned to their homes with fire-arms. This led to exaggerated fears on the European side of a 'united native rising'. Fortunately for the white men in South Africa the wars that did break out were no such thing, but they were extremely destructive because Africans as well as Europeans were using fire-arms.

In 1871 the Cape government assumed control over the Basuto, who had been involved in a bitter land struggle with the Free State farmers. Next, in 1877–8, it finally broke the fighting power of the Xhosa and other Nguni tribes on the eastern frontier – though at a great cost in men and money. Again, in 1877 the British government took over the Transvaal, where the forces of a poverty-stricken Boer government could make no headway in the war which had broken out against the Bapedi under their chief Sekukuni. This involved the British (who in Natal had been friendly with the Zulu) in a quarrel between the Transvaal Boers and Cetshwayo (pronounced Ketshwayo), the nephew and successor of Dingane, over an area of grazing land. Cetshwayo was now provoked by Sir Bartle Frere, the British high commissioner in South Africa, to armed conflict. The Zulu defeated one British army at Isandhlwana before being crushed by the reinforcements which the British hurriedly sent into Natal. The following year, 1880, saw the outbreak of a long war between the Cape government and the Basuto, sparked off by an attempt to disarm the Africans. The Cape had to be rescued from this disastrous war in 1884, when the British government took over direct responsibility for administering Basutoland. These were not the only troubles. Whites were also involved in clashes with some of the Tswana tribes and with the Korana (Khoi) people on the lower Orange river. In South-West Africa the mutual enmity of the Herero (Bantu) and Nama (Khoi) peoples, both pastoralists in a dry land, was inflamed by the activities of European traders, who took sides in their disputes and supplied them with both fire-arms and liquor.

Just before the outbreak of all these wars and while they were in progress, attempts were made, in Britain by the colonial secretary, Lord Carnarvon, and in the Cape by Frere, to unite the white states in South Africa into a single large territory under one government. By the end of the 1870s this attempt at confederation had failed. The Boers in the Orange Free State had never forgiven the British annexation of the diamond-bearing district of Griqualand West in 1871. At the end of 1880 the Transvaalers rose against the government imposed upon them by Britain three years previously and in 1881 defeated

64

10   Southern Africa, 1800–1885: Boer migrations

a British force sent to put them down in an action at Majuba Hill.

THE ROAD TO THE NORTH

Much of the hostility between the British government and the Boers was due to the presence of the Christian missionaries, whose activities among the Africans were regarded by the Boers with great suspicion. Missions were well established within the colonial borders of the Cape and Natal, though they could make little headway among the still independent and warlike Nguni peoples, especially the Zulu and the Ndebele. They were more influential among the Sotho and Tswana groups, however. The Paris Missionary Society established a close relationship with Moshesh, as we have seen, and, although neither he nor his successor was converted, many thousands of the Basuto became literate and Christian. Robert Moffat of the London Missionary Society had worked among the Griqua (a group of mixed Khoi and European descent) and Tswana peoples at Kuruman, beyond the northern frontier of the Cape, since the 1820s. Here Boer encroachment upon Tswana lands during and after the Great Trek added to the dislike of the missionaries for the Transvaal government and made them determined to keep open a way to the north which was free from Boer control. Livingstone began his career in Africa as a missionary and explorer, working to open up this 'missionary road' – the narrow strip of habitable Botswana between the Transvaal and Kalahari desert, which led northwards to Matabeleland and Barotseland. Through Livingstone's great journey from Barotseland to Luanda and from there across Africa to the Zambezi mouth (1853–6), European governments, traders and missionaries were made aware of the possibilities for Christianity and commerce in the lands north of the Limpopo. The British government in particular realised the vital importance of the 'missionary road' between South Africa and the interior. As soon as the Germans annexed the South-West African coast in 1883, the British replied by declaring a protectorate over Botswana (known during the colonial period as Bechuanaland). This paved the way for Rhodes's occupation of Zimbabwe a few years later.

6   East-Central Africa, 1800–1884

East Africa, for the purposes of this chapter, includes not only the modern states of Kenya, Uganda and Tanzania, but also northern Mozambique, Malawi, Burundi and Rwanda. All these lands were to come under some kind of European rule before the end of the century, but from 1800 till 1884 the predominant outside influences were not European, but Swahili–Arab or Egyptian–Sudanese. Before 1884 only a handful of Europeans attempted trading ventures of their own in the interior. In general, European and American enterprise was limited, like that of the Indians from the British empire in India, to supplying Arab and Egyptian merchants with manufactured goods, especially cloth and fire-arms, in exchange for ivory and a few less-important products such as hides, beeswax and gum arabic. It was the Muslim merchants who traded directly with the African peoples. The work of Christian missionaries was the main European activity in East Africa before the partition took place. The missionaries, however, arrived in this region much later than the Muslim traders, and their work was still in the pioneer stage when the colonial period began. They were not responsible for the establishment of European political control, which came, when it did, mainly as the result of happenings outside East Africa.

THE ARAB PENETRATION OF THE INTERIOR

The evolution of the Swahili–Arab population in the coastal belt of East Africa and on Zanzibar and the other offshore islands was described in Chapter 2, as were the origins of trade between the interior and the coast. This trade from the interlacustrine kingdoms and from Katanga, most of which was carried originally by the Nyamwezi, seems to have been mainly a peaceful activity. Early European travellers were much impressed by the prosperity and sufficiency of many of the inland districts they visited. For example, Sir Richard Burton, who was by no means prejudiced in favour of African achievements, wrote after his journey to Lake Tanganyika in 1858: 'The African is in these regions superior in comforts, better dressed, fed and lodged than the unhappy Ryot [peasant] of British

India. His condition, where the slave-trade is slack, may indeed be compared advantageously with that of the peasantry in some of the richest of European countries.' Traditions among peoples who were to suffer from the violence that was to come recall, in the exaggerated way that people often do, the good old days:

In the old times, long long ago, in their old homes, the Yao were in accord and united. If a quarrel arose they used to fight without rancour, avoiding bloodshed. If strangers came to a village, would they have to pay for their food? No, it was bestowed on them free; directly a man heard that a stranger was at his door, he would rejoice and say 'I have the plant of hospitality at my door, bringing guests'.[1]

As the nineteenth century approached, however, two factors combined to hasten changes in the old way of life. The first was the rapidly growing demand at the coast for ivory and slaves. The second was the great desire of the peoples in the interior for more and more fire-arms. There was still, as there had always been, a ready market for domestic and plantation slaves in all the east-coast settlements, as well as in Oman and the other states of Arabia and the Persian Gulf. From the mid-eighteenth century until the mid-nineteenth the French added greatly to the demand with their labour requirements for the sugar and coffee plantations in Réunion (and, until the Napoleonic wars, in Mauritius). In the early nineteenth century the Portuguese, because of the restrictions imposed on the West African slave-trade north of the equator, shipped an increasing number of slaves round the Cape from Mozambique to Brazil and Cuba. And, above all, the nineteenth century saw a vast development of the plantation agriculture of the Swahili-Arabs, and with it a growing demand for slaves from the interior. But, as the nineteenth century went on, the demand for ivory – and therefore the prices paid for it – became even greater than that for slaves. The age-old market for East African ivory was the Asian one. By the middle of the nineteenth century, however, demand in Europe and America had very greatly increased. Wealth derived from the industrial and commercial changes taking place in their countries had developed an almost insatiable appetite for the luxury objects made from ivory, such as knife-handles, piano-keys, billiard balls and ornaments of every kind.

A few of the Swahili-Arabs who had been settled on the coast for centuries began to respond to these opportunities at the end of the eighteenth century, soon after the Nyamwezi traders had pioneered the routes. The great advance of the coastmen, however, developed

[1] Yohannah B. Abdullah, *The Yaos*, ed. and tr. M. Sanderson (Zomba, 1919), p. 11. 67

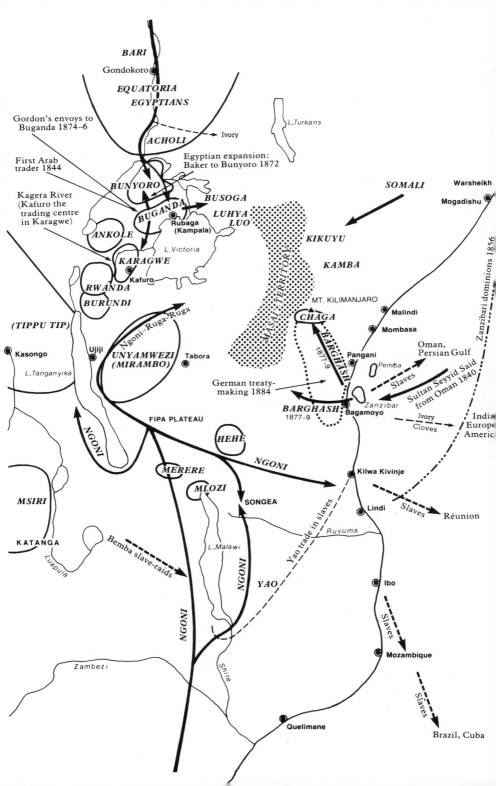

BARI

Gondokoro

EQUATORIA
EGYPTIANS

Gordon's envoys to
Buganda 1874-6

ACHOLI

→ Ivory

L.Turkana

First Arab
trader 1844

Egyptian expansion:
Baker to Bunyoro 1872

SOMALI

Warsheikh

Mogadishu

Kagera River
(Kafuro the
trading centre
in Karagwe)

BUNYORO

BUSOGA

BUGANDA

LUHYA
LUO

Rubaga
(Kampala)

ANKOLE

L. Victoria

KIKUYU

KAMBA

Zanzibari dominions 1856

KARAGWE

Kafuro

MT. KILIMANJARO

RWANDA

BURUNDI

Malindi

CHAGA

(TIPPU TIP)

Mombasa

Ngoni-Ruga-Ruga

BARGHASH

Pangani

Oman,
Persian Gulf

Kasongo

Ujiji

UNYAMWEZI
(MIRAMBO)

Tabora

1877-9

Pemba

Slaves

L.Tanganyika

MASAI TERRITORY

Sultan Seyyid Said
from Oman 1840

German treaty-
making 1884

Zanzibar

India
Europe
America

BARGHASH
1877-9

Bagamoyo

Ivory
Cloves

NGONI

FIPA PLATEAU

HEHE

NGONI

MSIRI

MERERE

MLOZI

Kilwa Kivinje

SONGEA

KATANGA

Luapula

Bemba slave-raids

L.Malawi

NGONI

YAO

Lindi

Slaves

Réunion

Ruvuma

Yao trade in slaves

Ibo

Slaves

NGONI

YAO

Zambezi

Shire

Mozambique

Slaves

Quelimane

Slaves

Brazil, Cuba

only during the long and brilliant reign (1806–56) of Seyyid Said, imam of Muscat and hereditary overlord of the Arab settlements along the Zanzibar coast. Said was both an able commander and an economic genius, and it did not take him long to see that his East African empire was more worthy of his attention than the rocks and deserts in his little state of Oman on the western shores of the Persian Gulf. But first he had to reconquer it. He possessed efficient armed forces. The ships of his navy had been provided by Britain under the terms of a treaty made with him, and his army consisted of Baluchi mercenaries recruited from the borders of Persia and India. With these he occupied Zanzibar and made effective his nominal control over the coastal towns from Warsheikh in the north to Lindi in the south, including the important cities of Mombasa and Kilwa, which had for long been practically independent. Under Said's influence Zanzibar became the central market for the whole of the East African coast. After his introduction of the clove-tree from the East Indies, the islands of Zanzibar and Pemba soon came to grow most of the world's supply of cloves. The plantations were invariably worked by slaves who were imported from the interior. In 1840, after a series of increasingly long visits to his African dominions, Said actually transferred his capital from Muscat to Zanzibar, where he was usually given the title of sultan. After his death in 1856, the scattered empire was divided, one son taking Oman, and another, Majid, becoming sultan of Zanzibar.

Sultans Said and Majid encouraged Arabs to settle in Zanzibar as plantation-owners, and they also encouraged the coastal people to trade in the interior. The sultanate provided the background of security necessary for large-scale trade: debts could be collected at Zanzibar and contracts enforced. The financial arrangements for the trade were made by Indian merchants of Zanzibar and the coastal towns, who had strong commercial ties with their fellow countrymen across the ocean in India. They supplied credit to Arab traders to enable them to stock up caravans with goods and journey up-country, sometimes not returning with their purchases of ivory and slaves until several years later. In a letter dated 21 November 1872 (which was sent back to England with his body) Livingstone wrote of these Indian traders, 'The Banians have the Custom House and all the public revenue of Zanzibar entirely in their hands and by their money, arms, ammunition and goods a large and cruel Slave trade had been carried on.'[2] The Nyamwezi traders resisted the competition of the new-

---

[2] Quoted in Zoë Marsh, *East Africa through Contemporary Records* (Cambridge, 1961), p. 44.

11   East-Central Africa: 1800–1884

comers and were able to retain a near monopoly of trade routes from central Tanzania to Katanga. But the Arabs were better organised and armed and had greater financial resources behind them. They were able to supply African rulers with guns and ammunition, which were beyond the means of the Nyamwezi traders. As the century went on, and as European armies were re-equipped with more and more modern varieties of fire-arms, so more and more of the out-of-date models found their way on to the African market. By the end of the 1830s Arab traders had penetrated to Lake Tanganyika, and in 1844 the first Arab visited the court of Buganda. So extensive was the Arab trading in the interior that it was said as a joke that 'when they pipe in Zanzibar, people dance on the shores of the great lakes'. Arabs established settlements at certain key points, such as Tabora in the Nyamwezi country and Ujiji on Lake Tanganyika. These were mainly commercial depots, but in time they grew to exercise a certain military and political control over the surrounding countryside. Burton and Speke visited Tabora in 1858 and the former wrote:

The Arabs live comfortably, and even splendidly. The houses, though single-storied, are large, substantial and capable of defence. Their gardens are extensive and well planted; they receive regular supplies from the coast; they are surrounded by troops of slaves, whom they train to divers crafts and callings; rich men have riding asses from Zanzibar, and even the poorest keep flocks and herds.[3]

Generally the Arabs obtained their ivory and slaves from the local rulers, who, armed with the imported guns, sent their warriors to hunt elephants and to raid the forests of neighbouring peoples, often capturing slaves in the process. In most of East Africa, however, slaving was more a by-product of the ivory rush than the primary object of the trade. Only the country around Lake Malawi was primarily a slaving region, where the powerful Yao chiefs raided the ill-organised and defenceless peoples of the eastern lakeshore. The Bemba, and later the Ngoni, did the same on the west. It was along the trade route from Lake Malawi to the coast that Livingstone noted some of the worst atrocities that he witnessed in all his long travels:

We passed a woman tied by the neck to a tree and dead . . . We saw others tied up in a similar manner, and one lying on the path shot or stabbed for she was in a pool of blood. The explanation we got invariably was that the Arab who owned these victims was enraged at losing his money by the slaves being unable to march . . . Today we came upon a man dead from starvation . . . One of our men wandered and found a number of slaves with slave-sticks on,

[3] R. F. Burton, *Lake Regions of Central Africa* (London, 1860), vol. 1, p. 328.

abandoned by their master from want of food . . . We passed village after village and gardens, all deserted.[4]

Elsewhere, however, the emphasis was on ivory, though slaves were bought and sold at every stage along the trade routes. The Nyamwezi, for example, were great buyers of slaves, whom they employed in agricultural work while they themselves were absent on long trading journeys.

THE NGONI AND MIRAMBO

The situation in Tanzania was complicated towards the middle of the nineteenth century by the incursions of the Ngoni from the south. Bands of warriors who had broken away from Shaka's Zulu kingdom (see Chapter 5) were swollen by the attachment of the remnants of peoples they had defeated on their long northward trek. They spread across much of western and southern Tanzania to the east and west of Lake Malawi, where they finally settled as ruling aristocracies. Far beyond the range of their settlement, their outlying raiders and their military tactics were absorbed into the new groupings of tribes that were taking place in Tanzania. Warrior bands, called *ruga-ruga* in Nyamwezi country, and *maviti* and *magwangwara* elsewhere, roamed the countryside, usually pillaging on their own account, but ready to be employed by ruthless war-lords or Arab traders. Sometimes their raids caused their victims to combine against them. The centralised state of the Hehe, for instance, in south-central Tanzania, was formed in this way. On the other hand a young Nyamwezi chief, Mirambo, actually took groups of Ngoni *ruga-ruga* into his service and used them to build up and extend his hereditary chiefdom in the western part of Unyamwezi. Mirambo became powerful enough, in the 1870s, to rival the Arab merchant princes. By 1880 he had gained control of the Ujiji trade route to Lake Tanganyika and was able to threaten even the route leading north-westwards to Buganda. It was with Mirambo and not with his fellow Arabs, that Tippu Tip allied himself in his commercial exploitation of eastern Zaïre, which was described in Chapter 4.

THE INTERLACUSTRINE REGION

North of the Nyamwezi country, the trade with the rich interlacustrine region developed, from the 1840s on, mainly under the control

[4] *Last Journals*, ed. Horace Waller (London, 1874), vol. I, p. 70.

of Swahili-Arab merchants. The main trade route ran from Tabora through Karagwe, where there was a large Arab commercial settlement at Kafuro near the capital, to the Kagera river. Here it divided, a westerly branch leading off through the plains of eastern Ankole to Bunyoro, and an easterly branch following near the shoreline of Lake Victoria towards the capital of Buganda. The Tutsi kingdom of Rwanda, though still at the height of its power, would admit no strangers within its frontiers, and such outside trade as there was passed by Rwanda caravans to and from Karagwe. Ankole was nearly as hostile to foreigners as Rwanda. The big trading countries were Bunyoro and Buganda. For, in addition to her powerful armies, Buganda was the chief naval power of Lake Victoria, and, as the nineteenth century went on, fleets of the great Buganda canoes made of planks sewn together, with their high prows visible far over the water, came regularly to the southern shores of the lake, competing with the overland trade routes. In this way Kabakas Suna and Mutesa, who reigned through the middle years of the century from about 1832 till 1884, steadily built up their stocks of cloth and guns, and used them to arm and pay ever more efficient armies, which harried the Basoga to the east and the Bahaya to the south and nibbled more cautiously at the renewed military power of Bunyoro to the north-west.

It was not from only the south-east, however, that the outside world was forcing itself upon the interlacustrine states. As we shall see in the next chapter, the trading frontier of the Egyptian Sudan had been established since the 1840s in the Bari country to the south of the Nile swamps, and by the 1860s the Khartoum-based ivory-traders were operating among the Acholi people of the northern province of modern Uganda. The Egyptians established their first contacts with Bunyoro by intervening in the succession struggle following the death of the ruler, Kamurasi, in 1869. In that year the Khedive Ismail of Egypt sent the British explorer Samuel Baker to be governor of this 'Equatorial Province' of the Sudan. Baker tried unsuccessfully to occupy Bunyoro and had to be content with establishing forts along its northern edge. In 1873, however, he was succeeded by Charles Gordon, who had definite instructions to extend the Egyptian dominions to the Great Lakes. Thus in 1874 Gordon's emissaries reached the court of Kabaka Mutesa of Buganda.

Mutesa knew enough of the outside world to guess what was afoot. An Egyptian garrison was detained by the Kabaka and given a taste of Buganda's power to hurt, and then allowed to retire unharmed. Meanwhile Mutesa strengthened his links with the strangers from the east coast, buying more arms, listening to the Islamic teachings of his

Arab friends, even learning to write the Swahili language in Arabic characters. His fears of the Egyptians were described by the Anglican missionary Alexander Mackay a few years later, in his biography which was written by his sister:

Egypt had always been an object of great suspicion in the eyes of the Baganda. Captain Speke, who formed Mtesa's acquaintance a dozen years before Stanley, tells how the king objected to his passing through Uganda to Egypt via the Nile . . . The Egyptian station of Mruli was regarded by Mtesa with very jealous feelings, and the Arabs lost no opportunity to fan the flame. Knowing well that with the presence of the white man the hope of their gains was gone, they told him that Colonel Gordon and the Turks (as they called the Egyptians) would soon come and 'eat the country'. The Baganda constantly had the word *Baturki* on their lips. Mtesa never wearied in narrating to Mackay all his intercourse with white men: how Speke brought Grant, and then sent Baker; how Colonel Long (Gordon's agent) came and was followed by Stanley. 'What do they all want?' asked Mtesa. 'Are they not coming to look for lakes, that they may put ships and guns on them? Did not Speke come here by the Queen's orders for that purpose?'[5]

It was almost certainly the presence of a second Egyptian delegation at his court at the time of the explorer Stanley's visit in 1875 which caused him to encourage Stanley to let it be known in Europe that he would like Christian missionaries to come and settle in his country. Mutesa was an exceptionally intelligent and open-minded man, and no doubt he was genuinely impressed by what his European visitors – first Speke (1862) and then Stanley – had told him of Christianity and European civilisation. As a statesman he realised that if Buganda was really threatened by the Egyptian advance from the north, it would be wise to increase the number of his other foreign contacts, so as to be able to play them off against the Egyptians. Church of England missionaries from Britain therefore arrived in Buganda in 1877, and Roman Catholic missionaries from France in 1879, and, so long as the Egyptian threat lasted, both received a warm welcome. In the course of the next six or seven years Christianity became so deeply established among a minority of the court circle in Buganda that it was able to survive a brief, but terrible, persecution at the hands of Mutesa's successor, Mwanga, in 1885–6.

PEOPLES AND TRADE ROUTES OF KENYA

Right up until the colonial period the main trade outlet of Buganda

---

[5] J. W. H. Mackay, *The Story of the Life of Mackay of Uganda* (London, 1898), pp. 132–4.

and the other interlacustrine states remained the south-easterly one, linking up with the trans-Tanzanian route at Tabora. It was difficult to set up a more direct route from Buganda to the coast at Mombasa because of the nomadic and warlike way of life of so many of the peoples, notably the Masai, in what became Kenya. With the Masai, it was not merely that they attacked strangers: throughout the nineteenth century they fought almost continuously among themselves. Thus the whole region of the Kenya highlands was in a perpetual state of unrest. Traders could only pass through this country at great danger to themselves and to their goods, and no regular trading links could be set up by the Swahili-Arabs with the densely populated lands of the Luo and the Abaluhya in the Kavirondo region to the north-east of Lake Victoria until several decades after they had taken over the Nyamwezi routes to the south and west of the lake. The equivalent among the Kenya peoples of the Nyamwezi were the Kamba, who lived some 300 kilometres inland from Mombasa. They made trading contacts with the Kikuyu on one side and with the coastmen on the other as early as the 1830s, when a series of disastrous famines caused them to leave their homelands in search of food. The German missionary traveller Johann Krapf noted how 'The Swahili purvey to the Wakamba cotton fabrics (Americani), blue calico, glass beads, copper and brass-wire, red ochre, black pepper, salt and blue vitriol (zinc), and receive in exchange, chiefly cattle and ivory.'[6] The Kamba continued to monopolise trade between Kikuyuland and Mombasa until, in the 1880s, the Arabs with their superior organisation and weapons drew off the Kikuyu trade into their own routes. The Arabs did not thrust into the hinterland of any part of the Kenyan or north Tanzanian coast until the 1860s, when they managed to open routes to the Chaga of the Kilimanjaro region. Thence they were able to work their way across the narrowest part of the Masai plain and on westwards to Kavirondo. By about 1880 these Arab ivory-traders and -hunters had reached the country to the west of Lake Turkana. Here, in the last unexploited ivory district of East Africa, they came into contact with Egyptians from the southern Sudan and with Ethiopians, all concerned with enriching themselves from the ivory-trade.

THE SUMMIT OF SWAHILI-ARAB POWER IN EAST AFRICA

We have seen that the most important development during the first three-quarters of the nineteenth century in East Africa was the commercial penetration of the whole region by the Swahili-Arabs from the

[6] J. L. Krapf, *Travels in Eastern Africa* (London, 1860), p. 353.

East Coast. And now for a brief period in the late 1870s and early 1880s it seemed that the commercial empire of Zanzibar might turn itself into a political one. In the eyes of the British consul-general at Zanzibar, Sir John Kirk, this was a development very much to be hoped for. Kirk had been in Zanzibar since 1864 and had built up a remarkable degree of influence, first with Sultan Majid and then with his brother, Sultan Barghash. Neither Kirk nor his masters in London wished for direct British intervention in East Africa. In their view a friendly and easily influenced sultan of Zanzibar would be both the cheapest and the most effective means of achieving their two objectives, which were to end the East African slave-trade and to prevent the intervention of other European powers in the area. In 1873 Barghash was persuaded to abolish the slave-trade within his dominions, and from then onwards, so far as the British government was concerned, the wider the sultan's dominions, the better. Inspired by Kirk, Barghash engaged a British officer to enlarge and train his army, and in the late 1870s he began to set up garrisons along the line of the main trans-Tanzanian trade route. As Kirk watched the growing interests of other European powers, especially of King Leopold of the Belgians, so he spurred Barghash to greater efforts. The Arab traders in the far interior were encouraged to turn from commerce to conquest, and did so – first Tippu Tip in the region round Lake Tanganyika; next the Arabs who were settled round the north end of Lake Malawi; and finally the Arabs in Buganda. In 1887 a special representative of Sultan Barghash arrived in Buganda, where the previous year the Kabaka Mwanga had executed a number of Christians at his court. This representative plotted with the Muslim party in the kingdom to depose Mwanga in 1888, and then to seize power for themselves. A younger brother of Mwanga was declared to be Kabaka. This Muslim success, however, was short-lived. By 1890 Mwanga had regained power, with the support of the Christian Baganda, in spite of his previous persecution of their religion.

The achievements of Tippu Tip and other Arab chiefs marked the summit of Arab power in East Africa; and to the European missionaries living scattered about in the interior this appeared in a very different light from that in which it had been conceived by Kirk at Zanzibar. Where Kirk had imagined a Zanzibar dominion recognised by the powers and responsive to British influence, the missionaries saw burning villages and starving refugees, and a new anti-European and anti-Christian attitude among the Arabs. The experience made them long for, and in some cases work for, European colonial occupation. In the event, however, Swahili-Arab imperialism did not last

75

long. Before any missionary condemnation of it had time to take effect, a handful of German adventurers had shown that the sultan's power in the interior of East Africa was nothing but a hollow sham. Neither Carl Peters nor his associates in the Society for German Colonisation had ever set foot in East Africa before 1884; but they had grasped the essential fact that a mere 50 or 60 kilometres inland from the coast there were African communities which owed no allegiance to the sultan of Zanzibar. They realised that the rulers of these could be persuaded without too much trouble to sign pieces of paper placing their lands under the protection of a European power. From that moment onwards Kirk's plan was doomed. The European scramble for East Africa had begun.

MADAGASCAR

King Nampoina's conquests at the end of the eighteenth and the beginning of the nineteenth centuries laid the foundations for the great Merina state. This must rank as one of the most remarkable political creations in the whole of Africa in the pre-colonial period. Nampoina's successor, Radama I (1810–28), transformed the warrior chiefdom into a nation comparable in many ways to the smaller states of Europe. He rounded off Nampoina's conquests, so that by the end of his reign two-thirds of the island was under Hova domination. The rich kingdom of Betsileo, in the highlands around Fianarantsoa to the south of Tananarive, recognised the control of Radama. The Merina army was equipped with fire-arms, largely supplied by the British from the Indian Ocean island of Mauritius, and Radama was advised on military matters by a strange trio – a Scotsman, a Jamaican and a Frenchman. The king, however, did not confine his attentions to conquests and military reforms. In 1820, with royal permission, the first Christian missionaries, belonging to the British London Missionary Society, arrived in Merina. The fruits of their efforts were astonishing – after seven years it was estimated that 4,000 Hova could read and write their own language, and many had been trained to perform European trades.

The pagan priests and the older Hova upper class naturally felt their positions threatened by the new religion and the young educated men, and there followed an almost inevitable reaction. Radama I was succeeded in 1828 by the first of the queens of nineteenth-century Merina, Ranavalona. In 1835 she closed the London Missionary Society's schools and only allowed those foreigners to enter her king-dom who could contribute directly towards its military and economic power. But the seeds of Christianity and of Western education could not easily be uprooted. After a violent struggle for power at the death of Queen Ranavalona in 1861, a most remarkable man became prime minister – Rainilaiarivony, who remained in office until the coming of the French expedition in 1894. He made certain of his position by becoming the husband of three successive queens. Missionary work was resumed, and in 1868 Rainilaiarivony himself became a Christian. By the 1880s (by which time French Roman Catholic missionaries were also active) there had been a massive conversion to Christianity, and the proportion of Malagasy children at school was comparable with that in western Europe. Pagan beliefs, however, did not wither away, and, indeed, continued to flourish, in many cases among converts to Christianity.

This continuation of traditional beliefs was one sign of the considerable strain that was building up within the Merina state. Its subject peoples resented the often harsh rule of the Hova aristocracy, and many of the Hova resented the huge personal power of the prime minister. Although the majority of Christians were converts of the London Missionary Society, and although Britain kept close diplomatic links with Merina, a great amount of the external trade of Madagascar was in French hands. The Hova were proudly independent and had no wish to be under the 'protection' of either Britain or France. However, the French were determined to secure their commercial interests, and in 1885, after the first of the Franco-Malagasy wars, forced a treaty upon Merina. As in the case of the Wichale Treaty between Italy and Ethiopia (see Chapter 10), the French and Malagasy versions of this treaty differed. The Malagasy considered that they had maintained their independence; the French thought that they had secured control over the external affairs of the island and had thereby set up a protectorate over it. As in the case of Ethiopia, the misunderstandings arising out of this treaty led to increased friction between France and the kingdom of Merina.

7 North-East Africa before partition

As we saw in Chapter 1, the states of North-East Africa at the end of the eighteenth century were suffering, without exception, from a serious decline in their political power and a stagnation in the economic and cultural activities of their subjects. The authority of rulers was much less than it had been in former times. Everywhere nomadic peoples were overrunning the lands of the settled agriculturalists, on whose production the power of kingdoms and chiefdoms very largely depended. North of the Swahili coast, the Somali with their herds of camels and goats (which were particularly destructive of vegetation) were steadily extending the desert region, which could only support a nomadic pastoral way of life. Behind them, all round the core of the Ethiopian highlands, the Galla (Oromo) were still spreading by infiltration and conquest into the Sidama kingdoms and other neighbouring areas which had once been part of the Ethiopian empire. What was left of Christian Ethiopia had fallen apart into the regions that had formerly been united under the rule of the emperors – these were Shoa and Lasta, Amhara and Tigre, and many more. The Red Sea was full of pirates, and the lack of security had reduced the flow of pilgrims to the holy places of Islam to a mere trickle. With the breakdown of orderly government, the trade of the whole region had suffered severely, especially that of Egypt, the Funj kingdom and Ethiopia. A further reason for commercial decline was that the trade of all these states had been linked to the larger trade of the Indian Ocean, which was now increasingly diverted round the Cape of Good Hope to western Europe.

MUHAMMAD ALI (1805–49): THE REVIVAL OF RED SEA TRADE

The turn of the tide in the fortunes of all the states in this part of Africa was Napoleon's invasion of Egypt in 1798. The French occupation, though it lasted little more than two years, showed up the weakness of the Muslim world in relation to the countries of Christian Europe which were forcing themselves upon it. In particular, it revealed the inability of the Ottoman sultan to control and defend the southern part of his vast empire. Above all, Napoleon's invasion threw up in Egypt an outstanding leader, who was able to understand these events and to apply the lesson he had learned. The history, not only of Egypt, but of the whole of North-East Africa and the Red Sea area, was dominated during the first half of the nineteenth century by the figure of Muhammad Ali Pasha. This remarkable man combined the talents of an oriental despot with a shrewd understanding of the very different world of Europe. Muhammad Ali was a man of great charm and utter ruthlessness, an able administrator, and a cunning diplomat. Although he himself was not an outstanding military leader, several of his many sons were extremely efficient commanders. He was concerned above all to secure his position as Ottoman viceroy in Egypt, and to make the office hereditary within his own family. In addition, however, he restored the beginnings of order and prosperity to the Red Sea area and provided Egypt with the framework of a modern state.

Muhammad Ali was born in 1769 in Macedonia, one of the Ottoman territories in the Balkans, and first entered Egypt as an officer in the Ottoman forces sent there to deal with the French invasion. With the support of a body of Albanian soldiers loyal to him personally rather than to the far-off Ottoman sultan, he made himself by 1805 the most powerful military boss in Cairo. The following year he was appointed *vali* (Turkish, viceroy, governor) by the sultan. His power was at first very uncertain, there being many other military groups opposed to his own. In 1811 he dealt with this opposition with characteristic ruthlessness by inviting the principal Mamluk *amirs* to a banquet in Cairo and then having some three hundred of them massacred in a narrow alley leading out of the citadel on their way home. His power in Egypt was now secure, and for the next eight years he devoted his main efforts to the pacification of the Red Sea area. First and foremost, this involved the suppression of the Wahhabis, the followers of a fanatical Muslim sect which had arisen among the bedouin tribesmen of the Arabian desert. The Wahhabi leaders denied the authority of the Ottoman government and disrupted the annual pilgrimage caravans travelling to the holy cities of Mecca and Medina. Muhammad Ali's armies cleared the Hijaz of the Wahhabis and in 1818 finally overcame the fanatical tribesmen in the heart of Arabia. The holy places were restored by Muhammad Ali to the authority of his overlord. The Ottoman garrison towns of Suakin and Massawa, on the African side of the Red Sea, remained under Ottoman control until the end of the viceroy's reign, when, in 1846, they

79

were leased by the sultan to Egypt; only in 1865 were they permanently annexed to the Egyptian Sudan.

Nevertheless, Muhammad Ali's early operations in the Red Sea area brought about a complete revival of the pilgrimage and an even more striking revival of trade. The Red Sea route began to be used by the British for rapid communications with India; and Jidda, the Ottoman port in the Hijaz, became temporarily the most important commercial town between Bombay and Cairo. This in turn revived all the local trade routes running inland on the African side of the Red Sea, especially those to the Ethiopian highlands. From this region the most highly valued female slaves were sent to the Hijaz, where they were bought as concubines by the more prosperous class of pilgrims. Also in great demand in the Hijaz and elsewhere in the Muslim world was the musk obtained from the glands of the civet-cat, which was the speciality of the Sidama kingdoms. There was a similar revival in the gold trade from Innarya in the south-western highlands, and also in the splendid coffee grown all over the highland region. The political recovery of the Ethiopian state (in the northern provinces of Tigre and Amhara) and of its powerful daughter state of Shoa, which began in earnest in the 1830s and 1840s, was made possible very largely through the revenue from this commercial revival. The increased trade enabled the rulers of these states to start re-equipping their soldiers with fire-arms in place of spears.

THE EGYPTIAN CONQUEST OF THE SUDAN

From the Red Sea, Muhammad Ali turned his eyes in 1820 towards the Sudan. The Arabian campaigns had been costly in troops, and he hoped to secure an inexhaustible supply of Negro slave recruits for his armies in the southern Sudan. The Funj sultanate was quite incapable of offering any resistance. It had already lost control of all the northern part of the Sudan; Dongola was in the hands of a group of Mamluk refugees who had escaped from Muhammad Ali's clutches in Egypt. With only 4,000 well-armed men, Muhammad Ali's son Ismail was able to make steady progress up the Nile, overcoming the Mamluks at Dongola and entering the Funj capital at Sennar unopposed in June 1821. The Funj sultan was deposed, and he and his family received an Egyptian pension. There was one brief rising in 1822, in which Ismail lost his life. After this had been suppressed, the Egyptian colonial capital was founded in 1824 at Khartoum, at the junction of the White and Blue Niles, and the Sudan remained under Egyptian rule until the Mahdi's rebellion of 1881–4.

The economic benefits which Muhammad Ali's reign conferred upon Egypt and the Red Sea coasts did not generally extend to the Sudan. Attempts made by the Egyptian administration to widen the range of agricultural production, such as the settlement of Egyptian peasants in the Gezira around Sennar, were not very successful. The Arabic-speaking groups living in the Nile valley in the north were regularly taxed by the government, and some of them became quite prosperous through their involvement in the considerable shipping traffic that developed on the river; others became even more wealthy by partaking in the slave- and ivory-trades in the southern Sudan. The nomadic tribes in the deserts to the east and west of the river supplied the large numbers of camels and other domestic animals which, after slaves and ivory, formed the main exports of the Sudan. All the serious efforts of the Egyptian government were concentrated, however, on the region to the south of Khartoum. 'You are aware', Muhammad Ali wrote to his treasurer in 1825, 'that the end of all our effort and of this expense is to procure negroes. Please show zeal in carrying out our wishes in this capital matter.' Every year the Khartoum government despatched military expeditions southwards to Dar Fung and westwards to Kordofan and the Nuba mountains on official slave-raids, which returned with as many as 5,000 captives each. For a time the Shilluk with their centralised kingdom on the White Nile above Fashoda made an effective limit to the Egyptians' southward penetration. But Muhammad Ali, hoping for the discovery of gold, was always urging his governors to press farther south. In 1838 he even visited the Sudan himself to encourage these efforts. From 1839 to 1841 one of his Turkish sea-captains, called Salim, broke through the opposition of the Shilluk in a series of expeditions up the White Nile. He proved the river to be navigable for 1,600 kilometres south of Khartoum, as far as Gondokoro in the land of the Bari near the modern Sudan–Uganda frontier. The dream of gold did not come true. In its place appeared the reality of a million or more square kilometres of elephant country, the human inhabitants of which were still ignorant of the value of ivory. From then on the penetration of the traders developed fast, with European firms based on Khartoum in the forefront. Through their consuls these firms resisted the attempt by the Egyptian government to set up a monopoly over the ivory-trade.

At first the forces at the disposal of the traders and of the local inhabitants were fairly evenly balanced. The traders with their armed sailing-boats were superior so long as they kept to the river, but on land the local people had the advantage. While these conditions 81

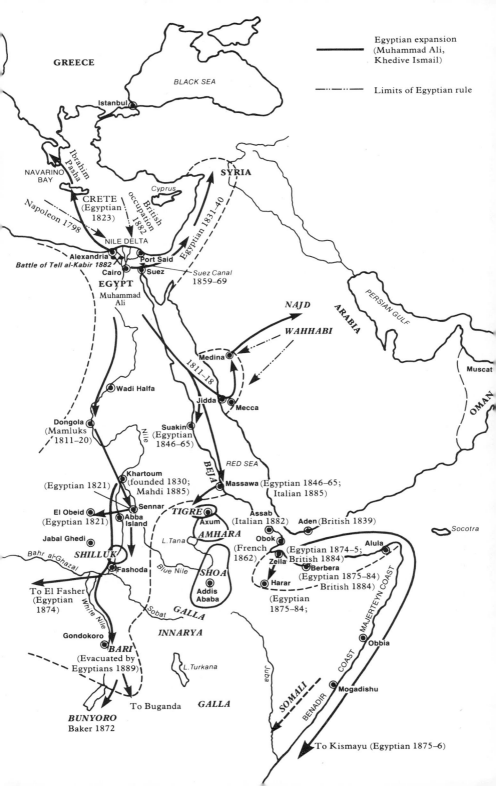

Egyptian expansion (Muhammad Ali, Khedive Ismail)

Limits of Egyptian rule

GREECE

BLACK SEA

Istanbul

NAVARINO BAY

Ibrāhīm Pasha

CRETE (Egyptian 1823)

Cyprus

British occupation 1882

SYRIA

Napoleon 1798

NILE DELTA

Egyptian 1831–40

Alexandria
Battle of Tell al-Kabir 1882

Port Said

Cairo   Suez

Suez Canal 1859–69

EGYPT

Muhammad Ali

NAJD

PERSIAN GULF

ARABIA

WAHHABI

1811–18

Medina

Muscat

Wadi Halfa

OMAN

Dongola (Mamluks 1811–20)

Nile

Suakin (Egyptian 1846–65)

Jidda   Mecca

BEJA

RED SEA

Khartoum (founded 1830; Mahdi 1885)

Massawa (Egyptian 1846–65; Italian 1885)

(Egyptian 1821)

El Obeid (Egyptian 1821)

Sennar

TIGRE

Axum

Assab (Italian 1882)

Aden (British 1839)

Socotra

Jabal Ghedi

Abba Island

AMHARA

L. Tana

Obok (French 1862)

(Egyptian 1874–5; British 1884)

Alula

Bahr al-Ghazal

SHILLUK

Fashoda

Blue Nile

SHOA

Zeila   Harar

Berbera (Egyptian 1875–84; British 1884)

MAJERTEYN COAST

To El Fasher (Egyptian 1874)

White Nile

Sobat

Addis Ababa

GALLA

(Egyptian 1875–84;

COAST

Gondokoro

BARI (Evacuated by Egyptians 1889)

INNARYA

L. Turkana

Obbia

BUNYORO
Baker 1872

To Buganda

L. Turkana

GALLA

Juba

SOMALI

BENADIR COAST

Mogadishu

To Kismayu (Egyptian 1875–6)

lasted, the exchange of goods, though unequal in value, was peaceful enough. There came a time, however, when few elephants could be shot near the river banks and when the local demand for beads and cheap trinkets was satisfied. To get ivory it now became necessary to leave the river banks and to try to find trade goods which would arouse the interest of the peoples of the back country, who were even less sophisticated than the groups alongside the rivers. The traders responded to the new conditions by bringing up bands of armed Arab followers, recruited mainly from the Nile valley north of Khartoum. They placed these men in fortified encampments called *zeribas* spread over the whole back-country of the White Nile and the Bahr al-Ghazal. There was little surplus food available for them, and they were often forced to raid the villages in order to feed themselves. The local people, being mostly Nilotic pastoralists with the simplest material needs, wanted only cattle and ever more cattle. Armed raiding-parties therefore scoured the countryside for cattle, and exchanged them (often with the people from whom they had been captured) for ivory and slaves. Petherick, the British Consul in Khartoum, described the situation in 1863: 'Instead of the introduction of more valuable and civilising merchandise, such as cutlery, or cloth for wearing apparel, as articles for barter – when the value of glass and copper ornaments began to decline and lose their charm – the traders disgraced themselves by descending to enrich themselves by the plunder and destruction of tribe after tribe.'[1]

MUHAMMAD ALI AND THE EUROPEAN POWERS

By the early 1820s Muhammad Ali was far stronger than his overlord, the Ottoman sultan. He realised the importance of sea-power in the military forces of the European states, and at great expense built an Egyptian navy in the Mediterranean. In 1821 the first major revolt broke out in the Ottoman empire, when the Greeks rose to claim their independence. The sultan was not strong enough to suppress the revolt and called upon Muhammad Ali to help him. Egyptian forces rapidly overwhelmed the rebels on the island of Crete, and in 1824 a great military expedition under the viceroy's eldest son, Ibrahim Pasha, set out for Greece from Alexandria. So successful was Ibrahim in the Morea (the southern part of Greece) that it seemed that the Greek revolt was doomed. At this point Russia threatened to intervene on the side of the Greek Christians. To prevent this a joint

[1] J. Petherick, *Travels in Central Africa, and explorations of the White Nile tributaries, 1869* (London, 1869), vol. 1, p. 229.

12   North-East Africa: Egyptian expansion

French and British naval force was sent to Greece in an attempt to enforce an armistice between the rebels and the Egyptian army. Almost by accident hostilities broke out, and at the battle of Navarino Bay in 1827 the Egyptian fleet was destroyed. The following year Ibrahim Pasha had to evacuate his troops from the Morea, and Greece became independent.

This was the first serious reverse suffered by Muhammad Ali, and he naturally wanted recompense from the sultan for the costly Greek campaigns. The sultan went back on a promise to make him *pasha* (governor) of Palestine and Syria, and so, in 1831, Ibrahim's army took over these provinces from direct Ottoman control. By now the sultan was thoroughly alarmed at the power of his over-mighty subject but could do nothing to curb it. In 1833 Muhammad Ali was officially recognised as governor of Syria and Palestine. A further attempt by the Ottomans in 1839 to drive him out of these provinces ended in the defeat of the sultan's forces by Ibrahim Pasha; the Egyptian forces seemed ready to march to Istanbul and dictate terms to a new sultan, who was only a young boy. Again the European powers intervened. Britain was committed to uphold the ramshackle Ottoman empire, and in 1840, in concert with other European countries and in spite of French support for Muhammad Ali, forced him to withdraw from Syria. Yet he obtained one solid gain – the viceroyalty of Egypt was made hereditary in his family, and with this his authority over the Sudan was tacitly recognised by the sultan.

To meet the shortage of recruits for the army after his Arabian and Sudanese campaigns, and because of the failure of his plan to obtain Negro slave soldiers, Muhammad Ali took in 1822 the new step of forcing into his army as conscripts the Egyptian *fellahin* (Arabic, peasants). Since the Arab conquests of the seventh century, all soldiers in Egypt had been foreigners. Now native Egyptians began to be recruited into the ranks, and later in the century they were even trained as officers. This was to have a great effect on the growth of nationalism in Egypt. Muhammad Ali also imported European – mostly French – military advisers and instructors to establish army medical, artillery and engineering schools. One result of this was that European text-books were translated into Turkish and Arabic, and some of the cleverest young Egyptian officers learned French and became familiar with western political as well as military ideas. In this period when European countries had a near-monopoly of the manufacture of modern weapons, Muhammad Ali was dependent on Europe for arms and military equipment. These were very expensive, and one factor in the tremendous drive towards economic and administrative reforms in Egypt, which characterised much of his reign and for which he is above all remembered, was the need to obtain money to pay for armaments. Muhammad Ali and his ministers were seriously concerned to modernise Egypt for the benefit of its people, who had for long been living under oppressive conditions. The amount of land under irrigation was greatly increased. Cotton and sugar were introduced as economic crops, and grain cultivation was expanded. The old Mamluk land-owning aristocracy was largely replaced by the family and favourites of the viceroy. This did not put an end to corruption and exploitation, but it helped to spread new ideas. Muhammad Ali is justly considered by Egyptians and many other historians to be the founder of modern Egypt. The main failing of Muhammad Ali's government was that all power remained so closely concentrated in his own hands. Weaker and less capable successors were unable to control the machine he had created.

THE KHEDIVE ISMAIL (1863-79)

Muhammad Ali died in 1849 and was followed as viceroy by undistinguished successors – the brilliant Ibrahim Pasha had died the year before. Abbas I (1849-54), Muhammad Ali's conservative grandson, was hostile to European ideas, and his son Muhammad Said (1854-63), the uncle of Abbas, a rather weak man, was by contrast too much under the influence of European favourites. During his reign, in 1859, the construction of the Suez Canal was begun. A new chapter, however, opened both for Egypt and for North-East Africa as a whole with the accession of another of Muhammad Ali's grandsons, Ismail. Ismail's ideas were large and enlightened, but they were not backed by good judgement or by any sense of financial prudence. At home Ismail lived the luxurious life of a mighty sovereign, and he was given the old Persian title of *khedive* by the Ottoman sultan. His public policies were undertaken in the same spirit, and were no doubt modelled upon the reforming drive of his grandfather. Egypt should be projected at one bound into the world of railways, telegraphs, factories, schools and town-planning. The Suez Canal, which Muhammad Ali had consistently refused to sanction, rightly foreseeing that it would place Egypt at the mercy of the much more powerful navies of the nations of Europe, was completed by Ismail (in 1869). A fleet of steamships was ordered, which were to ply between the Mediterranean and the Red Sea ports. In the year of Ismail's accession, the British explorers Speke and Grant passed through Cairo with the tale of the rich interlacustrine kingdoms at the head of the White Nile, and at once Ismail's imagination responded. He would pass round the Nile cataracts with a railway, and he would place steamers on the White Nile and the equatorial lakes. All the ivory flowing eastwards to Zanzibar would be diverted northwards to Cairo. In 1869 he commissioned Baker, the explorer of Lake Albert, at the huge salary of £10,000 a year, to put this immense scheme into effect. Baker in four years achieved little more than the assembling of some steamers on the White Nile, and was succeeded in 1873 by Gordon. Gordon insisted that the grand design could only work if Ismail occupied a base on the east coast of Africa. He noted in his diary on 21 January 1875:

I have proposed to the Khedive to send 150 men in a steamer to Mombaz Bay, 250 miles north of Zanzibar, and there to establish a station, and then to push towards M'tesa. If I can do that, I shall make my base at Mombaz, and give up Khartum and the bother of steamers, etc. The centre of Africa would be much more effectually opened out, as the only valuable parts of the country are the highlands near M'tesa, while south of Khartum is wretched marsh. I hope the Khedive will do it.[2]

Ismail agreed, and later the same year sent another expensive expedition, this time to Kismayu at the mouth of the Juba river. This expedition, however, was recalled as the result of British pressure exercised on behalf of the sultan of Zanzibar. At the same time Ismail's forces occupied Zeila in the Gulf of Aden and Harar inland, but attacks on Tigre from Massawa resulted in heavy defeats at the hands of the Ethiopian emperor, John.

Although Ismail's scheme for making Egypt the head of a great African empire collapsed, in many respects Egypt greatly benefited from the reign of the magnificent khedive. A considerable network of communications – railways, telegraphs, urban amenities – was built up, including of course the Suez Canal. Muhammad Ali had done much to modernise Egypt, but it was only in Ismail's time that the urban centres at least, Cairo, Alexandria and the Canal towns, achieved a distinctively modern aspect. But because Egypt was so dependent upon European capital for the implementation of these development policies, the khedive was forced to borrow money at exorbitant rates of interest. Already in 1875 he was forced to sell his own shares in the Suez Canal in order to meet his most pressing debts. By 1879 the Egyptian treasury was bankrupt, and later the same year Ismail himself was deposed by the sultan at the suggestion of the European powers. A committee representing the European countries to whom Egypt owed money took over the direction of the Egyptian

[2] *General Gordon in Central Africa, 1874–79*, ed. G. B. Hill (London, 1881), pp. 65–6.

finances. European financial experts took seats in the cabinet of Ismail's son and successor, Tawfiq.

The economy measures introduced by Tawfiq's European advisers hit the army officers hard, amongst other classes of Egyptians. Many were put on half-pay, and a group of them, led by Colonel Urabi Pasha, rebelled in 1881 and set up military control over the khedive's government. They threatened to repudiate the national debt. This military revolution led at last to the direct intervention of the European powers. Britain and France planned to act together to restore the weak authority of Tawfiq and to protect European financial interests. In the end France was prevented from taking part by an internal political crisis and by events in Tunisia and Indo-China. Thus Britain invaded Egypt alone in 1882 and defeated the forces of Urabi Pasha at the battle of Tell al-Kabir. Britain's occupation of Egypt was to be a major factor in the partition of Africa that followed.

THE SUDAN AND THE MAHDIYYA (1881–98)

Only a year before the British occupation of Egypt the Sudan revolted against its Egyptian government. This was not a movement originating in the Negro south of the Sudan, where Egyptian rule had been most oppressive. The core of the rebels came rather from the nomadic groups to the west of the Nile, especially the Baqqara, Arabic-speaking cattle-owning people of Kordofan and the Nuba mountains. The nomads were the first to rally to the standard of revolt. They resented the Egyptian government's attempts to tax and to control them more than did the settled agriculturists of the Nile valley north and south of Khartoum. These riverain Arabs, the descendants of the old population of the Funj kingdom, tended to sit on the fence, waiting until it was clear that the Mahdi was successful before joining him. Economically, their grievance was that the Egyptian government in the early days had conscripted many of their slaves, on whose labour they had depended for their livelihood. More recently, since the reign of Ismail, the government had prevented the importation of more slaves from the south, and had kept even the ivory-trade in its own hands. Religious grievances were also important. The Egyptians had increasingly brought into the Sudan their own Muslim teachers and religious dignitaries, whereas Sudanese Islam had its own strongly established *shaikhs* (holy men) and religious brotherhoods, who resented the newcomers and their different ways. Ismail's appointment of Gordon, a Christian deeply committed to the anti-slavery campaign, as governor-general of the whole Sudan, upset the local Muslims still further. The nomads, at least, were ready to follow a religious leader who promised to overthrow Egyptian rule, which in their eyes was impious and heretical as well as being at times harsh.

Such a religious leader appeared in the person of Muhammad Ahmad, who was born in 1844, the son of a boat-builder near Khartoum. After an intensely religious upbringing, he became a teacher and was granted the title of *shaikh*. In 1881 he proclaimed himself the *mahdi*, the Saviour of the Muslims, who would re-establish Islam in its primitive purity. At first the British authorities in Egypt took little notice of what seemed to be a local religious movement. When, after the capture of El Obeid by the Mahdi's Baqqara horsemen in 1883, they realised its seriousness, it was already too late to restrain it except by a major military expedition far beyond the means of the bankrupt Egyptian state. The British government had at this time no wish to extend its responsibilities in Egypt and therefore decided that the reconquest must wait until Egypt's own finances were sufficiently restored to undertake it. Meanwhile it was clear that the Mahdi had the enthusiastic support of most sections of the Muslim Sudanese. Khartoum fell to him in 1885, and Gordon, who had been sent to evacuate the garrison, was killed in the fighting. The Mahdi himself died shortly after the capture of Khartoum and was succeeded by his general, Abdallahi, who was known as the *khalifa* (Arabic, successor). Abdallahi established a strong secular administration in place of the Mahdi's dream of a society that would be organised on a religious basis similar to the Muslim state in the earliest days of Islam.

The Khalifa's rule lasted for thirteen years. It might have lasted longer if the European powers had not by then been partitioning Africa among themselves. As it was, the government of the Mahdiyya in the Sudan continued until almost the end of the nineteenth century. The reconquest of the Sudan by Anglo-Egyptian forces was almost the closing episode of the partition. It was one of the few cases in which a government that was still carrying out most of its functions had to be defeated and overthrown by an invading army in order to make way for colonial rule.

THE REUNIFICATION OF ETHIOPIA (1855–89)

The most remarkable development in the whole of Africa during the later nineteenth century was perhaps the reunification and development of Ethiopia into a state which could not merely survive the partition of Africa but even in a sense take part in it. As we have seen, the opportunity for this revival had been created by the reopening of

13   North-East Africa: Ethiopian expansion and the Mahdiyya

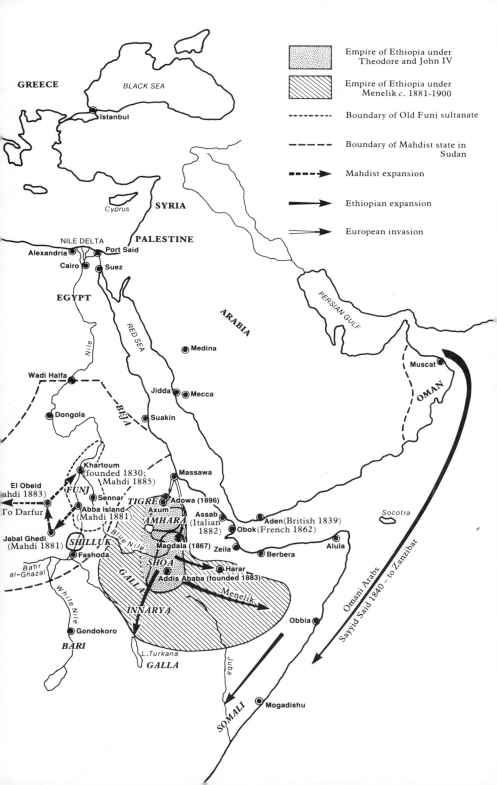

GREECE

BLACK SEA

Istanbul

Cyprus

SYRIA

PALESTINE

NILE DELTA

Alexandria   Port Said

Cairo   Suez

EGYPT

Nile

RED SEA

ARABIA

PERSIAN GULF

Medina

Wadi Halfa

BEJA

Jidda   Mecca

Dongola   Suakin

Khartoum
(founded 1830;
Mahdi 1885)   Massawa

El Obeid
(Mahdi 1883)   *FUNJ*   Sennar
To Darfur   Abba Island
(Mahdi 1881)   **TIGRE**   Adowa (1896)

Axum   Assab
AMHARA   (Italian
1882)   Obok
(French 1862)

Jabal Ghedi
(Mahdi 1881)

SHILLUK   Blue Nile   Magdala (1867)   Zeila

Fashoda   Berbera

Bahr
al-Ghazal   **SHOA**

White Nile   **GALLA**   Addis Ababa (founded 1883)   Harar

Menelik

INNARYA

Gondokoro

BARI   L.Turkana

GALLA   Juba

Muscat

OMAN

Socotra

Aden (British 1839)

Obbia

Omani Arabs
Sayyid Said 1840 – to Zanzibar

SOMALI   Mogadishu

Alula

Empire of Ethiopia under
Theodore and John IV

Empire of Ethiopia under
Menelik *c.* 1881-1900

- - - - - - -   Boundary of Old Funj sultanate

– – – – –   Boundary of Mahdist state in
Sudan

▪▪▪▪▶   Mahdist expansion

▬▬▶   Ethiopian expansion

──▶   European invasion

the Ethiopian region to external trade during the second quarter of the century. This enabled the more enterprising local rulers to build up their power by buying fire-arms. So far there was nothing essentially different from what was happening in all the more powerful native states of tropical Africa. In Ethiopia, however, there was in addition the memory of a great state which had existed in the past. The ancient Christian Church still existed as a single national organisation in Tigre, Amhara and Shoa and the other almost completely independent provinces of the old empire. It acted as a unifying influence. It marked off the Christian core of the country in the highlands from the Muslim states to the north and east and from the pagan Galla lands to the south. Because of the education provided by the Church, there was still a small class of literate and sophisticated people. This educated class had some idea of how to enter into diplomatic relations with the outside world and how to give foreigners the impression of a civilised power. All these factors were there to be used by a national leader as soon as one arose. The first to do so was Ras Kassa, a successful robber chief from the north-western frontier, who in 1855 managed to have himself crowned as emperor by the leaders of the Church at the ancient capital of Axum in Tigre. Ras Kassa took the name of Theodore. Two consuls from the British Foreign Office visited Theodore soon after his coronation and wrote their impressions of him in their official report:

King Theodorus is of a striking countenance, peculiarly polite and engaging when pleased, and mostly displaying great tact and delicacy. He is persuaded that he is destined to restore the glories of the Ethiopian Empire, and to achieve great conquests. Indefatigable in business, he takes little repose night or day; his ideas and language are clear and precise; hesitation is not known to him, and he has neither counsellors nor go-betweens. He is fond of splendour, and receives in state even on a campaign. He regards nothing with pleasure and desires but munitions of war for his soldiers.[3]

Though fanatically pious and utterly ruthless, he undoubtedly believed that it was his mission to revive the Ethiopian nation, and in the twelve years after 1855 he did much to achieve this ambition. He was, however, already subject to fits of madness when his career was cut short by a British military expedition, sent in 1867 in protest against the maltreatment by him of two British envoys. Surrounded by the British forces in his fortress at Magdala, he eventually shot himself.

His successor as emperor, John IV, fought his way to the throne

---

[3] Walter C. Plowden, *Travels in Abyssinia and the Galla Country* (London, 1868), pp. 455–6.

with arms obtained from the British, who had encouraged him as a rival to Theodore. In the 1870s the main external enemy of the empire of Ethiopia, which was still more a collection of semi-independent provinces than a unified kingdom, was Egypt. The expansionist policies of the khedive Ismail, directed towards the Red Sea and Somali coasts, threatened to revive the previous long isolation of the Christian lands in the interior mountains. As we have seen (pp. 80, 86), Egypt took over control of Suakin and Massawa in 1865 from the Ottoman sultan, and occupied much of Eritrea. In 1875 Ismail extended an Egyptian protection over the Muslim rulers of Zeila and Harar and launched an Egyptian attack upon Ethiopia from both the north and the east. The Emperor John was successful in halting the Egyptian invasion, but the continued Egyptian occupation of the more important Red Sea and Somali ports severely curtailed the supply of arms and other goods to Ethiopia. This weakened John in his conflicts with Menelik, the powerful young ruler of Shoa, with whom he had to contend for the title of emperor. Shoa, which lies to the south of Tigre and Amhara, had suffered greatly from the Galla invasions of the sixteenth to eighteenth centuries. The two rulers of Shoa before Menelik had been engaged during the previous fifty years on a course of rearmament and expansion (at the expense of the Galla and other pagan or Muslim peoples) similar to that undertaken by Theodore. In 1878 John had to make terms by which Menelik married his daughter and was recognised as his successor. Even so, concealed hostility and competition continued between the two until John's death in battle against the Khalifa Abdallahi in 1889, when Menelik at last became emperor. In the early years of his rule over the state established by the Mahdi, Abdallahi had attempted to extend his control over all the Sudanese lands formerly occupied by the Egyptians. This inevitably brought him into conflict with Ethiopia, which conflict resulted in the fulfilment of Menelik's ambitions.

In a long reign, which lasted until 1913, Menelik completed the process which had been begun by Theodore. He united the provinces of Tigre and Amhara with Shoa, and extended Ethiopian rule over the Muslim and pagan states to the east and to the south. He fully understood the importance of modern weapons, and long before he became emperor, he bought arms and ammunition from every available source, especially from the Italians. These changed places with the French (who operated from their Somali coast possession of Obok) in the 1880s as the principal external influence in Ethiopia. Italian consuls from Aden had made arrangements with Menelik in 1878–9, and after the establishment of a colony at the port of Assab in

1882 Italian envoys were in regular attendance at Menelik's court. As we shall see (Chapter 10), this Italian presence in Ethiopia led to the Wichale Treaty of 1889. Yet it was the Italians whom Menelik defeated in their attempted invasion of Ethiopia from their possessions in Eritrea, at the decisive battle of Adowa in 1896. To obtain money for his weapons, Menelik, like all his contemporary rulers in North-East Africa and in the interlacustrine lands, relied mainly on the profits of ivory, for which he raided deep into the pagan lands to the south-west and south-east of Shoa. He extended his political control behind the raiding armies. Ethiopian expansion at the expense of the Somali of Harar and the Ogaden was a factor in the last great southward migration of the Somali peoples. By the turn of the century they were spilling over into the dry northern province of Kenya.

Long before direct European intervention in East and North-East Africa, the Muslim and Christian rulers of the more powerful and wealthy states in Africa itself were using fire-arms obtained from Europe to extend their trade with the peoples of the interior. They followed up these commercial activities with an extension of their political control. Egyptian expansion in the Sudan and Shoan expansion in the lands to the south and east of the Ethiopian highlands are examples of this process in North-East Africa. The Swahili-Arab penetration of East Africa, based on the sultanate of Zanzibar, is an example in East Africa. Only the Ethiopian rulers, however, were skilful enough to use the advantages of contact with the outside world while avoiding the financial and diplomatic entanglements which could lead to European intervention.

8 North-West Africa, 1800–1881

We have seen that at the beginning of the nineteenth century North Africa west of Egypt consisted of four Muslim states. Three of them – Tripoli, Tunis and Algiers – were nominally dependencies of the Ottoman empire. The fourth – Morocco – was an independent kingdom. Though all of them traded extensively with western Europe, all their religious and cultural connections, as well as a great part of their trade, lay with the eastern Mediterranean on the one hand and with the Muslim states of the western Sudan on the other. In particular, the steady flow of Negro slaves across the Sahara desert was directed mainly to the Balkans, Turkey, Syria and Egypt. During the first third of the nineteenth century this basic pattern changed very little. Thereafter, the growing power of western Europe made itself felt in a variety of ways which in the long term introduced important changes in the lives of the people of North-West Africa. First there was the British campaign against the slave-trade, waged both in the Mediterranean and in the Atlantic. Next, there was the Greek war of independence (1820–9), fought with the support of the Christian powers. The success of the Greeks drove Muslim rule from a Christian country and provided an example later to be followed by the other Balkan states. Finally, with the invention of the steamship and the consequent growth in the power and mobility of European navies, there came the concentration of the nations of western Europe on the Mediterranean Sea. For Britain and France the Mediterranean was a route to the rich lands of India and the East Indies. It was also the outlet (through the narrow strait at Istanbul) for the Russian fleet in the Black Sea. It was to prevent the establishment of Russia as a Mediterranean power that Britain intervened against Muhammad Ali, in Greece in 1827 and in Syria in 1840. France's interests in the Mediterranean were more local, and less global, than were Britain's (as was to be expected from the geographical position of France). France was concerned with its commercial activities in the Levant and North Africa, and indeed welcomed the growth of a strong, friendly North African power based upon Egypt. In 1829, not long before the French attack upon Algiers, the French government encouraged Muhammad Ali to think of including the Maghrib in his sphere of influence. Thus governments in France, and in Spain and later Italy, were interested in North Africa both for its value as a counter in the Great Power game played by the European states and for its economic and commercial possibilities.

At the beginning of the nineteenth century there was little awareness in the Maghrib countries that Christian Europe would prove the main threat to their continued independent existence. Certainly there was no idea among them of presenting a united front to European advances. In Tripoli, for example, the hereditary pasha, Yusuf Karamanli, who ruled the country from 1795 till 1830, had begun his reign by aiding the British against the French in Egypt, and thereafter enjoyed British support in maintaining his freedom from Ottoman control. This freedom he used to extend his authority over the Fezzan, the semi-desert country to the south of Tripoli, through which ran the caravan routes to the central Sudan. By 1811 Yusuf was master of the Fezzan, and by 1818 he had established treaty relations with Muhammad al-Kanemi in Bornu and with Muhammad Bello, the son of Dan Fodio, at Sokoto. Tripoli supplied Bornu with arms and ammunition for her wars against Bagirmi, and received a greatly increased supply of slaves in exchange. In spite of her friendly relations with Britain, the city of Tripoli became at this time the greatest slave-market of the Mediterranean. Of the 10,000 slaves brought annually across the Sahara, over half passed through Tripoli or else through Benghazi, the port of Cyrenaica.

The rulers of Tunis, like Yusuf Karamanli of Tripoli, based their country's almost complete independence from the Ottoman sultan on their friendship with Britain. Algiers, in contrast, was linked more closely with France. During the wars which the Revolutionary government of France and the French Emperor Napoleon fought with most of the other European powers between 1792 and 1815, Algiers had supplied grain to the French forces, including those which had attacked Egypt. A large war-debt to the government of the dey of Algiers had been incurred by France during these years. After the defeat of Napoleon in 1815 the new French government refused to pay this debt. This poisoned relations between the two countries and led to the French invasion of Algeria in 1830. But for a long time, even after the French invasion, the majority of the people of what later became Algeria, as of Morocco and Tunisia, were little if at all concerned with the relations between the ruling groups and European powers. The political life of much of the Maghrib turned upon the authority and influence of holy men (*marabouts*) and religious brotherhoods or orders (*tariqas*). Islam, in its various forms, both provided the major focus of unity and partly accounted for the divisions in the Maghrib.

Alone among the North African countries, Morocco did not have the Ottoman sultan as a nominal master against whom it was necessary to seek an ally. Morocco therefore reacted to the increased European activity in the Mediterranean and the Atlantic by seeking to cut herself off from the outside world. Sultan Mawlai Sulaiman (1792–1832) forbade his subjects to leave the country and restricted their dealings with Christians to the very minimum. The European consuls and merchants were made to stay in the ports of Tangier and Mogador. The efforts of the British consuls to interest the sultans in anti-slavery measures met with blank refusals even to consider the matter. In 1841 Sulaiman's successor, Abd ar-Rahman, declared firmly that he would not forbid a practice which had been sanctioned by the laws of every sect and nation 'from the times of the sons of Adam up to this day'.

THE FRENCH IN ALGERIA (1830–79)

The French invasion of Algeria was one of the most unprincipled and ill-considered acts of policy in the whole of the nineteenth century. It was undertaken for no positive reason at all, but for the purely negative one of diverting the attention of the French people, by a spectacular military success abroad, from their resentment of the misgovernment of the kings Louis XVIII and Charles X. It did not even succeed in this object, for, within a few months of the attack on Algiers, Charles X had been overthrown by a popular revolution. But the French stayed in Algiers.

The excuse for the attack was a fit of anger by the dey of Algiers, Husain, who in 1827, in the course of one of the endless discussions about the war-debt, struck the French consul in the face with his fly-whisk. Three years later the French government, announcing that it would put an end to the piracy of the Algerian corsairs, landed troops and defeated Husain's forces. Algiers and Oran fell almost at once, and Bone, the port of eastern Algeria, fell in 1832. There remained for the French the far more difficult task of ruling what they had conquered.

Like all previous conquerors of Algeria, the French imagined that they would be able to confine their occupation to the coastal plain.

Indeed, the inhabitants of the coastal towns and those social group-ings which had traditionally made up the *makhzan* (Arabic, allies) of the dey proved friendly to the French and anxious to accept their protection. The reason was simply that the French were able to exploit the age-old rivalry between the townsfolk and the peasants of the coastal region on the one hand and the men of the hills and mountains on the other. The leader of the hill-folk was Abd al-Qadir, the son of a famous *marabout* (holy man) of the Atlas region, who in 1832 declared a great jihad against the French (and against the *makhzan*), saying:

> We have assumed this important charge [the office of *amir*, commander], hoping that it may be the means of uniting the great body of Muslims and preventing dissensions among them, of affording general security to all dwellers in the land and of driving back the enemy who had invaded our country with a view to placing his yoke upon our necks.[1]

With great skill and tact Abd al-Qadir held together the quarrelsome tribes of western and central Algeria, organised an administration similar to that of the old Ottoman government, and built up a standing army with which he inflicted a number of defeats upon the French. His jihad made it quite impossible for the French to limit their occupation to the coastal plain: like all other conquerors of North Africa, they were drawn, whether they liked it or not, into the interior.

In 1841 General Bugeaud began the systematic conquest of Abd al-Qadir's territory. District after district was occupied by French military posts and patrolled by flying columns of mounted soldiers. This was no longer a war of armies which, while fighting one another, could spare the civil population. These small campaigns were brutal. One of the sons of the French king, serving with the French army, wrote, 'Our soldiers returning from the expedition were themselves ashamed. About 18,000 trees had been cut down; houses had been burnt; women, children and old men had been killed.' Similar fer-ocity was shown by the Arabs towards French soldiers and civilians whenever the chance occurred. Resistance continued long after the capture of Abd al-Qadir himself in 1847, and great bitterness entered into the relations between conquerors and conquered.

In these circumstances, the settlement of French colonists, of whom there were by 1847 about 100,000, could not be a peaceful process. Bugeaud saw that the newcomers would have to be settled in concentrated areas, where they could be protected by the army. This

[1] Cited in Col. Churchill, *The Life of Abd el Kader* (London, 1867), p. 28.

meant the clearance (French, *refoulement*) of the more fertile regions in the coastal plains and movement of the former inhabitants into remoter, less fertile and already inhabited districts. This policy was carried out by force, and the fighting in Algeria continued until the 1870s. Once conquered, the Muslim areas were administered by a form of indirect rule. French officials governed the people through their territorial chiefs and councils. The system had much in common with the old Ottoman administration. Nevertheless, while the deys had maintained their government with a force of 15,000 men, the French required 100,000, and in the interior regions military government gave way to civil administration only in 1879. Even then, Kabylia and other mountain districts remained unpacified.

The colonists, who in 1880 numbered some 350,000, did little to bring prosperity to Algeria. Nearly all of them were poor people. Most of those who settled on the land were small wine-growers from the south of France whose vineyards had been attacked by disease. In the towns most of the settlers were not even French, but Spaniards, Italians and Maltese from overcrowded homelands, who came to seek paid employment and to engage in petty trade. As time went on, even the French agricultural settlers tended to drift into the towns, leaving the land which had been so expensively cleared for them to fall into the hands of a few wealthy individuals and companies who built up great estates. Unlike colonists in other parts of the world, the French settlers in Algeria, especially the wealthy ones, were able to keep close touch with their homeland across the Mediterranean. They came to have an influence on French politics out of all proportion to their numbers or real importance.

MOROCCO (1830–94)

Morocco was much affected by the French occupation of Algeria. Abd al-Qadir's resistance was conducted mainly from western Algeria, and Sultan Abd ar-Rahman (1822–59) supported him with arms and, on occasion, provided him with refuge in Morocco. This brought French action against him in 1845, when Moroccan forces, fighting a European enemy for the first time since the sixteenth century, were badly defeated at the battle on the river Isly. Fortunately for Morocco, the French were too busy with Algerian affairs to follow up their victory. In 1859 Morocco also became involved with Spain, which claimed that the ports of Ceuta and Melilla on the northern coast, which she had held since the sixteenth century, were being constantly raided by the sultan's subjects. A Spanish army invaded Morocco and inflicted a

97

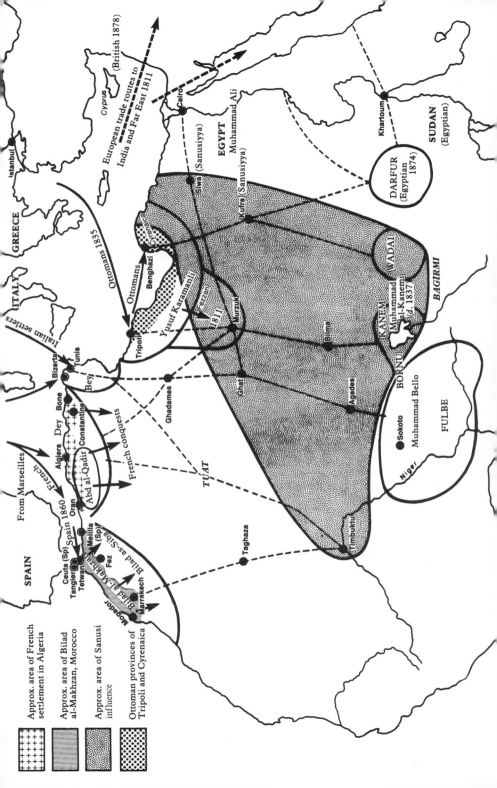

European trade routes to India and Far East 1811 (British 1878)

Cyprus

Istanbul

GREECE

ITALY

Italian settlers

French

From Marseilles

SPAIN

Ceuta (Sp)
Tangier
Tetwan
Melilla (Sp)
Bilad al-Makhzan
Fez
Spain 1860
Oran
Bilad as-Siba
Mogador
Marrakech

Bizerta
Tunis
Bey
Bone
Dey
Algiers
Constantine
Abd al-Qadir
French conquests

Ottomans 1835

Ottomans

Tripoli
Yusuf Karamanli
Fezzan
1811
Ghadames
TUAT

Benghazi
Cyrenaica (Sanusiyya)
Siwa
Kufra (Sanusiyya)

EGYPT
Muhammad Ali

Cairo

Khartoum

SUDAN
(Egyptian)

DARFUR
(Egyptian 1874)

Murzuq

Ghat

Bilma

Agades

KANEM
Muhammad al-Kanemi (d. 1837)

BORNU

WADAI

BAGIRMI

Sokoto
Muhammad Bello

FULBE

Niger

Timbuktu

Taghaza

Approx. area of French settlement in Algeria

Approx. area of Bilad al-Makhzan, Morocco

Approx. area of Sanusi influence

Ottoman provinces of Tripoli and Cyrenaica

series of defeats on the sultan's forces. The war was ended in 1860 by the Treaty of Tetuan, under which Morocco promised to pay Spain a huge indemnity. This indemnity opened Morocco to further European interference. To pay it, the sultan had to raise a loan in London on the security of the Moroccan customs and to accept control over these by foreign commissioners.

Within Morocco the government had the difficult task of upholding the sultan's authority against the religious movements of the *marabouts* and the hostility of the nomadic groups. Traditionally the country was divided into the *bilad al-makhzan* (the friendly country), which paid taxes into the sultan's treasury, and the *bilad as-siba* (the unfriendly country), where the government could exert its influence only by threats and bribes. The relative size of these two areas was something that depended very much on the personality of each particular sultan. Mawlai al-Hasan (1873–94), the last great sultan before the French occupation, was continually on campaign reducing the area of the unfriendly country. For the first time since the seventeenth century the sultan's authority was carried into the High Atlas region, and also deep into the Sahara in northern Mauritania. Mawlai al-Hasan was thus trying to make certain that no ungoverned groups existed which could cause frontier incidents of the kind which had led to the Spanish war. The fact that Morocco was able to keep its independence until 1912 is a tribute to Mawlai al-Hasan's enterprise and skill.

TRIPOLI UNDER OTTOMAN RULE (1835–1911): THE SANUSIYYA

After the death of Yusuf Karamanli in 1830 two parties contended for the office of pasha, one supported by the British, the other by the French. After several years of confusion, during which the bedouin of the Fezzan broke away from the control of any authority in Tripoli, the Ottoman government decided to reassert its authority over Tripoli, to counter Muhammad Ali's power in Egypt and the French presence in Algeria. In 1835 an Ottoman governor arrived in Tripoli and declared the Karamanli dynasty deposed. By 1842 this government had subdued most of the coastal tribes, but it could not control the Fezzan. The trans-Saharan trade suffered gravely, both from these events and from the wars which broke out all round the frontiers of Bornu after the death of al-Kanemi in 1837. During the 1830s and 1840s the central Sahara was so disturbed that traffic on the routes from Bornu and Wadai was restricted to a single annual caravan on each main route.

Peace returned to the central Sahara as a result of the rise of another Muslim brotherhood, that of the Sanusi. The founder of the order, Muhammad al-Sanusi, was born in Algeria about 1790 and studied in religious schools in Morocco before making the pilgrimage to Mecca. He established his first *zawiya* (Arabic, religious centre) among the bedouin of Cyrenaica in 1843. His simple teaching of a return to the original practices of Islam, and his great tact and diplomacy, appealed to the feuding tribesmen and held them together in a way in which neither the Karamanlis nor the Ottomans had been able to do. The order spread rapidly into the Sahara and the western Sudan, and its popularity was still increasing when Muhammad al-Mahdi (not to be confused with the Mahdi of the Egyptian Sudan) succeeded his father as *shaikh* in 1859. *Zawiyas* of the Sanusi order were set up all over Cyrenaica, the Fezzan, Wadai, Kanem–Bornu and as far west as Timbuktu. The followers of al-Sanusi were closely connected with trade, and paid regular dues out of their trading profits which went to enrich the *zawiyas*. These became the centres not only of religious propaganda but also of agricultural and commercial development. At the beginning of the nineteenth century the route from Benghazi to Wadai had been the least busy of the trans-Saharan routes. After the establishment of the Sanusi movement in Cyrenaica and in Wadai, at both ends of it, it became the most important. The Ottoman governors of Tripoli were forced to acknowledge the authority of the leaders (*ikhwan*) of the order over the desert peoples and to keep on good terms with them, since they controlled the trade on which the prosperity of Tripoli and Benghazi depended. As a result of British pressure at Istanbul, the Ottoman government abolished the trade in slaves throughout the empire (except the Hijaz) in 1857. In Tripoli and Cyrenaica this law could not be enforced against the determination of the Sanusi traders to continue their operations. In this region the trans-Saharan slave-trade survived until the French occupation of Niger and Tchad and the Italian occupation of Cyrenaica, at the beginning of the twentieth century.

THE REGENCY OF TUNIS (1830–81)

All through the nineteenth century the *beylikat* (regency) of Tunis was the most progressive and westernised of the Maghrib states. As early as 1819 the bey outlawed piracy. The beys were also the first Muslim rulers to abolish slavery and the first to adopt a constitutional form of government. The economy of Tunisia was varied enough to withstand the effects of the abolition of privateering and slavery. The plains of northern Tunisia provided rich harvests of grain and fruit, while Tunis and the other coastal cities produced many manufactured goods, such as cloth, leather goods and metalware. The political situation, however, was by no means so secure, especially after the French invasion of Algeria and the restoration of Ottoman authority in Tripoli. The Tunisian government felt itself in a trap between two sources of likely attack, and turned to Britain for protection. In 1837, after the French occupation of Constantine, the Algerian fortress city near the Tunisian border, the British government promised to support the bey not only against France but also against the Ottoman sultan. It was this reliance on Britain that led Ahmad Bey to abolish slavery in a series of decrees issued between 1841 and 1846. The bey's government had sufficient authority to enforce these laws throughout the country.

The constitutional decrees of 1857 and 1861 were passed, at the suggestion of the French and British consuls, in order to satisfy the ambitions of the wealthy, well-educated Tunisian middle-class and of the influential French and Italian trading communities. The constitution granted equality of all men before the law and guaranteed freedom of trade. It also set up nominated councils to advise the bey. In practice, the common people were not much helped by this constitution, which gave political power to the wealthy few. The government largely ignored the constitution and it soon fell into disuse. However, the memory of it survived, and when nationalist political parties emerged in Tunisia during the twentieth century they took the name Destour (Arabic, constitution).

During the 1860s and 1870s British influence in Tunisia declined in relation to that of France, which was determined that no other European country should occupy a position of strength on the borders of Algeria. After a prolonged diplomatic and commercial struggle with Italy, which was by the 1870s united and was beginning to show interest in North Africa, France decided to take strong action. A dispute between the bey's government and a French trading company, and the incursions of Tunisian hill-tribes across the Algerian frontier, provided the necessary excuse. In 1881 French forces captured Bizerta and Tunis. The bey was forced to sign a treaty allowing France to occupy Tunisia and to take charge of her finances and foreign affairs. Unlike the dey of Algiers fifty years earlier, the bey and his government continued to function under French supervision.

The French occupation of Tunis, as much as the British occupation of Egypt which occurred in the following year, was one of the opening moves in the partition of Africa among the European powers. It was in fact the result of an informal agreement made in 1877 between Britain, France and Russia, by which each of these powers was to 'take one bite at the Ottoman cherry' with the tacit support of the others. Britain's bite was Cyprus, which was ceded to her under pressure by the Ottoman government in 1878. Russia's bite consisted of three formerly Ottoman provinces in the Caucasus mountains. Though viewed by Britain and Russia as a Mediterranean and Middle Eastern agreement, the French were conscious of its African implications. In occupying Tunis they were not merely protecting the borders of Algeria but were extending a French North Africa which was ultimately to connect with the area of French conquests on the Senegal and the Niger.

9 The partition of Africa on paper, 1879–1891

During the last quarter of the nineteenth century events took place
which changed the face of Africa and which can only be understood by
tracing their origin and development outside Africa. In 1879 more
than 90 per cent of the continent was ruled by Africans. By 1900 all
but a tiny fraction of it was being governed by European powers. By
about 1914 the lives of almost all Africans were being deeply affected
by the changes brought about by these foreign rulers. The European
powers partitioned Africa among themselves with such haste, like
players in a rough game, that the process has been called 'the scramble
for Africa'. The motives for this partition, the reason why the European powers acted as they did, and when they did, are a part of
European history rather than African history, and it is to these European affairs that we must now turn our attention.

We have to remember, first of all, that throughout the first sixty-
five years of the nineteenth century the only great powers in western
Europe were Britain and France. Germany and Italy did not yet exist
as separate and unified states. Of the lesser powers, Holland and
Denmark actually abandoned their African possessions (trading posts
on the Gold Coast) during the nineteenth century, leaving only Portugal as a minor competitor with France and Britain. We have also to
remember that even France, despite her considerable military
strength, was well behind Britain in the race for commercial and
industrial development. Precisely because her manufactures were
inferior or more expensive than those of Britain, France pursued a
'protectionist policy' – that is to say, she tried to reserve the trade of
French colonies for her own merchants. In the Senegal from 1815,
and from the 1840s in Guinea, the Ivory Coast, Dahomey and Gabon
and in Madagascar, there were, therefore, French naval and commercial bases from which non-French traders were kept out. These areas
were, however, quite small. In the British possessions the same
customs dues were charged to British and foreign traders alike. In
fact, however, traders of all nations did the largest part of their

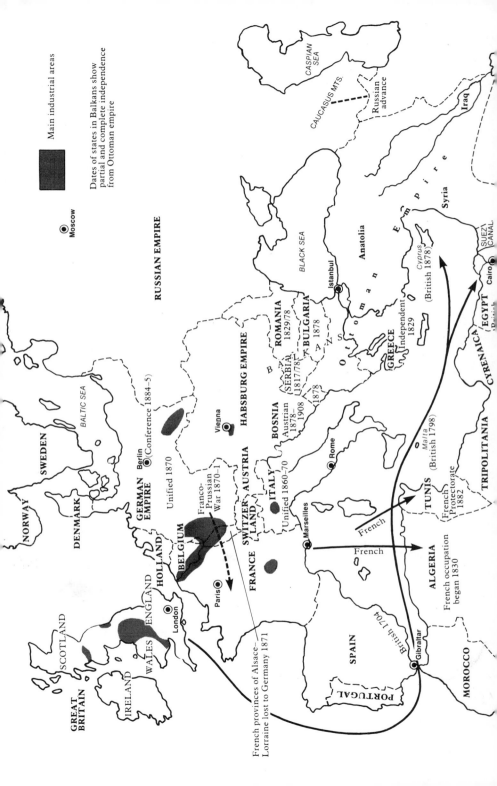

Main industrial areas

Dates of states in Balkans show partial and complete independence from Ottoman empire

Moscow

RUSSIAN EMPIRE

CASPIAN SEA

CAUCASUS MTS.

Russian advance

Iraq

Syria

Anatolia

BLACK SEA

Istanbul

O   t   t   o   m   a   n   E   m   p   i   r   e

Cyprus (British 1878)

SUEZ CANAL

Cairo

EGYPT

CYRENAICA

GREECE
Independent 1829

ROMANIA 1829/78

SERBIA 1817/78

BULGARIA 1878

BOSNIA
Austrian 1878–1908

1878

Malta (British 1798)

TRIPOLITANIA

HABSBURG EMPIRE

Vienna

Rome

ITALY
Unified 1860–70

TUNIS
French Protectorate 1882

Berlin
(Conference 1884–5)

Unified 1870

GERMAN EMPIRE

Franco-Prussian War 1870–1

SWITZER-LAND

AUSTRIA

French

French

Marseilles

ALGERIA
French occupation began 1830

NORWAY

SWEDEN

DENMARK

BALTIC SEA

HOLLAND

BELGIUM

FRANCE

Paris

French provinces of Alsace–Lorraine lost to Germany 1871

GREAT BRITAIN

SCOTLAND

IRELAND

WALES ENGLAND

London

SPAIN

PORTUGAL

British 1704

Gibraltar

MOROCCO

business in Africa on stretches of the coast over which no European flag yet flew. So long as most of the trade was carried on near the coast, and so long as most of the coastline was free to all comers, Britain, at least, had no economic motive to annex large territories in Africa. Even France found that her protected settlements were more of a financial burden than they were worth.

THE DEVELOPMENT OF ANGLO-FRENCH RIVALRY IN WEST AFRICA

By the 1870s, however, a new situation was beginning to develop in West Africa. The trade was no longer exclusively a coastal trade. At the few key points where railways or river steamships could be introduced, European trade was starting to penetrate the interior. The French were thrusting deep into the Senegal valley, and it was known that their objective was to connect the Senegal and the upper Niger by a railway, which would attract the trade of a great part of the West African interior into French hands. Here was a development which must affect the British trading posts on the Gambia and which might in time affect the trade routes leading to Sierra Leone and the Gold Coast. Again, on the lower Niger, the penetration of the interior markets by British firms trading up-river in their own steamers had reached a stage at which, to go further, it was necessary for them to come together and form a single company with a monopoly over the trade. Only by this means could the essential installations be afforded and a united front be maintained in dealing with the powerful Fulbe emirates of the interior. In 1879 George Goldie amalgamated the British firms trading up the Niger river, only to find himself facing competition from French traders. This he dealt with in a characteristically ruthless fashion, by undercutting their prices at a loss to himself and so forcing them to sell out their interests to his own company. Thus the French were left feeling that, for the future at least, their commercial companies must be given political support.

THE ENTRY OF NEW POWERS

Already, in the early 1870s, Britain and France had considered partitioning West Africa into 'spheres of influence', in each of which only the firms of one country would be allowed to trade. It had been suggested by the French that the Gambia should be given to France in exchange for British control over the coastline from Sierra Leone to Mount Cameroun. The scheme had fallen through in 1875, but, had it   105 not been for the intervention of other European powers, it would probably have been revived in the eighties, so as to leave the French in control of the upper Niger and the waterways leading to the Upper Guinea coast, and the British in control of the lower Niger and the coastlands of Lower Guinea. In the early 1880s, however, the slow movement towards an Anglo-French partition of West Africa, arising from the commercial penetration of the interior, was both speeded up and complicated by the appearance on the African scene of two new European powers which had not previously shown any great interest in Africa. The result of these interventions was to force all the European powers, including France and Britain, to look far beyond their immediate economic needs. What each power feared was that its rivals would keep the trade of their new colonies to themselves by enclosing them within high tariff (or customs) barriers. Therefore each power felt compelled to enter the scramble for territory in order to reserve the largest possible sphere for its own future activities.

KING LEOPOLD AND THE CONGO

The first of these newcomers was an individual rather than a nation state. It was Leopold II, King of Belgium, a little country situated uncomfortably between the European giants, France and Germany. The Belgian people did not share the expansionist dreams of their ruler. As early as 1861 Leopold had written, 'The sea bathes our coast, the world lies before us. Steam and electricity have annihilated distance. All the non-appropriated lands on the surface of the globe (mostly in Africa) can become the field of our operations and our success.' Leopold was a master diplomat, a man of boundless ambition, and in his younger days he had a genuine idealism – a belief in human progress and in the need to improve the conditions of less-privileged peoples. As he grew older, his idealism was largely submerged by a growing love of wealth and power. As we saw in Chapter 4, Leopold's opportunity came when Stanley's schemes for the opening up of the Congo basin, which the explorer had formed after his descent of the river in 1877, were rejected by the British government. In 1879 Leopold took Stanley into his service. During the next four years Stanley established road and river communications from the Congo estuary to Stanley Falls (Stanleyville, Kisangani). Leopold on the Congo, like Goldie on the Niger, was aiming at a commercial monopoly, which would attract all the trade of the Congo basin into his own river steamers and his own railway from Lake Malebo to the

106 coast.

Leopold did not at this stage attempt to obtain treaties of sovereignty or legal possession from the African rulers of the lower Congo area. He relied on his own mastery of the lines of communication. The immediate effect of his operations, however, was to stimulate the competition of a rival French group, whose agent, Savorgnan de Brazza, returned to Europe in the summer of 1882 with a treaty signed by Makoko, chief of the Bateke country on the northern shores of Lake Malebo. This treaty placed his territory under French sovereignty. De Brazza toured France, stirring up imperialist sentiment so successfully that he persuaded the French government both to ratify his treaty with Makoko and to set in motion a large programme of treaty-making and annexation along the Nigerian coast. This in turn led the British government to join in the race for Nigerian territory and forced King Leopold to seek treaties granting sovereign rights in the lower Congo area. The scramble for West and West-Central Africa had thus begun in earnest.

Once he had started upon territorial annexation, King Leopold skilfully prepared the way for international recognition of his claim to rule the Congo basin. He persuaded the French government to support him by a secret promise that the territory should revert to France if he himself should prove unable to govern it. He also gained the support of the German chancellor, Bismarck, just at the moment when Germany herself was about to enter the colonial field. To English merchants he held out tempting hopes of valuable contracts, and with their help he broke down the British government's plan to bar his access to the Congo by recognising Portuguese claims of sovereignty over the river mouth. Finally, his American secretary, Sanford, persuaded the United States to join France and Germany in giving recognition to the Congo Free State.

GERMANY ENTERS THE SCRAMBLE, 1883–5

During the 1850s and 1860s a great political and economic revolution had taken place in Germany, in which most of the independent states whose peoples spoke the German language became united around the North German state of Prussia, under the leadership of Bismarck. The basis of political unification was a customs union which enabled Germany to embark on industrialisation. This combination of political amalgamation or unification and modern industrial growth resulted in the emergence of a great power in Europe. By the 1870s the new Germany was able to rival France militarily and Britain industrially. The former rivalry led to the Franco-Prussian war of 1870–1, in 107

16*a*   Northern Africa on the eve of partition: African states and European settlements

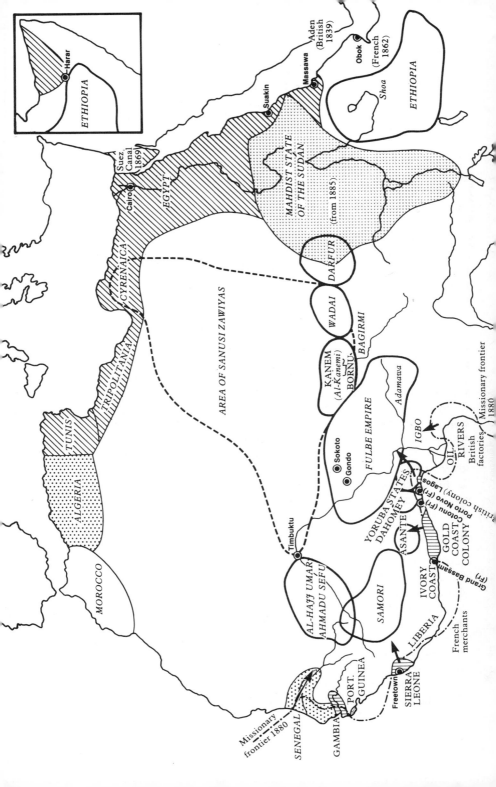

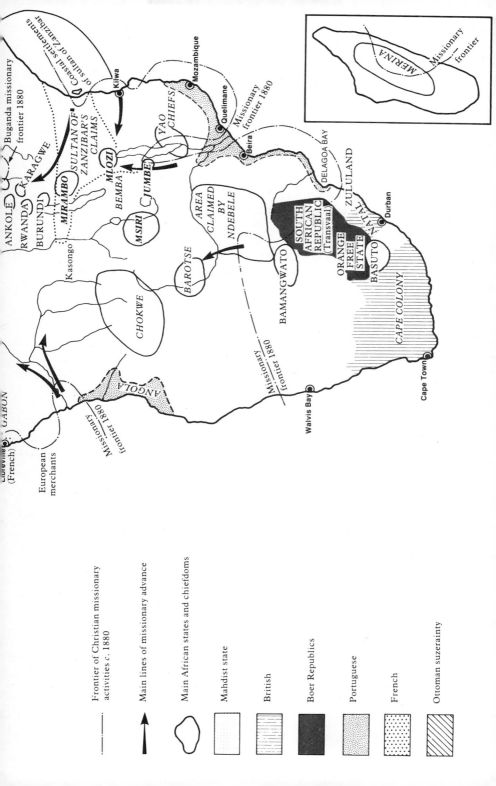

Frontier of Christian missionary activities c. 1880

Main lines of missionary advance

Main African states and chiefdoms

Mahdist state

British

Boer Republics

Portuguese

French

Ottoman suzerainty

Buganda missionary frontier 1880

Coastal settlements of Sultan of Zanzibar

Kilwa

Mozambique

Quelimane

Missionary frontier 1880

Beira

DELAGOA BAY

ZULULAND

Durban

SULTAN OF ZANZIBAR'S CLAIMS

YAO CHIEFS

ANKOLE

RWANDA

BURUNDI

KARAGWE

MIRAMBO

MLOZI

CJUMBE

BEMBA

MSIRI

Kasongo

CHOKWE

BAROTSE

AREA CLAIMED BY NDEBELE

BAMANGWATO

SOUTH AFRICAN REPUBLIC (Transvaal)

ORANGE FREE STATE

BASUTO

NATAL

CAPE COLONY

Cape Town

Walvis Bay

Missionary frontier 1880

ANGOLA

Missionary frontier 1880

GABON

Loeveme (French)

European merchants

MERINA

Missionary frontier

which France was overwhelmed and lost the frontier provinces of Alsace and Lorraine to Germany. In both France and Germany some political groups turned from this war to thoughts of colonial expansion, the French as a form of compensation for the humiliation of defeat, the Germans out of the realisation of new-found strength. For a long time yet, Bismarck personally refused to take any outward interest in the colonial question. It was left to merchant groups in the North German ports to stir up a national demand for colonies. These groups succeeded so well, however, that from 1883 to 1885 Bismarck, suddenly changing his attitude, was able to take the diplomats of Europe by surprise in declaring German protectorates in four widely scattered parts of Africa – Togo, Cameroun (known to the Germans as Kamerun), East Africa and South-West Africa.

Germany's bid for colonies was not based on any substantial interest built up in Africa beforehand. It was a simple assertion of her new position among the world powers. There is much truth in the view that Bismarck himself took part in the scramble mainly in order to dominate the international politics of the European powers which were connected with it. He wanted to turn French ambitions away from the recovery of her lost provinces, and the best way to do so was to involve her in rivalries with other powers for overseas territories. He therefore supported French claims in West Africa and the Congo basin and made his own African annexations in places which would threaten British claims rather than French ones.

It was now that Britain's peculiar position in Egypt became of such vital significance in the diplomacy of partition. The British occupation of Egypt, it will be remembered (Chapter 7), had been planned as a joint Anglo-French operation, to crush Urabi Pasha's revolt and to restore the authority of Khedive Tawfiq. It was originally intended to be only a temporary intervention, and therefore nothing was done to alter the control of Egypt's finances by the International Debt Commission. British rule in Egypt was thus dependent at every turn on the good will of the commission, on which, since French opposition to the continued British occupation was certain, the German vote was of the utmost importance. Bismarck, throughout the vital years of the partition, supported British rule in Egypt. His price was British acceptance of Germany's new annexations and of his support of the claims of France and King Leopold to the north and south of the lower Congo.

It was Bismarck, therefore, who dominated the first round of the scramble, which came to an end at the Berlin Conference (1884–5). The conference prepared the way for newcomers to the African scene

16*b* Southern Africa on the eve of partition: African states and European settlements

by requiring that claims to colonies or protectorates on any part of the African coastline should be formally notified to the other powers taking part in the conference, and by insisting that such claims must be backed by the establishment of an effective degree of authority in the areas concerned. This put an end to the British idea of informal empire. The conference also decreed that there should be freedom of navigation on the Niger and the Congo, thus in theory frustrating British attempts to close the Niger against the French and the Congo against King Leopold. The years 1883–5, therefore, saw Britain checked, surprised or forestalled in one part of Africa after another. The former large sphere of British influence in Lower Guinea was now broken up by a French protectorate in Dahomey (Bénin) and two German protectorates in Togo and Cameroun. The Congo and the Gabon coast, where British trade had flourished for so long, was divided between France and King Leopold. The unity of the southern African coastal regions, so long dominated by Britain, was broken by a German protectorate in the south-west. The Merina kingdom on Madagascar had signed a treaty with France, despite the fact that British missionary influence had been an outstanding feature in the island since the 1830s. And the old area of informal empire exercised through the sultan of Zanzibar in East Africa was shattered by the German annexations in the interior from Dar es Salaam. As bases from which Britain could build afresh, there remained only Egypt, the scattered possessions in West Africa, and the self-governing Cape Colony and Natal in the south.

LORD SALISBURY AND THE RESTORATION OF BRITISH INITIATIVE, 1885–91

The revival of British fortunes in Africa, and their conversion to the new conditions of formal as opposed to informal empire, was very largely the work of Lord Salisbury. Salisbury was prime minister of Britain from 1885 to 1892 and rivalled even Bismarck as a master of diplomacy. His first act was to open a way for northward expansion from the Cape Colony by declaring a protectorate over Bechuanaland (now Botswana) – the largely desert area lying between German South-West Africa and the independent Boer republic of the Transvaal (then known as the South African Republic). This action was to gain great significance from the discovery in the following year (1886) of the vast gold deposits of the Witwatersrand in the Transvaal. Although these were in Boer territory, the exploiters were nearly all English-speaking capitalists from the Cape Colony and from Britain itself. These British exploiters were led by Cecil Rhodes, who had already made a fortune in the diamonds of Kimberley. He shared the common belief that 'a second Rand' would be found in the highlands north of the Limpopo river and was determined that Britain should control this potentially rich area. Bechuanaland was his 'Suez Canal to the North', up which in 1890 there travelled the 'pioneer column' of white settlers who occupied Southern Rhodesia (now Zimbabwe). Salisbury disliked and distrusted Rhodes, but he was prepared to use his great wealth and energy to help carve out a belt of British territories in the highlands between the Portuguese colonies of Angola and Mozambique.

Salisbury's second action was to rescue for Britain what remained of East Africa after the German annexations of 1884. In 1886 he negotiated with Bismarck a division of the area into two 'spheres of influence', following the present boundary between Kenya and Tanzania. In 1890, by ceding to Germany the North Sea island of Heligoland, he persuaded Bismarck to sign a comprehensive series of boundary agreements, by which Germany recognised British claims to Zanzibar, Kenya, Uganda, Northern Rhodesia (now Zambia), Bechuanaland and eastern Nigeria. In the same year Salisbury concluded a treaty with France in respect of the western boundary of Nigeria, in return for British recognition of the French protectorate over Madagascar (which the rulers of the island did not acknowledge), and in 1891 an agreement with Portugal in respect of Nyasaland (now Malawi) and the two Rhodesias.

Thus, by the end of Salisbury's period of office in 1892, though many interior boundaries remained to be drawn, the broad outlines of the European partition of Africa had been sketched out. The cornerstone of Salisbury's African policy was the continued British occupation of Egypt. As he himself recognised, the consequence was that Britain should give way to French claims for the predominant place in West Africa. German claims, too, had to be admitted in the four regions where these had been staked. The British West African possessions were confined to a modest extension from their pre-partition footholds. The main British share in the partition had to be found in a northward expansion of British South Africa through Bechuanaland to the Rhodesias and Nyasaland, and in a slice of East Africa stretching from Mombasa to the upper Nile. Salisbury realised that Egypt, with British help, would soon be strong enough to undertake the reconquest of the Sudan from the Khalifa and that the final extension of British power would take place in this direction. Salisbury admitted in a memorandum to the British Cabinet that the slogan 'all British from the Cape to Cairo' was a rough expression of his African policy as a whole.

It is important to remember that the outline partition accomplished by 1891 was in large measure a partition which existed only on paper. Despite the insistence of the Berlin Conference that claims to African coastlines must be supported by effective occupation, most of the claims recognised by the powers were in fact based on a few scraps of paper obtained by consuls and concession-hunters from African chiefs who had very little idea of what they were doing and whose authority usually extended only over a very small part of the areas claimed. There was not a single territory in Africa where anything like effective occupation existed at the time of the partition. The final division of territories reflected not so much the strength of European interests on the ground as the political power of the claimants in Europe. The partition was nevertheless important. It represented the deliberate intention of powerful European states to carry their influence into the innermost parts of Africa, as they had already done in much of Asia, in the Americas and in Australasia. No one could doubt that they had the necessary power. The fact that they acted with so large a measure of mutual agreement that the partition did not cause an outbreak of war between them was probably of benefit to Africa as well as to themselves.

10   The partition of Africa on the ground, 1891–1901

EUROPEAN CONFLICTS IN AFRICA

The first stages of the partition, when European states were laying claim to coastal regions and navigable rivers, and were defining on paper the boundaries running inland from these first footholds, were accomplished with surprisingly little bloodshed and conflict. The reason for this was that very small numbers of European forces were used in Africa during this time. The first occupying groups consisted of small, mobile expeditions of European officers or chartered-company officials, accompanied by a few dozen lightly armed porters, scarcely distinguishable from the expeditions of the first explorers. Africa itself was so immense that these first little groups of Europeans seldom came into contact with each other. Their attitude to the African peoples had necessarily to be that of negotiators rather than conquerors. They entered into the local politics of every region that they came to, supporting the groups and factions which had some reason to be friendly, and avoiding those which were hostile. In the later stages of the scramble, however, towards the close of the nineteenth century, when forces were somewhat larger and when the final, interior frontiers were being claimed, meetings between rival European expeditions became more frequent. Collisions occurred between the occupying forces and those of the larger and more organised African states, which often fought desperately for their survival. Numerically, the armies of these states often outnumbered the European expeditions by many hundreds to one, but the superiority of European weapons was overwhelming. A single machine-gun could put to flight a whole army of undisciplined men armed only with ancient guns and spears. As it raced towards its conclusion, therefore, the scramble produced increasing bloodshed. At first there were small incidents in West Africa, in the Congo and in East Africa. Then came the French 'pacifications' of Madagascar and Morocco, the war between Ethiopia and Italy, and the reconquest of the Sudan. Finally came the deadly struggle in South Africa, in which white fought white.

THE FRENCH ADVANCE DOWN THE NIGER

After the Berlin Conference, the French took steps to consolidate their possessions on the West African coast. By 1893 the colonies of the Ivory Coast and French Guinea had been officially established. In the same year French troops entered Dahomey (Bénin) and deposed Behanzin, the last independent king of Dahomey. Dahomey became a French colony in 1900. The main French expansion in West Africa, however, took place from the basin of the Senegal river. Here, by 1879, the French advance up the river had brought them into contact with the empire of Ahmadu Sefu, the son of al-Hajj Umar (Chapter 3). Indecisive clashes between General Gallieni's Senegalese troops and Ahmadu's forces continued for many years, but Ahmadu's empire broke up once its military power had been destroyed. The French entered the upper Niger valley and captured Bamako in 1883. A more determined opposition to French penetration was put up by Samori, a Muslim Mandingo. This leader had, in a series of conquests begun in the early 1870s, succeeded in uniting under his rule most of the peoples in the vast area between the sources of the Niger and the upper Volta basin. Samori became the hero of the fiercely independent southern Mande peoples in his relentless opposition to the French. Although his homelands around Bissandugu were occupied in 1891, he was not finally defeated and exiled by the French until 1898.

Samori's resistance delayed but could not halt French penetration down the Niger. Timbuktu was taken in 1894, and Say in 1896. Beyond Say, the French advance was blocked by the British in Hausaland. Once in control of the upper and middle Niger, therefore, they turned their attention to filling in the gaps between the Niger valley and their possessions on the coast. This task was completed by the turn of the century. It was at this stage that frontier incidents with rival British expeditions in the Nigerian and Gold Coast interiors became frequent.

BRITISH EXPANSION IN THE GOLD COAST AND NIGERIA

We have seen (Chapter 9) that Britain was prevented by the wider pattern of the diplomatic partition of Africa from pressing claims to a large consolidated area of West Africa. All she could do was to extend, by effective occupation on the ground, her existing footholds in Sierra Leone, the Gold Coast and Nigeria. In the Gold Coast the local situation depended upon relations between the coastal 'colony' and

115

17   European partition: North-West Africa

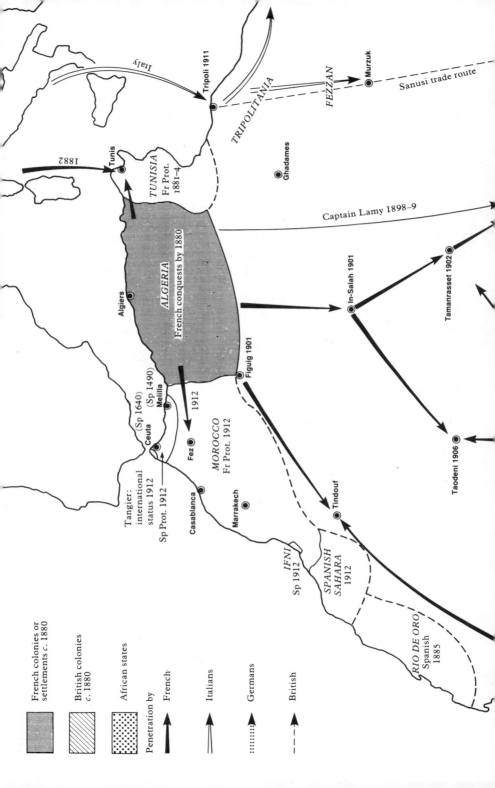

Italy

Tripoli 1911

TRIPOLITANIA

FEZZAN

Murzuk

Sanusi trade route

1882

Tunis

TUNISIA
Fr Prot.
1881–4

Ghadames

Captain Lamy 1898–9

ALGERIA
French conquests by 1880

Algiers

In-Salah 1901

Tamanrasset 1902

Figuig 1901

(Sp 1640)

(Sp 1490)
Melilla

1912

Taodeni 1906

Ceuta

MOROCCO
Fr Prot. 1912

Fez

Tangier:
international
status 1912

Sp Prot. 1912

Casablanca

Marrakech

Tindouf

IFNI
Sp 1912

SPANISH
SAHARA
1912

RIO DE ORO
Spanish
1885

French colonies or
settlements c. 1880

British colonies
c. 1880

African states

Penetration by

French:

Italians

Germans

British

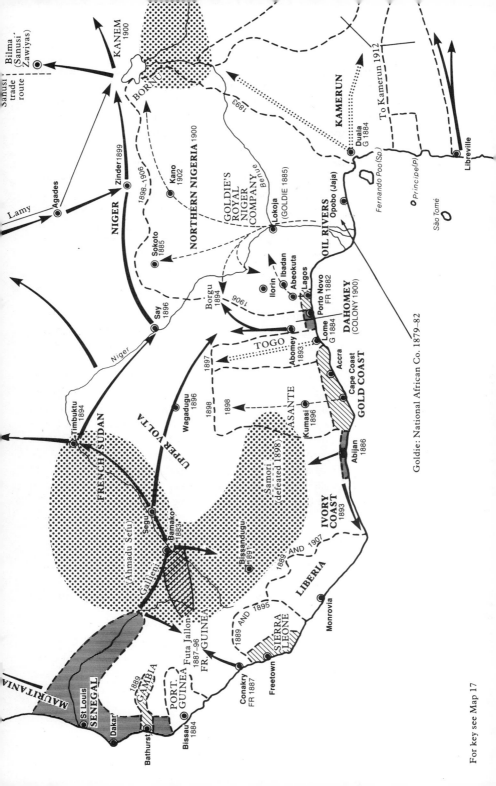

Bilma
(Sanusi
Zawiyas)

Sanusi
trade
route

KANEM
1900

BORNU

KAMERUN

To Kamerun 1912

Duala
G 1884

Libreville

1893

Fernando Poo (Sp.)

Principe (P)

São Tomé

Agades

Zinder 1899

1898–1906

Kano
1902

NORTHERN NIGERIA 1900

GOLDIE'S
ROYAL
NIGER
COMPANY

Lokoja
(GOLDIE 1885)

Opobo (Jaja)

OIL RIVERS

Lamy

NIGER

Sokoto
1885

Benue

Ilorin

Ibadan

Abeokuta

Lagos

Porto Novo
FR 1882

DAHOMEY
(COLONY 1900)

Say
1896

Borgu
1894

1906

1906

Lome
G 1884

Abomey
1893

TOGO

Accra

Cape Coast

GOLD COAST

Goldie: National African Co. 1879–82

Niger

Wagadugu
1896

1897

1898

1898

ASANTE

Kumasi
1896

Timbuktu
1894

UPPER VOLTA

Samori
(defeated 1898)

Abijan
1886

FRENCH SUDAN

(Ahmadu Sefu)

Segu

Bamako
1883

Bissandugu
1891

IVORY
COAST
1893

Galliéni

1889 AND 1907

LIBERIA

Monrovia

FR. GUINEA

Futa Jallon
1887–96

1889 AND 1895

SIERRA
LEONE

MAURITANIA

1889

GAMBIA

PORT.
GUINEA

Conakry
FR 1887

Freetown

St Louis

SENEGAL

Dakar

Bathurst

Bissau
1884

For key see Map 17

the Asante empire, whose outlying dependencies were detached from their allegiance by treaty-making expeditions as a preliminary to the military occupation of Asante itself in 1896. In 1898 the Northern Territories, part of which had been tributary to Samori, were declared a protectorate in order to forestall expansion by the French from the north.

Britain's occupation of Nigeria was more complicated and took place from three different spheres. The first was from Lagos, where the small island colony expanded into a protectorate covering most of Yorubaland. The second was from the Oil Rivers, where British consuls supported the Liverpool firms in breaking the power of the African middleman chiefs like Jaja of Opobo as soon as these tried to make treaties with other European nations. The third was from Nupe and southern Hausaland. Here, Sir George Goldie's National African Company, which in 1866 became the Royal Niger Company, had powers under its Royal Charter to administer justice and maintain order. Goldie secured the friendship of much of Hausaland by a treaty made with the sultan of Sokoto in 1885. Nupe and the emirate of Ilorin, however, had to be conquered by the Royal Niger Company's army, the West African Frontier Force. Goldie's officers, notably Captain Lugard, were involved in incidents with the French, who were advancing down the Niger and up from the coast into Dahomey. Borgu was occupied only after a French expedition there had been forced to withdraw. These military operations against a rival European colonial power soon proved too expensive and too dangerous for a private company. In 1898 the British government brought the charter to an end and two years later (1900) took over the control of northern Nigeria. British expansion continued in the direction of Bornu and Lake Chad. Kano was occupied in 1902.

THE FRENCH IN THE CENTRAL SUDAN: RABIH

The French moved into the central Sudan from three directions – from the Niger valley, from Gabon and from Algeria. By about 1900 expeditions from all three were converging on Lake Chad. Goldie's Royal Niger Company prevented the French from occupying any but the northern desert fringe of Hausaland as they moved eastwards from Say on the Niger. In Gabon the French government had begun to occupy the interior after the Berlin Conference, and by the late 1890s was in a position to start pushing northwards towards the Shari river basin. Finally, in the wake of Captain Lamy's pioneer trans-Saharan expedition of 1898–9, the French began to occupy the principal oases

118

18   European partition: West Africa

– Tuat, Tamanrasset, Aïr and Zinder. The nomadic Tuareg of the surrounding deserts, however, remained practically unaffected by the French presence until after the Second World War.

The final resistance to the French occupation of the central Sudan was put up by the Sanusi order from its fortified *zawiyas* in the Bilma region, and above all by Rabih, an Arab soldier from Sennar. He had earlier served the Egyptian government in the Bahr al-Ghazal. After refusing to submit to the Mahdi, he had set off westwards with his armed followers. He failed in an attack against the sultanate of Wadai in 1887, but by 1892 he had conquered Bagirmi and much of eastern Bornu. Here he set up a slave-raiding state, which disposed of its booty along the Sanusi trade routes leading to Tripoli and Benghazi. As the French closed in on him from all sides, he fiercely resisted their advance. He was finally defeated and killed in 1900.

THE RECONQUEST OF THE SUDAN: FASHODA

Before the French had defeated Rabih, the British in Egypt had reconquered the Mahdist state, which appeared to be threatened both by the Italians in Eritrea and by the French advance from the Congo. To forestall such moves, an Anglo-Egyptian military force, trained by the British commander Kitchener, moved into the Sudan in 1896. In 1898 this force defeated the Mahdist armies at the battle of Omdurman, in which 20,000 Sudanese were killed. Khartoum then fell to Kitchener. A week later news reached him that a French force of African soldiers led by Commandant Marchand had installed itself at Fashoda, some 300 kilometres further south, after an incredible march from Gabon, which had lasted nearly two years. Kitchener hastened up the White Nile with a much larger force. The hostile camps faced one another for several months, while telegraphic messages flashed to and fro between the Sudan and Europe. In the end the French gave way, and Marchand hauled down his flag; but not before France and Britain had been brought to the brink of a major war.

A brief mention can be made here of the last two territories in northern Africa to be seized by the European powers. In 1911 Italy launched an unprovoked, but not unexpected, invasion of the Ottoman province of Tripoli, and the next year pushed from there into Cyrenaica. Here the Italian armies met bitter opposition from the bedouin tribesmen who belonged to the Sanusi order. Their resistance continued until the 1930s (see Chapter 14). At the western end of North Africa, Morocco escaped European control until 1912, not because of the sultan's ability to oppose it, but because the European

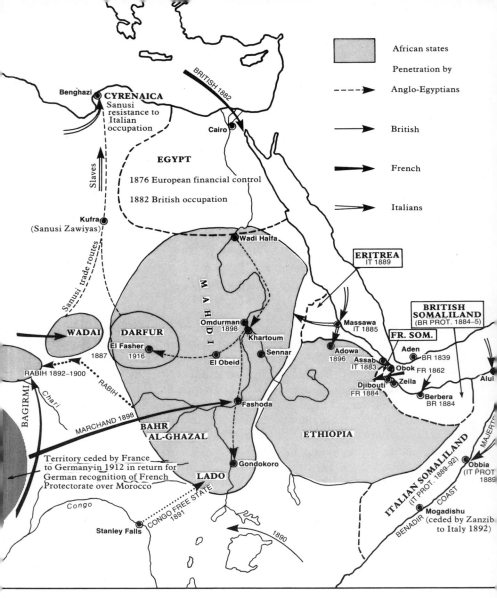

19   European partition: East Africa

powers quarrelled among themselves over which of them should occupy his kingdom. Their disagreements twice brought Europe within reach of war. Finally, the two powers most concerned, France and Spain, partitioned Morocco, Spain taking the smaller northern portion. Germany was bought off by being given extra territory in Cameroun. A French protectorate was declared over the main portion of the kingdom, the sultan remaining as the nominal head of his country.

EAST AFRICA AND THE CONGO BASIN

In East Africa and the Congo basin the Arabs put up the main opposition to the occupation forces of the Germans, the British and the Belgians. This opposition did not come openly from the sultan of Zanzibar. His capital would have been an easy target for the guns of European warships, and he therefore had to submit gracefully to the declaration of a British protectorate over the islands of Zanzibar and Pemba in 1890 and to the partition of his mainland territories. These were divided between the British and the German chartered companies, which were beginning to occupy what is now Kenya, the mainland of Tanzania and Uganda. In 1886 these mainland territories of the sultan were declared by an international commission to extend only 16 kilometres into the interior. The Germans then bought the coastal strip adjoining their treaty areas for a lump sum, while the British company leased the coastal strip of Kenya for an annual payment. That is why, throughout the colonial period, the red flag of the sultan continued to fly over Mombasa, Malindi, Lamu and other Kenya ports. It may also be the reason why there was no Arab revolt in the British coastal sphere.

The active opposition from the Swahili-Arabs came from two directions. The first was from the German part of the coast. The second was from the former slave- and ivory-traders scattered over the interior from Lake Malawi in the south, around both sides of Lake Tanganyika, and up into Uganda in the north. The movement probably stemmed from the attempt of Sultan Barghash to consolidate his mainland dominions on the eve of European partition. With its central leadership withdrawn, however, it exploded in a series of local risings, which the Europeans dealt with one by one. The sharpest of these struggles, though also the shortest, was that in 1888–9 between the Germans and the east-coast Arabs under their leader, Abushiri. Longer and more intermittent was that between the British and the Arabs of northern Nyasaland, which began in 1887 and was finally settled ten years later. King Leopold's officials fought their campaigns against the Arabs of eastern Zaïre between 1891 and 1894. In Uganda, as in Nyasaland, Arab opposition to European penetration, though strongly influenced by the German occupation of the coast, began while the only Europeans in the area were missionaries. This opposition was an aspect of the local political situation. The local Christians supported the entry of European influence; the local Muslims opposed it. In the kingdom of Buganda the Christian factions prevailed and made Buganda the principal ally of the British in their occupation of the region as a whole. The Arabs and the local Muslim faction retreated into the neighbouring kingdom of Bunyoro, which remained the centre of resistance to British rule. It was finally conquered by the British with the help of Buganda levies in a series of campaigns which lasted from 1894 till 1899 (see Chapter 12).

The one country in East Africa which successfully resisted European attempts at occupation was Ethiopia. The European nation involved in this attempt was Italy, which had entered late into the scramble. Italy had occupied a part of the Eritrean coast of the Red Sea in 1883 and in 1886 had participated in the division of the sultan of Zanzibar's mainland possessions by staking a claim to the eastern Somali coast. In 1889, immediately after becoming emperor, Menelik signed with the Italians the Treaty of Wichale. This treaty defined the boundary between Ethiopia and Italian Eritrea. It also stated in its Amharic version that Menelik's government might, if it wished, use Italian diplomatic channels for its contacts with the outside world. The Italian version of the treaty used a slightly more definite expression, implying that Menelik had agreed always to conduct his external affairs through Italian channels. It does not seem that the Italian negotiators deliberately intended to deceive Menelik – certainly they never intended to create a protectorate. Nevertheless it was on the basis of this phrase that the Italian Foreign Office two years later notified the powers which had taken part in the Berlin Conference of Italy's claim to a protectorate over Ethiopia. Italy now attempted to enforce this invalid protectorate upon Menelik, and disputes between the two sides resulted in the war of 1896. The Italian army was decisively defeated at Adowa, one of the first battles of modern times in which a non-European army beat one officered by, and partly consisting of, Europeans. Menelik turned from his victory over the Italians back to his lifelong interest, which was the extension of his kingdom to the south. Some of this country had paid tribute to the Ethiopian kings of the late medieval period and had been lost since the Galla invasions of the sixteenth century. Menelik's conquests, however, reaching to Lake Turkana in the south and to the ancient kingdom of Kaffa in the south-west, more than doubled the dominions which had come to him by inheritance and marriage. They made Ethiopia almost a participant in the scramble for Africa.

THE FRENCH CONQUEST OF MADAGASCAR

In the late 1880s the Merina kingdom began to break up under the pressure of French commercial and diplomatic influence. The prime minister, Rainilaiarivony, would not admit that the 1885 treaty gave France protectorate rights over the island. The French considered it did. Acting under what they understood were the terms of the treaty, the French in 1894 sent a large military expedition to Madagascar. This expedition entered Tananarive the following year and removed the prime minister. A definite treaty of protection was forced upon the queen. This foreign interference was the signal for one rebellion after another throughout Madagascar. Pagans turned upon Christians. The new religion was blamed for the troubles which had come upon the island. The people of the old Betsileo kingdom rid themselves of the hated Hova domination. French military actions against these rebellions only made matters worse. At one time Tananarive was the only place the French could hold. In 1895 General Gallieni came from his campaigns in West Africa to conquer (or 'pacify', as this action used to be called) Madagascar, which was declared to be a French colony. Nine years of bitter fighting passed before all the peoples of Madagascar had been forced by Gallieni and his second-in-command, Lyautey, to accept French rule. The Merina monarchy was overthrown, the last queen, Ranavalona III, being exiled in 1897. The French administered the island as a unit, thus completing the work of unification begun by Nampoina more than a century before.

RHODES AND CENTRAL AFRICA

The occupation of Central Africa was left by the British government very largely to Rhodes and his British South Africa Company. This was incorporated by Royal Charter in 1889 and was empowered to develop the region between Bechuanaland and the Zambezi which was later to bear Rhodes's name. In 1891 the company was allowed to extend into the lands north of the Zambezi which became Northern Rhodesia (Zambia). South of the Zambezi, Rhodes's agents had extracted concessions from Mzilikazi's successor, Lobengula, on the strength of which a body of farming and mining settlers was sent in

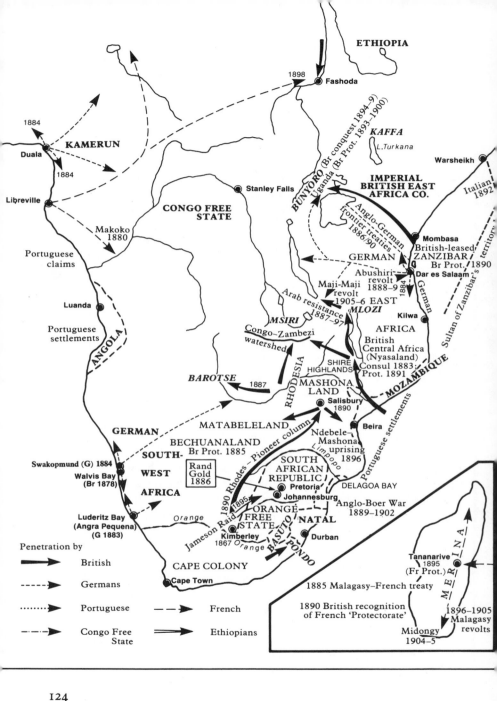

ETHIOPIA

1898 Fashoda

1884

KAMERUN

Duala

1884

Libreville

KAFFA

L.Turkana

Warsheikh

BUNYORO (Br conquest 1894–9)
Uganda (Br Prot. 1893–1900)

IMPERIAL
BRITISH EAST
AFRICA CO.

Italian
1892

Stanley Falls

CONGO FREE
STATE

Makoko
1880

Anglo-German
frontier treaties
1886/90

Mombasa
British-leased
ZANZIBAR
Br Prot. 1890

GERMAN

Portuguese
claims

Luanda

Abushiri
revolt
1888–9

Dar es Salaam

1884

Maji-Maji
revolt
1905–6

EAST

MLOZI

Arab resistance
1887–97

Kilwa

Sultan of Zanzibar's territory

Portuguese
settlements

MSIRI

ANGOLA

Congo–Zambezi
watershed

AFRICA
British
Central Africa
(Nyasaland)
Consul 1883;
Prot. 1891

MOZAMBIQUE

BAROTSE

1887

RHODESIA

SHIRE
HIGHLANDS

MASHONA
LAND

Salisbury
1890

Beira

MATABELELAND

Ndebele-
Mashona
uprising
1896

Portuguese settlements

GERMAN

BECHUANALAND
Br Prot. 1885

SOUTH-
WEST

Rand
Gold
1886

SOUTH
AFRICAN
REPUBLIC

Limpopo

Swakopmund (G) 1884

AFRICA

Pretoria

DELAGOA BAY

Walvis Bay
(Br 1878)

Johannesburg

Anglo-Boer War
1889–1902

Luderitz Bay
(Angra Pequena)
(G 1883)

Orange

ORANGE
FREE
STATE

NATAL

Jameson Raid 1895

Kimberley
1867

Orange

BASUTO

Durban

PONDO

Penetration by

British

CAPE COLONY

Cape Town

Germans

Portuguese

French

Congo Free
State

Ethiopians

M E R I N A

Tananarive
1895
(Fr Prot.)

1885 Malagasy–French treaty

1890 British recognition
of French 'Protectorate'

1896–1905
Malagasy
revolts

Midongy
1904–5

124

20*a* Southern Africa: the European partition – Britain, France and
Germany

ETHIOPIA

Adowa
(Italian defeat
1896)

Wichale
(Ethiopian–Italian
treaty 1889)

Fashoda

'KAFFA'   Ethiopian expansion

L. Turkana   Warsheikh

Duala

Libreville

CONGO

FREE

STATE

Stanley Falls

Portuguese
claims

Stanley 1879–84

Luanda

Portuguese
settlements

ANGOLA

Free State–
Arab War
1891–4

Msiri (killed
by Free State
forces 1891)

KATANGA
Congo–Zambezi watershed

Mombasa

Dar es Salaam

Kilwa

SHIRE   HIGHLANDS

GERMAN
SOUTH-WEST
AFRICA

Salisbury

MOZAMBIQUE

Beira

Portuguese settlements

Swakopmund (G) 1884
Walvis Bay (Br 1878)

Limpopo
SOUTH
AFRICAN
REPUBLIC

Pretoria

Luderitz Bay (Angra Pequena)
(G 1883)

Orange

ORANGE
FREE
STATE

Kimberley

DELAGOA BAY

BASUTO NATAL

Durban

CAPE COLONY

Cape Town

Tananarive

20b   Southern Africa: the European partition – Leopold and Portugal

1890 into Mashonaland, where they founded the Southern Rhodesian capital at Fort Salisbury. Further north Rhodes's agents raced those of King Leopold to secure possession of Katanga. The result of this scramble had in fact been decided beforehand by the international agreement of 1885 which fixed the Congo–Zambezi watershed as the limit of King Leopold's territory. Most of Msiri's kingdom (see Chapter 4) therefore passed to Leopold. Msiri himself was shot by a Belgian officer in a brawl arising from the treaty-making. The lands on the Zambezi side of the watershed became British and later proved to include a substantial part of the rich Copperbelt. The only part of Central Africa excluded from the company's sphere was Nyasaland (Malawi), where British missionaries and traders, who were hostile to the British South Africa Company, had been active since the later 1870s. This part of the country became a protectorate under the direct control of the British government in 1891.

The early years of the colonists' settlement in Southern Rhodesia were a time of constant fighting. There were unofficial wars between the settlers and the Portuguese on the Mozambique border. The settlers had to conquer the Ndebele, who soon became thoroughly resentful of their presence in neighbouring Mashonaland. It is not pleasant to read how the colonists deliberately provoked the conflict with the Ndebele, but the war was probably an inevitable consequence of the European settlement. Lobengula died shortly after his regiments had been defeated in 1893. The seizure of land and cattle by the victorious settlers provoked both the Ndebele and the Mashona to make a last attempt to drive them out in 1896, when the Africans' will to resist the white man was finally broken by the machine-gun.

THE ANGLO-BOER WAR

Rhodes was prime minister of the Cape Colony from 1890 to 1896. In addition he directed the activities of the British South Africa Company in the territories to the north. Rhodes had visions of uniting the whole of southern Africa, including the Boer republics, as a self-governing dominion under the British flag. He talked of 'equal rights for all civilised men south of the Zambezi'. It would seem that what he meant by this was primarily an alliance between Boer and Briton to develop the wealth of the country and to promote more white immigration. The Boer leader, Paul Kruger, president of the Transvaal, had very different ideas. He wanted a South Africa dominated by the Boers, who would retain their own language, Afrikaans (which had

126

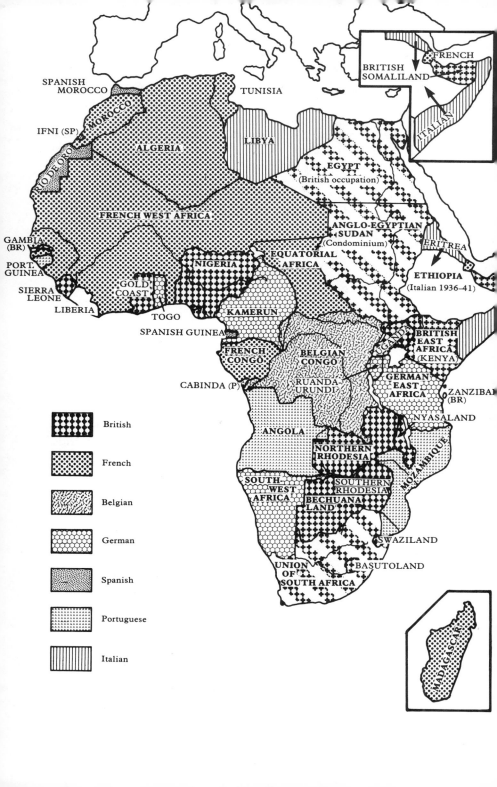

SPANISH
MOROCCO

TUNISIA

IFNI (SP)

ALGERIA

LIBYA

EGYPT
(British occupation)

FRENCH WEST AFRICA

ANGLO-EGYPTIAN
SUDAN
(Condominium)

GAMBIA
(BR)

PORT.
GUINEA

NIGERIA

EQUATORIAL
AFRICA

ERITREA

SIERRA
LEONE

GOLD
COAST

ETHIOPIA
(Italian 1936–41)

LIBERIA

TOGO

KAMERUN

SPANISH GUINEA

FRENCH
CONGO

BELGIAN
CONGO

UGANDA

BRITISH
EAST
AFRICA
(KENYA)

CABINDA (P)

RUANDA-
URUNDI

GERMAN
EAST
AFRICA

ZANZIBAR
(BR)

ANGOLA

NYASALAND

NORTHERN
RHODESIA

MOZAMBIQUE

SOUTH-
WEST
AFRICA

SOUTHERN
RHODESIA

BECHUANA-
LAND

SWAZILAND

UNION
OF
SOUTH AFRICA

BASUTOLAND

BRITISH
SOMALILAND

FRENCH

ITALIAN

British

French

Belgian

German

Spanish

Portuguese

Italian

MADAGASCAR

grown out of the Dutch of the original settlers), their old-fashioned pastoral way of life, and their refusal of political rights to Africans or to Cape Coloured peoples. Although glad of the wealth from the Witwatersrand gold-mines, Kruger was well aware that these were being developed mainly by British immigrants into the Transvaal, who might soon become a majority of the white population. While taxing them heavily, therefore, he denied them the vote. On the other hand he used the wealth with which they provided him to build up his defences and his railway links with the outside world.

Rhodes tried to persuade the disgruntled immigrants (Afrikaans, *uitlanders*) to stage a revolution and topple Kruger's government. A raid on the Transvaal from Bechuanaland in 1895, led by Rhodes's henchman Jameson, was a total failure, and no rising occurred. The raid ended Rhodes's political career, but elements in the British government which had been implicated in the plot were now determined on a decision with the Transvaal. The British high commissioner in South Africa, Sir Alfred Milner, deliberately incited the Transvaal to war. This broke out in 1899, and the Orange Free State stood beside its sister republic. The Boer armies – and after they were beaten, the irregular commandos – fought the whole might of Britain with tenacity and courage for more than two years. Destruction was widespread, and casualties on both sides were very high. Before peace finally came, the Boers had been inspired with an even greater bitterness against Britain and British institutions than they had had before. For the time being, however, the whole of South Africa was in British hands.

11   Colonial rule in tropical Africa (1):
Political and economic developments, 1885–1914

The colonial period in tropical Africa lasted for about seventy years. The first thirty years of this period may be called the years of establishment, the next thirty may be called the years of active development, and the last ten may be called the years of retreat. In this chapter we shall deal with the years of establishment mainly from the point of view of the colonial governments. In the next chapter we shall try to look at the same years mainly from the point of view of the African peoples, and to consider the changes which the colonial period introduced into everyday life.

THE POLICIES OF THE COLONIAL POWERS

Once Africa had been divided between them, the European governments lost much of their earlier interest in the continent. There were few parts of Africa which were expected to produce immediate wealth. The European nations had partitioned Africa mainly in order to ensure that they would not be excluded from regions which might prove valuable in the future. Possession was what mattered to them, not development.

At the end of the nineteenth century European states took a much narrower view of the functions of government, even within their own frontiers, than they do today. European states of those days had, for example, no public health services or old-age pensions, and no public housing other than the workhouse. In most European countries state education was still a recent introduction, and it was not yet provided for all children. Taxation was very much lower than it is today. Government spending was jealously controlled by the elected representatives of the voters, who were still, for the most part, the wealthy members of each community.

It is not surprising therefore that it was felt in Europe that the main duty of governments in the new African colonies was to maintain law and order, and to do so without expense to the European taxpayer. Education on the one hand and economic development on the other were left almost entirely to the private enterprise of Christian missions and commercial companies. Even the work of government was sometimes delegated to chartered companies, which were empowered to recruit their own officials and police forces, to collect taxes and administer justice. Where European governments assumed direct responsibility for the government of their new colonies, the most strict economy was practised. Officials were few in number; military and police forces consisted of ill-trained and poorly armed local recruits commanded by a few European officers.

Such governments were at first obliged to seek allies among their new subjects by entering into the web of intertribal politics and by aiding the friendly groups in their struggles with their traditional enemies. Unfriendly groups were often left severely alone for as long as possible. If action against such groups proved necessary, the small colonial forces, aided by their native allies, often burnt the villages of the resisters and seized their cattle. Such raids were continued until the authority of the colonial government was recognised. Only as local revenues were slowly built up from customs duties and head-taxes could colonial governments afford to employ regular civil services and police forces which could effectively occupy and administer the whole of the territories under their rule. In most African colonies this position had barely been reached by the time of the outbreak of the First World War in 1914.

Nevertheless, in most African colonies a surprising amount was achieved during this period, and this laid the foundation for the period of active development which was to follow. By 1914 the construction of railways and feeder roads had opened most of tropical Africa to some kind of wheeled traffic, with the result that cash crops could be grown and marketed profitably. The great number of small, tribal sovereignties which had been such a barrier to almost every kind of progress had been amalgamated into approximately forty separate territories, most of which were capable of growing into modern states with sufficient resources to stand on their own feet. The greatest benefit and that which impressed itself vividly on the memories of most Africans who had experienced the pre-colonial period was the relative peace and security imposed by all the colonial governments, even the harshest and most arbitrary ones. It was above all 'the colonial peace' which freed energies for new activities and which made possible not only economic development but also the spread of the universal religions of Christianity and Islam and the beginnings of modern education and learning. It is against this general background that we must now consider the various types of colonial government

Colonial rule: political and economic developments

which emerged in different parts of tropical Africa during the period between partition and the First World War.

WEST AFRICA: THE REALM OF THE PEASANT PRODUCER

The distinguishing feature of this region was that the peoples of the coast had been trading for more than three centuries with the peoples of Europe. Among them the demand for European goods had become so deeply ingrained that, after the abolition of the slave-trade, they had made the most strenuous efforts to develop for themselves cash crops which could be exchanged for the imports which they had come to regard as necessities. This meant that colonial governments in West Africa had one supreme advantage over governments in other parts of the continent. They could begin to build up their revenues by taxing an established trade. Even a light customs duty on imported spirits and fire-arms could yield them the revenue out of which to pay their first small bodies of officials and military forces. It could provide them with a basis on which they could borrow money. It was this fact, far more than any climatic differences from other parts of Africa, which caused colonial governments to seek to establish their revenues by building up peasant production rather than by trying to attract concessionaire companies or private settlers with gifts of land. They had inherited an economic system on which they could build. Most colonial administrations in Africa would have liked to build their economies on peasant production. In West Africa conditions enabled them to do so. At the beginning of the colonial period, even in West Africa, it was only a small part of the region that was affected by the growth of a cash economy. The basic economic activities of the majority of people still consisted in producing food-crops, housing materials, fuel and clothing, mostly for their own consumption. Although this involved a considerable amount of local trade and even some long-distance trade, the way of life was still of the kind called by economists a 'subsistence economy' as opposed to a 'cash economy'. It has been estimated that in 1900 such activities accounted for about 90 per cent of Nigerian production and 75 per cent of that of the Gold Coast. Yet in spite of the predominance of the 'subsistence economy', the beginnings of a cash economy were in existence and provided a growing-point for the future.

FRENCH WEST AFRICA

The most consistent pattern of colonial rule was that developed by the

131

French in their West African possessions. This was not the result of any imperial plan thought out beforehand. It was due to the fact that the seven younger colonies of Soudan, Mauritania, Upper Volta, Niger, Guinea, Ivory Coast and Dahomey were all in a sense extensions or offshoots of the old colony of Senegal. Access to the first four of these was at first mainly through the Senegal. In all of them the occupation was carried out by military forces, of which the backbone was the Senegalese army trained by Faidherbe and Gallieni in the course of their struggles with al-Hajj Umar, Ahmadu Sefu and Samori in the region between the upper Senegal and the Niger rivers (see Chapters 3 and 10). The fighting with Samori continued until 1898. Because the French had become so accustomed to fighting for the occupation of their territories, they were less willing than the British to negotiate with those African rulers who might have been open to such an approach. The kingdom of Dahomey, the Mossi states of Wagadugu and Yatenga, and other important states were broken up. The French administrative units (called *cercles*) which replaced them were more uniform in size and more directly controlled, first by military officers and later by civilian officials, than their counterparts in British territories.

The economic policy of the new French West African colonies was likewise based on the example of the Senegal, where Faidherbe and his successors had made the colonial administration self-supporting by encouraging the African population to grow ground-nuts on their own farms. This meant that the Senegalese peasants had a crop which they could sell for cash, with some of which they could pay the head-tax imposed by the government. As the French armies advanced into the interior, the civilian administration set up in the newly conquered districts at once sought to introduce similar cash crops. Particularly high hopes were set on the development of cotton-growing in the Niger basin. As in all other parts of the African interior, however, the great obstacle was the lack of transport. The first railway, built by the military as a strategic link between the upper Senegal and the upper Niger, though adequate for the movement of troops and supplies, proved useless for commercial cargoes. The railway terminals could only be reached by small steamers of shallow draught, and even they could only make the journey at certain seasons of the year. The difficulty of navigation on the Senegal was overcome only with the completion of the line from Dakar to Kayès in 1924. The uncertainties of navigation on the upper Niger remain to this day. In the coastal parts of Guinea, the Ivory Coast and Dahomey there was some early development in palm-oil, cocoa and other forest produce.

Here again the opening up of the interior had to await the building of railways, and this was not begun until the early years of the twentieth century. Indeed, the railways were only starting to make significant progress by about 1914. The earliest cash earnings of the people of Soudan and Upper Volta were in fact those of migrant labourers who went to seek work in the ground-nut areas of Senegal and the palm-oil and cocoa districts of the Gold and Ivory Coasts.

It was the problem of economic self-support which led the French to federate their West African territories in a single unit, in which the richer and more accessible regions could help to support the poorer and more remote. In 1895, the governor of Senegal had been given supervisory powers over his colleagues. This had been mainly in order to secure military co-ordination at a time when French armies were fighting with Samori around the interior frontiers of Soudan, Guinea and the Ivory Coast. Under French laws passed in 1902 and 1904, at the beginning of the great period of railway-building, all the West African territories were grouped under a government-general situated at Dakar. This government-general consisted of the governor-general, his officials and advisory councils. It took an important share of the customs duties levied in all the coastal colonies. With this revenue the government-general negotiated loans for railways leading to the interior. This meant, in the early days, that Senegal and Dahomey were between them contributing three-quarters of the federal budget of French West Africa, although to the great benefit of the region as a whole.

BRITISH WEST AFRICA

The British West African territories presented, at the beginning of the period, a rather confused appearance. Not only were they geographically separated from one another, but their longer and more divided history had left them under three different kinds of government. As explained in the previous chapter, there were the four Crown Colonies of the Gambia, Sierra Leone, the Gold Coast Colony and Lagos. In eastern Nigeria there was the Oil Rivers protectorate, administered by the Foreign Office. And, finally, in northern Nigeria, there was the territory administered under charter by the Royal Niger Company. These differences, however, were not as important as they appeared. The Royal Niger Company, as we have seen, surrendered its charter in 1898. In 1900 Northern Nigeria became a British protectorate, the same year as eastern Nigeria was taken over by the Colonial Office. Thereafter the British West African colonies came to resemble more

133

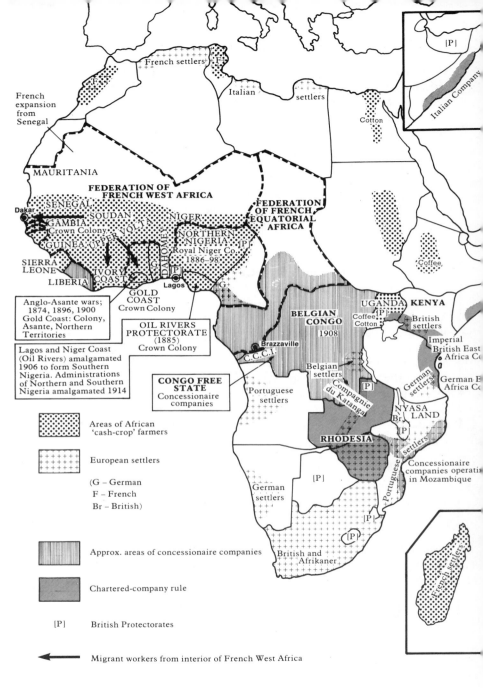

French settlers   F

French
expansion
from
Senegal

Italian   settlers

Cotton

Italian Company

[P]

MAURITANIA

FEDERATION OF
FRENCH WEST AFRICA

FEDERATION
OF FRENCH
EQUATORIAL
AFRICA

Dakar
SENEGAL
GAMBIA   SOUDAN   NIGER
Crown Colony
GUINEA   NORTHERN
                               NIGERIA
SIERRA   Royal Niger Co.
LEONE   IVORY   G   1886–98
LIBERIA   COAST   DAHOMEY
                     Lagos
             GOLD   G
             COAST
             Crown Colony

Coffee

UGANDA   KENYA
[P]

BELGIAN
CONGO   Coffee   British
                Cotton   settlers
1908   Imperial
                              British East
Belgian   Africa Co
settlers   German E
                             Africa Co
C.C.I.

Anglo-Asante wars;
1874, 1896, 1900
Gold Coast: Colony,
Asante, Northern
Territories

OIL RIVERS
PROTECTORATE
(1885)
Crown Colony

Brazzaville

Compagnie du Katanga

German
settlers

Lagos and Niger Coast
(Oil Rivers) amalgamated
1906 to form Southern
Nigeria. Administrations
of Northern and Southern
Nigeria amalgamated 1914

CONGO FREE
STATE
Concessionaire
companies

Portuguese
settlers

NYASA
LAND
Br

RHODESIA

[P]

Portuguese settlers

Concessionaire
companies operati
in Mozambique

Areas of African
'cash-crop' farmers

European settlers

(G – German
F – French
Br – British)

German
settlers

[P]

[P]

[P]

Approx. areas of concessionaire companies

British and
Afrikaner

[P]

Chartered-company rule

French settlers

[P]   British Protectorates

Migrant workers from interior of French West Africa

- - - - -   Federations of French West and Equatorial Africa

closely than any others in Africa their French neighbours. They resembled them above all in the fact that they were economically based on the production of cash crops by African peasants. They resembled them further in that the prosperity of the coastal regions was used to build up administration in, and communications with, the interior. Moreover, though geographically much smaller, the British West African territories had more than double the population, and perhaps three or four times the wealth, of the whole of French West Africa. And so, despite the lack of a federation between them, they went ahead faster than the French territories.

The Gold Coast moved quickest. Here the great political problem was the continued unity and strength of the Asante nation, which had largely recovered from its defeat of 1874. Two more serious military campaigns in 1896 and 1900 were fought before Asante would submit to the authority of the British colonial government. Even before the final defeat of the Asante, deep mining for gold by British companies had begun in Adansi and in parts of southern Asante which had been annexed by Britain after the war of 1874. Mining provided the impulse for the construction of the first railway in the colony, which reached the gold-mining district of Tarkwa from Sekondi by 1901. At the end of the nineteenth century gold exports from the Gold Coast were actually falling, from a value of some £80,000 in 1897 to £22,000 in 1901. After the railway reached Tarkwa, the value rose rapidly: £97,000 in 1902, £255,000 in 1903, £1,165,000 in 1907 and £1,687,000 in 1914. Within a few years of its extension to Kumasi in 1903, to ensure military and political control over Asante, the second great significance of the railway proved to be its opening up of the forest region, first to rubber-tapping and then to cocoa-farming. In 1901 the value of cocoa exported from the colony was £43,000; it was £95,000 in 1902, £515,000 in 1907 and £2,194,000 in 1914. By that year cocoa amounted to 49 per cent of all exports, and cocoa alone was already paying for all the Gold Coast's imports. The exportation of timber, worth £169,000 in 1907, also resulted from the building of the railway. Cocoa, gold and timber made the Gold Coast, by 1914, the most prosperous of all the African colonies.

In Nigeria, as in the rest of West Africa, it was the peasant producers of the coastal regions who, by the customs duties levied on their imports even more than by their direct taxes, provided the revenues out of which colonial administration and a modern system of communications were gradually extended over the interior. The Lagos protectorate in the south-west and the protectorate of Southern Nigeria (the old Oil Rivers) in the south-east were amalgamated in

1906 as the self-supporting colony of Southern Nigeria. The North, meanwhile, with its vast population, remained cut off from access to world markets save by the long and precarious line of river communications on the Niger and the Benue. The colonial administration there, despite continuing grants-in-aid from the British Treasury, was able to maintain itself only by making the utmost use of the existing Fulbe system of government. Under British overrule the Fulbe emirs continued to police, tax and administer justice to their Hausa subjects, while accepting advice from British residents posted at their courts. The system worked, but it was scarcely progressive. Even Lugard, the first governor of the North (1900–6), who was responsible for the system, realised that Northern Nigeria could be modernised only when it had been politically amalgamated with the South and linked by railways with the coast. Lugard returned to Nigeria in 1912, and two years later (1914) became governor-general of the whole territory. By this time the differences between north and south had hardened too much to be easily eliminated. Nevertheless, the administrative unification of the country marked a great step forward.

THE REALM OF THE CONCESSIONAIRE COMPANY: FRANCE
AND KING LEOPOLD IN THE CONGO BASIN

The region of Africa drained by the Congo and its tributaries was, as we have already seen, a very different one from West Africa. At its heart was the equatorial rain-forest, inhabited sparsely by Africa's most isolated and therefore most backward peoples. The denser and more civilised populations of the area lived around the rim of the river basin. Their former trading links had been in some cases northwards to Libya and Egypt, in some cases eastwards to the Zanzibar coast, in some cases westwards to Portuguese Luanda. Before the coming of river-steamers in the 1880s very little trade had passed by water through the forest centre to the Congo mouth. Along the West-Central African coast from Mount Cameroun to Luanda the trade established in the nineteenth century had been disrupted by the activities of the Free State officers on the lower Congo and of the French in Gabon. There was no worthwhile exchange of European manufactures against African produce on which the colonisers could build, as they had been able to do in West Africa. No government could support itself by levying customs on the trade passing through Boma or Libreville, still less raise a loan for the building of railways round the Congo cataracts or south from the upper Kasai to Katanga. The finance required for such projects was 'risk capital', which had to be attracted by the possibility of large long-term gains in order to offset the lack of immediate returns. In these circumstances the time-honoured solution was that followed in railway development in North and South America – private capital was attracted by grants of land and mineral rights in the area to be opened up.

Such was in fact the origin of the system of concessionaire companies which was to become the distinguishing feature of the colonial history of this region. In 1886 King Leopold made the first contract of this kind with the Compagnie du Congo pour le Commerce et l'Industrie (CCCI), under which the company agreed to build a railway round the lower Congo rapids from Matadi to Leopoldville, in exchange for which it could claim 1,500 hectares (a little over 14 square kilometres) for every kilometre of line constructed. Thus, the lower Congo railway alone involved the alienation of nearly 8,000 square kilometres. No sooner was it completed in 1898 than similar contracts were made with two other companies. These organisations undertook to build railways from the upper Congo to Lake Tanganyika and from the limit of navigation on the Kasai to the heart of Katanga. A variation on the railway concession was that given in 1891 to the Compagnie du Katanga. This was at the time when Rhodes was threatening to overrun Katanga from the south and when King Leopold could not himself afford to undertake the effective occupation of the region. He therefore chartered the Katanga Company to do so in exchange for one-third of the vacant lands and mineral rights in the area.

All the land conceded in this way was in theory 'waste land', the villages of the Congolese and the land actually under cultivation by them being excluded. But since land was useless without labour, every form of pressure was put upon the local inhabitants to work for the concessionaire companies. The worst abuses occurred during the period from about 1895 to 1905, when the invention of pneumatic rubber tyres for bicycles and motor-cars was causing a great demand for rubber. In the long term this demand was met by the development of rubber plantations in South-East Asia. While the boom in wild rubber lasted, however, very large profits indeed were made by the concessionaire companies in the Congo. In theory these companies employed, but in practice compelled, their Congolese neighbours to tap rubber in the forests, usually for very small rewards. The profits secured in this way aroused the greed of King Leopold, who took over and managed himself large areas of Crown land. Other areas he leased to private companies on a profit-sharing basis. The system proved so attractive that it spread into French Equatorial Africa. Here the French government saw in it a means of reducing the large annual deficits which had been accumulating since the beginning of colonial rule. In both territories the worst abuses of the system were brought to an end between 1906 and 1910, when the end of the wild rubber boom coincided with an outcry by international public opinion. In 1908 King Leopold was forced to cede the Congo to Belgium. In an effort to provide a more direct administration and to cut down expenses, France in 1910 joined the four territories of Gabon, Middle Congo, Oubangui-Chari and Tchad into the federation of French Equatorial Africa. This was modelled upon the government-general of French West Africa. Its capital was at Brazzaville. Both the French and Belgian governments, however, had contracts with the concessionaire companies which they could fulfil only by leaving the companies in possession of large areas of land and with commercial monopolies over still larger regions. The Belgian Congo was further burdened with an enormous debt which King Leopold had incurred by borrowing money on the Congo's account and spending it on his palaces and other public buildings in Belgium. The interest on this debt at one time absorbed nearly a fifth of the country's revenue.

Certainly the foundation of colonies in the Congo basin presented a very different problem from that faced in West Africa. The region was a very poor one, and the people who lived in it had practically no sources of income that could be taxed to pay for the expenses of government and of modern communications. The only possible way to create such wealth was to reorganise the labour of the people. In a very crude manner the concessionaire companies did achieve this end.

THE REALM OF THE EUROPEAN SETTLER: BRITAIN, GERMANY AND PORTUGAL IN EAST AND CENTRAL AFRICA

Like the Congo basin and unlike West Africa, the new colonies of East and Central Africa had at the time of their occupation no trade, other than the declining trade in ivory, on which colonial revenues could be built. Unlike the Congo territories, however, these colonies in East and Central Africa were mostly crossed by the chain of highland country running from the Kenya highlands south-westwards towards the Cape. Here were lands, sparsely occupied by Africans, on which Europeans could settle as farmers. To colonial governments in search of revenue, a policy of limited white settlement by Europeans who would act as employers and organisers of African labour appeared as an attractive solution.

The German government was committed in principle to promoting settlement for its own sake. Germany at the end of the nineteenth century had a large and growing rural population, and German peasants had been emigrating in hundreds of thousands to the United States for many years. One of the main aims of the promoters of the colonial movement had been to enable such emigrants to settle in German lands overseas. In German East and South-West Africa, therefore, and even to some extent in the West African colonies of Cameroun and Togo, settlers were encouraged to make claims. Land was set aside for them, particularly in the areas destined to be opened up by railways.

The British government in London had no such fixed inclination to favour European settlement. In Southern and Northern Rhodesia settlement was promoted by the British South Africa Company. This was done for two reasons. First, the idea agreed with the ideals of Cecil Rhodes, that the highlands of Central Africa would make an excellent home for English-speaking farmers. The second was that land grants were a means of rewarding the occupiers, who would otherwise have had to be paid out of company funds. But in Nyasaland, where a protectorate government was established in 1891, and in Uganda and Kenya, when these countries were taken over from the Imperial British East Africa Company in 1894–5, governors were left by the British government to solve their own problems in their own way. It is remarkable that the Uganda Railway, completed from Mombasa to Kisumu on Lake Victoria by 1901, was paid for by the imperial government out of an interest-free loan, which was later written off as a gift. In Uganda, after five years of mainly military activity the colonial government settled its account with its Baganda allies by signing a special agreement with them in 1900. This turned the Baganda chiefs into a land-owning aristocracy and gave the Buganda state a degree of recognition which would have made a policy of European settlement almost impossible to carry out. The Baganda responded to the situation by taking up the cultivation of cotton on a scale which soon made the country independent of grants-in-aid. Kenya, on the other hand, and also Nyasaland were thought to present revenue problems which could only be solved by encouraging settler plantations.

The scramble for Africa among the more powerful European nations put new life into the ancient Portuguese colonies of Angola and Mozambique. New settlers were encouraged to leave Portugal to become farmers in the interior of these colonies. The Portuguese looked upon this colonisation by settlers more as a means of controlling their huge African possessions than as a means of developing them. In many parts of Angola and Mozambique the settler landowner was more like a one-man concessionaire company than was his British or German opposite number. On his estate he collected taxes and administered summary justice to his African tenants, from among whom he recruited both his labour and his private police force. This was feudal Europe of the Middle Ages surviving in twentieth-century Africa.

The Europeans who settled in East and Central Africa during the period up to 1914 were very few in number – some ten thousand in what is now Zimbabwe, some three thousand each in what are now Zambia, Kenya, Tanzania and Namibia, probably not many more in Mozambique and Angola, and only a few hundred in Malawi and Uganda. Several thousand Frenchmen settled in the highlands of Madagascar and formed the largest group of French *colons* in Africa outside the Maghrib. Numerically the European settlers were much less significant than the Indians, who settled in the wake of the colonial occupation as artisans and petty traders all over East Africa and in parts of Central Africa also. The Indians settled in the towns and villages and lived by their own labour. The Europeans, on the other hand, settled in competition with the Africans, on the land, and lived as employers of African labour. Even so, only small areas were directly affected, and most of the areas of dense African population – for example, those around Lake Victoria and Lake Malawi – were untouched. Indeed, throughout the greater part of all these countries African communities lived their lives and were ruled by the colonial administrators on much the same lines as in West Africa. Unlike West Africa, however, instead of being encouraged to add cash crops to the subsistence crops grown on their own land, the Africans were encouraged to earn the money they needed to pay their taxes by working, usually as migrant labourers, on European farms. Like the concessionaire company in the Congo basin, the European farmer settler of East and Central Africa was at this time chiefly important for the part he played in reorganising African labour by bringing some of it into the market economy. Politically and socially, as we shall see in the next two chapters, the European settler introduced much more confusion into tropical Africa than the concessionaire company. Whereas the company thought mainly of its profits, the settler was apt to think mainly of his children and grandchildren and of the position they would occupy in society. This posed a problem which grew steadily more important during the years after the First World War. It had then to be decided whether these parts of tropical Africa were to be developed in the interests of the settlers or of the indigenous inhabitants. The result was a series of uneasy compromises, which we shall examine in Chapter 13.

12 Colonial rule in tropical Africa (2): Social and religious developments

The impact of colonial rule on African societies varied greatly, not only from one territory to another but also from one part of a territory to another. To some extent the reasons for this sprang from their social organisation or the way in which they made their living. For example, specialised pastoralists, like the Masai in Kenya or the Herero in South-West Africa, found it much more difficult to adapt themselves to the wishes of colonial governments than most of the peoples who lived by agriculture. Or again, warrior groups, like the Ndebele of Southern Rhodesia or the Ngoni of Northern Rhodesia and Nyasaland, themselves the colonialists of an earlier period, found it more difficult to work and pay taxes than their former subjects, the Mashona and the Chewa. Much more important than the sociological reasons, however, were the sheerly accidental circumstances under which each group in a particular territory made its first contacts with the colonial government.

There were people who gained from colonial rule. In nearly every territory there were 'favourite peoples', who by good luck or good judgement made common cause with the colonial power and received privileged treatment as a result. To such peoples the colonial period brought at first no shame, but on the contrary extended frontiers, enhanced prestige and a sense of prosperity and achievement. In Northern Rhodesia, for example, the Barotse, who under the influence of the missionary Coillard had written to ask for British protection, received quite special treatment from the British South Africa Company. Because of their readiness to sign treaties and concessions, they were recognised as the overlords of a wide surrounding region. By signing away the land and mineral rights of the peoples supposedly subject to them, they were able to protect their own country from most kinds of European interference.

In German East Africa it was the Swahili people of the coastal belt who were the most favoured by the German colonial government. The coastal Swahili were the first people in East Africa to experience the rule of the German East Africa Company. As Hemedi bin Abdullah, a poet from Tanga, put it,

> At Kilwa and Dar es Salaam
> There was a plague of Europeans;
> There was no free speech:
> They had throttled the country.

Under their leader Abushiri, the Swahili rebelled against the Germans, and after their defeat early in 1889 theirs was the first part of the country in which the Germans worked out a system of district administration. In this administration the Swahili played an important part. As the Germans later moved into the interior, they took with them a highly privileged class of Swahili soldiers and policemen, clerks and interpreters. These people understood their system of government and were able to turn it to their own advantage in a variety of ways.

In Uganda it was the Baganda who filled this intermediate role between the British and the other peoples of the protectorate. Baganda armies fought alongside the British in many early campaigns and received their reward in the extension of Buganda's boundaries at the expense of her neighbours. Far beyond even these extended boundaries, Baganda accompanied the expanding protectorate administration and were employed for a time as chiefs in nearly every district in the country. Buganda got in first with every colonial improvement. The new roads radiated from Buganda; the first schools and hospitals were built there; it was there that the first cash crops, coffee and cotton, were grown.

In Nigeria, to take one more example, there were two privileged groups: the Fulbe ruling class in the north, and the already educated townsmen of the coast – Yoruba from Lagos, Efiks and Ijaws from the city states of the Delta, Igbos from the river-ports of the lower Niger. The Fulbe were early resisters who swiftly came to terms with their conquerors and in consequence found their system of government supported, extended and made more profitable than it had been before. The success of the coastmen was more like that of the Swahili. They were the clerks, the merchants, the schoolmasters, who accompanied the British administrators as they moved inland, and who helped to transform the institutions of the Yoruba city states and the Igbo village communities into a pattern acceptable to the colonial government.

These then were the people who gained from colonial rule. Those who suffered from it were, by contrast, those who, through ill-luck or ill-judgement, or simply from an excess of patriotism, challenged the colonial power and found themselves disastrously overthrown. In Madagascar many of the people who had long been hostile to the Hova ruling group seized the opportunity of its decline in power at the time of the French invasion. They rose against the Hova and the French. But the rebellions were put down with a heavy hand by the French. The condition of many of these groups was no better under colonial rule than it had been under Hova domination. In Southern Rhodesia, first the Ndebele and then the Mashona very understandably rose in the attempt to drive out the white colonists, who were visibly settling down in their land and taking it over for their own use. The result of the war of 1893 and revolts of 1896–7 was that most Ndebele and Mashona found themselves driven off the land they had previously grazed or farmed, and herded roughly into 'reserves'. Here they had to start life afresh, often without their cattle, often without even the support of their old social groupings, which had been broken up as a result of warfare and flight. A still worse fate befell the Herero of South-West Africa, who in 1904 rose against the German settlers who had been infiltrating into their land. Two-thirds of the Herero were exterminated in the course of the German counter-measures. The Herero country was declared the property of the state, and the survivors were forbidden to keep cattle, since they no longer possessed any land on which to graze them. A handful of refugees escaped into Bechuanaland. The remainder passed into European employment.

Nowhere else in tropical Africa were settlement and resistance quite so unfortunately combined. North of the Zambezi, the areas required for European settlement were very small, and the earlier inhabitants of those areas were either left where they were or, at worst, moved only a few miles. The largest displacement was that of the northern Masai from the central part of the Kenya highlands, and this was brought about by agreement, not by force. The groups which suffered most by the colonial occupation were not those who lost a small part of their land to settlers. They were those who, for one reason or another, found themselves opposing rather than supporting the spread of colonial power. Of this the Banyoro of Uganda are a particularly unhappy example. These people opposed the British mainly because the British were supported by their traditional enemies, the Baganda. Between 1890 and 1897 Bunyoro became a place of retreat for Arab and Swahili traders, for Muslim Baganda, and for all those who opposed the pro-British, Christian parties dominating the Buganda scene. These refugees included the rebellious Kabaka of Buganda, Mwanga. Advised by their Baganda allies, 143

23*a* Northern Africa: resistance to European rule
23*b* Southern Africa: resistance to European rule

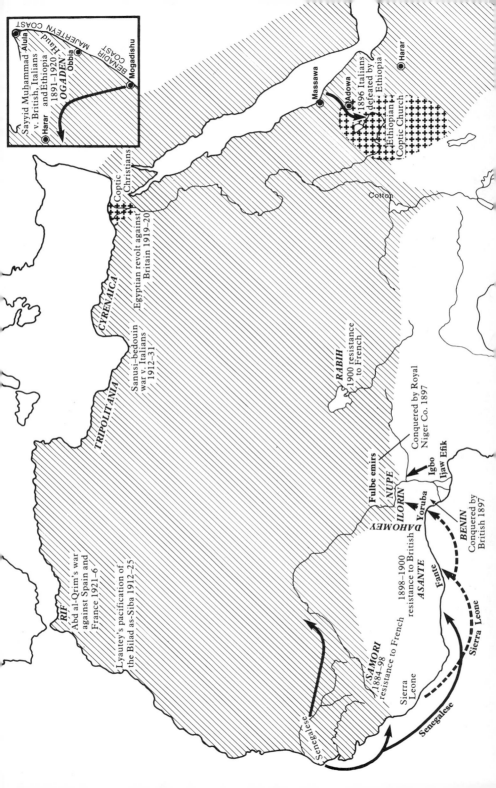

Sayyid Muhammad Alula
v. British, Italians
and Ethiopia
1891–1920

OGADEN
Haud
MAJEERTEEN COAST
BENADIR COAST

● Harar
Obbia ●
● Mogadishu

Coptic Christians

Massawa ●

● Adowa
1896 Italians
defeated by
Ethiopia
● Harar
Ethiopian
Coptic Church

Cotton

Egyptian revolt against
Britain 1919–20

CYRENAICA

Sanusi–bedouin
war v. Italians
1912–31

TRIPOLITANIA

RABIH
1900 resistance
to French

Conquered by Royal
Niger Co. 1897

Igbo
Ijaw Efik

Fulbe emirs

NUPE

ILORIN

Yoruba

BENIN
Conquered by
British 1897

DAHOMEY

ASANTE

Fante

RIF
Abd al-Qrim's war
against Spain and
France 1921–6

Lyautey's pacification of
the Bilad as-Siba 1912–25

SAMORI
1884–98
resistance to French

1898–1900
resistance to British

Sierra Leone

Sierra Leone

Senegalese

Senegalese

Series of uprisings by Malagasy people against French and Hova domination, 1885–1905

Abushiri revolt against Germans 1888–9

Displacement of Masai from Kenya highlands

KENYA HIGHLANDS

MASAI

BUNYORO

Busindwa

1890–8 Bunyoro resistance to British penetration

Swahili

HEHE
Maji-Maji revolt against Germans 1905–6

NGONI

Chewa

Nyanja

YAO

Chilembwe uprising against British in Nyasaland 1915

TIPPU TIP
Arab resistance to Congo Free State 1891–4

LUNDA
(Mwata Yamvo)

Barotse

MASHONA
Mashona revolt against S. Rhodesian settlers 1896

NDEBELE
Ndebele–settler war 1893
Ndebele revolt 1896

ZULU
Zulu revolt 1906

Anglo-Boer War 1899–1902

Pro-German Boer revolt 1914

BAKONGO
Uprising against Portuguese 1913

OVIMBUNDU
Bailundo revolt against Portuguese 1913

HERERO
Herero–German war 1904

NAMA
Hottentot resistance to Germans 1904–6

Bondelswarts–South African bombing of village 1922

Islamic regions

BUNYORO Peoples or rulers overthrown by colonial rule

Yoruba Peoples or rulers benefiting from colonial rule

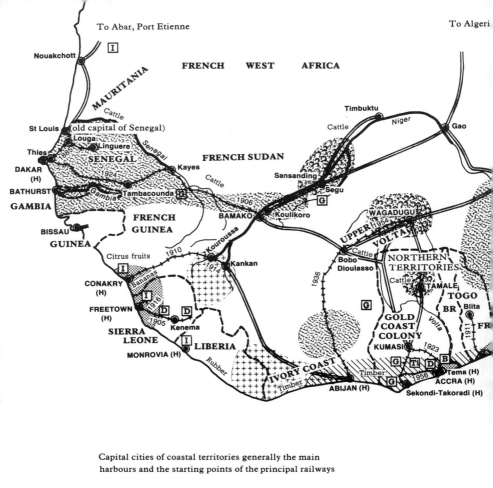

To Abar, Port Etienne

To Algeri

Nouakchott ☐I

MAURITANIA

FRENCH   WEST   AFRICA

Cattle

Timbuktu

Niger

Gao

St Louis (old capital of Senegal)

Cattle

Louga

Linguere

FRENCH SUDAN

Thies

SENEGAL

Senegal

Kayes

1855

1924

DAKAR
(H)

Cattle

Sansanding

BATHURST

Gambia

Tambacounda ☐

1906

Segu
☐G

GAMBIA

BAMAKO

Koulikoro

BISSAU

FRENCH
GUINEA

Kouroussa

WAGADUGU

UPPER   VOLTA

1954

GUINEA

Citrus fruits

1910

1914

Kankan

Cattle

NORTHERN
TERRITORIES

CONAKRY
(H)

☐I

Bananas

Bobo
Dioulasso

Cattle

1916

FREETOWN
(H)

☐I

1936

☐G

TAMALE

TOGO

Blita

1905

D D

GOLD
COAST
COLONY

BR

FR

SIERRA
LEONE

Kenema

KUMASI

1923

1911

MONROVIA (H)

☐I

LIBERIA

Rubber

IVORY COAST

Timber

G T D B

1956

Tema (H)

Timber

ABIDJAN (H)

G

ACCRA (H)

Sekondi-Takoradi (H)

Capital cities of coastal territories generally the main
harbours and the starting points of the principal railways

Capital cities of many inland territories situated at the
railheads of the lines to the coast; some situated on
rivers where navigable sections begin   **G**   Gold

CONAKRY   Capital cities   Cocoa   **D**   Diamonds

(H)   Principal modern harbours   Palm-oil and kernels   **Ti**   Tin

1912
+++++   Railways (dates of construction)   Groundnuts   **I**   Iron ore

Navigable rivers   Cotton   **Cl**   Coal

Some main roads
(especially from railheads)   Coffee   **B**   Bauxite

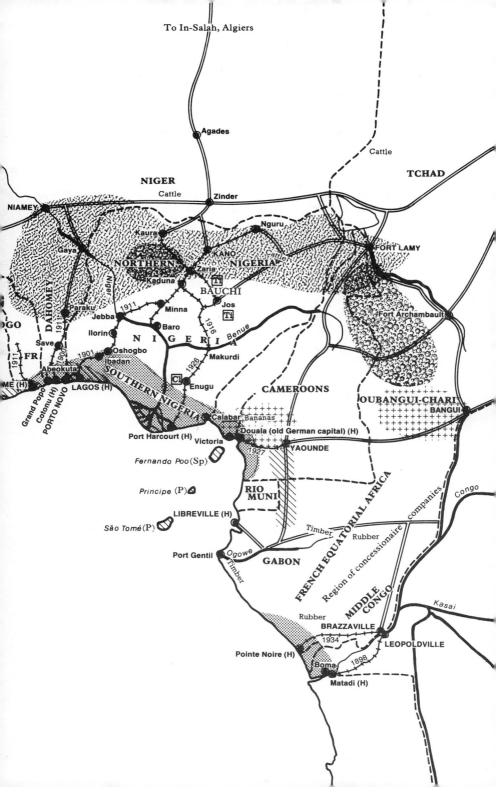

the British came to regard Bunyoro as ready for conquest. When this had been carried out with the assistance of Baganda levies, the British deposed the ruler in 1899, carved off the outlying districts of his kingdom and gave them to Buganda. For ten years or so the British even forced the Bunyoro government to employ a number of Baganda chiefs in key positions. The result of all this was a feeling of helplessness and frustration, which lasted right through the colonial period and which made Bunyoro the last district in Uganda to adopt any of the useful innovations that came with British rule. Bunyoro had its Tanzanian counterpart in the kingdom of Uhehe, its Zaïrian counterpart in the Lunda kingdom of Mwata Yamvo, its Nigerian counterpart in the kingdom of Benin, its French West African counterpart in the kingdom of Dahomey, its Ghanaian counterpart in the kingdom of Asante. And so on.

The basic question in the social and religious history of any particular African people at the beginning of the colonial period was whether it was swimming with the tide of advancing colonialism or against it. Eventually, no doubt, *all* African societies suffered a great blow through the loss of sovereignty, as the colonial governments progressively established the effectiveness of their overrule. In African societies, as in all others, the ultimate sanction behind authority was that of religion. The religious sanction began to be undermined as soon as the authority ceased to be absolute. Though the ordinary man in the ordinary village might continue to live his life much as before and to be ruled for all practical purposes by the same village headman, it could only be a matter of time before he realised that there had been a change in the ultimate authority which controlled his life. Sooner or later a murder would be committed, and the accused and the witnesses would be taken, not to the chief's court as of old, but to the court of the colonial power, with its strange procedures and punishments. Sooner or later the European district officer would appear on tour, with the local chief very much a subordinate in his train. There would be demands for labour to build roads, for porters to carry luggage or building materials or trade goods. There would be talk of taxes to come, payable at first in kind, but later only in the unfamiliar pieces of minted coinage. It might be necessary to obtain this money by working for others or by trading in markets far outside the tribal area. Against these demands the tribal authority offered no protection, and therefore its divine sanction was slowly undermined.

148

24a West Africa: economic development during the colonial period – western half
24b West Africa: economic development during the colonial period – eastern half

CHRISTIAN MISSIONS AND WESTERN EDUCATION

At this point in time the Christian missionary, or, in some parts of tropical Africa, the Muslim missionary, was fortunately available to help build up again what had been broken down. As we have seen, the missionary had entered most parts of tropical Africa ahead of the colonial governments. At any time up till 1914, and in most places long after, he would have been a much more familiar figure, in the rural areas at least, than the government official. With the coming of the colonial period his activities took on, almost everywhere, a new lease of life. It is a remarkable and often overlooked fact that the colonial expansion of the nineteenth century provoked among the young men and women of Europe a response not only from those who wished to rule, but even more from those who wished to serve, in the backward places of the world. Missionary societies of every denomination experienced a boom in recruitment and in financial support, with the result that missions all over tropical Africa were able to be strengthened very greatly during the years between 1890 and 1914.

The object of all missionaries was to bring African people into membership of the Churches to which they themselves belonged. At this period they at last began to be outstandingly successful in doing so. All over the previously pagan parts of tropical Africa, from about the seventh parallel of north latitude southwards, Africans flocked to join the Churches – and not only to join them, but also to serve them actively as evangelists and catechists and ordained ministers. Only where Islam was already well established – in Senegal and Guinea, in Soudan and Niger, in Northern Nigeria and the Tchad territories, in the northern Sudan and in Somalia, and in the coastal belt of East Africa – did Christian propaganda encounter any serious resistance. Only in these areas did Islam itself carry out a comparable expansion, spreading from its town bases into the surrounding countryside and consolidating itself through the development of Koranic schools and religious brotherhoods. In southern Nigeria, Yorubaland, poised between the Muslim north and the Christian coastlands, experienced both movements simultaneously.

The main means used by all the Christian missions in their evangelism was to found networks of village schools in which children of all ages could be given a very simple education in reading, writing and arithmetic alongside the religious instruction leading to baptism and Church membership. These 'bush-schools', as they were called, were not impressive places architecturally. This description, written   149

25*a* West-Central Africa: economic development during the colonial period – mineral deposits
25*b* East-Central Africa: economic development during the colonial period – mineral deposits

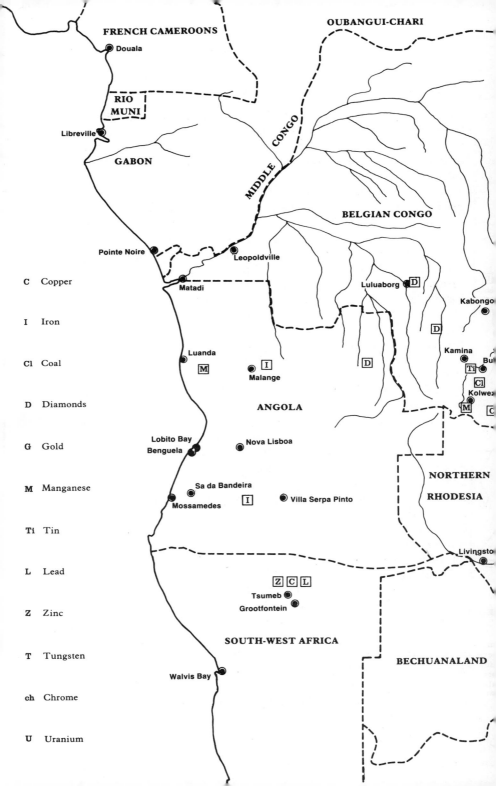

FRENCH CAMEROONS

Douala

OUBANGUI-CHARI

RIO MUNI

Libreville

GABON

CONGO

MIDDLE

BELGIAN CONGO

Pointe Noire

Leopoldville

Matadi

C   Copper

I   Iron

Cl   Coal

D   Diamonds

G   Gold

M   Manganese

Ti   Tin

L   Lead

Z   Zinc

T   Tungsten

ch   Chrome

U   Uranium

Luluaborg   D

Kabongo

Kamina
Ti   Bul
Cl
Kolwez
M   C

Luanda
M

Malange   I

ANGOLA

Lobito Bay
Benguela

Nova Lisboa

NORTHERN

RHODESIA

Sa da Bandeira

Mossamedes   I

Villa Serpa Pinto

Livingsto

Z   C   L

Tsumeb
Grootfontein

SOUTH-WEST AFRICA

BECHUANALAND

Walvis Bay

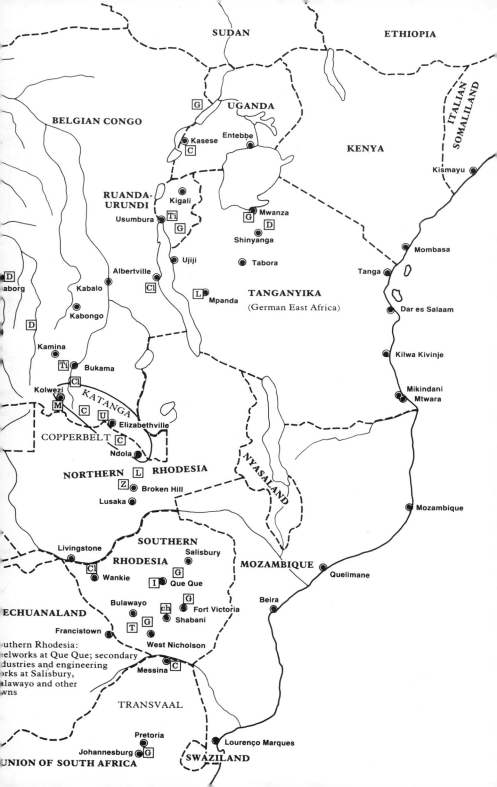

SUDAN

ETHIOPIA

BELGIAN CONGO

UGANDA

KENYA

ITALIAN SOMALILAND

[G]

Kasese
[C]

Entebbe

Kismayu

RUANDA-URUNDI

Kigali

Mwanza
[G]

Usumbura [Ti]
[G]

Shinyanga
[D]

Mombasa

Ujiji

Tabora

Tanga

Albertville

Dar es Salaam

[Cl]

Kabalo

[L] Mpanda

TANGANYIKA
(German East Africa)

[D]
aborg

[D]

Kabongo

Kilwa Kivinje

Kamina

Mikindani
Mtwara

[Ti] Bukama

[Cl]
Kolwezi

[M] KATANGA

[C] [U]

Elizabethville

COPPERBELT
[C]

NYASALAND

Ndola

NORTHERN [L] RHODESIA

Mozambique

[Z] Broken Hill

Lusaka

Livingstone

SOUTHERN

Salisbury

RHODESIA

MOZAMBIQUE

[Cl]
Wankie

[G]

[I] Que Que

Quelimane

BECHUANALAND

Bulawayo

[G]

[ch] Fort Victoria

Beira

Francistown

[T] [G] Shabani

West Nicholson

Southern Rhodesia:
eelworks at Que Que; secondary
dustries and engineering
orks at Salisbury,
lawayo and other
wns

Messina [C]

TRANSVAAL

Pretoria

Johannesburg [G]

Lourenço Marques

SWAZILAND

UNION OF SOUTH AFRICA

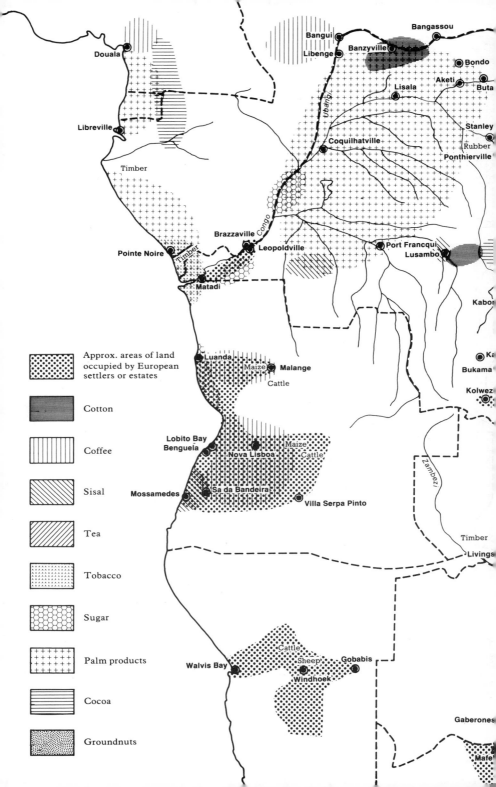

Douala

Libreville

Timber

Pointe Noire

Timber

Matadi

Brazzaville

Congo

Leopoldville

Bangui

Libenge

Banzyville

Bangassou

Bondo

Aketi

Buta

Lisala

Stanley

Coquilhatville

Ubangi

Rubber

Ponthierville

Port Francqui

Lusambo

Kabor

Ka

Bukama

Kolwezi

Luanda

Maize

Malange

Cattle

Lobito Bay

Benguela

Maize

Cattle

Nova Lisboa

Mossamedes

Sa da Bandeira

Villa Serpa Pinto

Zambezi

Timber

Livings

Cattle

Sheep

Gobabis

Walvis Bay

Windhoek

Gaberones

Mafe

Approx. areas of land occupied by European settlers or estates

Cotton

Coffee

Sisal

Tea

Tobacco

Sugar

Palm products

Cocoa

Groundnuts

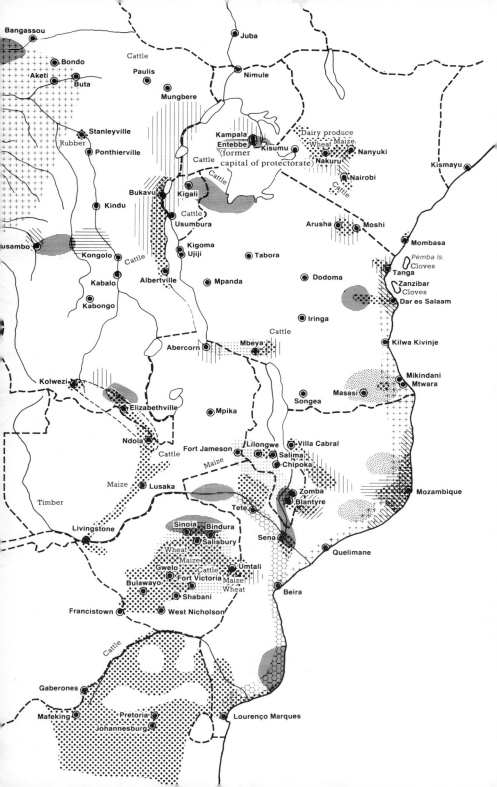

in Northern Rhodesia in 1912, would have been typical of much of Africa. 'The school consisted of a fence of grass, 6 feet high, surrounding a big tree, a few poles laid across short, forked sticks for seats, and a mass of wriggling, youthful humanity.' A little later, a school like this would probably have developed into a building of the kind so well described by Bishop Kitching in northern Uganda, which served as a school on weekdays and a church on Sundays. Kitching wrote:

Imagine a rough shed, built of mud and wattle and thatched with grass. Very likely it is leaning sideways and is propped up with extra poles at varied angles. A few gaps left in the mud serve for windows and doorways. At one end the floor is raised a few inches by way of a chancel, and a pole or bamboo runs across as a Communion rail. At each side a mud-walled enclosure does duty as reading-desk and pulpit. On the inside of the roof hang innumerable hornet's nests, and possibly a few bats. On the walls, suspended from little pegs, are sheets displaying the alphabet, or rows of syllables, some of them nibbled by intrusive goats or fretted by the ubiquitous termites. Look in at about 8.30 in the morning, and you will see groups of readers of mixed ages and sexes, seated on the floor in front of the sheets, saying over the letters or syllables in a sing-song voice. Somehow they get the syllables memorised, and are promoted to reading consecutive print.[1]

Such were the beginnings of western education in tropical Africa. The first instructors were, of course, European missionaries, but the brighter pupils who emerged from the system were given further training as catechists and teachers. As a result, education soon developed into a popular movement, in which foreign missionaries occupied only the supervisory positions and in which most of the teaching and evangelistic posts were held by Africans. These educated men constituted a new and very real kind of leadership rivalling that of the traditional chiefs. In the Africa of 1900–14 these mission teachers were the men and women who understood and felt at ease in the new world of the colonial period. To the tribal beliefs of their parents they had added a faith which they knew to be shared by people of all colours and all climates. Their religion taught them that all men had the same capacity for improvement in this life and salvation in the next. They were not therefore cast down by the changes which confronted them, but regarded them as opportunities to be seized. The development of the colonial administrations, of commercial and mining companies and of European plantations all increased the demand for clerks and skilled craftsmen, especially for those who

[1] A. L. Kitching, *From Darkness to Light* (London, 1935), p. 31.

26a West-Central Africa: economic development during the colonial period – agricultural products

26b East-Central Africa: economic development during the colonial period – agricultural products

knew a European language. The mission school soon emerged as a clear avenue for advancement, along which the ambitious could escape from the narrow discipline of village life into a wider world of well-paid urban employment.

THE BIRTH OF NATIONALISM

Part of the significance of the Christian missions was that, in their religious as well as their educational work, they were introducing Africans to the modern world into which they were now entering. They were showing them how they could succeed in that world. They were helping to make them into good colonial citizens. At the same time, however unconsciously, the missionaries were teaching the Africans to weigh up and criticise the influences of Europe *from within*. During the earliest years of the colonial period opposition to colonialism had been the opposition of the least-westernised groups, whose leaders simply wanted to drive out the Europeans and restore the situation which had previously existed. From the mission schools, however, there was beginning to emerge, even before 1914, a new kind of opposition to colonialism. This opposition did not aim to restore the pre-colonial situation. On the contrary, the aim of the mission-educated Africans was to capture the political and religious institutions introduced into Africa from the West. This they meant to do either by taking over these institutions from the inside and gradually replacing their European masters, or by imitating them from the outside and establishing similar alternatives to the colonial institutions.

These mission-educated Christians were, in fact, the first real African nationalists. Some of them believed that the way forward lay in joining the Churches planted by the missions and in seeking the best employment they could get in the service of colonial governments and commercial companies. They hoped that one day their children or grandchildren would rise naturally into the controlling positions. Others already believed that this hope was vain and that it would be necessary for Africans to found their own independent Churches and to prepare for an ultimate and revolutionary challenge to the colonial authorities. Either way, these new nationalists were thinking in modern terms – not in terms of a reversion to tribal beliefs and tribal organisations but in terms of Christian Churches under African leadership and of African successor states based on the existing colonial territories and governed along western rather than along traditional African lines.

155

27a   West-Central Africa: economic development during the colonial period – railways and waterways (bolder lines indicate navigable portions of rivers)

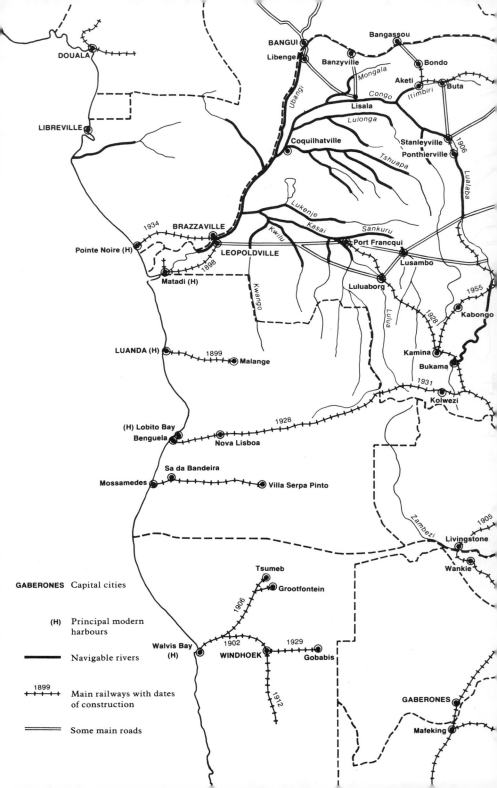

DOUALA

BANGUI
Libenge
Banzyville
Bangassou
Bondo
Aketi
Buta
Mongala
Congo
Itimbiri

LIBREVILLE

Ubangi

Lisala

Lulonga

Coquilhatville

Stanleyville
Ponthierville

Tshuapa

Lualaba

1906

Lukenje

1934 BRAZZAVILLE

Kwilu

Kasai

Sankuru

Port Francqui

Pointe Noire (H)

LEOPOLDVILLE

Lusambo

1898

Matadi (H)

Kwango

Luluaborg

1955

Kabongo

Lulua

1928

Kamina

LUANDA (H)

1899

Malange

Bukama

1931

Kolwezi

(H) Lobito Bay
Benguela

1928

Nova Lisboa

Sa da Bandeira

Mossamedes

Villa Serpa Pinto

Zambezi

1905

Livingstone

Wankie

Tsumeb
Grootfontein

1906

Walvis Bay
(H)

1902

WINDHOEK

1929

Gobabis

1912

GABERONES

Mafeking

There is a pamphlet written in 1911 by a Nyasaland African called Charles Domingo which gives a very good picture of the outlook of the more radical of these early nationalists. Domingo wrote:

There is too much failure among all Europeans in Nyasaland. The three combined bodies – Missionaries, Government and Companies or gainers of money – do form the same rule to look upon the native with mockery eyes. It sometimes startles us to see that the three combined bodies are from Europe, and along with them there is a title Christendom. And to compare and make a comparison between the Master of the title and his servants, it provokes any African away from believing in the Master of the title. If we had power enough to communicate ourselves to Europe, we would advise them not to call themselves Christendom, but Europeandom. Therefore the life of the three combined bodies is altogether too cheaty, too thefty, too mockery. Instead of 'Give', they say 'Take away from'. There is too much breakage of God's pure law as seen in James's Epistle, chapter five, verse four.[2]

As one can see, Charles Domingo was not a very highly educated man. His ideas were simple ideas. His use of English was far from perfect. But what is interesting about him is that he was judging the Europeans he had met according to their own professed standard of moral judgement, namely the New Testament. He evidently did not doubt that the Epistle of James represented 'God's pure law', nor did the people for whom he was writing. The conclusion he drew from the failure of Europeans to practise their Christianity was not that Africans should abandon it, though he realised that that was a danger, but that they could and should practise it better under their own leadership. Charles Domingo and those like him all over tropical Africa at this time represented the *most*-westernised element in the colonial societies. Even on the equator, most of them dressed in all the elaborate finery of early-twentieth-century Europe. In every aspect of their lives they were the pioneers of European taste and customs. The independent Churches founded at this period were mostly even more European in their ritual and procedure than the mission Churches. Yet, for all their imitativeness, these early African nationalists had learned one thing above all others from their mission education: they wanted to run their own lives for themselves.

Although historians now know that opinions such as these were forming under the surface, they were not, in the years before 1914, much in evidence to Europeans who lived or worked in Africa at the time. Outwardly, the colonial governments, the missionaries, the settlers and the commercial companies appeared to be in complete

[2] George Shepperson and Thomas Price, *Independent African* (Edinburgh, 1958), pp. 163–4.

27*b* East-Central Africa: economic development during the colonial period – railways and waterways (bolder lines indicate navigable portions of rivers)

control of their several spheres. Almost everywhere the first, military stage of colonial occupation had been succeeded by civil administration. Modern communications had penetrated to most districts. Cash crops were being widely grown. Migrant labourers were moving freely over long distances to various kinds of European employment. Taxes were being paid. At last, grants-in-aid from the governments of the European countries were being steadily eliminated. Most Europeans imagined that the foundations of empire were being laid down for a thousand years to come. To the extent that they were aware of the mission-educated Africans – the slowly developing intelligentsia – they wrote them off as an unrepresentative and unimportant minority. Even so great an administrator as Lugard referred to them contemptuously as 'trousered blacks', from whose exploitation the uneducated majority must be protected for a long time to come. The eyes of the colonial administrations were fixed upon the traditional chiefs and the old social hierarchy, whose influence they were unconsciously doing so much to destroy by their patronage. They ignored the new men, on whom the future of Africa was really to depend.

13 The inter-war period, 1918–1938

The First World War, fought between 1914 and 1918, marked an important turning-point in the history of the tropical African territories. Before the war these colonies had been backwaters, each connected with the mainstream of world events only through the single channel linking it to one or other of the colonial powers. There had been little overall policy. Each colony had been thought of as a separate problem, and mainly as a problem of economic self-support. After the war things moved faster. Most African colonies were by now sufficiently established to be able to think of more than mere survival. Their revenues were beginning to show modest surpluses over the bare cost of law and order. Colonial governments were able for the first time to contemplate expenditure on education, on health, on agricultural and veterinary services and on economic development of various kinds. After the war, too, colonial powers started to take their colonial responsibilities more seriously. They tried to work out consistent policies for the African colonies. They developed within their colonial ministries important specialist departments and advisory services designed to assist all the colonial governments under their control. This increasing centralisation did much to break down the previous isolation of individual territories.

The war also made the colonial powers somewhat responsible to international opinion. The former German colonies were divided among the victor nations. Britain took most of the former German East Africa as Tanganyika Territory, and Belgium the remainder as Ruanda-Urundi. South Africa took the former German South-West Africa, and France and Britain each took adjoining parts of Cameroun and Togo (the British called their part 'Togoland'; the French, 'Togo'). The changes were not outright annexations in the manner of the original partition. In the hope of avoiding further conflicts, the victorious powers had set up an international authority, the League of Nations. Largely on the initiative of the American president, Woodrow Wilson, it was agreed that those powers taking over German colonies should do so as 'mandatories' of the League. Those undertaking the task were required to recognise that the interests of the population concerned must have equal weight with those of the administering power. In spite of the lead taken by Wilson, the United States Congress would not agree to America joining the League. This gravely weakened the organisation from the very start of its life. Nevertheless, with strong British support, the establishment of a Mandates Commission of the League went forward. The mandatories agreed to govern their territories as 'a sacred trust of Civilisation' until such time as they were 'able to stand on their own feet in the strenuous conditions of the modern world'. Annual reports on each of the mandated territories had to be sent to the League at its headquarters at Geneva in Switzerland, and in the Mandates Commission of the League it was possible for international opinion to have some influence on the policy of the mandatory powers.

THE DUAL POLICY IN BRITISH AFRICA

In practice it turned out to be the mandatory powers themselves who made most of the running at the commission's meetings. This was significant because it showed that these powers were not merely concerned to defend their actions in the mandated territories but were also seeking a defensible policy of colonialism which could be applied to all their overseas possessions. Foremost among these practical thinkers about colonialism was Lord Lugard, who had ended his career as colonial administrator and had become the principal British representative on the Mandates Commission. In 1922 he published a book called *The Dual Mandate in British Tropical Africa*, which inspired a whole generation of colonial administrators and was accepted as a guide by politicians and civil servants in Britain. Lugard started from the doctrine that a colonial power had a double responsibility, on the one hand to the colonial peoples under its rule and on the other hand to the outside world. To the colonial peoples it owed material and moral advancement leading ultimately to self-government. To the outside world it had the obligation to see that the natural resources of its colonies were developed and that they found their way on to the world market. Lugard argued that, properly balanced, these two obligations need not conflict with one another. To secure a proper balance, it was necessary to ensure that in the economic field as well as in that of government the colonial peoples were encouraged to do as much as possible for themselves.

In the field of government Lugard prescribed a general adoption of the system of indirect rule, which he had first evolved in Northern 161

Nigeria and later adapted to the differing circumstances of the South. Indirect rule meant government through the traditional chiefs. In Lugard's words, a colonial official 'would consider it as irregular to issue direct orders to an individual native . . . as a General commanding a division would to a private soldier, except through his commanding officers'.[1] At the same time indirect rule was not just a system for concealing the exercise of power by the colonial government. It was basic to Lugard's thinking, though not always to that of his followers, that the traditional local government of the chiefs should be progressively modernised. The aim was that it should be able to take more and more responsibility, especially financial responsibility for the raising and spending of public funds. Under indirect rule taxes were collected by the chiefs, who passed on most of the money to the colonial government for national use. The chiefs were, however, allowed to keep a proportion of the taxes for their own 'Native Treasuries' and to spend the money on local needs and largely at their own discretion. This expenditure included the salaries of local government employees, such as clerks, messengers and policemen, and also local public works, such as offices, court-houses, dispensaries, markets, country roads and footpaths. Lugard looked forward to a time when the smaller traditional chiefdoms would federate with their neighbours to form larger units. In this way he imagined that a class of people would eventually emerge with the experience necessary to take responsibility at a national level.

In economic development Lugard was once again insistent that the largest possible place should be left free for the enterprise of Africans in their own countries. He recognised, of course, that large-scale and long-term economic investment, such as that required for railways and harbours, was clearly beyond the scope of local communities. Equally he thought that projects of this kind were too important to be left to outside private enterprise, and therefore in these matters he was a strong and early advocate of state ownership. In other kinds of large industry, such as mining, he saw a legitimate field for outside enterprise, though he stressed that not only colonial governments but also local 'Native' governments, should receive an interest in the profit. In the field of agricultural production, however, he was a firm opponent of the outside enterprise that was seeking to establish plantations for tropical produce in the West African countries. These European companies used arguments such as those put forward in 1924 by Lord Leverhulme when he said, 'The African native will be

---

[1] Lugard's Amalgamation Report, 1919, p. 14, cited in Margery Perham, *Lugard: the years of authority 1898–1945* (Oxford, 1960), pp. 469–70.

happier, produce the best, and live under the larger conditions of prosperity, when his labour is directed and organised by his white brother who has all these million years start ahead of him.'[2] Lugard in the 1920s regretted the policy of white settlement in East Africa, which he had himself advocated in the 1890s. He saw it had the effect of obstructing African enterprise of the kind which had flourished so successfully under the West African system of peasant production. That Lord Leverhulme's United Africa Company was refused permission to acquire plantations in any of the British West African colonies was due very largely to Lugard's influence.

THE DUAL POLICY IN EAST AND CENTRAL AFRICA

Obviously the part of tropical Africa where the dual policy was hardest to apply was in East and Central Africa, from Kenya south to Rhodesia. Here Europeans had been encouraged to settle, and here they were now claiming the right to take an increasing share in government. In Rhodesia this process had indeed gone too far to be stopped. When, in 1923, the British South Africa Company asked to be relieved of its governmental responsibilities, effective power was transferred to the 33,000 white settlers. North of the Zambezi, however, the British government was already by this time showing signs of its change of heart. The policy adopted in 1918 of encouraging demobilised army officers to settle in Kenya had led, within three years, to an acute labour crisis. During this crisis the colonial government had instructed its administrative officers to put pressure on the chiefs to direct their subjects into European employment. This led to such an agitation by missionaries and by the administrative officers themselves that public opinion in England was aroused. When the settlers pressed for further political powers in 1922–3 they were resisted. In July 1923 the British government issued a White Paper stating that

Primarily Kenya is an African territory, and His Majesty's Government think it necessary definitely to record their considered opinion that the interests of the African natives must be paramount, and that if and when these interests and the interests of the immigrant races should conflict, the former should prevail. As in the Uganda Protectorate, so in the Kenya Colony, the principle of Trusteeship for the Natives, no less than in the Mandated Territory of Tanganyika, is unassailable.[3]

The following year (1924) the British government sent an all-party parliamentary commission under the chairmanship of one of Lugard's

---

[2] Speech, cited in Michael Crowder, *The Story of Nigeria* (London, 1973), p. 264.
[3] *Indians in Kenya Memorandum* (HMSO, London, 1923), p. 9.

greatest admirers, William Ormsby-Gore (later Lord Harlech), to investigate the guiding principles of British policy in East Africa. In its report the commission reaffirmed that there need be no conflict between the interests of the settlers and those of the native inhabitants. White settlement should not be allowed to hold back the education of Africans or their training in economic skills, especially training in the best use of their own land. Though it did nothing to attack settlement, the Ormsby-Gore commission envisaged a great expansion in the functions of colonial governments, in the building up of health services, education services, agricultural and veterinary services. All these measures were directed towards the African population of the territories. It was this report which helped to set British policy in East Africa in line with that pursued in the west.

EDUCATION IN THE BRITISH COLONIES

In 1925 Ormsby-Gore, now under-secretary of state for the colonies, summoned the governors of the West and East African colonies to London. He ordered them to pursue a much more active policy of education, by entering into partnership with the Christian missions of all denominations and by subsidising the mission schools on condition that they conformed to the proper standards of efficiency. This did not result in a great increase in the total number of African children attending school, which remained at about one-third of those of school age. But, of those who did attend, the great majority now stayed at school for at least four years. And from this time onwards there were government inspectorates in every colony. Subsidies were given only on condition that teachers were trained and that the prescribed syllabuses were followed. In Muslim areas, like Northern Nigeria, local-authority schools were set up and staffed by government-trained teachers. As a result, during the fourteen years from 1925 to 1939 the standard of primary education was very much improved, and the effects were felt over the whole field of employment. The higher standards were noticed in government, and especially in local government, in the Churches, in commerce, in industry and in every walk of life where a little clerical skill and a little knowledge of the world was needed.

More revolutionary still, however, was the progress made in secondary education. Here the numbers involved were very small indeed. Nigeria was probably the only country in British Africa which in 1939 had more than a dozen secondary schools. In most countries the output was between a hundred and two hundred students a year.

Nevertheless it was these few hundreds of secondary-school students who demonstrated that tropical Africans were capable of filling a wide range of posts of skill and responsibility, for which it had previously been thought necessary to import Europeans. With the exception of a few West Africans from well-to-do families who had been educated abroad, it was from this generation that there emerged the first professional men. There were doctors and veterinary surgeons, the first agricultural and forest officers, the first managers of retail stores, the first secondary schoolmasters, and, above all, the first educated chiefs and local-government officials. Not all of these secondary-school students, however, consented to fill the occupations intended for them by the colonial authorities. It was in this generation that most of the leaders of the nationalist revolution received their secondary education: Kenyatta, Banda, Azikiwe towards the beginning of it, Nkrumah, Tafawa Balewa and Oginga Odinga towards the end of it. It is probably true that had the colonial governments and the Christian missions not provided the means of secondary education during this inter-war period, there could have been no successful nationalist revolution until long after the Second World War.

THE FRENCH POLICY OF ASSOCIATION

If it was Lugard and Ormsby-Gore who laid the foundations of British colonial policy between the wars, their French equivalent was Albert Sarraut, minister of colonies in 1920–4 and 1932–3. Sarraut's outlook was very different from that of the Englishmen. It was less respectful of the African personality and yet more fraternal towards the African. Sarraut never talked of 'allowing the African to develop along his own lines'. His dominant thought was rather that France and her African colonies must be kept as united in peace as they had been in war. The key to his plan was the rapid economic development of the colonies, to provide France with raw materials and with markets for French manufactured goods. 'Our colonies', he wrote, 'must be centres of production, and no longer museums for specimens.' Assimilation of Africans into French culture remained the ultimate objective, but no special effort was made to hurry it on. In 1936, apart from the four coastal *communes* of the Senegal with their 80,000 black *citoyens* (citizens with full political rights), only about 2,000 out of 14,000,000 French West Africans had received French citizenship. The immediate emphasis was on 'association' meaning the collective association of the French colonies with France. Economically the French empire was to become as centralised as it already was administratively. There 165

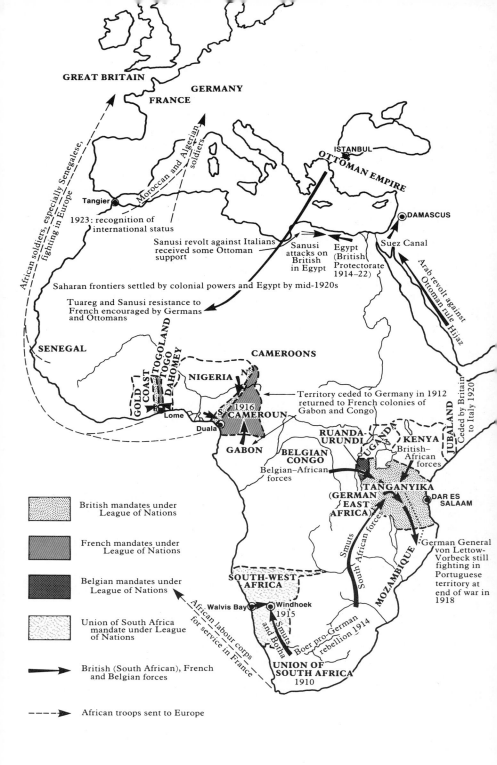

GREAT BRITAIN

GERMANY

FRANCE

ISTANBUL

OTTOMAN EMPIRE

African soldiers, especially Senegalese, fighting in Europe

Moroccan and Algerian soldiers

Tangier

1923: recognition of international status

Sanusi revolt against Italians received some Ottoman support

Sanusi attacks on British in Egypt

Egypt (British Protectorate 1914–22)

DAMASCUS

Suez Canal

Arab revolt against Ottoman rule Hijaz

Saharan frontiers settled by colonial powers and Egypt by mid-1920s

Tuareg and Sanusi resistance to French encouraged by Germans and Ottomans

SENEGAL

TOGOLAND
GOLD COAST
TOGO
DAHOMEY
Lome

CAMEROONS

NIGERIA

N

1916
Duala
CAMEROUN
S

Territory ceded to Germany in 1912 returned to French colonies of Gabon and Congo

GABON

RUANDA-URUNDI
BELGIAN CONGO
Belgian–African forces

UGANDA
British–African forces

KENYA

JUBALAND
Ceded by Britain to Italy 1920

TANGANYIKA (GERMAN EAST AFRICA)

DAR ES SALAAM

Smuts
South African forces

MOZAMBIQUE

German General von Lettow-Vorbeck still fighting in Portuguese territory at end of war in 1918

British mandates under League of Nations

French mandates under League of Nations

Belgian mandates under League of Nations

Union of South Africa mandate under League of Nations

SOUTH-WEST AFRICA

Walvis Bay

Windhoek
1915

African labour corps for service in France

Smuts and Botha

Boer pro-German rebellion 1914

UNION OF SOUTH AFRICA
1910

British (South African), French and Belgian forces

African troops sent to Europe

was no thought that any of the colonies would ever become independent. African chiefs were merely the 'agents' of the French administration, and there was no intention at all of allowing their powers to grow. Indeed, the top-grade chiefs, the *chefs de canton*, were really officials of the French administration. They were normally chosen from among the more efficient clerks and interpreters in the government service rather than on any hereditary principle.

It was above all in education that French policy differed from British. Although a few mission schools received government subsidies for exceptional efficiency, nine-tenths of the formal education given in French Africa between the wars was given by the state. Moreover, all teaching was in French. The aim of education was neatly defined by one governor-general of French West Africa as 'instruire la masse et dégager l'élite' (give primary education to the masses and win over the elite). Primary education was given in 'regional schools', of which there were by 1937 about eighty scattered over French West Africa. There were a very much smaller number in French Equatorial Africa. Secondary education was limited to filling the needs of the government service. Nearly all of it was given in three first-class institutions in Dakar. The best-known of these institutions, both academically and for its output of later nationalist leaders, was the teacher-training college called the École William Ponty.

In the Congo the Belgians pursued between the wars a policy which resembled the French policy in so far as rule was direct rather than indirect. In 1919 the colony was being administered in no fewer than 6,000 separate chiefdoms (*chefferies*). By 1934 this had been reduced by amalgamations to some 2,500, but even at this figure the African chief in the Belgian Congo was scarcely even the equivalent of the French *chef de canton*. Like his opposite number in French West Africa, he was strictly the agent of the colonial government. In the Belgian colonial service, as in the French, administrative districts were much smaller than in most British territories, and the administrative staff was larger. Control, therefore, was correspondingly closer. In education the Belgians, like the British, preferred to subsidise mission schools rather than to organise a state education service. Unlike the British, however, they subsidised only 'national', that is to say Roman Catholic, missions. Even more severely than the French, the Belgians limited schooling to primary education only. Their stated aim was to bring forward the inhabitants of the colony at a uniform pace and so to prevent the exploitation of the many by the few. Actually, as it turned out, the result was to leave the country with few 167 effective leaders at independence and with not nearly enough educated people to operate the machinery of government.

COLONIALISM AND NATIONALISM

Although by the 1920s the tropical African colonies of all the European powers were being run at least partly in the interests of their African inhabitants, developments were still dominated by European governors, administrators and commissions of inquiry. No important decisions were made by Africans, and in a sense there were fewer Africans of importance in this period than there had been in the period before 1914, when a few of the old leaders still survived from the pre-colonial period. By the 1920s most of these older men were either dead or in retirement. Their places had been taken by men who owed their promotion to Europeans and who tended to be the 'trusties' of the colonial administrations. A small but important number of educated men and women were leaving the secondary schools, but these were still young and inexperienced, and they held as yet only minor jobs in government and commerce. A very few were able to study in Europe and America, and became doctors and lawyers, but on their return to Africa they were often not given the status merited by their qualifications. Most such people considered that their attainments deserved greater rewards. Out of these individual grudges emerged a more general dissatisfaction with the way their countries were being governed.

The earliest political associations were formed, naturally, in West Africa, where the coastal people had been in contact with Europeans for centuries and where a tiny minority had enjoyed western education for several generations. In Sierra Leone the leading freed-slave families, and in Senegal the Creoles (descendants of marriages between Frenchmen and African women), had taken part in local politics since the middle of the nineteenth century. In the Gold Coast and in Lagos small associations had sprung up during the early twentieth century among the lawyers, doctors and businessmen. As early as 1918 a Gold Coast lawyer, J. E. Casely Hayford, founded the National Congress of British West Africa, which spread to Nigeria in 1920. The Congress demanded that Africans should participate in the government. For the most part, however, the activities of these early politicians were confined to local affairs, and they had little influence upon the colonial governments. In French West Africa political consciousness centred upon the four coastal *communes* of Senegal, where the 80,000 *citoyens* had as early as 1914 elected a black Senegalese, Blaise

Diagne, to the Chamber of Deputies in Paris. In 1917 Diagne became the under-secretary of state for the colonies of metropolitan France, and this helped to set the fashion that politically conscious Senegalese should join the political parties of France. From about 1936 onwards, increasingly left-wing governments were elected in France. Socialists and communists were now able to obtain appointments in the colonies, especially in the education service. As a result, considerable numbers of French West Africans joined the French socialist and communist parties.

In the field of pan-African politics, student organisations in Britain and France were the chief means of turning local and individual grievances into a true spirit of nationalism. Much of the inspiration of these organisations came from the writings and activities of American and West Indian Negroes, such as Edward Blyden, W. E. DuBois and Marcus Garvey, who stressed the similarities in the conditions of black people on both sides of the Atlantic. Under their influence, Africans began to think in terms of taking over control of the political units which the colonial powers had created and of uniting them after the manner of the United States of America or the Union of Soviet Socialist Republics. Foremost among the student organisations was the West African Students' Union, founded in 1925 in London by the Nigerian Ladipo Solanke. The Italian invasion of Ethiopia in 1935 added fuel to the growing fire of nationalist feelings. The decisive event in the history of nationalism in British West Africa was undoubtedly the return in 1935 of Nnamdi Azikiwe from his studies in America and his launching, first in the Gold Coast and then in his native Nigeria, of a popular press. This was the most essential step in getting the political ideas of pan-Africanism accepted by a mass audience. Soon after his return Azikiwe helped to send to America eight Nigerians and four Gold Coasters, all of whom grew into key figures of the post-war nationalist revolution. The most prominent of this group was a young Gold Coast teacher named Kwame Nkrumah.

Most of the West African politicians were men who had broken away from their tribal backgrounds. They organised their activities in a European way, using newspapers and popular agitation. These caused riots at times but were essentially non-violent. In East Africa discontent with European rule still assumed a mainly tribal form. The history of nationalism in Kenya, for example, is largely the history of Kikuyu dissatisfaction and resistance. The numbers of the Kikuyu were increasing rapidly. Their natural path of expansion out of the forests around Mount Kenya was blocked by the European settlers. Many became squatters and farm labourers on European estates, 169

while others left the land and joined the growing numbers of unemployed in Nairobi. In 1922 a clerk in government service, Harry
Thuku, started a political association which drew attention to these
problems. He was sacked from his job and arrested, whereupon a
large crowd assembled in Nairobi and was fired upon by the police.
Thuku was banished to the remote Northern Frontier District, but
political groups spread widely among the Kikuyu. When in the late
1920s some missionary societies attempted to interfere with Kikuyu
initiation customs, many teachers left the mission schools and formed
an Independent Schools Association. Jomo Kenyatta first came to
prominence as secretary of the main Kikuyu party, the Kikuyu
Central Association, before he left to study and work in Britain in the
1930s. When Thuku was released from detention in 1931, he formed a
moderate party which quarrelled bitterly with the Kikuyu Central
Association. The Kikuyu were thus unable to present a united front to
the government and the settlers, and this of course suited the Europeans very well.

Kenya was by far the most troubled territory in British Africa
between the wars, though the calm and slow pace of political and
economic change in much of the rest of the continent was deceptive.
Under the surface, African society was changing rapidly, and not in
the way Lugard had hoped it would. The 'trousered blacks' rather
than the long-robed chieftains were setting the pace. Africa was
seething with new ideas and new ambitions, making ready to exert its
will in opposition to the rule of European governments. Still, without
the added ferment of the Second World War, it is very doubtful if the
authority of the colonial governments would have been challenged
until very much later than in fact it was.

14 North and North-East Africa, 1900–1939

By 1914 North Africa and the Muslim lands of the Horn of Africa were all in European hands. Only Ethiopia clung to a precarious independence. The variety of political and social conditions in this region was staggering. The contrast between Somali pastoralists on one hand and the wealthy citizens of Cairo on the other was extreme. Yet they possessed a common faith and a single cultural tradition which set them apart from most of the people of tropical Africa. The European powers had to adapt their policies and their methods of administration to the institutions of Muslim society. These were too deeply rooted to be set aside. Warfare and political conflict loomed larger over these countries throughout the colonial period than in any other part of Africa. Resistance to the loss of independence was inflamed by the intense religious hostility long felt by Muslims for the Christian peoples of Europe. As a result, revolts led by *shaikhs* and holy men continued until the 1930s, by which time nationalist opposition organised on modern political lines had developed. Nationalism, here as elsewhere, was influenced by European political ideas absorbed in colonial schools and metropolitan universities. Throughout this region it was influenced also by the pan-Islamic reform movement.

The pan-Islamic movement was a reaction against the relentless encroachment of Christian Europe upon the lands of Islam. It began among groups of educated Turks in the Ottoman empire in the 1860s and the 1870s. The movement owed something to the example of the unification of Italy and Germany which was taking place about that time. The ideas spread to Cairo, Damascus and other Arabic-speaking cities of the Middle East. The central argument of the pan-Islamists was that the only way the Muslim world could survive in the face of European aggression was for all Muslims to sink their political and local differences and to unite against the common foe. Political unification could only be brought about through a thorough rethinking of the principles and practices of the Muslim religion. Al-Azhar University in Cairo became the main centre for the teaching of pan-Islamic

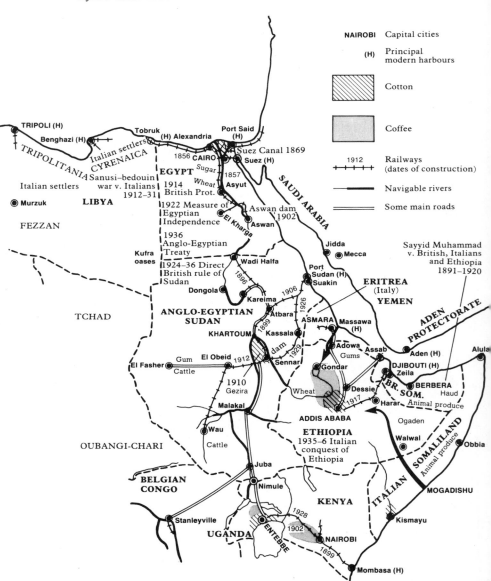

29   North-East Africa under colonial rule: economic and political development

ideas, in spite of the British occupation of Egypt after 1882. To al-Azhar came students from all over the Muslim world, including the Maghrib and the Sudanic lands. These students returned to their homes inspired by the reforming movement.

FRENCH RULE IN THE MAGHRIB

By the beginning of the twentieth century Algeria had already been governed for many years as if it were a part of France. In Tunisia and Morocco, however, the governments of the bey and the sultan survived the establishment of the protectorates. They were, however, increasingly staffed with French officials. All three countries were poor, suffering from perennial droughts, poor soils and, above all, difficulties of communication caused by the mountainous interior. The French now tackled these problems with determination, especially that of communications. By the 1930s it was possible to travel from Marrakech to Tunis by train, and Maghribi roads were the best in Africa. The growth of Casablanca offers an outstanding example of development under French rule. In 1900 it was a tiny fishing village. Even before the establishment of the protectorate in 1912 the French had constructed an artificial harbour, with rail links to the iron and phosphate-mines of the interior. By 1936 it had a population of a quarter of a million. Moroccans flocked to Casablanca (as Algerians did to Algiers and Oran) to work in the factories and port installations, the more poorly paid among them living in shanty towns on the outskirts of the city.

In all three countries Frenchmen were encouraged to settle as *colons*. In Algeria by the turn of the century there were more than 500,000, and by 1936 they had grown to nearly 1,000,000. In the same year there were more than 200,000 *colons* in Morocco, and nearly as many in Tunisia. Undoubtedly, most of the economic development which took place under French rule was attributable to these immigrants, though their presence in such numbers caused grave political and social difficulties. Not only did they occupy much of the land, but in every town they competed for jobs with the indigenous Muslim population. The Muslim population was also growing rapidly: in Algeria alone it doubled itself, rising from 4,500,000 to more than 9,000,000 during the first half of the century. With the best land and the highest paid jobs in European hands, the Muslims tended to become poorer as their numbers increased. By the 1930s many thousands of Maghribis had migrated to France in order to earn a better livelihood.

The *colons* of Algeria remained, in the fullest sense, citizens of France. They elected their own deputies to the National Assembly in Paris and exercised a steady pressure on French politics. Theoretically, the same rights of citizenship could be granted to educated Muslims, but only if they abandoned Muslim for Christian law, which few of them cared to do. The *colons*, needless to say, did nothing to encourage them. In 1913 a French writer summed up the settler point of view as follows: 'In a conquered country almost the only kind of co-operation that can occur between the two races is one in which the conquered work for the conquerors.'

MOROCCO: LYAUTEY AND ABD AL-QRIM

The territory which differed most from Algeria was Morocco. This was partly because French rule there did not begin until 1912. It was mainly because of the outstanding character of its first resident-general, Marshal Lyautey, who held the office for thirteen years, from 1912 till 1925. Lyautey was a colonial ruler of the highest order. He understood and respected the traditional institutions of North African Islam, and was determined that they should be preserved with dignity. At the same time he had a sure grasp of economic affairs, and the rapid modernisation of the Moroccan economy was largely his work. When he came to Morocco he found it 'submerged in a wave of anarchy'. In particular he had to take on the task of pacifying the tribes of the *bilad as-siba* (see Chapter 8). For centuries no sultan of Morocco had been able to subdue these tribes. Perhaps Lyautey's greatest achievement was the bringing of law and order to areas that had never previously been controlled by the central government of Morocco, and by means more humane than forceful conquest. His principle was 'to display force in order to avoid using it'. His policy of combining French interests with those of the sultan and the tribal *kaids* (chiefs) was similar to Lugard's work in Hausaland, and suffered from the same defects.

In the early 1920s Lyautey's pacification was rudely interrupted by the Rif War. The Berbers of the Rif mountains in the northern zone of Morocco rose against the inefficient and often unjust Spanish military government. Brilliantly led by a former *qadi* (Muslim judge) called Abd al-Qrim, they defeated a Spanish force in 1921 and followed this up by pushing the Spaniards into the coastal towns. Abd al-Qrim proclaimed a 'Republic of the Rif'. The term was modern, but he had a thoroughly old-fashioned ambition – to become sultan and found a new dynasty in Morocco. His military successes made him the hero of the Muslim world. This gave him the false confidence to extend his operations into the French zone. By doing so he brought the whole might of the French army against him. France and Spain, in the words of an American observer, 'had enveloped the Rif in a wall of steel, employing every device of scientific warfare against the embattled tribesmen'. Once this had happened, further resistance was futile. In May 1926 Abd al-Qrim

came riding astride a mule into the French lines. At one point he was crossing a stream in which French soldiers were bathing. As soon as they saw who he was, they came rushing towards him. Though naked, they saluted him in correct military fashion, and expressed their great admiration for his qualities as a soldier and a leader.[1]

The French exiled him to the island of Réunion, but years later he returned to play a part in the Moroccan nationalist movement.

In 1925 Lyautey sent in his resignation to the French government in protest against the delays in sending him the reinforcements which he had asked for during the crisis of the Rif War. To his surprise and grief, his resignation was accepted. It is said that he boarded his ship at Casablanca with tears streaming down his face. His successors, who were lesser men than he, soon pushed the old ruling classes into the background, giving them no further opportunity to modernise the traditional institutions. In 1927, when the old sultan died, the French arranged for a young prince, Sidi Muhammad, to accede to the throne of Morocco. The French imagined that they could educate the young sultan to rule entirely according to their wishes. They could not have been more mistaken, for after the Second World War Sidi Muhammad became the leader of the Moroccan nationalist movement. The French also attempted to play off the Berbers against the Arabs: the result was to unite them in opposition to French rule.

THE BEGINNINGS OF NATIONALISM IN THE MAGHRIB

Nationalism in the Maghrib was a reaction against the realities of French rule, which were at variance both with the theory of assimilation in Algeria and with the terms of the protectorate treaties in Tunisia and Morocco. As early as 1920 Lyautey had forecast that 'a young generation is coming along which is full of life, and which needs activity. Lacking the outlets, which our administration offers them so sparingly, they will find another way out, and will seek to form

[1] Rom Landau, *Moroccan Drama* (London, 1956), p. 128.

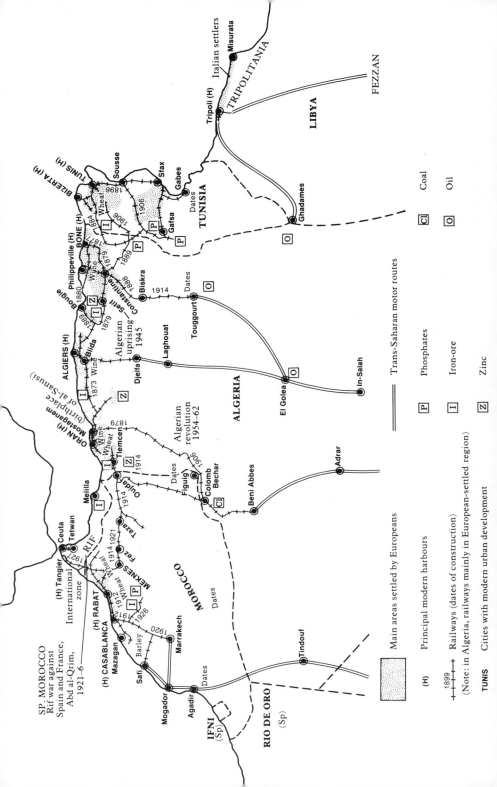

SP. MOROCCO
Rif war against
Spain and France,
Abd al-Qrim,
1921–6

(H) Tangier
International
zone

(H) RABAT

(H) CASABLANCA

Mazagan

Safi

Mogador

Agadir

IFNI
(Sp)

RIO DE ORO
(Sp)

Tindouf

Marrakech

Barley

Dates

MOROCCO

Ceuta
Tetwan

1922

RIF

Fez

MEKNES

Melilla

Taza

Oujda

Tlemcen

Figuig

Colomb
Bechar

Beni Abbes

Adrar

Mostaganem (birthplace of al-Sanusi)

ORAN (H)

Wine
Wheat

Algerian revolution
1954–62

Blida

ALGIERS (H)

Wine

Djelfa

Laghouat

El Golea

In-Salah

ALGERIA

Bougie

Philippeville (H)

Setif

Constantine

Biskra

Touggourt

BONE (H)

Wine

BIZERTA (H)

TUNIS (H)

Sousse

Sfax

Gafsa

Gabes

Dates

TUNISIA

Ghadames

Misurata

Italian settlers

Tripoli (H)

TRIPOLITANIA

LIBYA

FEZZAN

Algerian uprising 1945

Wheat

Dates

Dates

Dates

Dates

Main areas settled by Europeans

(H)   Principal modern harbours

1899 ⊢⊢⊢ Railways (dates of construction)

(Note: in Algeria, railways mainly in European-settled region)

TUNIS   Cities with modern urban development

═══ Trans-Saharan motor routes

P   Phosphates

I   Iron-ore

Z   Zinc

Cl   Coal

O   Oil

themselves into groups in order to voice their demand.' In Morocco and Tunisia it was possible to foresee the emergence of free, reformed, Muslim states. Moroccans looked back with pride over a long and glorious past. Their sultan claimed descent from the Prophet Muhammad and was the spiritual as well as the temporal leader of the country. The young Sidi Muhammad did not abandon his outward show of subservience to the French until after the Second World War, but his sympathies were known long before. The foundations of the nationalist movement, however, were laid by others. One summer's evening in 1926 ten young men met in a garden in Rabat, sipping mint tea under the boughs of a mulberry tree. They were addressed by an eighteen-year-old student, Ahmad Balafrej, who was one day to be prime minister of Morocco. 'Without freedom,' he said, 'the darkness of the grave is more comforting to the spirit than the light of the sun.' The ten agreed to form a secret association to oppose French rule by any and every means. Nearly twenty years of preparation by journalism and political organisation were to be necessary before early movements like this one were able to combine in 1943 as the Istiqlal, or Party of Independence. The Istiqlal Party had the support of the sultan and of a large section of the Moroccan people.

In Tunisia the beginnings of democratic political organisation went far back behind the colonial period to the middle of the nineteenth century, when, as we saw in Chapter 8, the Destour (Constitution) Party was formed to curb the power of the Ottoman bey. The Destour Party remained active during the early years of French rule, but represented mainly the wealthy citizens of the capital. In 1934, however, Habib Bourguiba broke away from the old party to found the Néo-Destour, composed of younger, more radical groups, with a modern secular policy. Bourguiba proclaimed that 'The Tunisia we mean to liberate will not be a Tunisia for Muslim, for Jew, or for Christian. It will be a Tunisia for all, without distinction of religion or race, who wish to have it as their country and to live in it under the protection of just laws.' But in 1934 Bourguiba and his supporters had still a long struggle ahead of them. Being generally sympathetic to France and French culture, they wanted to negotiate Tunisia's independence in a friendly way. The French and Italian settlers in Tunisia were opposed to such an independence, as were the French civil service who staffed the Tunisian administration in large numbers. Above all, the French military chiefs were determined that Tunisia should remain French. They saw Tunis and the naval station of Bizerta as a necessary base for the coming war against Fascist Italy. Until after the Second World War therefore the French dealt with the   177

30   The Maghrib: economic development during the colonial period

Néo-Destour by imprisoning its leaders, by banning its newspapers and finally by outlawing the party and closing its offices.

In Algeria, nationalism had to deal with an even more difficult situation. The political structure of the country had been entirely refashioned by the French. Most educated Muslims had been to French schools and spoke French better than they spoke Arabic. Yet the privilege of French citizenship was in practice denied to them. There was little surviving from the past on which they could build. In 1934 Ferhat Abbas wrote despairingly, 'Men who die for a patriotic ideal are honoured and respected. But I would not die for an Algerian fatherland, because no such fatherland exists. I search the history books and I cannot find it. You cannot build on air.' The sense of an Algerian nationhood was born only during the bitter war fought with France between 1954 and 1962, in which the more moderate nationalists of the 1920s and 1930s, like Ferhat Abbas, were swept aside by younger, more extreme leaders. Nationalism in Algeria could hardly make a beginning until nationalism in Tunisia and Morocco had all but gained the victory.

THE BRITISH IN EGYPT AND THE SUDAN

After the British occupation of 1882, Lord Dufferin, who had been ambassador in Istanbul, was sent to Egypt to report on a possible system of government. He advised that the country could not be administered from London with any prospect of success. 'Any attempt on our part to do so would at once render us objects of hatred and suspicion to its inhabitants.' Unfortunately for both countries, this warning went largely unheeded. As allies of the Ottoman sultan, who was still the nominal sovereign of Egypt, Britain could not annex the country outright. The khedive and his ministers continued outwardly to govern the country. In reality, the British consul-general in Cairo held absolute power in Egypt. Lord Granville, the British foreign minister, wrote, 'It is essential that in important questions affecting the administration and safety of Egypt, the advice of Her Majesty's Government should be followed, as long as the provisional occupation continues. Ministers and Governors must carry out this advice or forfeit their offices.' Compared with other African countries, Egypt was highly developed both socially and economically. Nevertheless, the British carried out many improvements, especially in irrigation. The Aswan dam was completed in 1902. It stored sufficient water to irrigate the Nile valley all the year round, and for the first time in five thousand years Egyptian agriculture became independent of variations in the annual Nile floods. In other fields, however, the problem was not the lack of modernisation but the fact that modernisation had outrun the financial resources of the country. Indeed, the foremost aim of Lord Cromer, who as consul-general from 1883 until 1907 held the position of supreme power, was to simplify the elaborate government of the khedives, and so to lighten the burden of taxation upon the peasant *fellahin*.

Material benefits, however, did not endear the British to the Egyptians, and discontent soon developed into nationalist demands for their withdrawal. Already by the 1890s most Egyptian politicians were nationalists, and from then on Anglo-Egyptian relations ran round in a vicious circle. The nationalists had only one demand: that the British should quit Egypt. The British replied that they could not do so until a really strong and financially stable government had been established. This was impossible because the nationalists would not co-operate with the khedive and the British to form one. Thus a growing gulf of misunderstanding and hostility separated the rulers from the ruled. In 1914, when Turkey sided with Germany in the First World War, and when Britain as a counter-measure declared a protectorate over Egypt, this gulf grew wider. Egypt became the base for all British military operations in the Middle East. Egyptians suffered real hardship from the foreign troops who were quartered among them. These troops requisitioned their labour, their animals and their produce for military purposes. They voiced their resentment against Wingate, the high commissioner for the protectorate, in a popular song:

> Woe on us Wingate,
> Who has carried off our corn,
> Carried off our cotton,
> Carried off our camels,
> Carried off our children,
> Leaving only our lives,
> For love of Allah, now leave us alone.[2]

Egyptian resentment boiled over into open revolt in 1919, when Britain and France failed to keep their promises to grant independence to the Arab provinces of the old Ottoman empire. Britain, now realising that she could only hold the country by force, decided to give way to Egyptian demands. But so suspicious had Egyptians become of British intentions that no politician was prepared to risk his reputation by signing a treaty with the occupying power. In 1922, therefore,

---

[2] George Young, *Egypt* (London, 1927), p. 228.

Britain issued a one-sided declaration, granting Egypt a modified form of independence. British forces still remained in the country, but under a new constitution the khedive was recognised as king, and the parliament was to be elected under a universal male franchise.

One of the immediate results of self-government in Egypt was to show how unreal was the joint rule of Britain and Egypt over the Sudan under the so-called condominium arrangement. The Sudan had been 'reconquered' in 1898 by the Egyptian army with the aid of British troops. The annual deficit in the Sudan's budget, which had persisted from then until 1913, had been met from the Egyptian, and not from the British, Treasury. For twenty-five years after the reconquest Egyptians had held all but a hundred or two of the most senior posts in the army and the civil service. Nevertheless, all real power in the Sudan was exercised by the British governor-general and by the senior British administrators and military officers. British power was exercised on the assumption that the Sudan was a separate country from Egypt, with interests of its own which were more important than those of Egypt. For example, education in the Sudan was launched along English lines, very distinct from the largely French tradition prevailing in Egypt. More sinister still from the Egyptian point of view, the British were planning to use the Nile waters for a great irrigation project in the cotton-growing district of the Gezira, south of Khartoum. This scheme was undoubtedly beneficial to the Sudan, but it emphasised to every Egyptian that the waters of the Nile, the life-line of Egypt, were in the control of another power. In fact, Egypt, which had ruled the Sudan in the nineteenth century, had been squeezed out of it by Britain in the twentieth.

This resentment over the Sudan led, in 1924, to the assassination by an Egyptian nationalist of the governor-general of the Sudan, Sir Lee Stack, when he was passing through Cairo on leave. The British reaction to the incident was severe. King Faud was given twenty-four hours in which to order the withdrawal of all Egyptian officers and army units from the Sudan, and there followed a replacement of nearly all the Egyptian civil officials by British or Sudanese. From this time the Sudan took on more and more the appearance of an ordinary British colony. 'Indirect rule' became the order of the day, and with it there grew up a new concern for the non-Muslim population of the southern Sudan. The British came to distrust the educated Sudanese emerging from the northern schools. They were felt to be disloyal to the government and sympathetic to Egypt. Just as the Egyptians had been excluded from the government of the north, so the northern Sudanese were now excluded from the government of the south, with

the result that the two halves of the country grew further apart instead
of closer together. The north was accessible to the outside world, and
most of the economic development took place there. The south,
though protected from northern and Islamic influences, remained
equally isolated from the economic and social developments which
might have enabled it to stand on its own feet. The results of this
policy were to be disastrous when, on Sudanese independence, a
mainly northern government had to undertake the administration of
the south.

Meanwhile, in Egypt, political power was alternating between the
Wafd party and the court party of the king. The Wafd party was led by
Zaghlul Pasha, a moderate nationalist, who had been forced by the
circumstances of the 1919 rebellion to take up a hostile attitude to the
British. By the 1930s disillusionment with the intrigue and corruption
of the professional politicians had become general. Rich Egyptians –
many of them of the old Mamluk, Turkish class – seemed to get
richer, while the lot of the urban workers and the *fellahin* grew harder.
The mood of the country in 1935 was expressed by the young Gamal
Nasser, then still a pupil at secondary school, who wrote in a school
essay, 'The nation is in danger, and the disputes among the Parties are
being fomented by Imperialism, the Palace, and the Party leaders
themselves. Thus they hope to keep the country divided and busy
with the race for lucrative posts, so that the Egyptians shall forget that
they have a right to freedom.' In their frustration many young people
turned to political groups actively hostile to parliamentary democracy. The most influential of these was the fiercely nationalistic
Muslim Brotherhood. This body aimed at re-establishing a truly
Muslim state in which the great extremes of riches and poverty would
disappear.

In 1936, after years of fruitless negotiations, Britain and Egypt
signed a treaty, the fundamental provision of which was that British
troops were to be confined to the Canal Zone. Although an attempt
was made to solve some of the problems of the Sudan, no real
understanding on this territory was possible. Britain and Egypt
agreed to administer the Sudan in the interests of the Sudanese.
Egyptian army units rejoined the Sudan garrison, and the virtual
exclusion of Egyptian civilians from the Sudan was brought to an end.
The Egyptians had to face the fact that, as a result of the Anglo-
Egyptian estrangement, the sense of Sudanese separateness from
Egypt had gone too far to be undone. This, no less than the temporary
return of British military government to Egypt during the Second
World War and the emergence of a western-supported Jewish state in

Israel, determined that in the long term Egyptian nationalism would continue to grow in hostility towards the West.

THE ITALIAN SPHERES OF INFLUENCE: LIBYA

The remaining parts of Arabic-speaking Muslim Africa were those subject to Italian domination, of which the most turbulent throughout this period was Libya. We have already seen (Chapter 10) how in 1911–12 Italy conquered the Ottoman provinces of Tripolitania and Cyrenaica. The elimination of the Turks, however, merely gave the Italians possession of the coastal towns. They soon came up against the real rulers of the interior, the *shaikhs* of the Sanusi *zawiyas* described in Chapter 8 (p. 100). These *zawiyas* were by now established in all the tribal territories of the nomadic bedouin of Cyrenaica and the Fezzan. The *shaikhs*, though still primarily religious leaders, had come to be regarded by the bedouin Arabs as their natural representatives in all their dealings with the outside world. The *shaikhs* had usually co-operated with the Turkish officials, who had been their fellow Muslims. When the Christian Italians conquered Tripoli and Benghazi they moved into solid opposition. What had been mainly a religious movement now became a nationalist and political one. In 1912 the head of the Sanusi brotherhood, Sayyid Ahmad, moved his headquarters from the Kufra Oasis into southern Cyrenaica and during the next six years concentrated all his energies on organising armed resistance to the Italians. His efforts were supported by Muslims throughout the Middle East. Gifts of money and arms flowed in from unofficial committees in Egypt, Turkey, Syria and the Hijaz. When Italy in 1915 entered the First World War on the side of the Allied Powers, Turkey, which was fighting on the side of Germany and Austria, began to give him official support. When the Allied Powers emerged victorious from the world struggle, Sayyid Ahmad retreated to Istanbul, retaining his position as head of the Sanusi brotherhood but relinquishing his temporal power in Cyrenaica to his nephew, Sayyid Idris, who was to become, twenty-five years later, the first king of Libya.

Idris, between 1918 and 1922, entered into a series of only half-sincere agreements with the Italians, in which he undertook to recognise Italian sovereignty in exchange for a large measure of autonomy in the bedouin areas. In 1922 the Fascist Party of Benito Mussolini seized power in Italy and denounced these agreements. The Arab leaders of Tripolitania and Cyrenaica thereupon met in conference and recognised Idris as *amir* of all Libya, and Idris, having accepted, withdrew to Egypt in anticipation of the expected military action of the Italians. This was launched at the end of the year. From then onwards for nine years, the Libyan bedouin fought a war which, on a smaller scale, can only be likened to the Algerian War of 1954–62. There were never more than 1,000 bedouin under arms, but with the secret support of the entire civil population they engaged the continuous attention of an Italian army of 20,000. They forced the Fascists to adopt methods, such as aerial bombardment and the isolation of the civilian population in concentration camps, which sickened the whole of the civilised world. The main organiser of this phase of Libyan resistance was a Sanusi *shaikh*, Sidi Umar al-Mukhtar, whose capture and public execution by the Italians by 1931 brought military operations to an end. Italy had thus only eight years of undisputed rule before her North African empire was submerged in the Second World War, from which the Libyans under Idris emerged with their right to independence recognised.

THE ITALIAN SPHERES: SOMALIA AND ETHIOPIA

We saw in Chapter 10 how the first round of Italian imperialist expansion in North-East Africa was brought to a halt in 1896 by the decisive victory of the Emperor Menelik at Adowa. In the peace treaty that followed this battle Italy managed to retain her foothold on the Red Sea coast in Eritrea. She also had her protectorate treaties signed in 1889 with the Majerteyn Somali sultans of Alula and Obbia, and her lease from the sultan of Zanzibar of the Benadir ports of Brava, Merka, Mogadishu and Warsheikh. This lease was changed in 1905 into an outright purchase. Until 1905 the Italian government did little to build upon these earlier foundations. Eritrea centred upon the declining port of Massawa, from which the Ethiopian trade was being increasingly diverted to the new harbour of Djibouti in French Somaliland. A railway from Djibouti to Addis Ababa was begun in 1896 and completed in 1918. In Somaliland the Alula and Obbia protectorates were left alone except for occasional visits by Italian gunboats. The Benadir ports were ineffectively administered by two Italian commercial companies, the first of which went bankrupt in 1896, the second in 1904.

In these circumstances the first outburst of Muslim Somali resentment against Christian imperialist domination fell not upon the Italians but upon the British. The small British protectorate on the southern shores of the Gulf of Aden was the home of a great religious leader of the nomadic Somali, Sayyid Muhammad Abdile Hassan. He was known to his British opponents as 'the mad mullah'. Born in 1864 in the region inland from Berbera, Sayyid Muhammad gained an early reputation for piety and learning. During his early travels as a wandering *shaikh* he visited Mogadishu, Nairobi and parts of the Sudan. In all these places he became aware of the threat to Islam of the expanding forces of western Christendom. When Sayyid Muhammad returned home in 1891, he began to preach resistance to the British and was declared by them to be an outlaw. He retreated with his followers into the Haud and the Ogaden, the unadministered no-man's-land between Ethiopia on the one hand and British and Italian Somaliland on the other. From the Haud and the Ogaden Sayyid Muhammad launched attacks on the three neighbouring governments. British, Italian and Ethiopian troops were continuously and expensively engaged in expeditions against him until his death in 1920. Sayyid Muhammad wrote a great number of letters to friends and enemies. His letters to the British were frequently most expressive in their defiance. In one of them he wrote,

> If the country were cultivated or if it contained houses or property, it would be worth your while to fight for it. But the country is all jungle [he meant that it was uncultivated], and that is no use to you. If you want bush and stones you can get these in plenty. There are also many ant-heaps, and the sun is very hot. All you can get from me is war and nothing else.[3]

It was from Sayyid Muhammad that the three or four million nomadic Somali, till then conscious only of their clan loyalties, derived their first sense of a wider national unity. Today he is rightly regarded in Somalia as the father of Somali nationalism. However, unlike the founder of the Sanusi movement, whom he so much resembled, Sayyid Muhammad left no successor. On his death Somali resistance to the British and Italians ceased. Normal colonial governments were developed in British and Italian Somaliland. The centre of political interest in North-East Africa now switched to the renewed plans of the Fascist government of Italy to conquer the kingdom of Ethiopia. This conquest had been long prepared, but it could not be put into operation until Italian troops were freed from the long war against the Sanusi in Libya. The excuse for the attack was found in the disputed frontier between Somali and Ethiopia in the Ogaden. Here the Italians intrigued with the Somali clans who lived within Ethiopian territory and gradually advanced their military posts far across the undemarcated border. At last, in December 1934, the expected clash occurred between an Ethiopian escort patrol accompanying a boundary com-

[3] D. Jardine, *The Mad Mullah of Somaliland* (London, 1923), p. 185.

mission and the garrison of an Italian military post at a place called Walwal. The Emperor Haile Selassie appealed to the League of Nations. Haile Selassie had been crowned in 1930, although he had been the real ruler of Ethiopia since 1916, under his old name of Ras Tafari. In the League of Nations, Britain and France supported his cause but did not show sufficient determination to prevent the Italian aggression. In 1935, therefore, Mussolini's armies marched up the already prepared military roads from Massawa in the north and Mogadishu in the south-east. With their vastly superior weapons they completed their conquest by May 1936. The emperor was forced to become a refugee in England. The Italian East African empire, made up of Eritrea, Ethiopia and Somalia, had become a reality, after being the dream of many Italians since the time of partition of Africa. It was, however, to last only five years.

The effects of Mussolini's militaristic colonialism of the 1920s and 1930s were very wide. Though it has been argued that Italy was only doing in a more ruthless way what other European countries had done in the rest of Africa twenty or thirty years earlier, both the place and the time in fact made a vast difference. By the 1920s and 1930s the other colonial powers had gone far in reforming their colonial policies in the interests of the governed. Britain, especially, had recognised the ultimate right of colonial subjects to govern themselves. In Libya and in Somalia, Italy had put the clock back. In Ethiopia she had committed naked aggression against an internationally recognised state which had shown considerable ability in modernising itself without any outside interference. This was the first occasion on which the peace-keeping activities of the League of Nations had been tested, and they had been found wanting. Adolf Hitler, who had recently come to power at the head of another fascist movement, in Germany, was not slow to read the lesson. In the year of Mussolini's victory over Ethiopia, Hitler set out on the path of aggression which was to lead directly to the Second World War. German troops invaded the Rhineland, the zone between France and Germany which had been demilitarised after the First World War. In the introduction to his history of the Second World War, Winston Churchill drew attention to the influence of Mussolini's action in Ethiopia. He wrote, 'If ever there was an opportunity of striking a decisive blow for a generous cause it was then. The fact that the nerve of the British government was not equal to the occasion, played a part in leading to a more terrible war.'

15 South Africa, 1902–1939

South Africa was the first African country to experience the social stresses resulting from the transformation of an agricultural into an industrial economy. The pace of change between 1900 and the outbreak of the Second World War was faster, and on a larger scale, than in any other part of the continent. By 1939 the concentration of mines and factories on the Witwatersrand was comparable to the industrial regions of Europe and North America. In the centre of the Rand was Johannesburg, the largest city in Africa except for Cairo. From the Rand gold flowed to the banking houses of the world, binding South Africa into the web of international finance and commerce. Yet the fruits of this material prosperity were unevenly distributed. Only gradually did even all the white people reach a high standard of living. Africans, because of their colour, were excluded from all but a meagre share. Political change in no way kept pace with economic advance. The white rulers were restricted by attitudes and policies which had taken root in the nineteenth century and earlier. They seemed incapable of any fresh approach to the racial tensions which became sharper as more and more Africans were integrated into the expanding economy.

SOUTH AFRICA AFTER THE BOER WAR

After defeating the South African Republic (Transvaal) and the Orange Free State in the Anglo-Boer War, the British felt guilty at the way in which they had bullied the two small Boer republics. They tried to conciliate the defeated enemy by yielding, amongst other things, to their demands on the political status of the Africans. Concession to the Boers was considered to be more urgent than protection of African interests. One of the clauses of the Peace of Vereeniging (1902) gave the white people in the conquered Transvaal and the Orange Free State the right to decide whether or not to extend the parliamentary franchise to Africans. When Britain granted self-government to the two territories in 1906 and 1907, political power passed once again into Boer hands, and non-whites were permanently excluded from the vote.

The debate on African rights now shifted from Britain to the four colonies themselves. The political leaders of these colonies wanted to set up a Union. They hoped by this means to put an end to the disputes which had caused the war and to promote the economic and political development of South Africa as a whole. At the heart of the whole idea of union was the necessity evident to every white politician of developing a single policy towards the Africans. As the future Boer leader and statesman Jan Smuts had written in 1892,

> The race struggle is destined to assume a magnitude on the African continent such as the world has never seen, and the imagination shrinks from contemplating; and in that appalling struggle for existence the unity of the white camp will not be the least necessary condition – we will not say of obtaining victory, but of warding off (or, at worst, postponing) annihilation.[1]

If union was to be achieved, three traditional white attitudes towards Africans had somehow to be reconciled. The first was the 'Liberal' tradition of the Cape. The second was *baaskap*, the uncompromising inequality practised in the Transvaal and the Orange Free State. The third was the policy of protective segregation which British governors had tried to adopt in parts of Natal and the Cape and also in the three protectorates of Basutoland, Bechuanaland and Swaziland.

Cape Liberalism was the tradition inherited from the British colonial government of the Cape Colony, which accepted as citizens those Africans and other coloured people who conformed to white standards. Under this system educated Africans who owned or leased property to a certain value could register as parliamentary voters. In 1909 Africans formed 4.7 per cent of the Cape electorate. Cape leaders defended this system not only on grounds of idealism, but also on grounds of expediency. Merriman, a distinguished liberal politician, argued that the colour-blind franchise was a 'safety valve', for 'to allow no African vote at all would be building on a volcano'. Sauer, another Cape leader, in 1904 expressed more genuinely liberal beliefs when he said, 'I do not believe that where representative institutions exist a class that is not represented will ever receive political justice, because after all it is material interests that will eventually prevail, and therefore the class having no political power will suffer.' The Cape Liberals were supported by many educated Africans, who were anxious to preserve their hard-won privileges (such as exemption from the pass laws). They felt they could no longer identify themselves with the mass of tribal Africans, from whom they had grown

[1] W. K. Hancock, *Smuts*, vol. 1 (Cambridge, 1962), p. 30.

187

Africa since 1800

apart. For nearly thirty years John Tengo Jabavu was the mouthpiece of these enfranchised Africans. As early as 1884 he had launched, with white financial backing, the newspaper *Imvo Zabantsundu* (African Opinion), stating that 'the time is ripe for the establishment of a journal in English and Xhosa, to give untrammelled expression to the feelings of the native population'. But *Imvo*'s criticism of white rule was very mild, and Jabavu's faith in the political future of the white Liberals became towards the end of his life (he died in 1921) rather pathetic.

Baaskap was the simple exercise of white domination, which had been evident from the earliest days of Dutch settlement on the Cape frontier. The Boers had taken this attitude with them when they trekked northwards, in the 1830s, and had written it into the constitution of the South African Republic (Transvaal), which proclaimed, 'There shall be no equality in State or Church between white and black.' The miners from England and elsewhere who flocked to South Africa after the discovery of diamonds and gold quickly adopted the *baaskap* attitude. They protected their high wages by an industrial 'colour bar' which prevented Africans from performing skilled work. *Baaskap* led to the intermingling of the races of South Africa, not to their separation. The Boers wanted as much African land as they could get. Like the miners, they thought of the Africans only as cheap labour which had no need of land of its own.

The physical separation of whites and Africans had been attempted in the Cape, first by the Dutch and later by the British colonial government. It had broken down because of the impossibility of controlling the frontier. By the end of the nineteenth century the frontier problem had been replaced by that of the various pockets of land or 'reserves' into which Africans had retreated before the white advance. Separation found a new wave of support among missionaries and administrators. This led to the demarcation of the Transkeian Territories by the Cape government. In addition the British protectorates of Basutoland, Bechuanaland and Swaziland were established. A commission set up after the Boer War by the British high commissioner, Lord Milner, reported in 1905 in favour of the widespread application of separation throughout South Africa. The Cape politician Merriman remarked that such a policy was at least a century too late to be practicable. The advocates of *baaskap* on the other hand, who opposed separation in 1905, were to adopt it some thirty years later. By then there was proportionately less land available on which Africans could lead a separate existence, because the African population had greatly increased.

188

1910: UNION

In the negotiations which led up to union the white people of the two northern colonies and Natal proved themselves more determined to prevent the spread of Liberalism than the Cape delegates were to promote it. At the National Convention of 1908–9 a compromise was reached by which the first Union Parliament was to be elected on the existing colonial franchises. This meant that qualified Africans in the Cape would retain the vote, whereas Africans in Natal, the Transvaal and the Orange Free State would have no political rights. It was further agreed that not even in the Cape should any African be able to stand as a parliamentary candidate. The Cape delegates did succeed in entrenching the franchise provisions in the constitution, so that they could only be amended by a two-thirds majority of both Houses of the Union Parliament sitting together. This, however, was not a very secure safeguard, and the compromise as a whole was certainly felt as a bitter blow by the educated Africans. For once even Jabavu joined forces with his more militant compatriots in trying to resist the form of union decided upon by the National Convention. One of the many meetings called by Africans at this time 'noted with regret that the contemplated Union is to be a Union of two races, namely the British and the Afrikaners – the African is to be excluded'. Only one white Liberal, W. P. Schreiner, supported these African protests. Alone in his community, he felt that human rights were more important than union:

> To embody in the South African constitution a vertical line or barrier separating its people upon the ground of colour into a privileged class or caste and an unprivileged inferior proletariat is as imprudent as it would be to build a grand building upon unsound and sinking foundations. In our South African nation there must be room for many free peoples, but no room for any that are not free, and free to rise.[2]

A delegation which included both Schreiner and Jabavu went to London but failed to persuade the British government to change the proposed Union constitution in any way. The Union of South Africa was established on 31 May 1910. The British government maintained that it could not interfere with the decisions of the National Convention. It declared, however, that the three protectorates of Basutoland, Bechuanaland and Swaziland would not be transferred to the new

---

[2] W. P. Schreiner to J. C. Smuts, 2 August 1908, *Selections from the Smuts Papers*, vol. 2, ed. W. K. Hancock and Jean van der Poel (Cambridge, 1966), p. 450.

South African state until it had become clear how the racial provisions of the constitution would work in practice.

Though Jabavu soon reverted to his alliance with the white politicians of the Cape, other more politically conscious Africans launched in 1912 the (South) African National Congress, as a Union-wide body to protect African interests. Solomon Plaatje, a highly cultured Tswana journalist and writer, became the secretary-general of the Congress. The first legislation denounced by the Congress was the Natives Land Act of 1913, which prevented Africans from acquiring land outside their own areas. Of this Act Plaatje wrote, 'Awakening on Friday morning, June 20th 1913, the South African Native found himself a pariah [outcast] in the land of his birth.' Javabu wrote in favour of the Act, because it had been introduced by Sauer, one of the Cape Liberals in the government. This proved the end of the old man's influence among his fellow Africans. His failure was but one sad facet of the failure of the Liberal cause in general. Liberalism became hopelessly compromised by the discriminatory legislation of the Union government. The attitudes that prevailed in South Africa were summed up by an Afrikaner historian fifty years later when he said,

Particularly significant was the fact that the act and 'compromise' of Union enabled the ex-Republics of the Transvaal and the Free State to indoctrinate the rest of the Union with their traditions and ideals. This was eminently true of the two great principles which counted as corner-stones of the national existence of the Afrikaner people: republicanism, and the practice and theory of the inequality between white men and black men.[3]

SMUTS AND HERTZOG

Smuts, who served under General Botha until 1919 and then became prime minister of the Union, was a man of great learning, with profound insights in the fields of religion, philosophy and science. In 1917 he became a member of the British War Cabinet in the war against Germany, and from then until his death in 1950 he was looked upon as a statesman of world renown. He was a close friend of Sir Winston Churchill during the Second World War and was one of the founders of the United Nations Organisation. Yet on the racial problem, which surely would have benefited from the application of such a penetrating mind, he lacked any constructive ideas. In 1906 he had written to Merriman

190   [3] D. W. Krüger, *The Age of the Generals* (Johannesburg, 1961), pp. 9–10.

I sympathise profoundly with the native races of South Africa, whose land it was long before we came here to force a policy of dispossession on them. And it ought to be the policy of all parties to do justice to the natives and to take all wise and prudent measures for their civilisation and improvement. But I don't believe in politics for them . . . When I consider the political future of the natives in South Africa, I must say I look into shadows and darkness; and then I feel inclined to shift the intolerable burden of solving the problem to the ampler shoulders and stronger brains of the future. Sufficient unto the day is the evil thereof.[4]

This timidity pervaded the first ten years of the Union's history. Meanwhile the racial problems were becoming more difficult, and the younger generation of white people seemed no more capable of solving them. The African policy of Botha and Smuts was muddled and indecisive. It consisted of a further dose of *baaskap*, of colour bar and pass laws, coupled with a half-hearted attempt to put into practice some of the recommendations of Milner's commission on the subject of separation.

In 1922 white mine-workers struck and seized control of the Rand, because the mine-owners threatened to employ Africans as skilled workers at lower wages than the whites enjoyed. Smuts had to use soldiers to put down this 'rebellion'. Consequently he was defeated in the 1924 election by a combination of the Labour Party, which represented the views of the rebellious white miners, and the Afrikaner National Party. This party had been formed by General Hertzog in 1913. Although he was one of the main architects of *apartheid*, Hertzog was one of the most honest of the white politicians. He rightly said that it was the fear of being overwhelmed and swept aside by the vastly superior number of Africans that was at the root of the white attitude: 'The European is severe and hard on the Native because he is afraid of him. It is the old instinct of self-preservation. And the immediate outcome of this is that so little has been done in the direction of helping the Native to advance.' His policy was to remove this fear by physically separating the races, so as to create two South Africas, one white, the other African. He believed that when Africans were deprived of political and other rights in the Union as a whole, they should be given compensation in the form of more land and of some measure of local self-government.

Hertzog never abandoned his Afrikaner principles. He stood for the primacy of the Afrikaans language in South Africa and for the abandonment of any deference to British policy in international affairs. Nevertheless he welcomed a reconciliation of the Dutch and British elements in the white population. When the world economic

[4] Hancock, *Smuts*, vol. I, p. 221.

31*a* Western South Africa from 1900: minerals, communications and industrial areas
31*b* Eastern South Africa from 1900: minerals, communications and industrial areas

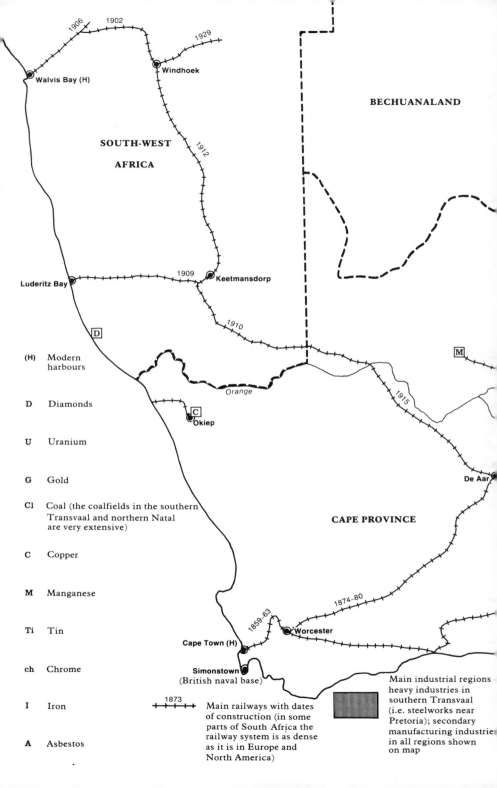

1906   1902

1929

Walvis Bay (H)

Windhoek

BECHUANALAND

SOUTH-WEST
AFRICA

1912

1909   Keetmansdorp

Luderitz Bay

1910

M

(H)   Modern
       harbours

Orange

1915

D   Diamonds

C
Okiep

U   Uranium

G   Gold

De Aar

Cl   Coal (the coalfields in the southern
       Transvaal and northern Natal
       are very extensive)

CAPE PROVINCE

C   Copper

M   Manganese

Ti   Tin

1874–80

ch   Chrome

1859–63

I   Iron

Worcester

Cape Town (H)

Simonstown
(British naval base)

Main industrial regions
heavy industries in
southern Transvaal
(i.e. steelworks near
Pretoria); secondary
manufacturing industries
in all regions shown
on map

A   Asbestos

1873

Main railways with dates
of construction (in some
parts of South Africa the
railway system is as dense
as it is in Europe and
North America)

Anglo-Boer War, 1899–1902, was fought over Transvaal, Orange Free State, northern Natal and parts of Cape Colony.

After the war the defeated Boer Republics, the South African Republic and the Orange Free State, became British Crown Colonies of the Transvaal and the Orange River Colony.

At Union, 1910, the four British colonies became provinces of the Union: the Cape province, Natal, the Transvaal – the Orange Free State reverted to its republican name.

The mandated territory of South-West Africa was administered like a fifth province of the Union until the 1970s.

In 1960 South Africa became a Republic, and in 1961 broke away from the Commonwealth. The word 'Union' was dropped from the title of the state.

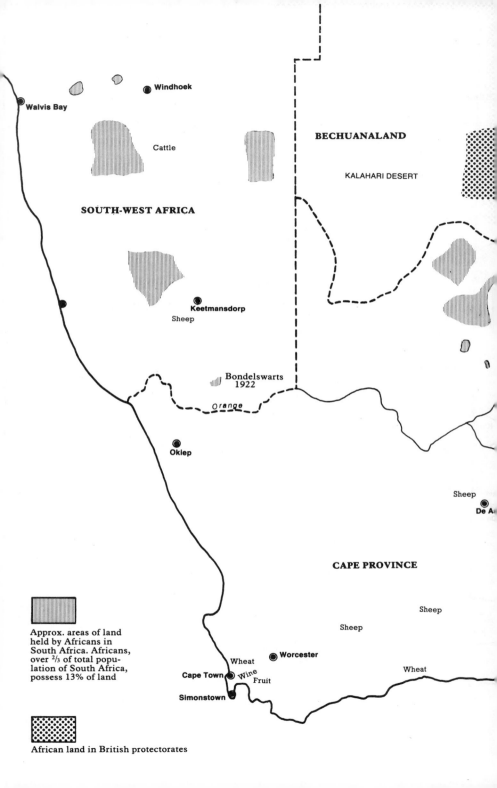

Walvis Bay

Windhoek

Cattle

SOUTH-WEST AFRICA

BECHUANALAND

KALAHARI DESERT

Keetmansdorp

Sheep

Bondelswarts
1922

Orange

Okiep

Sheep

De A

CAPE PROVINCE

Sheep

Sheep

Sheep

Worcester

Wheat

Cape Town

Wine

Fruit

Wheat

Simonstown

Approx. areas of land
held by Africans in
South Africa. Africans,
over ⅔ of total popu-
lation of South Africa,
possess 13% of land

African land in British protectorates

crisis of 1929–33 produced a demand among the white electorate for a 'national' government, composed of the leaders of the two main parties, Hertzog was prepared to enter a coalition with Smuts. In 1934 most of Hertzog's Afrikaner National Party joined with most of Smuts's South African Party to form the United Party, which was to remain in power till 1948. Smuts's side of the compromise was to support the Natives Representation Act, introduced in 1936, which brought to an end the registration of qualified Africans as voters on the common roll with whites in the Cape province. Hertzog's side of the compromise was to modify his anti-British line, both inside South Africa and in relation to the Commonwealth. Among Smuts's followers there was one, the brilliantly clever and deeply religious Jan Hofmeyr, who spoke against the 1936 Act. Hofmeyr said,

> By this Bill we are sowing the seeds of a far greater potential conflict than is being done by anything in existence today. We have many educated and semi-educated Natives in South Africa. Many of them have attained to, and many more of them are advancing towards, European standards. They have been trained on European lines. They have been taught to think and act as Europeans. We may not like it, but those are the plain facts. Now what is the political future for those people? This Bill says to these Natives 'There is no room for you. You must be driven back on your own people.' But we drive them back in hostility and disgruntlement, and do not let us forget this, that all this Bill is doing for these educated Natives is to make them the leaders of their own people, in disaffection and revolt.[5]

Although Hofmeyr was a cabinet minister in the governments of Hertzog and Smuts, his words were received in stony silence. Much more significant than Hofmeyr in South African electoral terms were the nineteen 'Purified Nationalists', led by D. F. Malan, who refused to follow Hertzog into the coalition. These followers of Malan advocated still sterner measures to ensure the survival of the white man in South Africa. In 1934 they were not very important politically. But in racially divided communities, where a minority race holds power, 'the enemy is always on the Right', that is, the racial extremists. The future in South Africa lay with those nineteen members, whose successors, in 1948, were to sweep the United Party from power and introduce yet another round of racialistic legislation.

THE AFRICAN PREDICAMENT

By 1939 the economic and political grievances of the African population in South Africa were already so great that a revolution would not

[5] Alan Paton, *Hofmeyr* (Cape Town, 1964), pp. 227–8.

32*a* Western South Africa from 1900: agricultural products; areas of African settlement
32*b* Eastern South Africa from 1900: agricultural products; areas of African settlement

have been surprising. The material prosperity of the country depended on the gold-mines; the gold-mines depended on African labour. Yet African workers in the mines, as also in the growing number of industrial jobs, received about one-eighth of the wages paid to white men. They were supposed to have their homes in the 'reserves' and to come and work in the white towns as migrant labourers without their families. The social and moral harm caused by this frequent disruption of family life was generally ignored by the white employers. Yet the land left to the Africans was totally inadequate to support them. In 1913 Africans, who formed nearly three-quarters of the population, possessed only 11 per cent of the land of South Africa, and this amount was only with great difficulty increased to 13 per cent by the late 1960s through government purchase under Hertzog's legislation of 1936. Many Africans had long before this abandoned the impoverished reserves to live permanently in slums on the outskirts of the white towns. By 1936 more than 1,000,000 (22 per cent) Africans had become urban dwellers. Another 2,000,000 were working on white farms, completely subject to their masters. They received wages that were so low that it was only just possible for them to pay their taxes. The prices of most things that Africans bought went up 50 per cent between the two world wars, yet African wages were nearly stationary. Africans had no means of increasing their wages or improving their conditions of work. The colour-bar laws prevented them from performing skilled work. Their wages were fixed by law. It was a criminal offence for them to combine in strike action. Their every movement was controlled by pass laws, which required that all Africans outside the reserves must carry a variety of permits. As early as 1919 a Johannesburg newspaper, *The Star*, had commented that 'the Native is crowded off the land, denied a permanent foothold in urban areas, exploited at every point, badgered from pillar to post, and under disabilities of all kinds, whether he stays at home or seeks work away from it'.

Nevertheless African reactions to these conditions of discrimination and restriction were still very far from revolutionary. During the inter-war years the African National Congress had little influence or authority even among Africans. It continued to hold its conventions year by year on the outskirts of Bloemfontein, but in 1938 it still had fewer than 4,000 members. Much more significant through most of this period was the Industrial and Commercial Union, founded in 1919 by Clements Kadalie, an ambitious clerk from Nyasaland. At one time the ICU could boast a membership of 200,000. But the ICU became unwieldy. Its central organisation was weak, and it was unable to operate effectively among the all-important mine-workers. The employers' control over the African mine-workers was extremely strict. Like its rival, the African National Congress, the ICU was rent by dissensions between communists and more moderate leaders. It failed to influence the government in labour matters, just as the ANC failed to divert Hertzog from his goal of territorial separation.

Even in 1940 Africans were still remarkably restrained and tolerant towards the white society in which, economically, they were becoming ever more integrated. This was due partly to the fact that South Africa was by far the richest country in Africa, and African wages, low though they were compared with those received by the whites, were still higher than in most of the continent. More money was available in South Africa to spend on African education, which, at the secondary level at least, was of a high standard. Africans therefore demanded no more than to receive a greater share in the wealth of the country and to be considered as citizens in their own land. Their nationalism was subdued – markedly so in comparison with the strident Afrikaner nationalism which was growing up at the same time. Many young Africans were hopeful about the future. There was still room for political adjustment between the races, and if the white people had earnestly desired to create a multiracial nation, they could still have done so. But, as we have seen, the opinion of white South Africans was in fact moving rapidly in the opposite direction. To secure election by a white constituency, an ambitious politician had to go one step further than his rivals on the racial issue, and always in the same extreme direction. Therefore, though all seemed peaceful enough on the surface, the sands of good will were in fact fast running out.

SOUTH-WEST AFRICA

We noted in Chapter 13 that the German colony of South-West Africa became a League of Nations mandated territory administered by South Africa. The country was in fact governed as if it were part of the Union, and local resistance was put down by force. In 1922 the Bondelswarts, a Nama group who had lost much of their land to the Germans, opposed the levying of a dog tax. Dogs were of great importance to them for herding and hunting. A police force was sent against them and their village was bombed. The police commented, 'The effects of the lesson taught in this short campaign will have an indelible impression not only on the minds of those who resorted to the use of arms in defiance of lawful authority, but on other native tribes in this territory as well.'

Land-hungry white South African farmers eagerly bought the cheap farms in the country, the government providing funds to enable them to purchase stock and equipment. By 1935 there were 32,000 settlers in the territory (some of them Germans who had stayed on), and nearly one-third of the land was in their possession. Much of the rest was desert. The Africans were forced to live in reserves and to labour for the white man to get enough money to pay their taxes. They had merely exchanged one hard master – the Germans – for another.

16 The Second World War

The Second World War is the great turning-point in the history of modern Africa. Before it broke out, the pace of change in Africa, since the establishment of colonial rule at the end of the nineteenth and the beginning of the twentieth century, had been steady and unhurried. After the war this gradual pace increased in momentum until it became uncontrollable.

In 1939 the whole of Africa was under European rule. The Italians were in occupation of Ethiopia. British troops remained in Egypt, in the Suez Canal Zone. Even Liberia was in practice dominated by the American Firestone Rubber Company. The Union of South Africa was an independent Dominion within the British Commonwealth, but the African population there had less freedom than the inhabitants of the colonial territories. Everywhere colonial rule appeared to be firmly rooted. Every colonial territory had by this time police and military forces adequate for all ordinary situations. With modern, fast communications, reinforcements could have been brought quickly from overseas to deal with any special emergency. But, for twenty years or more in most colonies, there had been no such emergencies. Colonial governments had come to be regarded as too strong to be successfully challenged.

Nevertheless, the concept of trusteeship in colonial policy had begun to produce some practical results during the twenty years since the end of the First World War. Trusteeship was linked with the policy of indirect rule in the British African territories. It had everywhere given African communities a considerable say in the management of their own affairs at the local level and through their traditional authorities. In the West African colonies a start had even been made in the Africanisation of the central institutions of the colonial government. Africans were recruited as administrative officers and some African members were included in the legislative councils and assemblies which advised the governors. Just after the war a former British colonial officer turned writer expressed the opinion that 'We shall not disappear tomorrow, nor the day after tomorrow [he meant for a long

200

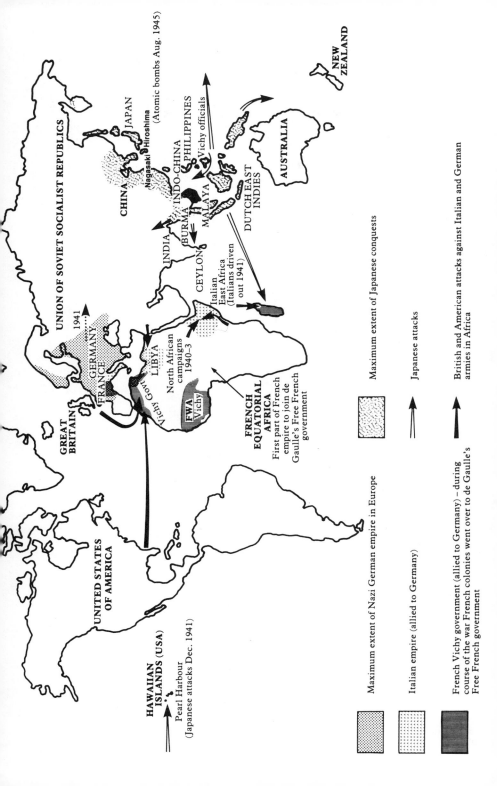

UNION OF SOVIET SOCIALIST REPUBLICS

JAPAN

(Atomic bombs Aug. 1945)
Hiroshima
Nagasaki

CHINA

INDO-CHINA

PHILIPPINES

Vichy officials

NEW ZEALAND

AUSTRALIA

DUTCH EAST INDIES

MALAYA

BURMA

INDIA

CEYLON

Italian East Africa (Italians driven out 1941)

1941

GERMANY

FRANCE

Vichy Govt.

LIBYA

North African campaigns 1940-3

FWA Vichy

FRENCH EQUATORIAL AFRICA
First part of French empire to join de Gaulle's Free French government

GREAT BRITAIN

UNITED STATES OF AMERICA

HAWAIIAN ISLANDS (USA)
Pearl Harbour
(Japanese attacks Dec. 1941)

Maximum extent of Japanese conquests

Japanese attacks

British and American attacks against Italian and German armies in Africa

Maximum extent of Nazi German empire in Europe

Italian empire (allied to Germany)

French Vichy government (allied to Germany) – during course of the war French colonies went over to de Gaulle's Free French government

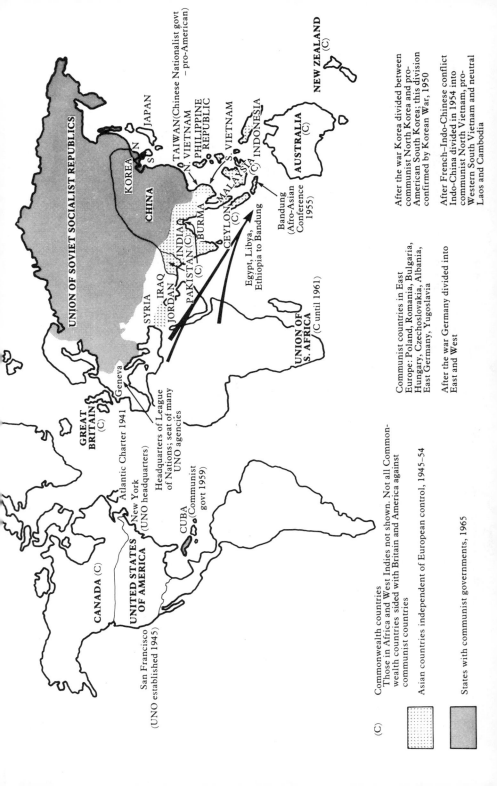

UNION OF SOVIET SOCIALIST REPUBLICS

JAPAN

KOREA

N. VIETNAM

TAIWAN (Chinese Nationalist govt – pro-American)

PHILIPPINE REPUBLIC

S. VIETNAM

INDONESIA

NEW ZEALAND (C)

CHINA

BURMA

MALAYSIA (C)

CEYLON (C)

INDIA (C)

PAKISTAN (C)

IRAQ

SYRIA

JORDAN

AUSTRALIA (C)

Bandung (Afro-Asian Conference 1955)

Egypt, Libya, Ethiopia to Bandung

UNION OF S. AFRICA (C until 1961)

GREAT BRITAIN (C)

Geneva

Atlantic Charter 1941

Headquarters of League of Nations; seat of many UNO agencies

New York (UNO headquarters)

CUBA (Communist govt 1959)

CANADA (C)

UNITED STATES OF AMERICA

San Francisco (UNO established 1945)

After the war Korea divided between communist North Korea and pro-American South Korea; this division confirmed by Korean War, 1950

After French-Indo-Chinese conflict Indo-China divided in 1954 into communist North Vietnam, pro-Western South Vietnam and neutral Laos and Cambodia

Communist countries in East Europe: Poland, Romania, Bulgaria, Hungary, Czechoslovakia, Albania, East Germany, Yugoslavia

After the war Germany divided into East and West

(C) Commonwealth countries
Those in Africa and West Indies not shown. Not all Commonwealth countries sided with Britain and America against communist countries

Asian countries independent of European control, 1945–54

States with communist governments, 1965

time to come], but the Governor of each British colony is in fact presiding over the liquidation of that colony – as a colony. It is to become a self-governing dominion.'[1] The French policies of cultural assimilation and economic association were designed to make France and her colonies permanently interdependent. No Frenchman seriously thought that any colony would ever achieve a political status independent of France. A few Africans, however, were rising to positions of power in France itself and were preparing to carry French political party organisation back into the French African territories.

The flaw in all colonial policies was the denial of scope for the political abilities and ambitions of the educated elite. In the British territories indirect rule gave status and often considerable power to hereditary chiefs and other members of the traditional, tribal aristocracies. On the other hand it left the new educated professional class without either political influence or social recognition. Under the French system, the educated African could rise higher in the government service and enjoy more social respect. He could do this, however, only at the price of complete identification with France and French culture. He had to cut most of his ties with his fellow Africans. The first generation of educated Africans – men like Casely Heyford of the Gold Coast or Blaise Diagne of Senegal, Herbert Macaulay of Lagos or Tengo Jabavu of the Cape Colony – while pressing for a greater participation in central government by the educated elite, accepted the existing gulf between educated and uneducated, between the traditional rural society and the modern, urban society. None of them tried to build up a mass following. Probably they would have been unable to do so had they tried. Certainly the attempt would have brought them into serious trouble with the colonial governments. Among the second generation of educated Africans there were a few, like Azikiwe, who understood that major reforms would not come until the educated had made political contact with the uneducated. Others younger still, like Nkrumah and Senghor, were in 1939 just setting out on their overseas studies and were to return with the same lesson even more firmly in mind. But, had it not been for the Second World War and for the profound change in the balance of world power that followed it, it is very doubtful whether even Nkrumah's generation would have lived to see African independence, let alone whether they themselves would have brought it about. The educational policies of both France and Britain had made it certain that independence would come to Africa within the twentieth century.

[1] W. R. Crocker, *On Governing Colonies* (London, 1947), pp. 66–7.

34 The post-war world

The fact that it came in the 1950s and 1960s was due very largely to the five-year struggle around the globe. The colonising nations emerged from this conflict only in the second rank of world powers. America and Russia, the two powers of first rank, had each of them a reason for speeding up the process of decolonisation. Another, though less important, reason why decolonisation came when it did was the direct involvement of large numbers of Africans in the war itself. Therefore, just as we had to look outside Africa in order to understand the beginning of the colonial period, so now we have to look outside Africa in order to understand its end.

THE WAR, 1939–45

The war that broke out in 1939 was in many ways a continuation of the great struggle of 1914–18. Germany was determined to reverse its military defeat in that war and to unite all German-speaking people, many of whom lived beyond the frontiers of Germany. Another German grievance was the loss of her African colonies after the First World War. Germany demanded the return of these colonies, so as to give her 'her rightful place in the tropical sun'. In 1933 Adolf Hitler, leader of the National Socialist (Nazi) Party, came to power in Germany. He turned the parliamentary democracy into a dictatorship. Nazi racial attitudes were even more extreme than those of Fascist Italy. German nationalism was stirred up and was deliberately directed against racial minorities, especially Jews. Britain and France failed either to put a stop to German aggression in its early days or to offer a constructive solution to the problems of Germany's relations with the small states of central Europe. German aggression against these countries led to a general European war, in the first year of which German armies overran most of the continent. France surrendered in June 1940 and was humiliatingly partitioned. The northern and western part was placed under German military rule. The southern part was ruled by the puppet Vichy government, which was subservient to German interests.

In Europe, only Britain and a few small, neutral countries remained outside the new German empire. Mussolini was the ally and tool of Hitler. One British success during the defeats and humiliations of the early years of the war was the expulsion in 1941 of Italy from Eritrea, Somalia and Ethiopia. Many African soldiers took part in the fighting in the Horn of Africa. The Emperor Haile Selassie returned to his kingdom at the beginning of the campaign and led his own guerrilla band into Addis Ababa. In spite of British attempts to set up a military administration for the period of the war, he was able to reassert his authority. Thus Ethiopia regained its independence after five years of Italian rule. In North Africa the German Afrika Korps joined the Italian army in an attack on Egypt and the Suez Canal, which was so vital to British supply lines. Meanwhile the vast military struggle was extending itself still further. In 1941 Hitler invaded Russia, despite an alliance which had been signed between the Soviet state and Nazi Germany as recently as 1939. German armies drove deep into Russia but were halted short of Moscow by the Red Army and by the terrible Russian winter. Even more fateful was Japan's entry into the war on the side of the Nazis.

The history of modern Japan had until that time provided an object lesson for non-European peoples all over the world. After two centuries of deliberate isolation from European influence, the rulers of Japan in the 1860s realised that the only way to avoid European domination was to modernise their country's economy and society along western lines – to beat the West at its own game. Consequently Japan became the industrial power of the Far East and entered upon a stage of imperial expansion similar to that of the West European powers. After defeating Russia in 1905, Japan acquired Korea and Manchuria and in the 1930s conquered large parts of China. Her attack on the American Pacific Fleet at Pearl Harbour in the Hawaiian Islands in December 1941, however, brought the United States into the war as the ally of Britain. This proved to be the turning-point of the war.

During the early part of 1942 the Japanese overwhelmed the European empires in South-East Asia. Within months of Pearl Harbour the Japanese had driven the British out of their possessions in Malaya and Burma, Sarawak, Borneo and Hong Kong, the Dutch out of Indonesia, and the Americans out of the Philippines. Japan also occupied Indo-China by agreement with the government of Vichy France, whose officials continued to administer the territory under Japanese supervision. India, Ceylon and even Madagascar were threatened with invasion. German and Japanese submarines made the seas of the world unsafe for Allied shipping. At last, however, in 1942, the tide of war started to turn, as Russia and America mobilised their huge resources. The Red Army pushed the Germans out of Russia. American and British forces landed in the Maghrib. They overthrew the Vichy governments of Morocco and Algeria and linked up in Tunisia with the British army that had chased the Germans and Italians out of Cyrenaica and Tripolitania. Then the allies landed in Italy and fought their way desperately northwards. Mussolini was deposed, and was murdered after the Italian government made peace. In June 1944 Hitler's European empire was invaded by a great Anglo-American task-force, which landed in northern France. After a year of bitter fighting and widespread destruction, the Allied and Russian forces met in central Germany. Hitler shot himself, and Germany surrendered in May 1945. In the Far East America defeated the Japanese in a series of mighty sea-battles and reoccupied the Philippines. Britain slowly pushed the Japanese out of Burma, using for the purpose many African troops. The war was brought to an abrupt end in August 1945 when the first atomic bombs were dropped on the Japanese cities of Hiroshima and Nagasaki.

THE WORLD AFTER THE WAR

The world of 1939 had been changed almost beyond recognition. Political, economic and military leadership had passed from the West European countries to the two super-states, America and Russia. Both had been dragged by the war out of their previous isolation from international affairs. Europe became divided into their allies or satellites. Eastern Europe passed under communist control, while Western Europe was defended by American armies and received massive American aid in reviving its shattered economies. The 'hot' war was now transformed into the 'cold' war, because of the enmity between the capitalist and communist systems. The 'Iron Curtain' split Europe down the middle. Outside Europe, South America remained under the economic and, more unwillingly, under the political influence of the United States. Africa was still the colonial possession of the old European states. In Asia, with the defeat of Japan, there developed a political vacuum. The way in which this vacuum was filled was to be of enormous significance for the rest of the world, including Africa.

THE WAR AND AFRICA

Soldiers from all over Africa were recruited by Britain and France. They went into action in Ethiopia, North Africa and Italy and against the Japanese in Burma. The colour bar operated in the South African army, as it did in that country's industries. In spite of not being allowed to bear arms, many Africans from the Union were eager to join up as drivers or labourers. As one leader of the African National Congress remarked, 'The country is in danger. Even if a man has quarrelled with his wife, when he sees an enemy approaching his home, he gets up to settle with that enemy.'

Most of the thousands of Africans who became soldiers had never before been out of their native lands. On active service, despite the dangers and hardships, they were well fed and clothed and comparatively well paid. Many of them learned to read newspapers, to listen to wireless bulletins and to take an interest in world affairs. They learned to see their own countries in perspective from the outside. On their return home, many of them became dissatisfied with conditions which were not so attractive as army life in countries more developed than their own. With the fighting in North Africa, and with the loss of the rich Far East colonies, Africa had become of vital strategic and economic importance to the Allies. The production of raw materials, such as vegetable oils and minerals, had gone ahead by leaps and bounds. New aerodromes, roads and harbours had been constructed. Labour was in great demand, and hundreds of thousands of people flocked to the towns. But because European and American industries were so closely geared to the war effort, and after the war to their own reconstruction, Africa's growing demand for consumer goods could not be met. The shortage of goods, and their high prices, resulted in disturbances and attacks on foreign shops. In the Gold Coast, for example, economic and political frustrations led to serious riots in 1948. The Watson Commission, which was sent out to investigate the causes of these riots, had this to say about the grievances of the ex-servicemen in particular:

The large number of African soldiers returning from service with the Forces, where they had lived under different and better conditions, made for a general, communicable state of unrest. Such Africans, by reason of their contacts with other peoples, including Europeans, had developed a political and national consciousness. The fact that they were disappointed at conditions on their return, either from specious promises made before demobilisation or a general expectancy of a golden age for heroes, made them the natural focal point for any general movement against authority.

Besides political unrest, the wartime and post-war boom in raw material prices had a most important effect on the economies of African countries. The colonial powers were unable to pay for these raw materials immediately in manufactured goods. Many African colonies became for a time the creditors of their colonial masters. These credits passed mostly into the hands of the colonial governments rather than into the hands of the individual producers. This happened because the colonial governments, in order to prevent rising prices and thus to control inflation, bought produce from the growers at one price and sold it on the world market at a higher price. The difference between these two prices was retained in government 207 funds. For good or ill, this marked a big step in the direction of socialism. On the one hand it enabled the colonial governments to embark upon big development schemes for the benefit of the community as a whole. On the other hand, by limiting so drastically the prices paid to the growers, it probably held back the growth of production, as it certainly did the growth of private savings and investment. Above all, it set a pattern of state control which most independent African governments were to follow.

THE WAR AND EUROPEAN PRESTIGE

Most significant for the subsequent spread of nationalism in Africa was what can be termed the psychological effects of the war. The mental attitudes of Europeans and Africans towards each other were greatly changed by the war. Previously Europeans had been able to dominate Africans, not only because of their more advanced military and economic techniques, but also because they *believed* that they were superior and invincible. And most Africans believed this too. The Second World War, even more than the First, completely shattered this myth. Several former colonial powers had been defeated and publicly humiliated. The South-East Asian empires of Britain, France and the Netherlands had collapsed before the Japanese onslaught like straw huts in a storm. The Italian empire in Africa had ceased to exist. The political dissensions which had so weakened France at the beginning of the war had been transferred to the French African colonies. Most of the French officials had sided at first with the racialist Vichy government. Nevertheless, the governor of Tchad, Felix Eboué, by birth a Negro from French Guiana in South America, had supported the Free French resistance to Germany which was led by General de Gaulle. By 1943 the whole of Equatorial Africa had joined de Gaulle, and Eboué had become governor-general at Brazzaville. Only after much intrigue and squabbling did French West Africa and Madagascar follow suit. In the Maghrib countries the civil war between Free France and Vichy had been even more intense. This dissension among Frenchmen lowered their prestige in the eyes of their African subjects. The Maghribis in particular looked upon the American invaders, with their anti-colonial traditions, as liberators. After Sultan Sidi Muhammad of Morocco had met President Roosevelt at Casablanca in 1943 he began to give open support to the nationalist cause.

In British Africa, the contact with British troops in training or in transit in the various African colonies was an important element in the undermining of colonial prestige. It was quickly noticed that the behaviour of these soldiers towards Africans was not the same as that of the colonial officers and traders. They went out with African girls in the same way as African troops abroad made friends with local women. As a result the white man – and white woman – ceased to appear as a lofty, superior being and was seen to be a similar kind of person to the African himself. The Zimbabwean African leader, Ndabaningi Sithole, has described in his book *African Nationalism* how the first Europeans contacted by Africans had appeared to them like spirits or like gods:

The African was simply overawed and perplexed. The white man's 'houses that move on the water', his 'bird that is not like other birds', his 'monster that spits fire and smoke' (these are all Sindebele expressions) amazed him. The dynamite that exploded the huge rocks in the mines confirmed the belief that the white man was a god possessing all power and knowledge.[2]

Disillusionment soon set in, but the prestige of the white man was not finally shattered till the Second World War. Sithole went on:

The girls of England, France and Italy who went out with African soldiers, did not help the preservation of the white myth. The African soldiers found themselves at the front line of war with one purpose in view; to kill every white enemy soldier they could get hold of. African soldiers saw white soldiers wounded, dying and dead. The bullet had the same effect on black and white alike. After spending four years hunting white enemy soldiers, the African never again regarded them as gods.[3]

THE INDEPENDENCE OF ASIA, THE UNITED NATIONS AND BANDUNG

After the war was over, by far the most important world event for the future of Africa was the momentous step taken by Britain in 1947 of liquidating her huge Indian empire. The subcontinent was partitioned between India and Pakistan, which became independent states within the Commonwealth. Ceylon did the same. Burma, on becoming independent, did not even join the Commonwealth. These countries between them were inhabited by well over 500 million people, about one-seventh of mankind. Much of the area had been ruled by Britain since the eighteenth century, and many ancient civilisations had flourished there before the British came. To the indigenous traditions of learning there had been added a powerful

---

[2] Ndabaningi Sithole, *African Nationalism* (2nd edn, London, 1968), pp. 157, 159.
[3] Ibid. pp. 162, 163.

stream of western education, beside which the primary and secondary schools of colonial Africa represented the merest trickle. In India and Pakistan, Burma and Ceylon university graduates existed in tens of thousands. They had long filled the learned professions and occupied all but the very highest positions in the state. Political parties of a modern nationalist kind had been growing up through half a century. The active supporters of these parties amounted to hundreds of thousands or even millions of people. So long as this vast region remained obedient to European rule, it must have seemed hard for any African nationalist to believe that the authority of British or French colonial governments in Africa could be successfully challenged. With the sudden liberation of South Asia the obstacle to African independence at once assumed a completely new look. Not only had the precedents been set, but four powerful outside allies had been added to the cause.

The liberation of the British Indian empire did not carry such revolutionary implications to the colonial powers as it did to Africans. The colonial powers considered that South Asia was ready for independence, but that South-East Asia and Africa were not. In 1941, before America was drawn into the war, Roosevelt and Churchill had met on a battleship off the Canadian coast and had signed the Atlantic Charter as a statement of their hopes for the future of mankind. They had then declared that they would 'respect the right of all peoples to choose the form of government under which they will live' and that they wished to see 'sovereign rights and self-government restored to those who had been deprived of them'. In Africa, as in Asia, many of the people who were politically conscious imagined that this statement applied to them. Churchill, however, later qualified it, saying, 'At the Atlantic meeting we had in mind, primarily, the restoration of sovereignty to the nations of Europe now under Nazi yoke. So that is quite a separate problem from the progressive evolution of self-governing institutions in the regions and peoples which owe allegiance to the British Crown.' In 1944 Arthur Creech Jones, later to be colonial secretary in the post-war Labour Government, stated, 'Britain today is in the Colonies and she cannot withdraw; nor do I think it desirable that she should. We are pledged to the pursuit of a policy of constructive trusteeship, a policy which is to lead, we hope, to partnership inside the British Commonwealth.'

France was even more forthright in her intention to remain a colonial power, not only in Africa but in South-East Asia as well. In 1944 de Gaulle replaced the old empire by the new French Union, in which the former colonial 'subjects' now became 'citizens'. In the same year a conference of Free French officials was held at Brazzaville. These officials whole-heartedly agreed with the colonial minister, Réné Pléven, when, in a speech to the conference, he said:

We read at one time or another that this war must be ended with what is called a liberation of colonial peoples. In the greater France which includes the colonies there are no peoples to liberate. There are only populations which feel themselves to be French and which wish to take a greater part in the life and democratic institutions of the French community.[4]

In South-East Asia, however, de Gaulle's Free French government took over Indo-China from the discredited Vichy administration, only to become engaged in a long and bitter war against Ho Chi Minh and his communist guerrillas. This ended in military defeat for the French. In 1954 Indo-China became three independent states, one of which, Vietnam, was further partitioned between the communist-dominated North and the pro-western South. In the former Dutch East Indies, Indonesian nationalist groups declared their territory to be independent as early as 1945 and fought against the Dutch when they attempted to move back into their East Indian empire. After several years of conflict, the Indonesians finally achieved full independence as the result of a series of conferences held between 1949 and 1951. Meanwhile, the British had returned to Hong Kong and to Malaysia. In Malaya they, too, had had to fight a long war with communist guerrillas. In this case the colonial power was successful.

During this post-war period the influence of America became decisive for the developing Afro-Asian liberation movement. The main instrument through which American influence operated was the United Nations Organisation, which was founded in 1945 as the successor to the League of Nations. The Charter of the UNO included a comprehensive statement of the rights of all peoples to freedom and justice. This was adopted largely because of American pressure and against the wishes of the colonial powers. It was likewise agreed that the former mandated territories should now come under the supervision of the Trusteeship Council of the United Nations, although South Africa refused point blank to make this transfer in respect of the mandated territory of South-West Africa. One of the conquered Italian colonies – Somalia – was also placed under the Trusteeship Council, which entrusted it to Italy to administer for a limited period only. Eritrea was joined to Ethiopia. When the smaller countries, such as those of Latin America, took their seats in the

[4] 30 January 1944, *Conférence africaine de Brazzaville, 36 janvier–8 février* (Ministère des Colonies, Paris, 1945), p. 22.

United Nations, they fell in enthusiastically behind the attitude of the United States. There is little doubt that the United States encouraged the Indonesian demand for independence and persuaded the Dutch to give way to it.

The independence of the new Asian states radically altered the composition of the United Nations. There was now a large group of lesser powers at the United Nations which demanded the speedy end of colonialism everywhere. The undoubted leader of this group was India. The leaders of India were then developing the idea of 'positive neutralism' as between the capitalist and communist sides of the Cold War. The first big conference of these non-aligned nations was held at Bandung in Indonesia in 1955, with Communist China also taking part. The only African countries then independent were Egypt, Libya and Ethiopia; but observers were sent by the main nationalist parties in the Sudan, the Gold Coast, South Africa and Algeria. The conference declared in its manifesto that 'Colonialism in all its manifestations is an evil, which should be speedily brought to an end', and it called upon the colonial powers to 'grant freedom and independence to subject peoples'. The sense of solidarity among Asian and Middle Eastern countries had now spread to nationalists all over Africa south of the Sahara, who knew that from henceforward they had friends to support them in their struggle. As one Indonesian commented, 'Before Bandung, many had struggled alone, unaided and often unnoticed, fighting first for independence and then for survival. Now it is clear that these hitherto disregarded peoples were no longer alone.' For Asian countries Bandung marked the end of the transition from colonial rule to independence; for Africans it marked the beginning of the last, decisive phase in this revolutionary movement.

17 The last years of colonial rule, 1940–1960

It is very important to remember that the years from 1940 till 1960 were not only the period when African nationalism was building up to its final triumph. They were also by far the most active period in the history of colonial rule. To some extent this was a natural development from what had gone before. During the period up to 1918, as we have seen, colonial governments had had to concentrate on making themselves financially self-supporting on the simplest possible scale. During the 1920s and 1930s there had at least been a little revenue left over from the basic functions of government. With this extra money a start had been made in establishing social services in health, education and welfare. This start had been terribly slowed up by the world slump of the early 1930s. In the course of the great depression the prices of African products had fallen to very low levels for four or five years in succession. The revenues of colonial governments had been drastically reduced because of this. For example, between 1929 and 1932 the European establishment of the Gold Coast was cut from 1,281 officers to 427. However, with the booming prices and revenues of the wartime and post-war years, colonial governments all over Africa could at last make up for 'the years that the locust had eaten'.

Quite apart from the increasing amount of internal development, colonial governments all over tropical Africa were able, for the first time in their history, to obtain very large amounts of financial aid from the colonial powers. The reasons for this are complex. Perhaps the most important element in the new situation was that during the war western governments learned to take a very much larger proportion of their own citizens' incomes in taxation. After the war was over, instead of lowering this taxation to its former levels, these governments turned themselves into 'welfare states'. Western governments spent their greatly increased revenues on social benefits. Pensions and unemployment allowances, health services, subsidised housing and state education were introduced at all levels. From this vastly expanded scale of public expenditure it was much easier than formerly to spare a small proportion for overseas aid. It was consistent with the philosophy underlying the 'welfare state' that the fortunate should assist the less fortunate. At the same time there were reasons of self-interest why colonies should be actively developed at the expense of the colonial power. Colonialism was under international attack. Its continuance could only be defended if the colonies could be shown to be benefiting by the association. Even so, the continuance of colonialism could only be defended on a temporary basis. It was clear even to the most reactionary person in Europe that decolonisation was on the way. In the post-colonial world, former colonies would be safer neighbours if their economies were developing than if they were abandoned in a state of impoverished stagnation. So far as British Africa was concerned, the Colonial Development and Welfare Act of 1940 expressed the new reforming principles in the following terms:

> If full and balanced development is to be obtained, some assistance from outside is necessary at this stage. Few of the colonies possess substantial mineral wealth. The majority are almost wholly dependent on the more limited resources derived from agriculture. Many colonies cannot finance out of their own resources the research and survey work, the schemes of major capital enterprise, and the expansion of administrative and technical staffs which are necessary for their full and vigorous development. Nor can they always afford, in the absence of such development, an adequate standard of health and education services.[1]

A second Colonial Development and Welfare Act passed in 1945 sanctioned the spending of even larger sums of money. Between 1946 and 1955 £210 million, from funds provided by the Act, from private investment, and from money raised by the colonial governments themselves, was spent on development plans in the British territories. Before the war French colonies had been even poorer than the British colonies. Therefore, when money began to pour in, the change was even more startling. Investment came from private sources and from a government fund set up in 1946. This fund, which was known by the initial letters of its French title as FIDES, provided official aid on a scale even larger than the British. The development plans of the nine West African territories alone totalled £277 million for the period 1946–55.

ECONOMIC DEVELOPMENT

This new flow of money, both from expanding internal revenues and from external aid, revolutionised the activities of colonial govern-

[1] *Statement of Policy on Colonial Development and Welfare*, Cmd. 6175 (HMSO, London, 1940), p. 4.

ments during the post-war period. From this time every colony had its planning staff and its development programme. Among the more spectacular projects started were the hydroelectric schemes. The largest of these were on the Nile at Jinja in Uganda, at Kariba on the Zambezi between Northern and Southern Rhodesia, on the Volta river at Akasombo in the Gold Coast, and at Fria and Kimbo in Guinea. The main purpose of all these projects was to supply power for industrialisation. Industries supported in this way were cotton-spinning in Uganda; the extension of copper-mining in Northern Rhodesia; factories in Southern Rhodesia; the smelting of bauxite into aluminium, as well as a whole range of light industries, in the Gold Coast and Guinea. The largest project of all was the Inga scheme for damming the lower Congo. This was brought to a halt by the crisis that followed the independence of the Belgian Congo. The Inga scheme would have supplied half as much electricity as is produced in the whole of Western Europe; construction work on this huge project was resumed by Zaïre once it had become independent and settled its internal conflicts.

Hydroelectric power for industrialisation was, however, only one particularly striking feature of the development programmes with which every colonial government was concerned after the Second World War. Central to every programme was the expansion and diversification of agricultural production. Not only was the production of cash crops for the world market expanded; even more significantly, food for local consumption, especially by the growing populations of the new towns, was increased and improved. Agricultural and veterinary services extended their operations into almost every administrative district. Strenuous efforts were made to educate farmers to adopt improved methods. These included the rotation of crops, contour-bunding to prevent erosion in hilly areas, the consolidation of scattered holdings and the introduction of better tools and simple machinery. Pastoral farmers who had hitherto bred cattle largely for prestige, concentrating on numbers rather than on the yield of milk and meat, were persuaded to accept scientific breeding methods and to produce regularly for the market. This meant using co-operative creameries and abattoirs in the grazing districts instead of moving large herds on the hoof to distant selling-points. Again, fish-marketing organisations were set up in many countries, and refrigerated vans began to visit the fishing communities of the sea-board, lakes and rivers to buy their produce and distribute it to the towns. All these activities demanded in turn a corresponding revolution in transport. The old dirt roads of pre-war Africa could no longer stand up to the weight of traffic that now passed over them. A very large proportion of most development budgets was spent on reconstructing and tarring the main trunk roads.

PROGRESS IN EDUCATION

It was soon realised by all colonial governments in the post-war period that if one limitation on development was money, another and more serious one was the shortage of educated people. Because there had been so few secondary schools in colonial Africa before the war, a large number of Europeans had to be employed to operate the new development plans. These people were expensive. They had to be induced to come to Africa by high salaries, subsidised housing and frequent home leave with free travel. On the political side these new 'invaders' of Africa undid much of the good which they contributed by their skills. Their presence widened the gap between European and Africans. It created the impression that the colonial grip on Africa was tightening, and it intensified political unrest and made all government activities suspect to the people. Education therefore soon became the cornerstone of every development plan.

At the end of the war the vast majority of schools were still mission schools, except in the French territories and in the Muslim parts of British territories. Nearly all of them were primary schools, and most of them provided only four years of education in one or other of the African languages. The first priority for advance was to extend the four-year period to six, the two additional years being devoted very largely to the study of a European language. The main problem here was to train enough primary-school teachers who had the necessary qualifications in English or French. The most significant educational development of the 1940s was the establishment throughout colonial Africa of primary teachers' training centres. In their early days these training centres were essentially schools of English or French. This problem of European languages had to be solved before it was possible to press on with the provision of a more adequate number of secondary schools. Before the war these had been very few indeed. Most territories had only two or three secondary schools, staffed mainly by European teachers. Now these schools had to be multiplied. This could only be done very gradually, by bringing in more teachers from Europe and by employing the fortunate few Africans who had passed through the existing schools. Whereas the reform of primary education had involved only the addition of two years, six new years of education were required for a secondary school. Even if a school was able to add a new class every year, a full secondary school could not be established in less than six years. In fact most schools took much longer than this to grow. Although the 1950s saw a great increase in the number of secondary schools, most of them were dismissing their pupils after only three or four years. The fifth and sixth years of secondary school are still today the greatest bottleneck in African education systems.

The secondary-school output determined the possibilities for higher education. Nevertheless the British government, at least, did not allow the secondary-school bottleneck to hold up the foundation of universities in colonial Africa. A commission set up in 1943 reported two years later that the development of universities was 'an inescapable corollary of any policy which aims at the achievement of colonial self-government'.[2] During the four years after 1945 four university colleges were set up, at Ibadan in Nigeria, at Khartoum in the Sudan, at Achimota in the Gold Coast and at Makerere in Uganda. Some of the money for these universities came from Colonial Development and Welfare funds. The university college at Salisbury in Southern Rhodesia was added in 1953, and that of Fourah Bay (which had been giving some post-secondary education in Sierra Leone since 1827) in 1960. The entrants to these university colleges were inevitably limited to the young people who had passed through the few long-established secondary schools. In all of them fearfully expensive European staffs were built up, while the output of graduates climbed slowly from a hundred to two or three hundred a year. Nevertheless, these were the few hundreds of highly trained people whose existence enabled independence to work when the time arrived. These were the people who would become the senior civil servants, the directors of public corporations, the headmasters and the doctors. The French also trained such people. At this period, however, they trained them almost exclusively in France. It may be that, for those who went, the experience of a great and long-established European university was more worth while from an educational point of view than the somewhat artificial and self-conscious atmosphere of the young universities of British Africa. On the other hand, this policy has left the French-speaking African countries more dependent on France during the period since independence.

It was perhaps in their steady support of educational development at the higher levels that British and French governments showed their awareness of how close they were to decolonisation and their good

[2] *Report of the Commission on Higher Education in the Colonies*, Cmd. 6647 (HMSO, London, 1945), p. 104.

faith in preparing for it. This was in contrast with the Belgians and Portuguese. The most tragic failure in educational development at this period was the Belgian one. Neither in the Congo nor in Belgium itself was a single Congolese given a university education until the very eve of independence. Even secondary education in the Congo remained much scarcer than elsewhere. What makes it more tragic was that it was not a failure of neglect but a failure to estimate the pace of history. In 1955 Pierre Ryckmans, who had been governor-general of the Congo from 1934 until 1947, and who then became the Belgian representative on the United Nations Trusteeship Council, wrote,

> Everyone who knows the Congo is convinced that Belgian rule is indispensable there, and that the end of it would be the end of all that we have built up during three quarters of a century. We have preferred to give primary education to the mass of children, and to organise secondary education later, as soon as available resources allow. French West Africa has a thousand young people studying in France, while we have just a handful studying in Belgium. But we have ten times more children than they have in primary schools. I sincerely believe that in thirty years' time we shall have in the Congo at least as many university graduates, and at least as many high-school graduates, and infinitely fewer illiterates than do our French neighbours in West Africa, even though the first university in the Congo opened its doors only last year. But will thirty years of peaceful progress be given us?[3]

Ryckmans answered his question with a cautious affirmative: he was 'full of hope'. In the event, four years later, both he and his government were proved terribly mistaken when the Congolese were quite unprepared for the responsibilities of an independence which was thrust upon them rather than struggled for.

PREPARING FOR DEMOCRATIC SELF-GOVERNMENT

A field in which nearly all colonial governments were most active during the time that remained to them in the post-war years was that of local government. In the British territories indirect rule was quietly abandoned as too gradual for the world situation. There was clearly not going to be time in which to allow African systems of local government 'to evolve along their own lines'. Democratic local government had to be attained within a very few years. The only thing to do was to follow western models. Every chief was surrounded by an elected council. The supervision of many local services was handed over to these councils. These services had previously been adminis-

[3] 'Belgian Colonialism', *Foreign Affairs*, October 1955, cited in Joan G. Roland, *Africa: the heritage and the challenge* (Greenwich, Conn., 1974), pp. 205, 211.

tered autocratically by the chief or by the district commissioner. The English county council was the model followed increasingly in British territories. The French aimed to reproduce the system of *communes*, which were the principal units of representative local government in France. Roads, local police, prisons, dispensaries and primary schools became the main concerns of these reformed local authorities. In the employment of the district councils and *communes* many Africans learned to take administrative responsibility in ways that were not yet open to them in the service of the colonial central governments. Many future national politicians gained their political training through membership of the local councils.

When it came to the creation of representative institutions at the colonial level, British and French policy still showed hesitations and contradictions. It was this that soon caused Britain and France to lose the initiative to the African nationalist movements which we shall be considering in the next four chapters. So far as the British were concerned, the intention to decolonise was not in doubt. Oliver Stanley, the wartime colonial secretary, had stated already in June 1943, 'We are pledged to guide colonial peoples along the road to self-government within the British empire.' Whether this meant the full, sovereign independence of every individual colonial unit, large or small, no one yet knew. There were still many people in Britain who hoped that federations of West, East and Central African territories would emerge. But the immediate course seemed clear. It was to repeat the pattern of constitutional development followed earlier in the European-settled lands in Canada, Australia and South Africa. Political power would be given gradually to the Legislative Councils which had already been set up in all the colonies. At the same time the membership of these councils would be widened by increasing African representation, through nominees of the governors and of the chiefs. Later the Legislative Councils would become even more representative by giving the vote to a wider and wider circle of people in the colonies.

Such a plan raised no special difficulties in relation to the West African colonies, where all the British people employed were temporary residents only. The complications arose on the eastern side of Africa. Here, from Kenya all the way down to Southern Rhodesia, there lived small colonies of British settlers. These settlers thought of themselves as permanent residents of these countries. They had already been given varying degrees of privilege in their government. The advance of the African majorities to full voting rights would mean the end of the privileged positions of these settlers. To understand their attitude one has to remember that South Africa had gained independence with a franchise virtually limited to white people, and that in 1923 Southern Rhodesia, with a much smaller proportion of whites to blacks, had gained internal self-government on the same basis. British views had changed greatly since 1923. All the same, the British governments of 1945–55 felt that they had an obligation to protect the settlers of East and Central Africa from a too-rapid transference of power to the African majorities. Britain therefore experimented for ten years with a variety of so-called 'multiracial constitutions' in these areas. The typical 'multiracial constitution' was one in which each racial group in the community elected a certain fixed number of representatives to the legislature. In this way the various groups were more or less evenly represented, regardless of their actual size. The hope was that a democratic moderation would emerge from the balancing of one group against another in the legislature. As we shall see in Chapter 20, few Africans could see any justice in such a system. Nevertheless, the multiracial constitutions did perform a useful function in providing a transitional stage between white-settler privilege and majority rule. The great gap between the two might have been very difficult to bridge without this multiracial stage.

French hesitations and contradictions turned less upon the number of Frenchmen resident in any particular one of their African territories than upon the future relations of the French overseas territories to France. Right up until 1960 the French plan for decolonisation envisaged nothing more than a local autonomy for the ex-colonies within a centralised imperial system. This imperial system was represented first by the French Union and later by the French Community. Whereas the French Union had been intended to include all the French overseas territories, Indo-China as well as Africa, the French Community was limited to Africa south of the Sahara and to those small island territories, like Martinique (West Indies) and St Pierre et Miquelon (off the coast of Canada), which had accepted full integration with metropolitan France. Algeria was within the Community only while it remained a part of France. Tunisia and Morocco were never members of it. In practice, however, French Africa from 1945 to 1955 was passing through a phase of decolonisation very similar to the 'multiracial' period in British East Africa. In French West and Equatorial Africa and Madagascar legislative assemblies were being developed both at the federal and at the territorial level. During this transitional stage half the seats in these assemblies were elected by the *citoyens de plein exercise*, that is to say in effect by the locally resident French population.

Except for the Belgian and Portuguese possessions, the rulers of colonial Africa from the Sahara to the Zambezi realised that they had entered into the last period of European colonisation. Yet French and British colonial governments acted their parts in this final act of the imperial drama with unprecedented vigour and even enthusiasm. Development money was being poured into the tropical African colonies. Agriculture and industry were being actively stimulated, and education was being given a decisive push forward. Local government was being made quickly and surely more democratic. Central government was also being made more democratic and representative, but less rapidly and less certainly. The colonial rulers were preparing to leave. There was no more time for political experiments. Therefore western models were increasingly used for the developing political institutions in the African colonies. All over British Africa Speakers in their traditional wigs presided over the rectangular debating chambers of the Westminster model, in which 'government' and 'opposition' sat facing each other. All over French Africa assemblies sat in semicircular chambers on the Paris model, in which the 'left wing' merged imperceptibly into the 'right wing', without a dividing 'floor'. These were the 'old bottles' imported hastily from Europe to contain the 'new wine' of African nationalism. They were not completely successful, but, as comparison with the Belgian Congo was to prove, they were a great deal better than nothing.

18 The road to independence (1): West Africa

African nationalism is like a great forest tree. Its trunk is the Pan-African movement, which gives a sense of solidarity to all the different people of the continent. Its branches are the independent states of Africa. As the roots of a tree reach deep into the soil, so the origins of African nationalism spread in many directions back into history. We saw in Chapter 12 how nationalism was born in the questioning minds of some of the first mission-educated Africans. In the early days of colonialism a few Africans ceased to think in terms of merely tribal institutions. They began to think of imitating, or of capturing from the inside, Western-type Churches and states of a wider than tribal kind. In Chapter 13 we described how some of the earliest generation of Africans to receive a secondary education in colonial schools during the inter-war period later went overseas to continue their studies. Those who then went to America made contact with a large, progressive modern state which had thrown off European colonialism a hundred and fifty years before. They also made contact with a stream of Negro racial consciousness and political discontent which had grown up in the days of slavery and gained strength after emancipation. Those who went to Europe made contact with socialism and communism. These radical political movements rose out of the discontents of the underprivileged sections of European societies.

The influence of trans-Atlantic slavery on modern African nationalism has been immense. At a time when Africa was still divided politically and culturally into hundreds of tribal units, Negro slaves in the New World were already detribalised. Nevertheless, because of the sufferings they had all experienced, they remained conscious of their common continent of origin. The idea of emancipation was linked from the first with the idea of a return to Africa, and although only a handful of people actually made the journey, Africa remained as a kind of mystical homeland in the minds of millions more. The symbol of that homeland was colour, the blackness of the Africans' skin. Edward Blyden, the West Indian Negro who settled in Liberia as early as 1850, thought out a philosophy which foreshadowed many of the ideas of present-day African leaders. He was probably the first man to use the term 'African personality'. 'Every race', he wrote, 'has a soul, and the soul of a race finds expression in its institutions.' Or again, 'I would rather be a member of the African race now [he was writing in 1888] than a Greek in the time of Alexander, a Roman in the Augustan period, or an Anglo-Saxon in the nineteenth century.' Blyden, however, could not greatly influence the Africa of his own time, even by going to live there. He was a prophet speaking from Africa to the Negroes of the New World. It was only there that his ideas could be kept alive until the mid-twentieth century.

Throughout the later nineteenth century there was a growing ferment of unrest and discontent among the Negro peoples of the United States and the West Indies. At first religion and politics were indistinguishable. 'The preachers of the Negroes', stated a white observer in Virginia in 1889, 'are their most active politicians. They play alternately upon the political passions and the religious fears of their congregations.' By the end of the century distinctly political movements had arisen. Two of these especially affected the later course of African nationalism. One was the 'Negro Empire' proclaimed by the Jamaican Marcus Aurelius Garvey, with its slogan 'Africa for the Africans' and its plans to transport Negroes back to Africa. Garvey was as racially exclusive as the white settlers in colonial Africa. Despite the failure of all his schemes, he stirred the imagination of Africans as no black man had ever done before. The idea of 'Pan-Africanism' was even more influential. The term was first used in 1900, at a conference summoned in London by a West Indian lawyer to denounce British imperialism. It was not used again, however, until it was revived by William DuBois, a radical American Negro, after the First World War. Throughout the 1920s and 1930s DuBois organised Pan-African Congresses, at which the common sufferings of black people on both sides of the Atlantic were stressed, and also their common cultural background. Unlike Garvey, DuBois did not preach African racialism. He saw the problems of the Negroes of the New World and of the Africans as part of a world-wide struggle of oppressed, underprivileged people for freedom and justice. Yet both men were working for the same end, 'to raise the status of the Negro, materially and spiritually, in his own eyes and in the eyes of the world at large'.[1] Many Africans from British territories who were studying

---

[1] Quoted in G. Shepperson and T. Price, *Independent African* (Edinburgh, 1958), p. 435.

in the United States were caught up in the excitement of these ideas and schemes. However, until the Second World War, the majority of those who attended the Pan-African Congresses were American Negroes. Only in the late 1940s did Africans themselves take over DuBois's movement and fully inherit all the diverse strands of thought from across the Atlantic.

The other main strand in the web of African nationalist ideas was that stemming from European socialism and communism. The prophet of both movements was Karl Marx (1818–83), a German Jew, who spent most of his working life as a political refugee in England. Essentially Marx's thought was addressed to the social evils accompanying the spread of industrialism in Europe. He believed that these evils could be cured only if the means of production were taken out of private ownership and put under the control of governments which truly represented 'the workers'. Common ownership was the keystone of Marx's philosophy. In the course of attacking private ownership (capitalism) he turned against all forms of religion. Religion he described as 'the opium of the people', fostered by 'capitalists' in order to distract the 'workers' from the evils of their present lot by false hopes of compensation in a future life. The generation following Marx's death saw an increasing division among his followers between socialists and communists. Many socialists kept their religious beliefs and pursued their objectives by peaceful persuasion. The communists believed that 'socialism' was only attainable by violent revolutions led by carefully indoctrinated, atheist 'party members'. These would seize power, establish a 'dictatorship of the proletariat [workers]' and carry out a fundamental re-education of the whole community. Socialists and communists agreed in denouncing the colonial system, which they believed to be the creation of capitalist property-owners seeking ever-greater numbers of 'workers' on whose labour they could make ever increasing profits. Communists, however, went further than mere condemnation of colonialism. Lenin, the leader of the Russian communists, demanded the forceful overthrow of colonial rule in the interests of 'world revolution'. As soon as the October Revolution of 1917 had established communism in power in Russia, the Soviet government, working through its supporters in western Europe, gave not only money but also training in political organisation and revolutionary methods to colonial nationalists who were seeking to overthrow their alien governments. Politically conscious Africans studying in European countries could not fail to be interested in communism. In the communist movement they found friends in a world that too often seemed hostile or indifferent to their aims. They found people who sympathised with their humiliations, and a whole philosophy which denounced imperialism as evil. They discovered in communism techniques of political action suited to their needs, a call to heroism in a world struggle and a promise of future freedom and prosperity. What is surprising is that so few Africans committed themselves whole-heartedly to the communist cause and that for most of them the milder path of socialism remained the more attractive.

To see how these complex strands were woven together to produce the political activity that resulted in independence, we can look for an example at the early career of Kwame Nkrumah, which is so well told in his autobiography, *Ghana*. Nkrumah was born, probably in 1909, the son of a goldsmith of the Nzima tribe in the south-western corner of the Gold Coast. Members of the Nzima tribe had long been active in the commerce of the west coast. Nkrumah was educated at a Roman Catholic mission school and then at the great secondary school at Achimota, near Accra. He thought of the priesthood and eventually became a mission teacher, but this did not satisfy his ambitions. In 1935, with the help of an uncle working in Lagos and with the encouragement of the Nigerian nationalist, Dr Azikiwe, he went to the United States. There he spent ten years, first studying and then teaching at Lincoln University in Pennsylvania. He read widely and stated that the writings of communists and socialists did much to influence him in his revolutionary ideas and activities, 'but of all the literature that I studied, the book that did more than any other to fire my enthusiasm was the *Philosophy and Opinions* of Marcus Garvey'. In 1945 Nkrumah left America for London and there met for the first time the West Indian journalist George Padmore, who became one of his closest friends and advisers. The two men played a prominent part in the Fifth Pan-African Congress held at Manchester in that year. The majority of delegates at this congress were Africans, although it was presided over by DuBois, then seventy-three, the 'Grand Old Man' of the movement. In Padmore's words, DuBois 'had done more than any other to inspire and influence by his writings and political philosophy all the young men who had forgathered from far distant corners of the earth'.[2] The congress adopted strongly worded resolutions condemning colonialism: 'We are determined to be free. We want education. We want the right to earn a decent living, the right to express our thoughts and emotions, to adopt and create forms of beauty. We demand for Black Africa autonomy and independence. We will fight in every way we can for freedom, democracy and social betterment.' At the congress, and later in London, Nkrumah worked closely with Jomo Kenyatta and had meetings with Africans from the French territories, such as Senghor and Houphouet-Boigny. At this stage, most of the political activity among Africans took place in London or Paris and not in Africa itself. It was then that the foundations of a continent-wide movement were laid. 'The political conscience of African students was aroused, and whenever they met they talked of little else but nationalist politics and colonial liberation movements' (Nkrumah).

THE GOLD COAST: THE FIRST BREAKTHROUGH

Until 1947 the Pan-African movement, though it had won the allegiance of the young African intellectuals studying abroad, had achieved little or nothing in Africa itself. Only Dr Azikiwe's newspapers, which were read by a small group of educated people throughout British West Africa, did something to prepare the ground for a more radical approach to politics. The colonial governments, to the extent that they had even heard of Pan-Africanism, thought of it as mere 'students' talk'. The African leaders whom they recognised, and to whom they were preparing to make limited political concessions, were men of an older generation who had done well under colonial rule – the chiefs, lawyers, businessmen and rich farmers. It was men of this sort who in 1947 founded the United Gold Coast Convention, in an attempt to face 'the problem of reconciling the leadership of the intelligentsia with the broad mass of the people' (Nkrumah). These were men of substance and experience. They were Gold Coast patriots too. They looked forward to independence in the shortest possible time – some of them thought in about ten years' time. They even realised that, to keep up pressure on the colonial government, it would be necessary to organise widespread support among the people. But they did not themselves know how to do so. They had their own professions to pursue. Politics to them was a spare-time occupation, as it was for most politicians in Europe. In western European countries the only whole-time political organisers were the paid agents of the political parties, who did not themselves stand for election. This was why the UGCC leaders in 1947 invited Nkrumah to come home and be their general secretary. Here, they thought, was a man who knew the techniques of organisation and who would take the rough work off their hands.

No sooner had Nkrumah arrived back in the Gold Coast than he began to pursue an activist policy designed to seize the initiative from

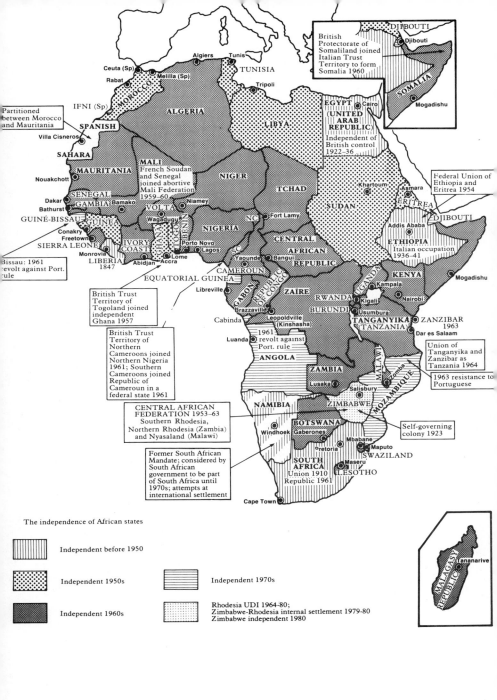

British Protectorate of Somaliland joined Italian Trust Territory to form Somalia 1960

DJIBOUTI
Djibouti

SOMALIA
Mogadishu

Algiers   Tunis
Ceuta (Sp)
Rabat   Melilla (Sp)
MOROCCO
TUNISIA
Tripoli

IFNI (Sp)
SPANISH
ALGERIA
LIBYA
EGYPT (UNITED ARAB REPUBLIC)   Cairo
Independent of British control 1922–36

Partitioned between Morocco and Mauritania

Villa Cisneros
SAHARA
MAURITANIA
MALI
French Soudan and Senegal joined abortive Mali Federation 1959–60
NIGER
TCHAD
SUDAN
Khartoum
Asmara
ERITREA

Federal Union of Ethiopia and Eritrea 1954

Nouakchott
Dakar
SENEGAL   GAMBIA   Bamako
Bathurst
GUINÉ-BISSAU   GUINEA
VOLTA
Niamey
NC   Fort Lamy
Addis Ababa
DJIBOUTI
ETHIOPIA
Italian occupation 1936–41

Conakry
Freetown
SIERRA LEONE
Wagadugu
IVORY COAST
TOGO   BENIN
NIGERIA
Porto Novo
Lagos
CENTRAL AFRICAN REPUBLIC
Bangui
KENYA
Mogadishu

Bissau: 1961 revolt against Port. rule

Monrovia
Abidjan   Accra   Lome
LIBERIA 1847
Yaounde
CAMEROUN
UGANDA
Kampala
Nairobi

British Trust Territory of Togoland joined independent Ghana 1957

EQUATORIAL GUINEA
Libreville
GABON
REPUBLIC OF CONGO
ZAIRE
RWANDA
BURUNDI
Kigali
Usumbura
TANGANYIKA (TANZANIA)
ZANZIBAR 1963
Dar es Salaam

British Trust Territory of Northern Cameroons joined Northern Nigeria 1961; Southern Cameroons joined Republic of Cameroun in a federal state 1961

Brazzaville
Cabinda
Leopoldville (Kinshasha)
Luanda
1961 revolt against Port. rule
ANGOLA
ZAMBIA
Lusaka
MALAWI
Zomba
MOZAMBIQUE

Union of Tanganyika and Zanzibar as Tanzania 1964

1963 resistance to Portuguese

CENTRAL AFRICAN FEDERATION 1953–63
Southern Rhodesia, Northern Rhodesia (Zambia) and Nyasaland (Malawi)

Salisbury
ZIMBABWE
NAMIBIA
BOTSWANA
Gaberones
Windhoek
Self-governing colony 1923

Former South African Mandate; considered by South African government to be part of South Africa until 1970s; attempts at international settlement

Mbabane   Maputo
SWAZILAND
Pretoria
Maseru   LESOTHO
SOUTH AFRICA
Union 1910
Republic 1961
Cape Town

The independence of African states

||||| Independent before 1950

⸬⸬⸬ Independent 1950s

≡≡≡ Independent 1970s

▓▓▓ Independent 1960s

⸳⸳⸳ Rhodesia UDI 1964-80; Zimbabwe-Rhodesia internal settlement 1979-80 Zimbabwe independent 1980

MALAGASY REPUBLIC
Tananarive

the colonial government. He started to reform the inefficient party organisation:

I found on going through the minute book, that thirteen branches had been formed throughout the country. In actual fact just a couple had been established and these were inactive. I saw at once the urgency of a country-wide tour. The results of this were most successful, for within six months I had established 500 branches in the [original] Colony alone. I issued membership cards, collected dues and started raising funds.[3]

The leaders of the UGCC became involved in violent demonstrations by ex-servicemen in Accra (see Chapter 16). The six top men of the party, including Nkrumah, were placed in detention by the government. This was the beginning of the split between Nkrumah and the UGCC. Nkrumah welcomed such violent activities; his colleagues had second thoughts about their value in achieving independence. The British government responded to the disturbances by inviting an all-African committee under Sir Henley Coussey to make recommendations for constitutional reform. The other five leaders of the UGCC joined the committee: Nkrumah alone was not invited.

The Coussey constitution, which was accepted by the British government, was a real landmark in the history of British moves towards decolonisation in Africa. It was implemented by the new governor, Sir Charles Arden-Clarke, as soon as he took up his duties in 1949. It provided for an all-African Legislative Assembly, directly elected in the more developed parts of the country and indirectly elected elsewhere. An Executive Council or cabinet was formed with eight ministers chosen from the Assembly and three more to be nominated by the governor from the ranks of the European civil service. It was in fact the constitution under which Nkrumah was to begin his rule, first as leader of government business and later as prime minister, from 1951 till 1954. In 1949, however, Nkrumah had just founded his own Convention People's Party in opposition to the UGCC. He denounced the Coussey constitution as 'an imperialist fraud', demanding instead 'Self-Government Now'. He followed up his claim with a campaign of 'Positive Action'. This was a movement of strikes and boycotts, designed to create a sense of struggle throughout the country. For their part in the Positive Action campaign, Nkrumah and other CPP leaders were arrested and condemned to imprisonment on various charges of incitement, libel and sedition. They remained in prison for a year, while the colonial government proceeded with its preparations for a general election in February 1951. This was won by the CPP, led

[3] *Ghana* (London, 1959), p. 61.

during Nkrumah's enforced absence from the scene by K. A. Gbedemah. This electoral victory of the CPP was the result of such political efficiency that the party won the respect and admiration of the formerly very hostile colonial government. Arden-Clarke therefore decided to release Nkrumah and to invite him to form a government. Nkrumah, for his part, agreed to abandon his claim for 'Self-Government Now' and to work for a period under the Coussey constitution. This gave the CPP ministers the great advantage of learning to operate the machinery of government from the inside before taking the full responsibilities of independence. On Arden-Clarke's side, this bargain, struck in February 1951, committed the colonial government to working, for only a brief transitional period, with the representatives of a radical party with a great popular following. The CPP was very different in its aims and leadership from the moderate, middle-class people to whom the colonial government had previously hoped to hand over power. The government in Britain, and indeed the outside world as a whole, watched with amazement the steadily growing friendship between these two very different men as they steered the Gold Coast towards independence. Nkrumah tells in moving terms how he received from Arden-Clarke the news of the date, 6 March 1957, fixed by the British government for the Gold Coast's independence under the new name of Ghana:

He handed me a dispatch from the Secretary of State. When I reached the fifth paragraph the tears of joy that I had difficulty in hiding blurred the rest of the document. After a few minutes I raised my eyes to meet those of the Governor. For some moments there was nothing either of us could say. Perhaps we were both looking back over the seven years of our association, beginning with doubts, suspicions and misunderstandings, then acknowledging the growth of trust, sincerity and friendship, and now, finally, this moment of victory for us both, a moment beyond description.

'Prime Minister,' the Governor said, as he extended his hand to me, 'this is a great day for you. It is the end of what you have struggled for.'

'It is the end of what *we* have been struggling for, Sir Charles,' I corrected him. 'You have contributed a great deal towards this; in fact I might not have succeeded without your help and co-operation. This is a very happy day for us both!'[4]

THE SEQUEL TO GHANA IN BRITISH WEST AFRICA

So far as the rest of British West Africa was concerned, the decision to decolonise followed automatically from the decision to do so in the

4 Ibid. p. 282.

Gold Coast. In Nigeria the course towards independence was firmly set by a new constitution which came into operation in 1951. This was the same year as Arden-Clarke's bargain with Nkrumah. That the process of independence took three years longer to achieve in Nigeria than in the Gold Coast was due to the special problems created by the differences in education, wealth and outlook among the three regions of Nigeria. The Northern region was largely Muslim and Hausa-speaking. The traditional Fulbe ruling class still exercised the predominant influence. The mainly Yoruba-speaking Western region was traditionally organised into a number of states ruled by kingly chiefs, while the Eastern region consisted largely of Igbo-speaking people who had never been bound together into powerful political units. The problems created by these differences could not be solved by setting up a unitary state covering the whole of Nigeria. This the 1951 constitution partly tried to do, and it was proved to be unworkable. Dr Azikiwe, who had become chief minister of the Eastern region, was especially critical of the attempt to minimise regional powers. The problems of Nigeria could only be settled by the compromise solution of a federal system of government. This more complicated structure took longer to develop than the unitary government of independent Ghana. A new constitution came into force in 1954. Under it, Nigeria became a truly federal state, with clearly defined powers granted to the federal government and all other powers given to the regional governments. Each region had to become internally self-governing before the territory as a whole could become independent. The most backward region politically was the North. When, however, this immense region came to play its full part in Nigerian affairs, it dominated the territory politically. No federal government could be formed without members of the Northern People's Congress party, and the first federal prime minister, Sir Abubakar Tafawa Balewa, was a northerner.

The strains and stresses produced by the interactions of regional interests in Nigeria delayed the granting of full independence until 1960. The major problem in Sierra Leone and, especially, in the Gambia, was the very opposite to Nigeria's. Both territories were very small and, consequently, relatively poor. Nevertheless, the process started in the Gold Coast could not be halted. Sierra Leone became independent in 1961, and the Gambia in 1965. The Gambia is one of the smallest countries in Africa. It is merely the narrow strip of land along the banks of the Gambia river and is completely surrounded by the French-speaking state of Senegal. The granting of independence to the Gambia raised the question as to whether a country of this size could afford to stand on its own feet as a sovereign state in the modern world.

THE INDEPENDENCE OF FRENCH WEST AFRICA

The difference in attitude towards the growth of nationalism between French-speaking and English-speaking West Africans may be seen in a comparison between the life of Senghor and that of Nkrumah. French Africans were at first concerned more with the cultural than with the political aspects of colonialism. English-speaking nationalists, it has been said, wrote constitutions, while their French-speaking contemporaries wrote poetry. Léopold Sédar Senghor was born in 1906 in a coastal village south of Dakar. His prosperous Catholic parents sent him to schools in the colony and later to Paris. The poems he wrote while in France are full of homesick memories of his childhood days. From 1935, after becoming the first African *agrégé* (qualified secondary-school teacher) in France, he taught in French *lycées* (grammar schools). On the outbreak of the war in 1939 he joined the army and was captured by the Germans, who tried unsuccessfully to persuade him to turn against France. His years in Paris had brought Senghor into contact with a wealth of political and literary ideas. He knew many outstanding French West Indians and became the close friend of Aimé Césaire from Martinique, who was to become like himself a poet and a politician. Before directly tackling political problems, these young men felt the need to produce a creed, or statement of cultural values. Between them, Senghor and Césaire created the concept of *Négritude*, 'the affirmation', as they described it, 'of the values of African culture'. In 1947 Senghor and a fellow Senegalese, Alioune Diop, founded *Présence Africaine* in Paris, a magazine devoted to the renewal of these values. Meanwhile, Senghor was turning to practical politics. After the war he returned to Senegal as a socialist politician, and took part in the events which led up to the formation of the French Union in 1946. He refused to attend the Bamako conference of that year which founded the Rassemblement Démocratique Africaine. He rightly believed that the new party would be dominated by communists. Instead, he led a popular political movement in Senegal and was elected as a deputy to the French Assembly. Under his influence many young Africans devoted themselves seriously to writing, poetry and the arts. This engagement of some of the best minds in French West Africa with cultural affairs partly explains why, in the early 1950s, these territories were not so politically conscious as their English-speaking neighbours.

Support for Senghor's party extended into Upper Volta and other territories, where it came into direct collision with the RDA. The main issue between the two parties from 1955 onwards was that between the federal policy of Senghor and the territorial policy of Houphouet-Boigny. Houphouet, who was born in the Ivory Coast in 1905, went to France for the first time when elected a deputy in 1945. Previously he had been a medical assistant, a prosperous cocoa-farmer and a local chief. He had entered politics as the spokesman of a farmers' association. Although a highly sophisticated man, he retained a good measure of the peasant's 'down-to-earth' common sense. He became the first president of the RDA. After the breakaway of the RDA from its communist alliance in 1950, he held cabinet posts in several French governments. After the war, the Ivory Coast had become the richest of the French West African territories, providing over 40 per cent of the Federation's exports. Houphouet argued that in the federal Union, supported by Senghor, the Ivory Coast would always be subsidising its poorer neighbours. As a minister in the French government, therefore, he was influential in preparing the Loi Cadre (Outline Law) of 1956. Under the Loi Cadre France kept control of foreign policy, defence and overall economic development. All other aspects of government became the responsibility, not of the existing federal governments of French West and Equatorial Africa, but of the twelve individual colonies of which they were composed. The Loi Cadre was deeply influenced by the approaching independence of the Gold Coast and Nigeria. France understood that the French Union, the plan for a kind of super-state, would have to be replaced by something much looser and more like the British Commonwealth. But, partly thanks to Houphouet, the autonomy offered was to units so small (in population, if not in size) that their practical dependence on France was bound to remain very great. Senghor unsuccessfully opposed these constitutional changes, which he considered would result in splitting up West Africa into too many small, weak states. In this opposition he was supported by Sékou Touré of Guinea, a prominent figure in the RDA.

Sékou Touré was born in 1922 and was therefore a much younger man than either Senghor or Houphouet. Although he was a descendant of the famous Samori, his family was poor. His first visit to France had been as a delegate to the Communist Trades Union Conference in 1946. Sékou Touré soon became the leading trade unionist in French West Africa. In 1956 he led a breakaway movement from the French parent body of the Union, although he still held communist views, and formed a new Federation of African Trades

Unions, free from outside ties. While most of his contemporaries concentrated upon increasing their influence in Paris, Sékou Touré realised that it was in Africa that the foundations of real power were to be laid. He favoured the retention of the federal government at Dakar. In 1958 it looked as though a regrouping of political parties was about to take place, with Sékou Touré leaving the RDA and joining Senghor. At this moment, however, General de Gaulle came to power in France as a result of the revolt of the French army in Algeria in May 1958. De Gaulle established a new constitution in France, the Fifth Republic. He offered the colonial peoples the choice between autonomy (self-government) as separate republics within a French Community, which now replaced the earlier Union, or else immediate independence, with the severance of all links with France. In the referendum held in September 1958, all the colonies of French West and Equatorial Africa voted acceptance of de Gaulle's proposals, except for Guinea, whose people followed Sékou Touré in voting 'No'. Sékou Touré was bitterly disappointed with the failure of French West Africa to achieve independence as a federation. He considered that the new Community was little more than a disguise for the continuing domination of France.

When Guinea decided to become independent, France immediately stopped all economic aid and withdrew her civil servants and technicians. Faced with an economic collapse, Sékou Touré turned to Russia and to other communist countries for assistance. Nkrumah offered him at once a loan of £10 million, and the two statesmen declared the formation of a union between their two countries. This was a gesture of solidarity, however, rather than a real constitutional measure. As a gesture, it was effective, for the other territories, which had voted 'Yes' in the referendum, began at once to readjust their positions. Senegal and French Soudan came together to form the Mali Federation, and in 1959 demanded and obtained complete independence while remaining members of the Community. The Ivory Coast joined in a looser grouping, the 'Entente Council', with Dahomey, Upper Volta and Niger, each member of which demanded its individual independence of France. By November 1960 all the French West and Equatorial African territories had become independent, as had the Malagasy Republic (Madagascar). After a matter of months the Mali Federation divided again into its two parts, French Soudan now taking to itself the name of Mali. The Community, as de Gaulle had envisaged it, was a dead letter, though French aid, and therefore French influence, remained very great.

The United Nations Trusteeship Territories in West Africa   233 followed the same broad path as the colonies proper. British Togoland decided by plebiscite (a direct vote of the whole people) to join Ghana in 1957, while French Togo became an independent republic in 1960. The history of Cameroun was the stormiest of all West African countries. Civil war between communist and anti-communist groups broke out in 1956 and had not been completely resolved when the territory became independent in 1960. In 1961 plebiscites were held in British Cameroun. The northern part voted to remain within Northern Nigeria. The southern part, however, voted for union with its French-speaking neighbour. Thus the Federal Republic of Cameroun combined for the first time areas which had been under different colonial rules and defied the language gulf which separates the English-speaking and French-speaking states of West Africa.

19 The road to independence (2): Northern Africa: independence and after

As we saw in Chapter 14, nationalism in the Muslim north of Africa had developed much earlier than in Africa south of the Sahara. Egypt, indeed, had been self-governing since 1922. Yet it was not until forty years later – after all of West Africa and most of East Africa had become independent – that the emancipation of North and North-East Africa was completed by the withdrawal of the French from Algeria. The emergence of this region from the colonial period was thus a much longer-drawn-out and more piecemeal process than that of the regions to the south. And although it became in its final stage increasingly linked with the rest of the Pan-African freedom movement, its origins were different and must be separately treated.

THE MAGHRIB

The Maghrib was divided, during the colonial period, into Algeria, which was administered as a part of France, and the two flanking protectorates of Morocco and Tunisia. There was no essential difference between the state of nationalist opinion in the three countries. The vast majority of all their populations were solidly Muslim and Arabic-speaking. Their leaders looked to Cairo and the Arab League for support in their struggle and were also affected by developments towards independence in Libya, the Sudan and Somalia. The difference between them was mainly one of strategy, which arose from the differing degrees of French commitment. It was obvious to all that if France would adopt delaying tactics in the protectorates, in Algeria she would fight to the bitter end.

In Morocco, the sultan had made himself the central figure of the nationalist movement. He refused to give his consent to French laws to ban the Istiqlal and other nationalist parties. In a desperate effort to overcome the resistance to their rule in Morocco, the French sided with the nomadic groups in the Atlas mountains, who were traditionally hostile to the sultan. In 1953 the French deposed Muhammad V and exiled him, first to Corsica and then to Madagascar. In his place 235 the tribal *kaid* Thami al-Glawi was made sultan. This act made Muhammad V the popular hero of Morocco and more than ever the symbol of the country's hopes. Unrest broke out with the formation of an Army of Liberation by the nationalist groups. The French were forced to acknowledge defeat and agreed to the principle of independence. In November 1955 Muhammad V returned to his country and was reinstated as sultan. A broadly representative government under the sultan, including the Istiqlal Party, negotiated with the French, and Morocco became independent in March 1956. A similar agreement was made with the Spanish government over the northern zone. After only forty-four years under European control, Morocco once more became a united independent monarchy. In 1961 Muhammad was succeeded as king by his son Hassan. Under pressure from the Moroccan army, Spain ceded the small enclave of Ifni to Morocco in 1969. However, the future of the much larger Spanish territory of the Western Sahara (called by the Spaniards Rio de Oro) was more complex.

A liberation movement, the Polisario Front, emerged in the sparsely inhabited territory in the 1970s, to fight for independence, and the UN agreed to hold a plebiscite to decide the future of the country. But Morocco and Mauritania had already made their plans for the desert lands, which are rich in phosphates. In 1975, before the UN could take any action, King Hassan led the dramatic 'Green March' of Moroccans into Western Sahara. The crowd of civilians was followed by units of the Moroccan army. The UN Visiting Mission in 1976 asserted that 'the Frente Polisario appeared as a dominant political force in the territory'. In spite of the mission's report, and in spite of a ruling of the International Court, Spain – rather than have a colonial war on its hands – agreed that the territory should be partitioned between Morocco and Mauritania. Since 1976 Morocco and Mauritania have occupied the northern and southern coastal areas respectively, while the Polisario guerrillas, with Algerian help, have attacked from the desert hinterland. In 1976 the Polisario Front proclaimed a Saharawi Arab Democratic Republic. The military coup in Mauritania in 1978 showed signs of a weakening resolve in that country to hold on to the south of Western Sahara. King Hassan, however, seemed unlikely to give way to the Polisario demands, if for no other reason than the finely balanced situation facing the king in Morocco.

Here, a new constitution in 1970 paved the way for the resumption of political activity, albeit on a limited basis. After that, King Hassan survived a number of attempts on his life by disgruntled soldiers. In the 1977 elections a majority of Moroccans voted in favour of the monarchy, but there was considerable opposition, both civilian and military, which was dealt with in a characteristically tough way. Towards the end of the 1970s Hassan felt secure enough to intervene further afield in Africa, south of the Sahara, by sending military forces to Zaïre (in close association with France) to help President Mobutu repel the Katangese invasions of Shaba (see p. 342). Morocco has thus emerged as one of the most forceful of 'moderate' African countries.

Immediately after the Second World War it seemed that France would allow Tunisia to become autonomous within the French Union at a fairly early date. Bourguiba returned to his country in 1949, after four years of self-imposed exile. The following year he was able to state that 'with independence accepted as a principle, there are no more problems'. Such optimism was misplaced. Increasing resistance to constitutional changes came from the French and Italian settlers in Tunisia. It also came from the governor-general of Algeria. The French in Algeria feared the effect on that country of having an independent Tunisia as a neighbour. In 1952 Bourguiba was arrested, and disturbances broke out which the French were unable to control. By 1954, however, France was fighting a full-scale war against the nationalists in Algeria and had neither the will nor the military forces to break the Tunisian nationalists. As in Morocco, France had to give way to the nationalist movement. In 1955 Bourguiba was released, and Tunisia became independent in March 1956, at the same time as Morocco. Relations with France became strained once more in 1961, when, at the time of the Évian negotiations between France and the Algerian nationalists, Bourguiba demanded the evacuation of French troops from the military base of Bizerta. Violent fighting broke out and continued until France agreed to the evacuation in June 1962. By that time a large proportion of the European community in Tunisia had left the country. Since the Bizerta crisis, Tunisia and France have grown closer together. There has been substantial French investment in the development of Tunisia's varied agricultural resources, and this has ensured a measure of economic and social stability. The 1970s have seen the consolidation in power of the aging president, the result being a kind of beneficent dictatorship, which allows for little opposition. In 1973 Bourguiba paid scant attention to Colonel Gaddafy's attempt to unite Libya and Tunisia – this caused a rift between the two countries – and in 1974 he was proclaimed president for life. The impression of Tunisia as the 1970s drew to an end was of a fairly prosperous and vigorous country, much bound up in Mediterranean political and economic affairs (including tourism), being kept on a tight rein by an elderly father-figure.

The first outbreak of violence in Algeria occurred within a few days of the end of the war in Europe in 1945, when police fired upon a procession at Sétif. Enraged Muslims turned upon the *colons*, and the French replied with ruthless retaliation; more than one hundred Europeans and many thousands of Muslims were killed. This grim experience gave many Algerians a sense of nationhood for the first time. In 1946 Ferhat Abbas could claim, 'The Algerian personality, the Algerian fatherhood, which I did not find in 1936 among the Muslims [see Chapter 14], I find there today. The change that has taken place is visible to the naked eye, and cannot be ignored.' The French tried to ignore this growing Algerian nationalism. They maintained that Algeria was a part of France. Finally, the nationalist organisation, the Front de Libération Nationale, began the Algerian rebellion in November 1954. This uprising was influenced by events in Morocco and Tunisia. In a sense, the French only withdrew from these neighbouring countries with the object of being the better able to hold Algeria. The million Frenchmen in Algeria had relations all over the mother country. No French ministry in the long series of weak governments which followed one another at frequent intervals from 1945 till 1958 could face the unpopularity of abandoning the hopeless Algerian war. The Egyptian triumph in the Suez crisis encouraged the FLN greatly. It also paved the way for the return to French politics of General de Gaulle. The French people desired a strong ruler to rescue them from disastrous overseas adventures. They were at last prepared greatly to increase the presidential powers. During his election campaign the general promised victory in Algeria. No sooner was he in power, however, than he started to pursue his *politique de l'artichaut*. This was his 'artichoke policy' of stripping off, leaf by leaf, the strong combination of right-wing generals, embattled settlers and reactionary administrators which had defied the peace-making efforts of all his predecessors. A ceasefire was finally arranged with the FLN at Évian in 1962, after seven and a half years of bitter fighting. By this time older leaders like Ferhat Abbas had been pushed aside by younger, more radical men. After a short period of civil war, during which most of the French settlers left the country, Muhammad Ben Bella emerged as the strong man of independent Algeria. But the FLN as an organisation did not survive the end of the fighting. Unlike other liberation movements – Frelimo in Mozambique, for example – it did not develop either the political apparatus or the popular support to enable it to become a peacetime government.

238

36 African unity and disunity since independence

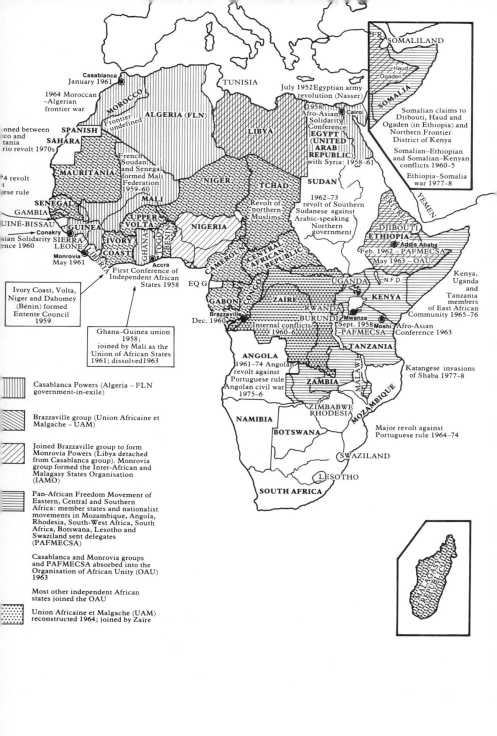

Casablanca
January 1961

1964 Moroccan
–Algerian
frontier war

...oned between
...co and
...tania
...rio revolt 1970s

SPANISH
SAHARA

...'4 revolt
...t
...ese rule

GAMBIA

...UINÉ-BISSAU

...sian Solidarity
...ence 1960

Monrovia
May 1961

Ivory Coast, Volta,
Niger and Dahomey
(Bénin) formed
Entente Council
1959

Ghana–Guinea union
1958;
joined by Mali as the
Union of African States
1961; dissolved1963

TUNISIA

MOROCCO
Frontier
undefined

ALGERIA (FLN)

MAURITANIA

French
Soudan
and Senegal
formed Mali
Federation
1959–60

SENEGAL

GUINEA
Conakry

SIERRA
LEONE

IVORY
COAST

MALI

UPPER
VOLTA

GHANA

TOGO

BENIN

NIGER

NIGERIA

CAMEROUN

Accra
First Conference of
Independent African
States 1958

EQ G

GABON

Brazzaville
Dec. 1960

CONGO

ZAIRE

CENTRAL
AFRICAN
REPUBLIC

Internal conflicts
1960–6

ANGOLA
1961–74 Angolan
revolt against
Portuguese rule
Angolan civil war
1975–6

NAMIBIA

LIBYA

July 1952 Egyptian army
revolution (Nasser)

1958
Afro-Asian
Solidarity
Conference

Cairo

EGYPT
(UNITED
ARAB
REPUBLIC)
with Syria: 1958–61

TCHAD

SUDAN

1962–73
revolt of Southern
Sudanese against
Arabic-speaking
Northern
government

FR. SOMALILAND

Haud
Ogaden

SOMALIA

Somalian claims to
Djibouti, Haud and
Ogaden (in Ethiopia) and
Northern Frontier
District of Kenya

Somalian–Ethiopian
and Somalian–Kenyan
conflicts 1960–5

Ethiopia–Somalia
war 1977–8

YEMEN

DJIBOUTI

ETHIOPIA
Addis Ababa
Feb. 1962 – PAFMECSA
May 1963 – OAU

UGANDA

N.F.D.

KENYA

Kenya,
Uganda
and
Tanzania
members
of East African
Community 1965–76

Afro-Asian
Conference 1963

RWANDA

BURUNDI

Mwanza

Sept. 1958
PAFMECSA

Moshi
Afro-Asian
Conference 1963

TANZANIA

Katangese invasions
of Shaba 1977–8

ZAMBIA

MALAWI

MOZAMBIQUE

Major revolt against
Portuguese rule 1964–74

ZIMBABWE
RHODESIA

BOTSWANA

SWAZILAND

LESOTHO

SOUTH AFRICA

Casablanca Powers (Algeria – FLN
government-in-exile)

Brazzaville group (Union Africaine et
Malgache – UAM)

Joined Brazzaville group to form
Monrovia Powers (Libya detached
from Casablanca group). Monrovia
group formed the Inter-African and
Malagasy States Organisation
(IAMO)

Pan-African Freedom Movement of
Eastern, Central and Southern
Africa: member states and nationalist
movements in Mozambique, Angola,
Rhodesia, South-West Africa, South
Africa, Botswana, Lesotho and
Swaziland sent delegates
(PAFMECSA)

Casablanca and Monrovia groups
and PAFMECSA absorbed into the
Organisation of African Unity (OAU)
1963

Most other independent African
states joined the OAU

Union Africaine et Malgache (UAM)
reconstructed 1964; joined by Zaire

MALGASY REPUBLIC

Political power in Algeria tended rather to polarise around the leaders of powerful civil or military interest groups.Under the leadership of Ben Bella Algeria achieved a prominent position in the Pan-African movement and in the affairs of the Organisation for African Unity (see Chapter 24). As one of the few African countries to gain independence by means of violent revolution, it was only natural that Algeria should adopt sweeping socialist policies to cope with the many problems left by the long war against France. Ben Bella was an outspoken critic of all manifestations of neo-colonialism and was particularly hostile to the European minority governments of southern Africa. He aligned himself closely with Russia and with her communist allies, especially Cuba. Yet despite embittering memories of the recent struggle, Algeria retained many links with France. Several thousand French teachers were employed in the schools, and the French continued to exploit the oil of the Algerian Sahara.

In spite of his great international prestige, however, Ben Bella's position within Algeria soon became less secure. The civil war which had followed the winning of independence had left wounds in many parts of the country, particularly among the freedom-loving Berbers of the Kabylia district, whose opposition had been ruthlessly crushed by Ben Bella; many other Algerians resented his dictatorial methods. He had spent most of the Algerian war in a French jail, and had never really won the confidence of the former soldiers of the FLN, who disliked taking orders from one whom they regarded as a non-combatant. It was the commander of an army group, Colonel Boumedienne, who, feeling his own position threatened by the president, staged an almost bloodless coup d'état in 1965, which toppled Ben Bella from power. The new government represented a compromise in Algerian politics. It contained members of Ben Bella's former administration, as well as army leaders and representatives of other sectional interests. Internal problems were given more attention than under the regime of his predecessor, and Algeria pursued a less-flamboyant and less-expensive foreign policy. The coup d'état led to the indefinite postponement of the much-heralded conference of the Afro-Asian countries, which was to have been a second Bandung and which was to have been held in Algiers in June 1965. China and other countries of the extreme left refused to attend, claiming that there were too many deep divisions among the Afro-Asian states for such a large-scale meeting to produce any useful results.

Under Boumedienne Algeria built up powerful military forces, which were largely supplied by Russia, and pushed ahead with the nationalisation of foreign companies which operated in the country.

Many of these companies were French-owned. In 1971 Algeria broke further away from France by unilaterally imposing increased charges for oil, an operation which was repeated in 1973–4, when Algeria, along with the other Organisation of Petroleum Exporting Countries member states, pushed up the price of oil threefold or more. With the increased flow of oil revenue, Boumedienne's government took measures to diversify the country's economy; Algeria became one of the few African states to construct a steel-mill, which was built with Russian help. Algeria continued to support radical movements in African countries, especially the southern African liberation groups. Men from these movements received military training in Algeria, often with Cuban instructors. Indeed, Algeria was one of the first African countries to encourage Cuban military involvement in the nationalist and Marxist liberation of African lands.

Since 1976 Algeria has actively supported the Polisario Front in attempting to create an independent state in the Western Sahara. Algeria would welcome access to the Atlantic coast and participation in the exploitation of the region's mineral resources. This policy brought Algeria into further conflict with Morocco (there had been intermittent skirmishing with Morocco in the later 1960s and early 1970s over the ill-defined southern border between the two countries – an area rich in minerals) and with Mauritania. Algeria has likewise remained in the forefront of 'radical' Arab states in its support of a Palestinian settlement of the Arab–Israeli strife. In 1976 a new constitution was proclaimed, which was markedly Marxist in character and which was a reflection of Boumedienne's thinking. Boumedienne received an overwhelming vote of confidence in a national referendum, and when he died in 1978, after a long illness, he was greatly mourned by the Algerian people.

Between the Maghrib and Egypt lay the sprawling country of Libya, which had formed part of the African empire of Italy, and whose independence was determined primarily by the results of the Second World War. The British, during their North African campaigns of 1942 and 1943, had entered into close and secret relations with Sayyid Idris, the temporal head of the Sanusi order, which had organised the bedouin resistance to the Italians during the 1920s and 1930s (Chapter 14, pp. 182–3). As a result the Sanusi co-operated with the British during the war, and as soon as the Italians had been expelled, Idris returned to his country. There were still, however, a number of problems which had to be solved before he could be recognised as king of a united and independent Libya. The Italians had found their main difficulty in extending their rule from the settled, mainly Berber

241

populations of the coastal cities to the nomadic Arab pastoralists of the interior. Idris now encountered the reverse problem, that of making the rule of the bedouin acceptable to the more sophisticated and cosmopolitan peoples of the coast. While this problem was being resolved, the country remained, with the consent of the United Nations, under the administration of its war-time conquerors. The southern province of Libya, the Fezzan, had been occupied during the war by the Free French, who had operated a supply road across the desert from Nigeria through Tchad to the North African battle-fields. This occupation continued after the war, and, especially since the Sanusi order was as powerful in Tchad as in Libya, the French were in no hurry to move out of the frontier region. The two northern provinces of Cyrenaica and Tripolitania likewise remained under a British administration, which, while strongly favouring Idris's claims, was anxious to keep control until those claims were firmly established. In 1949, therefore, the United Nations began to play a hurrying role, sending its own commissioner to work out a constitution acceptable to the country as a whole. At last in 1951 a constituent assembly drawn from all three provinces declared Idris king of Libya, and the new state began its independent existence in December of that year. The discovery of large oil resources in the 1960s gave Libya unexpected wealth.

In 1969 the government of King Idris was overthrown by the armed forces which set up a radical, more anti-western and more strictly Muslim regime, under a Revolutionary Command Council led by Colonel Gaddafy. The new Libyan government rapidly assumed one of the leading positions among Arab countries and in 1971 took the first steps towards forming a political union with the United Arab Republic and Syria. Neither this union nor the one projected with Tunisia materialised, mainly as a result of the volatile behaviour of Colonel Gaddafy. He set himself up as the leader of a radical Muslim jihad, directed against Israel and its supporters, but encompassing support for many 'liberation' movements, such as that of the Muslims of northern Tchad, the nationalists in southern Africa, and the Canary Island liberation group. In the early days of his rule, his fierce Islamic faith made him hostile to Russian communism, but after both his and Russia's break with Egypt, he moved closer to the Soviet bloc. Gaddafy's politics isolated him from most of his neighbours – Tunisia, Tchad, Sudan and Egypt – but he found an ally in Field Marshal Amin of Uganda and in 1977 switched his support from the Eritrean Liberation Front to the revolutionary Ethiopian government. Between 1974 and 1976 Gaddafy took a rest from active politics, but he returned and in 1977 staged a minor coup, dissolving the Revolutionary Council and proclaiming himself president. Gaddafy's volatile politics had to be taken seriously by the international community because he could back up his rhetoric with the military punch derived from Libya's oil wealth.

There thus emerged a peculiarly contrasting group of North African states: a radical Saharawi Republic (if this ever achieves independent status), the traditionalist monarchy in Morocco, a Marxist-oriented Algeria, a very conservative Tunisian republic, an 'ultra radical Islamic' Libya, and (as we shall see) a 'moderate' Egypt – all responses to different colonial experiences and to different contemporary situations.

EGYPT AND THE SUDAN

The key country of the whole North African region was Egypt. As soon as the British war-time occupation ended in 1944 it was fully independent. A British garrison remained in the Canal Zone, however, in accordance with the terms of the 1936 treaty. Egypt had by far the largest population and by far the most developed industry and commerce of any Muslim country in Africa. It was also the intellectual capital of the Arabic-speaking world. The two universities of Cairo had between them a student population of 20,000. It was there that Arabic-speaking students from the Maghrib met those from the Sudan and Somalia and formed the same kind of associations as English- and French-speaking African students were forming at the same time in London and Paris. At least for those North African nationalists whose primary loyalty was still to Islam, Egypt was both a place of refuge and a nursery of revolt.

At the same time post-war Egypt itself presented, in the words of John Hatch, 'a classic picture of a society moving inexorably towards revolution'.

Less than five per cent of the total land area of Egypt was productively habitable, the Nile Valley alone providing means of life in this vast desert. Yet, not only were eighty-five per cent of the 19,000,000 inhabitants landless, but over a third of the cultivable land was owned by one half per cent of the population. There were 2,700,000 landowners in the country; of these over 2,000,000 owned less than an acre each. The Egyptian fellahin were among the most downtrodden peoples in the world. Living out their miserable short lives in slime and squalor, racked by dysentery, bilharzia and trachoma, existence for the Egyptian masses reached the lowest depths of brutishness in human experience. Yet the ruling class, the land-owning pashas, descended   243 from Turks and without interest in the country which gave them wealth, were among the most ostentatiously opulent group of human beings. King Farouk was the richest, grossest and greediest of them.[1]

It was clear that the traditional rulers of such a society would adopt the classic tactics of trying to divert internal discontent into the channels of external aggression. In 1944 they joined with other Arab countries in forming the Arab League, the earliest and most persistent object of which was to prevent the emergence of a Jewish state in Palestine as soon as Britain fulfilled its declared intention of laying down its mandate. The United Nations in 1947 decreed the partition of the country between Israel and Jordan. In 1948 the Arab League armies went to war against Israel and were humiliatingly defeated by the one-year-old state. Egyptians especially felt this blow to Muslim prestige, which showed up the corruption and inefficiency of the monarchy and the politicians. Frustrated in their attempts against Israel, the politicians now responded by turning the hatred of the foreigner against the British, in the Canal Zone and in the Sudan. In covert defiance of the 1936 treaty (see p. 181), armed bands of Egyptians were encouraged to attack British troops and installations. In 1951 the Egyptian government declared the 1936 treaty to be at an end. This was important for the Sudan, as well as for Egypt, as the treaty had re-established the condominium over the Sudan. Under pressure from Sudanese nationalists, who were not sure that they wanted to be united with Egypt, Britain responded to the Egyptian move by setting a rapid course towards Sudanese independence.

Meanwhile, British reprisals to Egyptian terrorist attacks led to an outburst of popular feeling in Cairo, in which British and other foreign property was destroyed. Six months later, on 23 July 1952, a group of young army officers seized power. They were led by Colonel Gamal Abdul Nasser, but used an older man, General Neguib, as a figurehead. In a short time the Revolutionary Command Council swept away the discredited monarchy and parliament. The new rulers of Egypt quickly came to an agreement with Britain over the future of the Sudan. Neguib and Nasser had both served in the Sudan. They knew the strength of Sudanese nationalism. They realised that a friendly Sudan, even though independent of Egypt, was preferable to a hostile dependency. The new Egypt therefore accepted the British proposals. These were that the Sudanese people should hold elections under a constitution providing internal self-government for a period

[1] John Hatch, *A History of Post-War Africa* (London, 1965), p. 149.

of three years before deciding upon complete independence or union with Egypt. When the time came, in January 1956, the Sudan voted to become an independent republic, though outside the Commonwealth. Apart from Egypt and Ethiopia, Sudan was thus one of the first colonial territories to achieve independence (forestalling Ghana by one year). Sudan's initial two decades of independence, however, proved to be rough and difficult. The Muslim Arabic-speaking northern Sudan, which dominated the whole country politically and economically, was divided into a number of religious, economic and tribal interest groups, and was unstable politically. The army intervened only two years after independence when General Abboud and his leading officers seized power from the politicians. This military regime was overthrown in 1964, to be succeeded by a series of conflicting civilian governments. There was another military coup against the civilian government of the day in 1969, by a young and radical group of officers who set up a National Revolutionary Council under the leadership of General Nimeiri.

The political instability of northern Sudan was in part a response to the conflict in the south. The differences between the Arabic-speaking Muslim northerners and the pagan and Christian peoples of the south were more extreme than those between groups in most other states. The British had until 1946 ruled the two halves of the country as separate compartments. After independence northern administrators and northern soldiers moved into the south and pursued an injudicious policy of Islamisation and Arabicisation. To the southerners this appeared like a new form of colonialism. At last in 1963, after several years of unrest, the southerners rose against the Khartoum government, which suppressed them with a heavy hand. More than a quarter of a million southern Sudanese took refuge in neighbouring Uganda, Zaïre, Ethiopia and Tchad, while many of those remaining in the country retreated into the bush, leaving only the towns and administrative centres in government control. Like Africans in the white-dominated parts of central and southern Africa, the southerners formed liberation movements and demanded either secession from Sudan, or, at the very least, an autonomous position within it. In 1967 the Khartoum government attempted to reincorporate the south politically with the rest of the country, and elections to the central parliament were held in those regions which were under army control. But successive changes of the central government, culminating in the 1969 Nimeiri coup, did not succeed in reconciling the south. In 1966 unrest against the central authorities broke out in Darfur and Kordofan. At the beginning of the 1970s military operations against the dissident southerners continued, with the Sudanese forces using Russian military equipment, and the southerners (the military wing of the Southern Sudan Liberation Movement, known as the Anyanya) being accused of receiving Israeli aid. Aspects not only of the world-wide contest between capitalism and communism, but also of the Arab–Israeli conflict, were apparent in the southern Sudan, one of the most isolated regions of Africa.

Finally Emperor Haile Selassie of Ethiopia stepped in as a mediator, and the Addis Ababa Agreement of 1972 brought the civil war in the southern Sudan to an end. The Anyanya forces were absorbed into the Sudan army, and Nimeiri accepted a form of federal structure for the two parts of the country, with the south having its own regional government (under Abel Alier), with its headquarters at Juba, and with southerners as ministers in the central government at Khartoum. Although some southerners were still not satisfied with these arrangements, the agreement has held firm, and the break-up of Sudan, which seemed possible in the late 1960s, has not taken place.

Meanwhile, Nimeiri and his government have survived a number of attempted coups, one by the Umma party (the old Mahdists) in 1970, a communist-inspired coup in 1971 and two supported by Libya in 1975 and 1976. Since 1976 there have also been border conflicts with the revolutionary Ethiopian government. The effect of this opposition, inside and outside the country, has been to turn Nimeiri into a supporter of 'moderate' Arab states such as Egypt and Saudi Arabia in their relations with Israel, Libya, Russia and the West. Given political stability and an ambitious development programme, the rulers of the Sudan see the country becoming one of the major agricultural producers of the whole Red Sea area.

By 1954, Nasser had ousted Neguib as President of Egypt. The following year he attended the Bandung Conference. Under his rule Egypt became for the first time openly identified with independence movements in the rest of Africa. Internally, Nasser's Egypt was the first country in Africa to put radical socialist policies into practice, by limiting severely the amount of land which an individual could own and by redistributing the large estates among the peasants. Exter-nally, he succeeded in ridding Egypt of the last traces of European domination. Britain agreed to withdraw her troops from the Canal Zone, leaving the canal to be operated as before by the mainly Anglo-French company that had built it. Nasser then turned to his plan for extending the area of irrigated land by building a huge new dam across the Nile at Aswan. This was to have been financed mainly from an American loan. America, however, became increasingly annoyed by his neutralist policies and in 1956 withdrew its offer of the loan. Nasser responded by nationalising the Suez Canal, announcing that he would finance the 'high dam' from its profits. Britain and France, with Israeli help, thereupon attacked Egypt. They withdrew only under the strongest pressure from international opinion, expressed through the United Nations. Egyptian control over the Canal was confirmed, and Nasser seized British and French property in Egypt. Construction of the new Aswan dam was begun, financed not so much from canal profits as from massive Russian aid.

The Suez incident proved a sweeping victory for Nasser which greatly enhanced his standing in other African states and in the Muslim countries of the Middle East. In 1958 Egypt formed a political union with Syria, known as the United Arab Republic. Although the union was short-lived – it collapsed in 1961 – Egypt retained the new name. The enmity between the Arab countries and Israel broke out once again into open hostilities in June 1967. The resultant heavy defeat of Nasser's Egypt and its allies profoundly altered the power balance of the whole area, forcing Russia into more open support of the Arab cause. Russia provided aid to build the Aswan high dam and to equip the steelworks at Helwan, which, when finished, would make the UAR the biggest steel-producer in Africa outside the Republic of South Africa. President Nasser managed to navigate successfully the stormy waters of both Egyptian (UAR) and Middle Eastern politics. His sudden death in September 1970 was not only the occasion for grief throughout the Arab world and beyond but also ushered in a period of uncertainty in the UAR. Nasser was succeeded by Anwar Sadat, who initially found the UAR and its international policies inherited from Nasser difficult to manage, but who gradually built up his stature as a world statesman and as a ruler of Egypt until he became, in his own less flamboyant manner, as popular and as unassailable a figure as Nasser. He found it necessary to purge the republic politically by means of a treason trial of many of his erstwhile colleagues, including the vice-president. By 1975 he had introduced a number of 'liberalising' measures, including the easing of press censorship, more political participation for ordinary Egyptians and a reduction of state control in the economy.

Egypt's relations with Israel, and consequently with the superpowers Russia and the United States, remained, however, the country's chief preoccupation. The cease-fire at the end of the 1967 war wore very thin, with almost continuous artillery bombardments taking place across the Suez Canal, and there were Israeli air-raids on Egyptian positions, including installations around Cairo. Sadat pressed Russia to supply Egypt not only with arms to make up the earlier heavy losses but also with modern offensive weapons. This Russia was reluctant to do, and relations between the two countries cooled during the long period of stalemate with Israel. In 1972 the president announced that most of the Russian military personnel and advisers in Egypt were to withdraw. In the same year, the massacre of Israeli athletes by Palestinian terrorists at the Munich Olympic Games hardened the attitude of Israel. Finally, in October 1973 Egypt and Syria attacked Israel. After a few weeks of the most bitter fighting, during which Egyptian troops crossed the Canal into Sinai and Israeli soldiers crossed in the opposite direction, a cease-fire came into operation. Although neither side won or lost the Yom Kippur War, so called because of the Jewish religious festival on the day it broke out, the Egyptian soldiers more than held their own, and this reflected greatly to the advantage of Sadat; the invincibility of the Israeli military forces was shown to be a thing of the past.

There were two very important consequences of the Yom Kippur War, the first of which immediately affected most countries of the world, including those in Africa. The oil-producing states, the largest of which were the Arab members of the Organisation of Petroleum Exporting Countries (OPEC), took advantage of the war to increase drastically the price of oil; between October and December 1973 the price of oil trebled, and it continued to increase in subsequent years. Suddenly the world had moved from a long period of cheap energy to a much more difficult economic situation of very expensive supplies. The oil price increase played havoc with the economies of the rich industrialised nations, because these consumed such vast quantities of oil. But it also hit the poorer, underdeveloped countries very hard, including many in Africa. Although they did not use so much oil, they did not have the resources to meet the extra cost, and their economies suffered. Moves by the oil-producers, including Nigeria, to provide oil at somewhat reduced rates to some of these poor countries, and efforts by Arab producers, notably Saudi Arabia, to channel some of their new-found riches as development aid, did not compensate many African states; those that were poor before October 1973 became even poorer afterwards.

The other consequence of the Yom Kippur War was a marked improvement in Egypt's relations with the United States. This was in part a US response to the use made by the Arab producers of oil as an economic weapon of war – supplies to countries considered by the Arabs as being pro-Israeli were cut off. Secretary of State Henry Kissinger entered into months of 'shuttle diplomacy' which bore fruit in the 1974 Geneva agreements between Egypt and Israel. Israeli forces withdrew from the Canal area and from a strip of Sinai (which included the small Sinai oil-fields), and Egypt occupied most of this land; a demilitarised zone between the two armies was supervised by UN forces. US relations with Egypt continued to improve, until by the end of the decade the western super-power (together with countries like France) was supplying Egypt with weapons. In 1977 President Sadat made a dramatic visit to Israel, pleading for peace between the two countries, and in 1978 tentative peace proposals were worked out, with great difficulty, between the two heads of state meeting with President Carter at Camp David in Maryland, USA. But if there was now a genuine hope for peace between Egypt and Israel, this was at the cost of almost complete Egyptian isolation in the Arab world.

Although perhaps not apparent to outside observers (who seemed aware only of the conflict between Israel and Egypt and the rest of the Arab world), it was the dangerous state of the economy which was the chief problem to Sadat and his colleagues. The population of Egypt continued to increase rapidly (by the late 1970s it was well over 40 million, as compared to the 19 million just after the Second World War, the time of which John Hatch was writing). The burden of defence expenditure was crushing, and at times inflation was as high as 50 per cent. Industrialisation projects were not very successful; the steelworks at Helwan seldom operated at full capacity, and its products could not compete in price with imported steel. Early in 1977 the government was forced to reduce its subsidies on some foods, and this produced the most serious urban riots, in Cairo and elsewhere, since the days of the monarchy. There was a danger of what in the Middle East is called a 'Lebanese' situation emerging, in which a small middle class, strongly entrenched in political and economic power, becomes indifferent to the plight of the masses of poor people. Sadat's wish to get a peace settlement was partly a response to Egypt's grave economic situation; peace would greatly lessen the cost of armaments and would allow the government to spend money in a more positive manner.

The 1970s were marked by a continuously changing pattern of Egyptian relations with other Arab countries. In 1971 Egypt – still officially called the United Arab Republic – entered into a federal scheme with Syria and Libya, and the country's name was formally changed to the Arab Republic of Egypt; some time later there was a plan for a complete merger with Libya, but thereafter relations with Syria and in particular with Libya deteriorated, and in 1973 Sadat had forcibly to prevent a mass march or invasion of Libyans into Egypt, 249 which was organised by Colonel Gaddafy to push through the union. As Egypt distanced itself from Russia, and, during the middle 1970s, attempted to find a peace settlement with Israel, so Gaddafy, who saw himself as the champion of the cause of Islam, became more hostile, joining the ranks of the 'radical' Arab states (including Algeria, Syria and South Yemen). One consequence of the hostility between Egypt and Libya was a growing friendship between the former and Sudan, including agreements to control the water flow of the Nile (the construction of the Aswan high dam was completed in 1970).

During the 1970s – the Sadat decade – Egyptian relations with most black African countries were low-keyed, especially when compared with the heyday of Nasser's pan-Africanist policy. One thing Egypt managed to do, along with other Arab countries, was to persuade nearly all African states to take a distinctly pro-Arab stand in the Middle Eastern conflict, in many instances to break off diplomatic relations with Israel, and to reject Israeli military and other aid. Israel was compared, for propaganda purposes, with South Africa, and, as if to acknowledge its rejection by black African states and to give some substance to the Arab propaganda, Israel established very amicable relations with South Africa by the end of the 1970s – Israel supplying South Africa with arms, among other things. A further consequence of the shifting politics of the Middle Eastern conflict was the realisation by Russia of its diplomatic set-back in Egypt (which might have been deliberately contrived by Russia) and the need of the Soviet leaders to find other allies in Africa. The case of Libya has been mentioned already, but the crucial Russian move came in 1976–7, when Russia switched its support from Somalia to Ethiopia.

The growing Soviet influence in the Red Sea–Arabian Gulf area (to which we shall be turning later in this chapter) had long been a cause of concern, not only for western states, but also for those in the immediate area, Egypt, Sudan and Saudi Arabia. With Russia closely allied with South Yemen (Aden) and initially with Somalia and latterly with Ethiopia, and supporting one of the two Eritrean Liberation Fronts, the threat of Russian control over the Red Sea and the Indian Ocean coasts of the Horn and of Arabia was very real to the rulers of Egypt and Saudi Arabia, and brought them into close alliance. Saudi Arabia (by the mid-1970s one of the richest states in the world because of its huge oil revenue) supplied direct financial aid to Egypt to shore up its parlous economy and to pay some of its great armaments bills. In respect to the Soviet presence in the Horn of Africa, Egypt reverted to a much older role than the pan-African one briefly played by Nasser – concern over its African hinterland, the

250

Nile valley and the Red Sea area, which was of vital importance to the economic livelihood of its large population and to the political survival of the Sadat regime.

ETHIOPIA AND SOMALIA

We have seen (Chapter 16, pp. 204–5) that Ethiopia regained its independence, thanks to the action of British troops, in 1941. The two older Italian colonies of Somalia and Eritrea were conquered by the British during the same campaign, and both of them remained under British administration for the rest of the war and for some time afterwards. They were the subject of many disputes played out at the United Nations by interested parties. At least three different plans were proposed for Eritrea, with its population of one million people divided almost equally between the hill-dwelling Tigreans, who were Ethiopian Christians, and the Afar and Danakil of the coastal plains, who were Muslims. The Arab countries wanted Eritrea to be independent; the British wanted it partitioned between Ethiopia and the Sudan; the Ethiopians, wishing to recover a seaport of their own in Massawa, wanted to annex the whole. At length, in 1952, the Ethiopian view prevailed, though under a federal constitution which gave the Eritreans a considerable say in their own affairs. Ten years later Eritrea was more tightly integrated within Ethiopia, an arrangement which did not satisfy all Eritreans. Opposition to Ethiopia was split between the Muslim Eritrean Liberation Movement and the Marxist Eritrean People's Liberation Front, both of which received help from outside sources.

After he reassumed the reins of power at the end of the Second World War, the Emperor Haile Selassie ruled Ethiopia very much as he had done in the 1920s and 1930s, that is as the autocratic monarch of a vast feudal empire. The trappings of democracy were introduced, and some aspects of Ethiopia's economy and administration were modernised. Large amounts of aid from the West flowed in. From 1953 the United States became the main supplier of aid and of military equipment. By the mid-1960s this was augmented in order to counterbalance the Soviet supply of armaments to neighbouring Somalia. In 1960 Haile Selassie survived an attempted military coup staged by some elements of the palace guard while the emperor was visiting the United States. He went on to play a major role in pan-African affairs, mediating in disputes (the most notable being the ending of the Sudan civil war in 1972), to the extent that he persuaded his fellow heads of state to site at Addis Ababa the headquarters of the

Organisation for African Unity when this was founded in 1963. Throughout the 1960s and early 1970s the aging emperor ruled over his disparate subjects, introducing all manner of reforms, none of which affected the basic feudal structure of the state, but all of which added to a growing sense of frustration, dissatisfaction and unrest.

During this time, the army, supplied and partly trained by the United States, was pinned down in the north by the Eritreans and in the south by the Somali liberation forces. In 1973 Ethiopia was particularly hard hit by the great drought that caused such huge distress to African lands from the Senegal river to the Red Sea. The emperor's government was shown not only to be incapable of bringing relief to its starving subjects but also of apparently being indifferent to their suffering. In September 1974 the army intervened to overthrow Haile Selassie, who had ruled Ethiopia for nearly four decades (he had been emperor since 1930). A Provisional Military Administrative Council was formed, consisting of a large number of officers, and known as the Dergue. The Dergue announced that it would eradicate the old feudal system and turn Ethiopia into a socialist state. The removal of Haile Selassie's regime unleashed a period of almost unprecedented confusion and violence, during which it seemed likely that the ancient empire would disintegrate completely. The central government almost lost control of several provinces, in some of which powerful secessionist movements emerged, as in Tigre. Once freed of the control of their landlords, leaderless bands of peasants roamed the countryside. The drought continued. The situation in the towns, especially the capital Addis Ababa, was no better. A number of non-military political groups came into being, ranging from western-type liberal democratic parties to radical Marxist movements. The most influential of these was the Ethiopian Democratic Union. In order to fight the Eritreans, the Dergue recruited the Ethiopian People's Revolutionary Army, but this became yet another movement opposed to the authority of the military regime. Members of the Dergue became distrustful not only of all these uncontrollable activities but of one another. Purge followed purge. It is probable that an early victim was the former emperor, who died in prison in August 1975. Members of the Dergue engaged in mutual assassination and the wholesale slaughter of their opponents. By 1976 the original 120 members of the council had been reduced to fewer than half by such means; but also by then, a new strong man, Brigadier Mengistu Haile Mariam, was gradually feeling his way to power. Addis Ababa became utterly lawless; demonstrations of anti-Dergue feeling were frequent, but the inhabitants were terrorised by night-time executions by government-hired young thugs, the so-called Flame Squads (*nebalbal*). In 1976–7 the Ethiopian revolution had reached what has been termed 'the classic stage of devouring its own children'. Early in 1977 Mengistu staged his own coup.

The new regime's external relations were at a low point. The council quarrelled with Sudan; if the two Eritrean liberation movements had united, the whole of Eritrea would have broken away – as it was, only a few towns remained in Ethiopian hands. The Somali living in the Ogaden had risen to free themselves from Ethiopian rule and were receiving open help from Somalia. Between 1975 and 1976 the United States decided to cut off practically all aid to Ethiopia, including military equipment. Then, suddenly, Russia switched sides in the conflict in the Horn, withdrawing its aid from Somalia and in September 1977 starting a massive military build-up in Ethiopia. Cuban and Russian military advisers were sent in, and later large numbers of Cuban fighting forces arrived. In 1978 Ethiopian and Cuban troops successfully cleared the Ogaden of Somali regular soldiers and guerrillas. Ethiopian control of the vital rail and road link to the former French colony of Djibouti, newly independent, was assured. Only Cuban reluctance to become involved against the Eritreans, who still had powerful friends in the Arab world (though Libya and South Yemen had changed sides), prevented Mengistu from launching a large-scale campaign against them. Russia and Cuba favoured a federal solution to the long conflict between Ethiopia and the Eritreans. Internally, the Russian and Cuban presence considerably strengthened Mengistu's position, and the situation stabilised somewhat; the worst of the violence came to an end. Clearly the Ethiopian revolution and the Russian and Cuban intervention on its behalf introduced a new and dynamic situation in the Horn of Africa and the adjacent Red Sea area.

Somalia was the immediate loser from this dramatic turn of events. In 1950 Somalia was assigned by the UN to Italy as a Trust Territory, but for ten years only, at the end of which time it was to become independent. All observers are agreed that Italian rule during this period was exceptionally enlightened and successful.

The Italian Administration showed initiative and courage in opening a School of Politics and Administration at Mogadishu in 1950 as a training centre for Somali officials and political leaders. This bracketing together of the two skills most needed in an emergent country was also reflected in later legislation which, in marked contrast to the British tradition, encouraged members of the civil service to stand as candidates for the legislature, secure in the knowledge that if they failed they could resume their administrative careers without handicap. By 1957 the School of Politics had provided a cadre of officials with basic training in administration, and the emphasis then switched to the concomitant need for technically qualified staff in other fields. The School was transformed into a Technical and Commercial Institute. Meanwhile, in 1954, a Higher Institute of Law and Economics, later to become Somalia's University College, was opened to provide a two-year Rome University diploma course . . . These developments did much to dissipate what remained of Somali scepticism over Italian intentions, and this effect was greatly enhanced by the progressive opening of senior posts in all branches of the civil service to Somali officials. Here advancement proceeded with rapidity, to such an extent indeed that by 1956 all Districts and Provinces were in the direct charge of Somali administrative officers.[2]

Without any doubt the deliberate and rapid decolonisation of Italian Somalia was greatly helped by the fact that all the inhabitants of the country spoke a single language and felt themselves to be a nation. Most African countries had to go through a process of nationalist unification, for which some delaying tactics by the colonial powers was absolutely necessary. With the Somalis the problem was rather that the sense of Somali nationalism existed over a wider area than that of the Trust Territory. It extended clearly over the whole of British Somaliland, where the colonial government, though less active than the Italian trusteeship administration in its preparations for decolonisation, at least did nothing to prevent the unification of the two territories. Although in a hurried and disorganised way, British Somaliland was brought to independence five days before the Italian Trust Territory, and on 1 July 1960 the legislative assemblies of the two countries met in joint session at Mogadishu and constituted themselves into the National Assembly of the independent and sovereign Republic of Somalia. Still, however, there remained substantial Somali communities outside the boundaries of the new state, in the lowlands of eastern Ethiopia, in the Northern Frontier District of Kenya, and in the tiny but important French territory of the Somali Coast, whose capital at Djibouti was the coastal terminus of the Addis Ababa railway. In 1967 the inhabitants of French Somaliland voted to remain attached to France; the country was known as the Afar and Issa Territory. In 1977 this tiny area around Djibouti became independent in its own right, with a continued French military presence. In Somalia itself the democratic government of Mohammed Egal, which had even abandoned the concept of 'Greater Somalia', was overthrown by a military coup in 1969, led by Major-General Mohammed Siyad Barre. General Barre managed to survive the cut-

[2] I. M. Lewis, *The Modern History of Somaliland* (London, 1964), p. 141.

ting off of Russian aid and the humiliating military defeat at the hands of the Ethiopians and Cubans in the Ogaden.

The Russian and Cuban involvement in the Horn of Africa seems to have been a decision on the part of the Soviet leaders not to get too directly involved in the Middle Eastern conflict (in particular that between the Arabs and Israel), where the potential gains for Russia were never very great, but to develop a much larger theatre of operations in the Indian Ocean, with important implications for the whole of the eastern half of Africa. The violence in Ethiopia and the Great Power involvement there ties in with the violence in southern Africa and the direct or indirect involvement of the western capitalist bloc on the one hand and the eastern communist powers on the other. Whether they like it or not, many African countries are being drawn into this larger international confrontation.

20 The road to independence (3): East Africa and Zaïre

The timing of independence in East and Central Africa was influenced to some extent by developments in North Africa, particularly by the achievement of independence in Somalia. But these influences were late ones. The beginnings of the freedom movement in East Africa were much more closely connected with events in West Africa than in North Africa.

THE INFLUENCE OF NKRUMAH

Nkrumah had always made it clear that, once Ghana had achieved its independence, it would be his main objective to lead the rest of Africa to independence and unity. Accordingly, in December 1958 he invited representatives of nationalist movements in twenty-eight territories still under colonial rule to meet at Accra for the first All-African People's Conference. Nkrumah was at that time at the height of his influence. He was the undisputed leader of the Pan-African movement. At the conference, however, he deliberately shared the limelight with Tom Mboya of Kenya, who proved to be a brilliant chairman. This was the first real demonstration that East Africa was beginning to play a significant part in the African revolution. A few months before, Mboya and Julius Nyerere of Tanganyika had formed the Pan-African Freedom Movement of East and Central Africa, which sent its own delegate to Accra. Kenya and Tanganyika were both, according to Mboya, 'facing a rough patch in the independence struggle' and felt the need for Pan-African support. The Accra conference set up a body to direct and assist anti-colonial struggles and planned to establish other regional organisations on the same lines as PAFMECA. Some African leaders, previously unknown to one another, came away from Accra with a new sense of solidarity and purpose. In particular, Patrice Lumumba returned to the Belgian Congo tremendously impressed by the contacts he had made. The Belgians later admitted that the Accra conference 'brought decisive results for the Congo. There Lumumba got the support which he needed to implement his demand for independence.'

EAST AFRICA: MAU MAU AND MULTIRACIALISM

The 'rough patch in the independence struggle' alluded to by Tom Mboya was largely the result of the uncertainty of British policy towards East Africa during the years 1948–58. The British government was slow to understand that the appeal and compulsion of African nationalism were bound to spread from one end of the continent to the other. It knew that the East African territories were economically much poorer, and educationally more backward, than the West African countries. Britain therefore assumed that nationalism in East Africa would be correspondingly slower to develop. Moreover, British thinking about its East African policy was complicated by the settler problem. It was considered that the presence of the settlers demanded that some alternative should be found to the normal pattern of one-man–one-vote democracy. This alternative was to be along the lines of the 'multiracial' type of constitution which we described in Chapter 17. It was thought that this stage of political development would need to last for at least twenty years. This meant for as long ahead as anyone needed to think.

This distinction between the preparedness of West and East Africa for independence seemed to most European minds to be fully justified when, in 1951, there broke out in Kenya the violent insurrection of the Kikuyu people, known as Mau Mau. No observer of the situation denied that the Kikuyu had exceptional grievances. Their numbers had grown steadily throughout the colonial period, and yet the land into which they might have expanded was occupied by settlers' farms. As the East African Royal Commission of 1955 reported, 'Throughout our inquiry we were impressed by the recurring evidence that particular areas were carrying so large a population that agricultural production in them was being retarded, that the natural resources were being destroyed, and that families were unable to find access to new land.' In face of this land shortage, large numbers of Kikuyu were driven to seek inadequately paid jobs in the towns or else on the European farms. In the towns many were unemployed and took to living by crime. These poverty-stricken and land-hungry people looked with understandable envy and resentment upon the settlers' estates. These were large, well tended and rich. Many of them nevertheless included large areas of uncultivated land.

The Mau Mau rebellion began with the murder of a few British farmers. Their cattle were mutilated and other acts of violence carried out. All these demonstrations were intended to instil such terror into the settler community that most would leave the country. Very similar 257 events had taken place in Ireland during the nineteenth century. There the landlords had been Englishmen, and the Irish peasants poor and landless. In Kenya the government responded by arresting Jomo Kenyatta and other well-known Kikuyu leaders. They were charged with organising the revolt and were condemned to long terms of imprisonment. Kenyatta strenuously denied the accusation. Certainly his removal from the scene had no obvious effect on the course of events. The active insurgents were comparatively few in number. They had their bases in the almost impenetrable forests high up the slopes of Mount Kenya and the Nyandarua range. From these forests they ventured forth in small bands in the dead of night to swoop on outlying farms, to attack the soldiers who had been sent against them, and, very frequently, to take bloody reprisals against fellow Kikuyu suspected of co-operating with the government. The British would not give way in the face of such tactics. The fact that the enemy was unseen made a resort to counter-terrorism almost inevitable. The Kikuyu peasantry were rounded up from their scattered homesteads and made to live in villages which could be defended and policed. People suspected of collaborating with the insurgents were very roughly interrogated in the attempt to get information. The detention camps for captured insurgents used brutal methods to break the psychological resistance of their inmates – that is, their clinging to ideas that the government considered dangerous. Such is the nature of all secret warfare – it is the same in South Africa today. By the end of 1955 the back of the revolt had been broken, at a cost to Britain of more than £20 million and some hundred British lives. The casualties of the civil war between insurgents and collaborators among the Kikuyu were officially estimated at 3,000 but were reckoned by some reputable observers at ten times that number. Nothing like this had ever happened in West Africa. It was akin to the war in Algeria between the nationalists and the French. Obviously not much progress towards self-government was possible in Kenya while the struggle lasted. On the other hand, the Mau Mau revolt did serve to demonstrate that small bodies of British settlers, like those in Kenya, Tanganyika, Nyasaland and Northern Rhodesia, were quite incapable of defending themselves. It also showed that the multiracial constitutions in these countries would be effective only for so long as British force was available to keep them in being.

Immediately, the most important effect of the Mau Mau revolt on political development in Kenya was to prevent the emergence (until after independence) of a single mass party. While the insurrection lasted, the colonial government, fearing that it would spread to the whole country, permitted political organisations on a regional basis only. By the time the emergency was over, regionalism had developed so far that a deep rift had opened between the Kikuyu and the Luo politicians on the one hand and those of the Kalenjin (Paranilotic) and coastal Bantu peoples on the other. When national politics were again permitted, two rival parties emerged – the Kenya African National Union (KANU) and the Kenya African Democratic Union (KADU). Because of their mutual distrust, Kenya, which might have been the first, proved in fact to be the last of the East African countries to achieve independence.

Although for different reasons, Uganda was almost as deeply divided as Kenya. There were three contending interests in the territory. The first was the exclusiveness of the kingdom of Buganda. Buganda feared to lose its privileged position in the territory, which it owed to the settlement established by the colonial power. Most of the Buganda politicians found it difficult to work with those from other parts of the country. Secondly, there was the moderate nationalism of the other traditional kingdoms of the south and west. They resented the privileges and aloofness of Buganda yet felt that they, too, had much to lose from rapid change. Thirdly, there was the less hesitant radicalism of the north and east, where the socialist Uganda People's Congress soon found its main support. The alliance which eventually brought about the independence of Uganda was one between the first of these three interests and the third. This, however, was slow to emerge. So Uganda, despite the absence of a settler problem, was by no means in the forefront of the nationalist struggle in East Africa.

The pacemaker on the eastern side of Africa turned out, surprisingly enough, to be Tanganyika, which was economically and educationally far behind its two northern neighbours. Also political consciousness had been much slower to emerge in Tanganyika during the early years of the African revolution. Yet, between 1956 and 1959, Tanganyika not only pushed through from the backward ranks of colonies to the front, but actually set the pattern for all the British territories from Kenya to the Zambezi. Without any doubt, Tanganyika's sudden success was due to the fact that the Tanganyika African National Union (TANU), founded by Julius Nyerere in 1954, was by far the most efficiently organised mass party to emerge anywhere in Africa since Nkrumah's CPP. Within three or four years of returning to Tanganyika from his studies in Edinburgh, Nyerere had created a nation-wide party structure, with active branches in almost every district in the country. He was helped, as he said himself, by the 259 fact that the population was divided among more than 120 tribal groupings, of which none had been large enough, or central enough, to acquire a predominant position. He was helped, too, by the Swahili language. As a result of the Arab penetration of the nineteenth century and the educational policies of the German and British colonial governments, Swahili was understood throughout the length of the land. He was helped, finally, by the fact that so little in the way of political organisation had been attempted before. He was able to start with a clean slate.

From the first, the weight of Nyerere's attack was directed against the 'multiracial' conception of constitutional advance. As the United Nations Mission of 1954 stated in its report, 'The Africans of this country would like to be assured, both by the United Nations Organisation and by the Administering Authority, that this territory, though multi-racial in population, is primarily an African country and must be developed as such.' During the next four years Nyerere strove by a remarkable moderation to show that, while TANU stood for government by the African majority, non-Africans would have nothing to fear from such a government. Nyerere preached this doctrine with such success that in the elections of 1958, held under the existing 'multiracial' constitution, all of the contested seats were won either by TANU candidates or by those non-Africans who received TANU support in exchange for an undertaking to collaborate with TANU when elected. The result of the elections coincided with the appointment of a new governor, Sir Richard Turnbull, who saw, as Arden-Clarke had seen in the Gold Coast in 1951, that the turning-point in the country's development had now been reached. In October 1958 Turnbull announced that, when self-government was attained, Tanganyika would be ruled by its African majority. Nyerere enthusiastically welcomed this statement, saying,

We have always waited for a Governor of this country even to indicate that it was the government's policy that, when self-government is eventually achieved, the Africans will have a predominant say in the affairs of the country. Now the Africans have this assurance, I am confident that it is going to be the endeavour of the Africans, if non-Africans have any fears left, to remove them quickly.

Under the guidance of Nyerere and Turnbull, who worked together in the same spirit as Nkrumah and Arden-Clarke, Tanganyika fairly rushed out of the colonial era. Full independence was achieved in December 1961, after an apprenticeship of little more than three years. This was in a country with a population larger than Ghana's but with less than a tenth of the number of university and secondary-school graduates.

Obviously, once the multiracial system had been abandoned in Tanganyika, it could no longer be seriously defended in Kenya or Uganda. Nor could it be defended in Nyasaland or Northern Rhodesia, the two northern territories of the Central African Federation which had been formed in 1953 (see Chapter 21). The new trend in British policy as a whole was recognised when, early in 1959, Iain Macleod succeeded Alan Lennox-Boyd as colonial secretary. Whereas Lennox-Boyd's policy had been to strive for every additional year of colonial rule that could be gained, Macleod's was to free Britain from responsibilities in Africa with all possible speed. The 1960 Kenya constitution which bears his name provided for an African majority in the Legislative Assembly. 'At one swift blow,' said a leader of the settlers, 'power was transferred to the Africans.' Further political changes in Kenya, as also in Uganda, were delayed only by disagreements among the Africans themselves. In Kenya, not even the release of Kenyatta in August 1961 could break the deadlock between KANU and KADU. When the country became independent in December 1963, it was under a compromise constitution which provided for considerable regional autonomy. In Uganda Milton Obote, the founder of the Uganda People's Congress, succeeded in 1962 in making an alliance with the royalist Buganda Kabaka Yekka Party. This alliance at last carried the country to independence with the Kabaka of Buganda as head of state.

Britain completed her decolonisation of East Africa in December 1963 by granting independence to Zanzibar under a constitution which left the Arab sultan as head of state. The government was formed by an obviously precarious alliance between the political party directed by the old Arab ruling minority and the smaller of two parties representing the African majority of the population. As we shall see in Chapter 24, this government was to last less than two months before being violently overthrown by a communist-inspired revolution. Here at least, the British were to blame for moving out too soon before ensuring the transfer of political power to a stable regime.

ZAÏRE

While East Africa was hurrying along the path to independence, an even more sudden and perilous emancipation from colonial rule was taking place in Zaïre. Until 1957 the Belgians had continued to rule their huge colony as if it were completely isolated from the changes 261 taking place elsewhere in Africa. When in 1956 a lecturer at the Colonial University in Antwerp, Dr A. A. J. van Bilsen, published a 'Thirty Year Plan for the Political Emancipation of Belgian Africa', he was attacked in Belgium as a dangerous revolutionary. Van Bilsen based his time-table on the perfectly correct notion that 'in the Congo and Ruanda-Urundi the formation of an *élite* and of responsible, directing *cadres* is a generation behind the British and French territories'. Yet, four years after van Bilsen had made this statement, the Belgian authorities who had attacked him for his imprudent haste had left Zaïre to fend for itself. On the eve of the independence of Zaïre in 1960, the Belgian prime minister implicitly acknowledged his country's failure: 'if we could have counted at this moment on proper organisations at a provincial level, the political solutions for the Congo would have been greatly facilitated'.

The independence of Zaïre was in fact far from being a triumph of African nationalism. It was, rather, a result of Belgian irresolution and of the inability of a small country like Belgium to stand up to international pressures. The first crack in the wall of Belgian paternalism came in 1957, when Africans first took part in municipal elections. Joseph Kasavubu, who had built up a position of political leadership among the Bakongo people of the lower Congo, was returned as mayor of one of the Leopoldville *communes* (municipalities). This was typical of what happened elsewhere. An American observer wrote, 'Almost every party formed in the Congo had its origin in a tribal group, and since there were many tribes, there were many parties. Local interests were paramount and never ceased to be a powerful factor in politics.' Patrice Lumumba, who emerged at the same period as a political leader in Stanleyville, was the only Congolese politician who had a clear vision of the importance of creating a single, nation-wide party. To succeed, he would have needed not only time but also some prolonged resistance from the Belgian colonial government in order to force other Congolese politicians to see the necessity for such a party. This resistance, however, was not forthcoming.

In August 1958 de Gaulle visited Brazzaville, just across the river from Leopoldville, to proclaim autonomy within the French Community for the four colonies which had formed the Federation of French Equatorial Africa. Naturally, this provoked unrest on the Belgian side of the Congo river. Many of the little tribal parties began to demand independence for the Belgian Congo. Strikes and disorders broke out, and in January 1959, less than a month after Lumumba's return from the Accra conference, there was a serious riot in Leopoldville. Mobs of unemployed people sacked European shops and mission schools. The situation in the capital was brought under control in less than a week, but the blow to Belgian prestige was great. During the year that followed it became evident that law and order in many parts of the country were on the verge of breakdown. Some of the most dangerous situations were the result of tension between rival groups of Congolese. In Kasai province, for example, a civil war threatened between the Kasai Baluba, who worked on the oil-palm plantations, and the Benelulua who regarded the Baluba as intruders into their country. Again, in the mandated territory of Ruanda-Urundi an extreme state of tension was developing between the Batutsi ruling class and the Bahutu majority of the population. The Batutsi had maintained their social and political predominance under both German and Belgian rule, and their object, like that of the settlers in Rhodesia, was to gain political independence for the territory before the introduction of a universal franchise destroyed their ascendancy. The Belgians reacted to the steadily growing defiance of the Batutsi by suddenly switching their support to the newly formed Bahutu political movement, but they were unable to control the situation which resulted. All over the country, but especially in the north, the Batutsi were massacred by their former subjects, their houses burnt, their possessions looted, while the Belgian administration looked on, unable or unwilling to intervene. By the end of 1959, therefore, Belgian Africa presented a very different picture from that of 1956. It is true that the disorders had all been local ones. It is also true that to a larger power than Belgium these disorders would not have appeared impossible to suppress. But to Belgium, in the words of a government spokesman, they presented a terrifying alternative: 'to try to organise independence as quickly as possible, or to accept responsibility for the bloodshed which any delay would probably bring about. A colonial war entails heavy financial losses, which a small nation cannot afford. We are fearful lest another Algeria might develop in the Congo.'

At the beginning of 1960, therefore, the Belgian government summoned a group of Congolese political leaders to a 'Round Table Conference' in Ostend. Several of the Africans who took part have stated that they went to Belgium expecting to settle for a five-year transitional period leading up to independence. They would have been willing to accept this. But Belgium was by this time disillusioned with the Congo. It was not prepared to take the responsibility of continuing to govern the country while Congolese political parties united themselves or while Congolese civil servants were trained to 263 take over administrative duties from the Belgians. Above all, Belgium was not prepared to send any more troops to suppress the disorders that would certainly grow worse. While the conference was meeting, a cry went up throughout the country of 'Pas un soldat au Congo' ('Not a single soldier to Congo'). The Congolese negotiators at the Round Table Conference found no resistance against which they could bargain, no strength that would force them to unite. They came away with a date for independence which was less than six months away – 30 June 1960.

In May 1960 there were held the first national elections ever to take place in the Belgian Congo. The results were indecisive, but a few days before the end of Belgian rule Lumumba, after lengthy negotiations, succeeded in forming a government with himself as prime minister and Kasavubu, his chief rival, as president. Even the independence ceremonies were a disaster. A paternal speech from King Baudouin provoked the bitter reply from Lumumba, 'Nous ne sommes plus vos singes' ('We are no longer your monkeys'). Six days later the Congolese army, the Force Publique, mutinied, 'It all started', said Lumumba, 'when General Janssens, the Belgian Commander, refused to promote Congolese to the rank of officer.' The soldiers turned upon the Belgian officers and their families, whereupon Belgian troops intervened to protect Europeans and their property. With the collapse of law and order, all the old hatreds and humiliations came to the surface. Africans avenged themselves on Europeans, and different peoples within Zaïre fought each other. The worst inter-African conflict took place in Kasai, where the tension between Baluba and Benelulua now broke out into open warfare. The political struggle between the regionalists and the centralists, which was so much a feature of this period of African history (in Kenya and French West Africa, for example), became charged with danger in Zaïre. Kasavubu of the Bakongo, Kalonji of the Baluba and Tshombe in Katanga all wanted to set up a loose federal structure, in which real power would reside with the provincial and tribal groups. Lumumba, on the other hand, tried to work for a strong, centralised state. On 11 July Tshombe withdrew Katanga from Zaïre and declared its independence. This move received the backing of the Union Minière, the huge company which controlled the Katanga copper-mines. The Zaïre government thus lost the greater part of its revenues. Lumumba called upon the United Nations for military help to halt the disintegration of the country and to rid the country of the Belgian troops which had intervened in the mutiny. Thus the United Nations entered the most critical operation in its history. Wisely, it called for most of its contingents of soldiers to be sent from the African states. But when these forces did not do exactly as Lumumba wished, he turned to Russia for assistance. The chaotic situation in Zaïre thus became a matter for world-wide concern, introducing the rivalries between communism and capitalism into the heart of the African continent. This made the African states more determined to follow a neutral path, but the 'Congo crisis' produced deep divisions in their ranks, as we shall see in subsequent chapters. As early as 1960 Nkrumah remarked prophetically, 'Once we admit our impotence to solve the question of the Congo primarily with our African resources, we tacitly admit that real self-government on the African continent is impossible.'

The calling in of the Russians proved the downfall of Lumumba. Hitherto Belgian and other western influences had been confined to a veiled support of Tshombe's secessionist movement in Katanga. Henceforward, these influences, with American backing, began to intervene in the affairs of the central Congolese government. Lumumba was overthrown by an alliance between the army, led by Colonel Mobutu, and many of the regional politicians, headed by Kasavubu. The Russians were expelled. Lumumba was arrested and handed over to Tshombe, in whose custody he was murdered in March 1961. Faced with the problem of the central government's bankruptcy, the United Nations at last began to intervene more forcefully to break the secession of Katanga. It was only in 1963, however, after much heavy fighting, that this province was occupied and reunited with the Congo state. By this time it was the United Nations that was bankrupt. A number of its richer member states, including Russia and France, had refused to contribute to the Congo operations. Those who did contribute (Britain and America especially) were suspected of paying the piper in order to call the tune; that is, of using the United Nations in order to achieve their own aims. The United Nations had no option but to withdraw from the Congo. Left to itself, the central government could not hope to hold the all-important Katanga region by force. The unity and the solvency of the country could only be maintained by admitting Tshombe and his supporters to the central government on their own terms.

Meanwhile in Rwanda, and to a lesser extent in Burundi, tension between the Batutsi and the Bahutu continued to grow. Attempts to form the two little countries into one independent state failed, and they went their separate ways. The United Nations supervised the final stages of the transition to independence. In Rwanda the previously subservient majority of the population overthrew with fearful violence the Batutsi monarchy and proclaimed a republic. In Burundi the monarchy survived but was constitutionalised. Both states achieved independence in 1962. In Rwanda this at first served merely to intensify the harrying of the Batutsi, most of whom were driven as refugees into neighbouring countries.

MADAGASCAR

As we have seen in previous chapters, Madagascar has had in many ways a history rather separate from that of the African mainland. The population of the island is largely non-African, the language entirely so. At least since the beginning of the nineteenth century, there has been little coming and going across the Mozambique Channel. During the colonial period, when it was under French rule, Madagascar was a kind of halfway house between the French territories in West Africa and those in South-East Asia and the Pacific. From the time of the Second World War, however, the isolation of Madagascar from the rest of Africa began at last to be broken down. During the war the island experienced the occupation of British forces, many of them African. After the war Malagasy students began to go in some numbers to France. There they encountered French-speaking students from the West African territories, to whom they felt more akin than to the South-East Asians. Most important of all, perhaps, was the fact that the timing of Madagascar's struggle for independence coincided with the African revolution rather than with the Asian one. The first modern political party with independence as its object was founded in 1946. This party had its first trial of strength with the French in the following year, when a famine caused by the mismanagement of the government-controlled Rice Board gave rise to a violent rebellion. The revolt sprang up all over the island, among many different groups, including the aristocratic Hova, as a spontaneous reaction to colonial rule. The ferocity of the French military action against the rebels led to a still more widespread insurrection, which took nearly a year to repress. Many aspects of the Malagasy rebellion were similar to the earliest anti-colonial rebellions, such as the Maji-Maji outbreak in German East Africa in 1905–6. The Maji-Maji rebels thought that the German bullets would be harmlessly turned into water. Similarly, during the Malagasy rebellion,

When the rebels, armed only with pointed sticks, went in to attack troops armed with rifles and machine-guns, they advanced in step in serried ranks shouting 'Rano, Rano', which means 'Water, Water', as a magical formula intended to turn the bullets into water as they left the guns. Even some of the

Independence: East Africa and Zaïre

French soldiers began to have doubts and to panic when their fire proved ineffective through faulty aiming or the use of old cartridges.[1]

After the great rebellion, Madagascar entered upon an unusually smooth transition from colonial rule to self-government and then to independence. Much of the credit for this is due to the moderation of one remarkable personality, Philibert Tsiranana, who, in common with many other African leaders, began his career as a teacher. He was opposed to the rebellion and, after its repression, used all his gifts to heal the deep scars. His Social Democratic Party co-operated with the French in implementing reforms introduced under the Loi Cadre of 1956, and some of the Malagasy who had been sentenced by the French to long terms of imprisonment for instigating the rebellion became ministers in his cabinet. In the de Gaulle referendum of 1958 he was supported not only by the Malagasy but also by many of the 80,000 French settlers on the island. When the country became independent in June 1960, Tsiranana became the first president. The only serious opposition to his government came from the Hova people of the highlands around the capital. These former rulers of the island are still the best educated and the most sophisticated group. They were mainly protestant, while the majority of the population was Roman Catholic. These religious and social tensions took time to be resolved. Nevertheless, Madagascar became an important and unequivocal member of the community of African states. It played a leading part both in the union of French-speaking states, the Afro-Malagasy Joint Organisation (OCAM) and in the Organisation for African Unity. Madagascar also responded to the economic overtures made by South Africa. The Malagasy, ancient colonists from across the Indian Ocean, had at long last been assimilated into Africa.

[1] O. Mannoni, *Prospero and Caliban* (London, 1956), p. 59.

21   Independence: southern Central Africa

In the 1950s the colonial territories of southern Central Africa appeared to be moving in an opposite, or at least very different, direction from those of Middle Africa. The colonies of West, Central and East Africa, as we have seen, were advancing, albeit at an uneven pace, towards political independence. In 1953 the British government decided to create a constitutional arrangement for its southern Central African territories which set them apart from its other African lands. The protectorates of Northern Rhodesia and Nyasaland, which were predominantly African, were joined with Southern Rhodesia, which had been effectively controlled by its white settlers since 1891, to form the Central African Federation.

It was hoped that this would grow into an economically powerful, multiracial state, big enough to act as a counterweight to the power of white-dominated South Africa and as a buffer to any expansionist aims still aspired to by the National Party government which came into power in that country in 1948. One of the many compromises built into the Central African Federation was a division of ultimate responsibility between the metropolitan colonial country and a locally based settler government. After ten years, the Federation broke upon the rock of this unresolved conflict: London could not resist the tide of African nationalism in the northern territories, while Salisbury was determined to hang on for a much longer time.

Along either side of the Central African Federation, and controlling its main lines of access to the Atlantic and to the Indian Ocean, lay the Portuguese colonies of Angola and Mozambique. For the thirty years after the Second World War, the Portuguese empire in Africa proved an exception to the rule that a colonial system based in Europe would not resist the onslaught of African nationalism. The reasons for this are interesting. First, Portugal was one of the poorest countries of Europe. It had few industries and a standard of living not much higher than many African countries. Unlike other colonial powers, its colonial interests were considered to be not marginal but central to its economic existence. Secondly, the Portuguese state was a dictatorship. The Portuguese people, accustomed to authoritarianism at home, were unmoved by authoritarian rule in the colonies. Dr Salazar, who was prime minister of Portugal from 1932 to 1968, consistently played upon feelings of national pride and glorified the achievements of the Portuguese imperial past as an indu ement to future greatness.

However, Portuguese Africa was in the 1930s almost completely undeveloped and was a financial burden to Portugal. Public works, sugar and other estates, and the few mines were operated largely by forced labour. In the 1930s and 1940s a spate of colonial legislation from Lisbon gave the impression of great change, but there was very little economic development in Angola and Mozambique until the 1950s. The motives for this development were suggested by Salazar in 1943: 'The rich extensive colonial lands, underdeveloped and sparsely populated, are the natural complement for metropolitan agriculture. In addition they will take care of Portugal's excessive population.' Large numbers of Portuguese migrated to the African territories. By the late 1960s there were over 250,000 settlers in Angola and 130,000 in Mozambique. The African populations were 5 million and 8 million respectively. Agricultural and mining development (the most important being the Angolan diamond mines) remained firmly in European hands.

Portugal's racial policy was in theory similar to the French policy of assimilation. The status of citizen, however, conferred few political rights, in Portugal or in the colonies. To become a citizen, an African had to comply with a whole range of educational and economic opportunities so lacking for Africans that only a small number became *assimilados* (assimilated people). By 1950 there were only 30,000 *assimilados* in Angola and 25,000 in Mozambique. The vast majority of the population were *indigenas* (natives), whose main function in the eyes of the administration was to provide labour. Much was made of the virtue of work. In 1943 a colonial minister said, 'If we want to civilise the native we must make him adopt, as an elementary moral precept, the notion that he has no right to live without working.' The economic expansion of the colonies greatly benefited Portugal itself, and by the early 1960s about 25 per cent of the national budget was derived from Africa. In 1951 the colonies were theoretically incorporated into Portugal as overseas 'provinces', but the inferior status of the African *indigenas* continued.

Like the Belgians in the Congo, but with far more determination, the Portuguese refused to heed the course of events in the rest of Africa. In November 1960, a few months after Macmillan's Cape Town 'Wind of Change' speech (see below, p. 273), it was declared, 'We are not in Africa like so many others. We will continue as always   269 our policy of integration. To this end it is necessary for us to be what we have always been, and we will not change.'

THE CENTRAL AFRICAN FEDERATION

During the war years, both Southern and Northern Rhodesia had shared in the economic boom conditions experienced by South Africa. The demand for copper – a vital component of many armaments – soared, and good prices were obtained by Northern Rhodesia. A number of manufacturing industries were established in Southern Rhodesia, and its agricultural production, particularly of tobacco, cattle and maize, increased. Southern Rhodesia was used by the British as a training area for Royal Air Force pilots, and after the war considerable numbers of British ex-servicemen and their families settled in the country. The white population in 1954 was 80,500; by 1960 it had reached 220,000, compared to a total African population of over 4 million. The great majority of these whites lived in the towns, particularly Salisbury and Bulawayo, where they were joined by a large influx of Africans from the rural areas. The settler-dominated Southern Rhodesian government had divided the country along racial lines in very much the same manner as contemporary South African governments: urban Africans were forced to live in overcrowded 'townships', while the 1930 Land Apportionment Act had effects similar to the 1913 and 1936 Land Acts of South Africa. In the case of Southern Rhodesia, roughly half the land (and most of it the best land) was reserved for white occupation. Whites were employed in the top jobs and received much higher salaries than Africans.

The coming to power of the National Party in 1948 finally alienated English-speaking Rhodesians (there were only a small number of Afrikaners in the country) from the idea of joining South Africa. This had been considered off and on for many years, especially in the early 1920s, as a solution to their basic problem, that of being outnumbered by about fifteen to one by the African population. White Rhodesian settlers objected not so much to the extreme racial policies of the South African government as to its anti-British and republican sentiments. Sir Godfrey Huggins (later Lord Malvern), leader of the Southern Rhodesian settlers, now joined forces with Sir Roy Welensky of Northern Rhodesia in reviving schemes for the union of their territories. They argued that although in Northern Rhodesia and Nyasaland the European populations were even smaller than in Southern Rhodesia, it would be preferable to control these predominantly African lands, difficult though this might be, than have them as independent neighbours. The settlers hoped that a large Federation would soon become a fully amalgamated Dominion free from British control. They also wanted the economic benefits that were expected to result from a federation of the three territories, with the opportunities for further white settlement which this would create.

The British government supported the federal scheme for wider reasons. Certainly the economic advantages counted for much and were used to try to persuade Africans to consent to the plan. It was stressed how interdependent the three territories had become. The Rhodesias were dependent upon Nyasaland for labour, the two northern countries upon Southern Rhodesia for manufactured goods and some agricultural products, and the copper-mines upon Southern Rhodesian coal and transport. An even closer economic union, it was argued, must result in improved living standards for all the inhabitants, African as well as European. Further, Britain was at this time fostering multiracial constitutions in the East African territories (see Chapter 17), and the Federation that came into being in 1953 was an attempt to swing Central Africa out of the South African into the East African orbit. The British government was well aware of the racialism of the Rhodesian settlers and of the opposition of the majority of Africans to the idea of Federation, but it hoped that the benefits of political stability and economic expansion would soften the former and allay the latter. Moreover, by stopping short of amalgamation, at Federation, it kept alive interest in the administration of the two northern territories, which gave it the ultimate power to put the process into reverse.

The economic growth of the Federation was, as expected, rapid. New industries were developed in Southern Rhodesia, and towns (especially Salisbury, the federal capital) increased in size. One of the world's largest dams was constructed at Kariba on the Zambezi, to provide cheap electricity for the copper-mines of Northern Rhodesia and the industries of Southern Rhodesia. Africans shared less in this expansion than did Europeans. In 1961 the average annual income of wage-earning Africans was still only £87, and many Africans were not even wage-earners. In particular, Nyasaland had reasons to be dissatisfied, as all it got economically from the federal government was a comparatively small annual subsidy.

In Southern Rhodesia modern African nationalist opposition to white rule dated back to the 1940s and 1950s, when labour movements were formed, including a union of railway workers led by Joshua Nkomo. The Reverend Ndabaningi Sithole and Robert Mugabe were leading members of a teachers' association. In 1957 a revived African National Congress came into being, under Nkomo, but this was banned by the Whitehead administration two years later. By 1961 a new party, the Zimbabwe African People's Union, ZAPU, had emerged, again under Nkomo's leadership (the name Zimbabwe chosen for the country when it had achieved majority rule was deliberately taken from that of the renowned capital of the great Shona state of medieval times). In 1963 Nkomo attempted to set up a government-in-exile in Dar es Salaam. In response to this, Sithole founded the Zimbabwe African National Union, ZANU, within Rhodesia. Thus was created the initial critical split in the nationalist movement. ZAPU was largely supported by Ndebele people and had Bulawayo as its base, while ZANU had big Shona support and operated from Salisbury. In Northern Rhodesia and Nyasaland, African nationalist activity also predated the establishment of the Federation, but it was this that gave nationalism in the two territories its focus and its sense of urgency.

Within ten years, the two contending forces of settler intransigence and African nationalism had destroyed the new state. The European politicians who controlled both the federal and the Southern Rhodesian Parliaments were determined to maintain European supremacy. 'Political control', wrote Lord Malvern in 1956, 'must remain in the hands of civilised people, which for the foreseeable future means the Europeans.' Welensky likened the Federation not to a partnership of equals but to the relationship existing between rider and horse. He was a skilful politician, and when the franchise qualifications were amended in 1957 he appeared to give Africans a greater representation while in fact decreasing the value of the African vote. He made it clear that, at the 1960 conference to revise the federal constitution, he would demand independence from the last traces of British control. African resentment at Welensky's past performance and future threats came to a head early in 1959, soon after the return of Dr Banda to Nyasaland after an absence of over forty years. Demonstrations, strikes and riots led to states of emergency being proclaimed in Southern Rhodesia and Nyasaland, and to the detention without trial of many African nationalist politicians.

The federal government maintained that opposition to the Federation came only from a handful of 'extremists'. Many people in Britain shared this belief. The Devlin Commission, which inquired into the Nyasaland troubles, rejected it:

The government's view is that these nationalist aspirations are the thoughts of only a small minority of political Africans, mainly of self-seekers who think their prospects of office will be worse under Federation; and that the great majority of the people are indifferent to the issue. We have not found this to be so. It was generally acknowledged that the opposition to Federation was there, that it was deeply rooted and almost universally held.

The 1959 emergencies were the dividing-line in the fortunes of the Federation. Early the following year the Belgians decided to pull out of the neighbouring Congo. By this time the British government had lost faith in the multiracial experiments in Tanganyika and Kenya. Harold Macmillan, the British prime minister, during his 1960 African tour, was critical of the lack of progress towards genuine partnership in the Federation. He ended his tour in Cape Town, where he delivered his famous 'Wind of Change' speech before the white South African members of parliament:

We have seen the awakening of national consciousness in peoples who have for centuries lived in dependence upon some other power. Fifteen years ago this movement spread through Asia. Many countries there of different races and civilisations pressed their claim to an independent life. Today the same thing is happening in Africa and the most striking of all the impressions I have formed since I left London a month ago is of the strength of this African national consciousness. The wind of change is blowing through the continent, and whether we like it or not this growth of national consciousness is a political fact, and our national policies must take account of it.

Macmillan's speech surprised and annoyed white South Africans, and was possibly one of the factors which led to the Sharpeville and other incidents of violence later that year. North of the Limpopo it marked a further stage in the decline of the Federation. The Monckton Commission, which was sent to look into the workings of the Federation, reported that, for Africans, 'partnership was a sham'. The commission recommended that if all else failed, the territories should have the right to secede. Iain Macleod, the colonial secretary who was responsible for the departure from the multiracial idea in Kenya (see Chapter 20), decided that the Federation should not stand in the way of the two northern territories attaining African majority rule. Under Banda's leadership, Africans in Nyasaland achieved this in 1961. The Northern Rhodesian settlers, with Welensky's help, delayed a similar development in that country for two years longer. By 1963, however, Kenneth Kaunda, who had built up a great reputation for his statesmanship, led Northern Rhodesia to this position. He and Banda made it clear that they would take the earliest opportunity to withdraw from the Federation.

In Southern Rhodesia the picture was equally bleak for supporters of Federation. In 1961 African nationalist leaders rejected a new 273 constitution which would have given them a limited voice in the government, and in 1962 the white electorate voted the Rhodesian Front, a new right-wing party under the leadership of Winston Field, into power. This party was committed to the maintenance of white rule in the country. A supporter of the Rhodesian Front wrote,

I have faithfully followed the Huggins–Welensky line for over twenty-five years. But at the next election, I shall be asked to vote away the Europeans' long-standing protection against their swamping by hordes of primitive people, and agree to having them live next door to me and attending school with my children. This I cannot do . . . call it prejudice if you will but however liberal-minded we are, we can never cease to shrink from close and intimate contact with the Africans.[1]

The British government appointed Mr R. A. Butler as a special minister to preside over the dismantling of the Federation, and on the last day of 1963 it came to an end. Nyasaland became independent as Malawi in July 1964, and Northern Rhodesia followed as the Republic of Zambia in October of the same year. Southern Rhodesia reverted to its pre-Federation position, but with the immense advantage of retaining control over most of the Federation's not inconsiderable armed forces, including some quite modern aircraft.

Faced with the unscrambling of the Federation and the rapid transition to independence by the two northern territories, Winston Field's RF government demanded the same treatment for Southern Rhodesia, under the 1961 constitution. Even if Africans were prepared to participate in the operation of this constitution – which the majority were not – its complicated income and educational franchise qualifications (and its even more complicated two-'roll' system) meant that Africans would not have been within sight of majority rule for very many years; and white politicians were adept at constitutional manipulations in favour of maintaining white rule. Under these circumstances the British Conservative government refused to grant independence to Southern Rhodesia.

The Rhodesian Front government for its part used increasingly harsh methods to break up the nationalist movements, and by 1964 there was much violence in Rhodesia, particularly in the African 'townships', between the nationalists and the police and among supporters of the rival groups. The government banned both parties, placed the leadership, including Nkomo and Sithole, under restriction without trial, and temporarily broke the back of the nationalist

---

[1] *The Citizen*, 2 November 1962, quoted in James Barber, *Rhodesia: the road to rebellion* (Oxford, 1967), pp. 160–1.

movement. During 1965 both groups were reorganising from the safety of Lusaka.

Throughout 1963 and into 1964 Field tried to negotiate independence with the Westminster government and failed – a failure which caused him to resign in April 1964 and to be replaced as prime minister by the tougher and more resilient Ian Smith who continued negotiations with the British Labour government, which came into office in October 1964. Finally, after repeated threats to do so, on 11 November 1965 Smith's government made its Unilateral Declaration of Independence, the opening paragraph of which intentionally echoed the American Declaration of Independence of 1776:

Whereas in the course of human affairs history has shown it may become necessary for a people to resolve the political affiliations which have connected them with another people and to assume among other nations the separate and equal status to which they are entitled . . .

These and other sentiments in Smith's declaration must have seemed bitterly ironic to the African majority of Rhodesians. White Rhodesia's Unilateral Declaration of Independence failed to secure the recognition of any other country in the world. Nevertheless, thanks to the practical co-operation of South Africa and Portugal, it was able to survive for more than ten years without encountering any serious challenge to its authority.

THE COLONIAL WARS IN ANGOLA AND MOZAMBIQUE

In February 1961 serious rioting occurred in Luanda, the capital of Angola, after armed members of the Movimento Popular de Libertação de Angola (MPLA) had tried to free political prisoners from the city's prison. This had been timed to coincide with an abortive plan to attack Luanda by a Portuguese dissident, Henique Galvao, who seized the liner *Santa Maria* and hoped to enlist the support of anti-Salazar whites in Angola. In fact many Luanda whites went on the rampage against blacks after the failure of the MPLA attempt. Throughout the fifteen years of struggle, only a few whites in either Angola or Mozambique, however much they detested the Salazar dictatorship, sided with the nationalist movements. In March 1961 a much more serious revolt broke out in northern Angola, by supporters of the Uniao das Populações de Angola (UPA), which had been formed in 1958 by Holden Roberto. The UPA operated from Zaïre, and Roberto was much influenced by Patrice Lumumba. The party was largely supported by Bakongo people, who lived on both sides of 275 the Angola–Zaïre border; in 1962 the UPA merged with another party to form the Frente Nacional de Libertação de Angola (FNLA).

The 1961 insurrection in northern Angola was extremely serious for the Portuguese. Over 6,000 'loyal' Africans were killed by the nationalist guerrilla forces, and some 2,000 whites – the largest single number of European civilians killed in any African territory during the anti-colonial struggles. In spite of the Luanda riots and the troubles in neighbouring Zaïre, the Portuguese were totally unprepared for the outbreak of hostilities and had to rush military reinforcements (50,000 troops in all) from Portugal. These largely succeeded in suppressing the uprising by the end of 1961, but only after about 50,000 local Africans had been killed. This, however, was but the first stage in the Angolan revolt, and by 1962 and 1964 similar nationalist insurrections had broken out in Portuguese Guinea and Mozambique respectively.

Portuguese colonial policy was attacked in the United Nations by all countries except South Africa and Spain. A UN sub-committee (which was not allowed to enter Angola) reported at the end of 1961: 'The Portuguese authorities face a historic choice; whether to continue to rely on the use of force, with its inevitable miseries, or to respond to world opinion and take measures to build a new relationship with the people of Angola. What is needed is readiness to understand the new forces in the world.' Portugal, however, showed few signs of understanding these forces. After the outbreak of the revolt in Angola, reforming legislation was rushed through by the government. The status of *indigenas* was formally abolished, and all colonial inhabitants became in law Portuguese citizens. The local Legislative Councils were given slightly increased powers. Yet the Portuguese resolve to remain an imperial power was undiminished. Further immigration was encouraged. 'We believe it necessary', said the overseas minister, 'to continue the settlement of our Africa by European Portuguese, who will make their homes there and find in Africa a true extension of their country.' Such measures, he said, 'prove the sureness with which we contemplate the future, the serenity with which we face the difficulties of the present, and our faithfulness to the course of history'.

There were three main reasons for the long-drawn-out nature of the revolts in Portuguese Africa. One was Portugal's determination to suppress them. Another was the resolve of the nationalist movements to continue the struggles (and the support these movements received from outside). But the third was the disunity among the nationalist movements themselves, especially in Angola. In 1962 Roberto set up a government-in-exile (based on Leopoldville/Kinshasa) with himself as prime minister, and an Ovimbundu, Jonas Savimbi, as foreign minister. This was an attempt to widen FNLA support beyond the northern Bakongo. But the MPLA, which had been founded in 1956 as an urban-based movement, largely by *mestiços* (mixed African–European), with considerable communist influence, remained hostile. This was particularly because Roberto was known to be obtaining American support (this had to be clandestine, because the United States and Portugal were NATO allies). At the end of 1962 Dr Agostinho Neto, a physician and poet, was elected president of MPLA, which operated from Brazzaville in the Congo Republic (the former French colony of Middle Congo). Numbers of other ephemeral groups came and went, but in 1966 the third main Angolan movement was formed by Savimbi, who had left FNLA two years before; this was the União Nacional para a Independência Total de Angola (UNITA). As far as military activity was concerned, the struggle went through a number of stages. Early on, the MPLA started operations in the Cabinda enclave (where in 1965 a separatist independence movement had emerged), but by the mid-1960s the efforts of the Portuguese army and secret police (PIDE) had largely crippled the nationalists' initiatives. There was a resurgence of activity, however, in the late 1960s, with MPLA operating in a mountainous area north-east of Luanda and in the eastern district, from across the Zambian frontier, along the line of the Benguela railway; UNITA, on a very small scale, in the south and also near the railway; and FNLA from various points across the Zaïre frontier in the north. In 1968 Neto took a leaf out of Savimbi's book and set up his headquarters within Angola. By this time many African states and the OAU had withdrawn their initial support from FNLA and were more enthusiastic about MPLA, while continuing attempts to reconcile the hostile groups so as to present a united front to the Portuguese.

The military activities of these guerrillas pinned down large numbers of Portuguese forces, which by the early 1970s were becoming increasingly Africanised, but they did not seriously threaten the main rural centres of population or the towns or, generally, the Angolan economy. The same could be said for the revolt in the tiny West African colony of Guinea. By the early 1970s it was the fighting in Mozambique that was causing the Portuguese the greatest problems. The Frente de Libertação do Moçambique (Frelimo) was formed in 1962 in Dar es Salaam by the joining of three earlier-established parties, under the presidency of Eduardo Mondlane. Mondlane was born in southern Mozambique and studied in the United States; later he worked for the UN in New York for five years and then taught at an American university. In the early years Frelimo was supported mainly by Makonde and Nyanja peoples. The Portuguese had learned from their bitter experiences in Angola and had prepared militarily for a nationalist revolt in Mozambique, in particular in the north, along the border with Tanzania. But these preparations disturbed the Makonde, many of whom fled across the frontier. They formed the first recruits into Frelimo's army. In 1964 Frelimo started making attacks across the Rovuma river against Portuguese installations on the Makonde plateau. The guerrillas tried to move south along the coast but could make little progress because of the traditional hostility of the Makua. Instead, in 1965 they spread their operations into Niassa district (bordering Malawi), and by 1968 had infiltrated as far south as Tete. Up to this time the scale of the revolt had been quite small and had not unduly worried the Portuguese. Mondlane was disappointed not to have achieved his initial aim of a Mozambique-wide insurrection, set off by Frelimo's 1964 military actions. However, the presence of Frelimo guerrillas in Tete district was a more serious matter.

In 1966 the Portuguese announced plans for a dam and hydro-electric power station on the Zambezi river at the Cabora Bassa gorge. This is some 95 kilometres long and 300 metres wide, and lies about halfway between Zumbo, on the Zambian frontier, and the town of Tete. An international consortium, Zamco, was set up, organised by the Anglo-American Corporation of South Africa and made up of French, West German and South African concerns. Work on the dam started in 1969 and it was completed in 1974; the first generators were tested in early 1975. Cabora Bassa was the fourth largest hydro-electric scheme in the world, and when fully operational would pro-duce far more power than Mozambique could use. Under an agree-ment drawn up with the Portuguese in 1969, a large proportion of the electrical power would be sold to South Africa. A high-tension line 1,400 kilometres long was erected to link Cabora Bassa with the South African grid system at Middelburg.

The Cabora Bassa scheme had far-reaching implications for south-ern Africa; it amounted, in effect, to a declaration by Portugal that she was there to stay in Mozambique, with South Africa supporting this resolve. Naturally Frelimo tried to impede or harass the construction of this scheme, Mondlane saying that it was his intention 'to paralyse the work on the dam, or to make it more costly than the contractors had calculated'. For their part, the Portuguese, with some South African military or police support, vigorously defended the project.

278

Mondlane, who had led Frelimo so resolutely, did not live to see the successful outcome of the revolt in Mozambique. Early in 1969 he was killed by a parcel bomb, rumoured to have been sent by Portuguese agents, while working at his office desk in Dar es Salaam. He was succeeded as president of Frelimo by Samora Machel, the army commander in the field.

If Frelimo could not prevent work on the dam, its forces made their presence felt widely over Tete district. In 1973 they moved their guerrilla operations yet further south, into Manica district, where they seriously disrupted the rail and road links between Beira and Rhodesia. So critical was the Portuguese military position in what by then were four 'operational areas' that in March 1974 it was decided to airlift 10,000 more troops to Mozambique to join the 60,000 already there. It was the intensification of the fighting in Mozambique that broke the back of the Portuguese resolve. In 1963 Dr Caetano had succeeded Salazar as prime minister and had introduced some devolution of power between metropolitan Portugal and the so-called overseas provinces. But there were no signs of any moves towards granting eventual independence. Indeed, the Cabora Bassa scheme showed how determined the Portuguese government was to remain in Africa.

The guerrilla wars in Angola, Mozambique and Guinea were, however, very costly to the weak Portuguese economy in terms of money and manpower. People in Portugal increasingly suffered from war-weariness, and many individuals, in the army and in industry and commerce, considered that the country's best chance of economic recovery lay in associating with the European Economic Community rather than in pursuing pipe-dreams of an African empire. On 25 April 1974 officers of the Movimento das Forcas Armadas overthrew the Caetano regime and installed General Spinola as president. The new government announced that Portugal would grant some form of self-government to its overseas possessions. Within a few months Guinea (Bissau) achieved full independence, but the situations within Angola and Mozambique were more complex.

After the April coup, the Portuguese had to adopt the unfamiliar role of peacemakers between the three hostile nationalist groups in Angola. Finally, after a meeting at Alvor in Portugal, a provisional government was set up to prepare the way for independence in November 1975. But during the intervening period, the movements consolidated their military and political positions, FNLA occupying the north, MPLA at last getting a firm foothold in Luanda and the Mbundu hinterland, while UNITA built up its support in the central-southern districts, amongst the Ovimbundu, the largest   279 ethnic group in Angola. By June 1975 the transitional government had collapsed. The great powers intervened, not to bring about a peaceful solution, but to make the situation even more dangerous. The United States and China provided support to FNLA and UNITA, while the Soviet Union backed MPLA. By the middle of 1975, if not earlier, Cuba had sent instructors to the MPLA forces. In August South African troops occupied hydro-electric installations near the South-West African border, to protect them from attacks by MPLA and the South-West African People's Organisation (SWAPO); by this time considerable numbers of Cubans, and some Russians, were helping MPLA. By September it appeared that MPLA had won the increasingly bitter Angolan civil war. It was known that Cuban fighting troops were on their way by sea. Small numbers of South African advisers moved into southern Angola to support UNITA forces. At the end of October a South African mobile column rapidly advanced north, capturing Benguela and Lobito and other towns, and reaching as far as the Cuanza river to the south of Luanda. Meanwhile, FNLA forces, including mercenaries and with Zaïrean support, had advanced from the north to within striking distance of Luanda.

By the middle of November, however, massive amounts of Russian and Cuban equipment had arrived at Luanda, including heavy tanks and artillery, and many thousands of Cuban troops were airlifted in (there were never more than 2,000 South African soldiers in Angola). The South Africans and Savimbi were reluctant to attack Luanda, the inhabitants of which were strongly pro-MPLA, but their caution was not shared by Roberto, who launched the ill-equipped FNLA forces against the Cubans and was decisively defeated. FNLA soldiers were in full retreat, and Roberto and Savimbi quarrelled violently over future tactics.

South Africa had failed to obtain US and other western support for its military presence in Angola, and had been left, so white South African politicians considered, 'scandalously in the lurch'. By the end of January 1976 South African forces began to withdraw, and within a few weeks had left Angolan territory altogether, after receiving an undertaking from Neto's government that there would be no interference with the hydro-electric works on the Kunene river. As the South Africans withdrew, UNITA's positions crumbled before the advance of MPLA and Cuban forces. Apart from some anti-MPLA guerrilla activity, which has continued sporadically, Angola was henceforward controlled by Neto and the MPLA.

280   The implications of the Angolan civil war for the rest of southern

Africa (and for other parts of the continent as well) were considerable. While its roots can be traced back to the 1961 revolt and indeed much earlier in Angolan history, its immediate cause was probably external – the failure of the United States and the Russians to agree to support the Alvor Accords and to refrain from factional support and intervention. The South African adventure in Angola was not the cause of the Soviet Union and Cuba helping MPLA, but it was responsible for the really massive Cuban presence. This was by far the largest foreign military build-up in Africa since the withdrawal of the old colonial forces. The South Africans were not defeated; indeed, their small force performed well militarily – but the withdrawal was a humiliating experience which was appreciated particularly by Africans and Coloured people in South Africa. There was undoubtedly a connection between events in Angola (and in Mozambique) and the African and Coloured uprisings in Soweto, Cape Town and elsewhere.

In Mozambique the Portuguese military government had originally planned to hold a referendum to decide the territory's future. It soon became apparent, however, that the morale of the Portuguese forces, white and black, was too low to control the situation for even a few months. There were strikes in the docks at Beira and Lourenço Marques and rural uprisings directed against white-owned farms. Portugal's new rulers accordingly gave up the attempt to negotiate a constitutional settlement, and in mid-1974 signed the Lusaka Accords with Machel, which left Frelimo squarely in charge of the country. In spite of some resistance from Portuguese settlers, mainly in Lourenço Marques, independence was achieved in June 1975, with Machel heading a Frelimo government as president. Most of the Portuguese settlers fled the country, as they were also to do in Angola.

After the victory of Neto's MPLA in Angola and of Machel's Frelimo in Mozambique, both countries were governed along fairly rigid Marxist lines, with much emphasis placed on the mobilisation of the whole population to create new, socialist societies, free both of their colonial and of much of their older, African inheritance. Both governments, however, showed themselves to be pragmatic, in particular as far as their immediate external relations were concerned. President Neto patched up his quarrel with President Kaunda of Zambia, and to some extent with Mobutu of Zaïre, although Angola provided some support for the invasion of Zaïre's Shaba province by Katangese guerrillas in 1977 and 1978. MPLA also honoured the understanding not to interfere with the Kunene power stations along the Namibian border, but it provided considerable help to the SWAPO guerrillas (in 1978 South African forces retaliated by raiding the SWAPO base at Cassinga, 200 kilometres inside Angola). Angola retained its commercial agreement with the US Gulf Oil Company to exploit Cabinda's oil. Neto's policies did not satisfy all the leadership of MPLA, and in 1977 his government survived a left-wing coup; but the economic situation of the country, after the withdrawal of Portuguese expertise, remained precarious. In 1979 Agostinho Neto, who had played such a prominent part in his country's political development since the early 1960s, died after an unsuccessful operation in Russia. This was a major loss for a newly independent state like Angola.

For its part, Mozambique retained diplomatically 'proper' relations with South Africa. Because of the extreme economic difficulties experienced by Mozambique since independence, Machel had to agree to the continuing employment of large numbers of Mozambique migrant workers in the South African gold-mines and also to allow South African staff to help run the railway and harbour facilities of Maputo (the new name for Lourenço Marques). Machel provided a large amount of support to Mugabe's Patriotic Front forces, who continued to operate from bases in Mozambique in launching their offensives inside Zimbabwe Rhodesia. The country had to suffer the consequences of this in the form of destructive reprisal raids by Rhodesian troops. The concessions made to western capitalist interests in general, and to white South Africa in particular, do not detract from the fact that Angola and Mozambique are the most radical countries in southern Africa, dedicated not only to the overthrow of white rule in the rest of the sub-continent but also to a Marxist restructuring of all the societies there.

RHODESIAN UDI AND THE EMERGENCE OF ZIMBABWE

As was to be expected, the Rhodesian Unilateral Declaration of Independence produced a crisis of world-wide proportions. Here, as the finale to the long chapter of African liberation movements, was a minority of 250,000 white Rhodesians asserting their right to rule in independence over 4 million Africans. Yet no country in the outside world was prepared to intervene by force of arms – certainly not Britain, who was legally responsible for Rhodesia. The British government refused to recognise the declaration, and successfully prevented its recognition in all other capitals of the world, including (formally) those of South Africa and Portugal. Working through the UN, it went on to organise a series of financial and commercial sanctions, which were agreed to by most governments, but which were not always enforced by those governments upon their own citizens. South Africa and Portugal (until the coup of 1974) refused to operate sanctions against Rhodesia. There is no doubt that this continued South African and Portuguese support was what mainly enabled Rhodesia to survive economically. In particular oil, the one external commodity really vital to the Rhodesian economy, continued to reach the country. Without oil, Smith's regime would probably have collapsed; assured of supplies of oil, it could survive almost indefinitely. Much of this oil was taken to Rhodesia by subsidiaries of British oil companies. In 1966 the UN authorised Britain to use force against tankers carrying oil to the Mozambique port of Beira, whence there was a pipe-line to Rhodesia, but an alternative route was developed, using the port of Lourenço Marques and the railway from there to Beitbridge on the South African–Rhodesian frontier. In 1978 it became apparent that as early as 1967 the British government was aware of the activities of the oil companies, but decided not to do anything about the deception for fear of a confrontation with South Africa. A successful blockade of South African ports would have involved a substantial proportion of the navies of the great powers, and no such blockade was seriously considered. Sanctions against Rhodesia were thus something of a sham, and by encouraging import substitution they actually stimulated the growth of some sections of the Rhodesian economy.

After UDI, the British and Rhodesian governments continued to try to resolve the crisis. The British government formulated its 'No Independence Before Majority African Rule' principles, which Smith refused to accept. Fruitless negotiations between the British prime minister, Harold Wilson, and Smith took place between 1966 and 1968. Failure to find a way out of the impasse hardened Smith's attitude. In 1969 a new constitution was accepted by the Rhodesian electorate, which intensified segregation and made even a gradual transition to African majority rule all but impossible. In 1970 Rhodesia was declared a republic and the powerless British governor in Salisbury sent packing. The United States became concerned about the supplies of chrome, a metal vital for military armaments, and the Byrd Amendment of 1971 permitted this to be imported from Rhodesia, thus legitimising the breaking of UN sanctions. Also in 1971 the British Conservative government opened up a new round of negotiations and reached a compromise agreement with Smith which appeared not to breach the five principles. The British sent a commission, headed by Lord Pearce, to find out what the inhabitants of Rhodesia, black and white, thought of these proposals.

The appearance in Rhodesia of the Pearce Commission led to renewed political activity by Africans. This was centred on a newly formed movement, the African National Council (ANC) led by Bishop Abel Muzorewa, to oppose the new constitutional proposals. The ANC was joined by former ZAPU and ZANU members and attempted to reconcile the rival groups. The majority of Africans in Rhodesia signified a clear rejection of the proposals (with or without ANC prompting), and this the Pearce Commission reported in mid-1972. The British then left it to the Smith regime and the ANC to come to an 'internal settlement', but meetings between Smith and Muzorewa produced no result.

In the meantime, however, more militant action was being launched against Rhodesia from the outside. Between 1967 and 1970 ZAPU and the South African National Congress were responsible for a number of guerrilla incursions into the Zambezi valley from Zambia, to counter which South Africa sent a force of paramilitary police to help the Rhodesian security forces. Then, late in 1972, ZANU started a more intensive offensive, with Frelimo support, from the Tete district of Mozambique into north-east Rhodesia. As the scale of guerrilla attacks increased, so did that of the regime's counter-insurgency measures. These were helped for a time (until 1975) by South African forces, and included the construction of security fences along the Mozambique border, the herding of the local population into 'protected villages', and the proclaiming of 'no-go' areas, where anyone breaking the curfew could be shot on sight. Early in 1973 Smith closed the border with Zambia in retaliation for President Kaunda's support of the guerrillas; this was meant to be only a temporary measure, but Kaunda's response was to make the closure permanent. The coup in Portugal in April 1974 implied that Mozambique would soon be an independent state, hostile to Rhodesia. Rhodesia thus became considerably more isolated.

The Rhodesian conflict became more and more complicated, revolving as it did around a number of closely related elements. First there was the situation inside the country, with white politics dominated by the RF and that party dominated by Ian Smith. Rhodesia's 'siege' economy managed to survive, but under increasing difficulties. It was critically short of foreign exchange to pay for goods breaking sanctions and had to support more and more costly security operations. Secondly, there was the ever-widening scope and intensity of the nationalist guerrilla activities. From about 1974 these were conducted by armies which were distinct from the political parties which

formally controlled them – ZAPU's Zimbabwe Independence

People's Army (Zipra) and ZANU's Zimbabwe African National Liberation Army (Zanla). In 1975 Robert Mugabe, a ZANU leader, left Rhodesia for Mozambique, where he played an important part in directing operations, working closely with President Machel. By 1976 the guerrilla actions had escalated into an outright war, fought on a number of fronts, and by 1979 the nationalist forces had succeeded in penetrating deep into Rhodesia, up to Salisbury itself. Thirdly, there were the responses of Rhodesia's neighbours – on the one hand, Zambia, Mozambique and Botswana, which provided bases for the nationalists, closely backed by Angola and Tanzania, and on the other hand, South Africa, which was increasingly concerned by the scale of the conflict, and which wanted to see a 'friendly' black government installed in an independent Zimbabwe. In providing bases for the nationalists, the three major Front Line States, especially Mozambique, incurred devastating invasions of their territory by 'hot pursuit' raids by the Rhodesian forces. Fourthly, there were the great powers, the United States and Britain on one side, and Russia (together with its ally Cuba) and to some extent China on the other. The main concern of the western powers was to prevent Rhodesia from becoming the stage for an international conflict. The main concern of Russia and China was much the same (though Russia wanted to extract as much political advantage out of the situation as possible), with both countries trying to stop the other from gaining too strong a position in the area.

As early as 1974 the South African prime minister, Vorster, tried unsuccessfully to persuade Smith to negotiate with the nationalist leaders, and the next year he even joined forces with President Kaunda of Zambia to put pressure on the Rhodesians. Nothing, however, came of the bizarre meeting in a railway carriage on the Victoria Falls bridge across the Zambezi. In 1976 Smith launched one of his several attempts at an 'internal settlement' by having a series of fruitless talks with Joshua Nkomo, who subsequently left Rhodesia for Zambia. During 1975 and 1976 Britain made a number of attempts to find a way out of the impasse, before the United States intervened.

The United States had been badly shaken by the outcome of the Angola civil war and by the presence in that country of Cuban troops and Russian advisers. Henry Kissinger, the secretary of state, visited southern Africa in 1976, and met all the main actors in the Rhodesian drama. The result of this 'shuttle diplomacy' was that Smith announced his agreement to African majority rule within two years, but the nationalist politicians and the Front Line presidents remained unconvinced. Indeed, the response of Nkomo and Mugabe was to step up the scale of the fighting and to form a Patriotic Front to unite ZAPU and ZANU. The next move was a conference, convened by the British government towards the end of 1976. The Geneva Conference lasted several weeks, but the attitudes of both sides had become so embittered that it broke down without any agreement being reached. In 1977 Britain and the United States produced a further set of peace proposals, which gained some approval by the Patriotic Front.

In reply, Smith concluded, early in 1978, an internal settlement with 'moderate' black leaders. The RF government 'shared' power with Muzorewa, Sithole and Chief Chirau, until elections could be held. But the fighting continued unabated. The strains of the mounting struggle were, by early 1979, clearly beginning to tell upon the European population. Most adult male whites were conscripted at least for part-time service in the defence forces. Whites were emigrating in significant numbers, even though compelled to leave most of their property behind them when they did so. Despite strenuous attempts to Africanise the army, it became increasingly doubtful how whole-heartedly such forces would fight against their fellow countrymen in the nationalist forces. The Rhodesian economy showed signs of disintegrating under the burden of war.

Thus, when Bishop Muzorewa emerged victorious from the elections of April 1979, it was apparent that, even though Rhodesia had taken the momentous step to a mainly black government, there would be no lasting peace and no international recognition until the nationalists in exile had been accommodated. Lord Carrington, who became British foreign secretary in May 1979, at once addressed himself to this problem. Essentially, it was a matter of persuading Muzorewa and his colleagues to submit themselves to a fresh election to be held after a brief period of resumed British rule, during which the exiles would be permitted to return to the country and join fully in the electoral campaign. Equally it was necessary to persuade the exiles to drop their military activities in favour of political action and to trust in the fair conduct of this election. Carrington's initiative received much support at the routine meeting of Commonwealth prime ministers held at Lusaka in August. Leaders of the Front Line States joined in putting pressure on the various parties to attend a Constitutional Conference in London (it was held at Lancaster House), which in the event dragged on from September until December. Just before Christmas it was judged that sufficient mutual trust had been achieved for Lord Soames to be sent as governor, with wide powers but no force other than a contingent of military 'monitors' 1,400 strong, to preside over the reabsorption of some 25,000 guerrilla fighters and the fair conduct of the election held only two months later.

The result of the election of February 1980 was probably a surprise to all who took part in it, as well as to most of the foreign observers. Of one hundred seats in the new Parliament, Bishop Muzorewa's party won three and Sithole's party none. Of the former exiles, Joshua Nkomo's party, which had enjoyed the hospitality of Zambian bases and the material support of the Soviet Union, won twenty seats, all in Matabeleland. The overwhelming victory (fifty-seven seats) went to the ZANU/PF party of Robert Mugabe, the Shona leader with a reputation for uncompromising Marxism, whose host in exile had been President Machel of Mozambique. The remaining twenty seats were reserved for whites, and all went to Smith's RF. If there was momentary dismay felt in the western countries, this was certainly reciprocated in those of the Soviet bloc, whose satellites were not even invited to the independence ceremonies which followed on 18 April. Meanwhile, Mugabe's speeches and public statements had been curiously reminiscent of Jomo Kenyatta when he assumed power in the Kenya of 1963. Reconciliation was the keynote. Pragmatism rather than dogma was to be the guiding light. Black and white would walk into the future arm in arm and in full confidence.

22   The white-dominated South

During the years between the end of the Second World War and 1975, while the rest of Africa was passing through the transitional period between the last years of colonial rule and the first years of independence under African governments, most of southern Africa was moving still further in the opposite direction. To understand why this was so, one has first of all to imagine the difference in outlook between a democratic power based in Europe (we have seen that Portugal was in this respect an exception) and a self-governing community of white people living as a ruling minority in an African country. The government of a colonial power had many things to worry about besides its colonies. It had to rule its own country to the satisfaction of the electorate, and it had to conduct its relations successfully with the outside world. Its colonies were a very marginal interest. Colonial affairs did not sway many votes at a general election, and if colonies were troubled, the government was more likely to lose votes on their account than to gain them. Troubled colonies were expensive. Colonial wars were unpopular, both internally with the electorate and externally with foreign powers. It was difficult to recruit civil servants to go and work in troubled colonies. For all these reasons the staying-power of a European-based colonial system was very slight. As soon as a colony became more troublesome to rule than it was worth, the politicians of the colonising country would want to cut their losses and leave.

The outlook of a self-governing minority was, and is, quite different. Here the centre of power is locally based. Here the soldiers, the policemen and the civil servants are all employed by the local government, which is elected by the local white community. This local community has one overriding interest, which is the maintenance of its own highly privileged way of life. Beside this, all other considerations are subsidiary. It does not mind antagonising the outside world. In the transfer of power to the black majority it sees the certain end of the life it has always known. It sees the abolition of privilege, the confiscation of property and a general turning of the tables which will leave most of its members with no option but to try and start life afresh as refugees in another continent. To prevent this, it is prepared to fight and to kill and if need be to be killed. If there are a few people in such a community who can see further than their own immediate interest, their voices are not heard and they do not become members of parliament. It is therefore not surprising that in southern Africa the main result of the African revolution in the lands to the north was to stiffen the forces of white supremacy. Only in Northern Rhodesia and Nyasaland, where the British Colonial Office shared power with the government of the Central African Federation, and in the three small High Commission Territories bordering South Africa, did African majorities succeed in winning independence and majority rule, with only a comparatively short and mild period of political struggle. Elsewhere, this African revolution was fiercely resisted. Minority governments existed less and less on consent and more and more on coercion.

It is important to remember that in 1945 even South Africa was by no means the odd man out in world affairs which it is today. In 1945 all the rest of black Africa, except Ethiopia and Liberia, was under colonial rule. That meant, in the first place, that South Africa's relations with the rest of Africa consisted essentially of her relations with the metropolitan governments of the colonial powers. And by these powers South Africa, and also Rhodesia, were regarded more or less as honorary members of the colonial club. They, too, were engaged in the common task of governing Africans, and in this respect their administrative policies, their education policies, their health policies and their labour policies were felt to be variants of, rather than opposites of, the policies of the colonial powers. Differences were thought to be those of method and timing rather than of fundamental ideology. Again, in 1945 South Africa had a very large proportion of the best-educated Africans in the continent. Missionary education in South Africa went back to the early nineteenth century. By 1945 there were black professors, black doctors, black clergy and a host of other black professional people. As we saw in Chapter 15, a major black political party, the African National Congress, had been founded in 1912, and had organised large demonstrations against the pass laws as early as 1919. By 1945 its leaders were at least as well able as their contemporaries in other African countries to see the significance of the United Nations Charter and the coming withdrawal of the British from India. Black South African delegates had attended the Fifth Pan-African Congress in Manchester in 1945 and were in touch with the emerging political leaders of tropical Africa like Nkrumah and Kenyatta. By December 1945 the ANC had formally and publicly demanded one man one vote and freedom of movement, residence   289 and land-ownership; its officials were already lobbying at the United Nations and even presenting petitions from the Africans of South-West Africa in favour of a UN Trusteeship to replace the League of Nations mandate. All this helps to explain the reactions of the white minority in the post-war years.

The years 1958 to 1960 marked a turning-point in the history of post-war Africa. In 1957 Ghana, as we have seen (Chapter 18), became fully independent. Between 1956 and 1958, the French West and Equatorial African colonies were given internal self-government. In 1958 Nkrumah held the All-African People's Conference in Accra, which was attended amongst many other people by Patrice Lumumba from the Belgian Congo and by Tom Mboya from Kenya. Mboya returned to Nairobi to found the Pan-African Freedom Movement of East and Central Africa, and Lumumba returned to Leopoldville to organise the first wider-than-tribal political party in the Congo – which became independent just eighteen months later, in June 1960. These eighteen months from the Accra conference to Congo independence constituted the heart of the African revolution. With the independence of French and Belgian Africa, the British could no longer think of West Africa as a separate, self-contained world. With the Congo moving from full colonial administration to full independence in a single year, the multiracial policy in East Africa was clearly doomed.

Already in 1958 this policy had been badly dented in Tanzania, where Julius Nyerere had fought and won an election in combination with the local white colonists' party against the multiracial party sponsored by the colonial government. Developments in the Congo made it clear to British ministers that Britain could no longer hope to support small and highly privileged minorities of European and Asian colonists in Kenya through a long transition period. Above all, Congo independence brought independent Africa to the borders of the Central African Federation, where political disturbances in Malawi had already in 1959 caused the intervention of federal military forces and the creation of what a Royal Commission under Lord Devlin called 'a police state'. In 1960, the Monckton Commission sent to investigate the future of the Federation made it quite clear that both Malawi and Zambia would have to be allowed to develop quickly towards self-government on the basis of majority rule and be given the right to secede from the Federation if they wished to. Finally, 1960 was, though in a completely different sense, the decisive year in South Africa. Mr Macmillan told a stunned South African parliament that the winds of change were blowing through Africa (see p. 273). On 21 March, six weeks later, came the tragedy of Sharpeville.

SOUTH AFRICA: THE SECOND WORLD WAR TO SHARPEVILLE

The Afrikaans- and English-speaking sections of the white population of South Africa had been deeply divided by the outbreak of the war in Europe. They had weathered the storms of the depression years, and the economy, still dominated by the gold-mining industry, was on the upturn. A large group of Afrikaners, led by General Hertzog, had wanted South Africa to be neutral; and a smaller group of extreme nationalists had been sympathetic to Nazi Germany and had wanted South Africa to join the war on Germany's side. Africans, Coloured people and Indians, in so far as they could express their opinion, had been strongly pro-British. In a crucial vote in the all-white parliament, Smuts and his United Party had narrowly defeated the Hertzogites, and South Africa joined the other Commonwealth countries in becoming an ally of Britain.

The war-time situation had a number of consequences for South Africa. Considerable numbers of white men (mainly English-speaking) joined the South African armed services and fought in campaigns in North Africa and Europe. Africans – not only from South Africa, but also from the High Commission Territories – Coloured people and Indians joined the non-combatant medical and labour services. The white soldiers' jobs in industry and commerce were taken partly by 'poor white' Afrikaners being pushed off the land and partly by Africans from the rural areas. Afrikaners consolidated the important position they were already playing in the industrial sector of the economy, while Africans moved into skilled or semi-skilled jobs from which they had previously been legally debarred.

These changes in the structure of the labour force went hand in hand with other developments. To a large extent, the South African economy was put on a war footing, and the war years witnessed an immense growth of mining but even more of manufacturing industries. South African factories became one of the largest suppliers of small arms to the Allied armies. As a result, the size of the labour force increased, almost entirely from the non-white population groups. The new factories and the increased mining activities were nearly all in the established urban centres – the Witwatersrand in the Transvaal, the hub of South Africa's industrial economy, and the ports of Cape Town, Port Elizabeth and Durban. Cape Town harbour, for example, was completely rebuilt and new fortifications constructed, and for this work large numbers of Africans were brought from the eastern regions of the Cape. The number of people of all groups living in South

Africa's burgeoning cities vastly increased. During the war the South African economy boomed.

In 1943 Smuts held a war-time election, which was won by his United Party, though with a smaller majority; the whites in a number of urban constituencies voted, for the first time, for Afrikaner National Party (NP) candidates. During the war Smuts, being close to Churchill, operated as a major figure in the direction of the Allied war effort, as he had done in the First World War. After the war he was one of the prime movers in the formation of the United Nations, with its Declaration of Human Rights. As in the past, Smuts's grasp of world politics was more sure than his appreciation of the trends of South African affairs; there was a yawning gap between what he said and what he did. He made a number of statements to non-white soldiers which seemed to promise them better treatment after the war.

After 1945 Smuts and his colleagues, including the able and liberal J. H. Hofmeyr, appeared uncertain and vacillating in the face of the mounting political and economic pressures. By turns liberal and authoritarian, they adhered to no clear-cut policy to deal with South Africa's problems. Smuts realised that something would have to be done to alleviate the misery of South Africa's huge African urban population and the bitterness and confusion brought about by discrimination. In 1946 he appointed the Fagan Commission to inquire into the pass laws, migrant labour and the position of Africans in towns and industry. Later the same year the African Mine Workers' Union called out its members on strike. This lasted four days, and 74,000 workers were involved. The government responded by arresting the leaders and forcibly smashed the strike. Nine Africans were killed, and some 1,200 injured. Smuts said, 'The native strike was not caused by legitimate grievances but by agitators.'

In the 1948 elections Smuts's United Party was narrowly defeated by the National Party led by Dr D. F. Malan (in coalition with a smaller party). The Smuts administration had performed poorly, and the Nationalists frightened the electorate by claiming that some of the more liberal ministers were in favour of full political equality, which, it was alleged, would produce a 'coffee-coloured race'. The determination to remain the dominant race and the opposite fear of being 'swamped' by the African majority motivated nearly all whites: only a handful believed in, and worked for, a free and equal society. Basically, most whites clung to the notion of *baaskap*, racial domination, and most were prepared to see the government of their choice use force to maintain this. There were, nevertheless, crucial differences of approach. Immediately after the election, the Fagan Commission report appeared. It stated, first, that 'the idea of total segregation is utterly impracticable; secondly, that the movement from country to town has a background of economic necessity – that it may, so one hopes, be guided and regulated, and may perhaps also be limited, but that it cannot be stopped or be turned in the opposite direction; and thirdly, that in our urban areas there are not only Native migrant labourers, but there is also a settled, permanent Native population' (*Fagan Report*, para. 28). The National Party's rejoinder to this admission of economic (but not, it should be noted, political) integration was the overall policy of *apartheid*, separation.

The term 'apartheid' has several meanings, as used by different people at different times; it has in the 1970s been replaced in official South African usage by synonymous terms (such as 'separate development'). At the theoretical level of political science, apartheid emerged amongst Afrikaner intellectuals of the late 1930s and 1940s as a portmanteau concept, embodying notions that can be traced back to the nineteenth-century Cape and Natal, to the recommendations of the 1903–5 British Imperial South African Native Affairs Commission, and to the ideas of Hertzog and other Nationalists in the early years of the Union. At its most ideal, the doctrine of apartheid looked forward to a South Africa which would be geographically divided (unequally) between the white 'race' and the various African 'nations' – Xhosa, Zulu, Sotho:

The policy of apartheid has grown out of the experience of the established white population of the country, and is based on the Christian principle of right and justice. This aimed at the maintenance and protection of the white population as a pure white race, the maintenance and protection of the indigenous race groups as separate national communities, with possibilities of developing in their own areas to self-protecting national unities. The reserved areas should become the Africans' true fatherland. The National Party realizes the danger of the flood of Africans to the cities and undertakes to protect the white character of our cities . . .[1]

Among most whites, apartheid was little more than a dignified name for *baaskap*; as the Nationalist Prime Minister Strijdom put it, 'Call it paramountcy, *baaskap* or what you will, it is still domination. I am being as blunt as I can. I am making no excuses. Either the white man dominates or the black man takes over.'

Once in office, Malan's National Party rejected the Fagan Commission recommendations and set up its own commission under Professor Tomlinson to report on the socio-economic conditions of

---

[1] Report of Sauer Commission, *Die Burger*, 29 and 30 March 1948.

the African-held land (the reserves) and on what could be done with this land in the way of development. The Tomlinson Commission did not report until 1954, and then in such unpromising terms that its recommendations were quietly shelved. The commission said that only huge amounts of capital could develop the reserves (it suggested that some of this could be provided by white capitalists operating in the reserves – which contradicted the basic premise of apartheid), but considered that even if so developed over the following forty years, the reserves would be able to support only about half the total African population of that time (it has since been found that Tomlinson was wildly optimistic even in this reckoning). No white government in South Africa was prepared to spend large amounts of money for Africans in the reserves. Indeed, the early National Party governments showed little interest in implementing the main proposals of the apartheid programme. Instead, they smothered the non-white people of South Africa with a mass of purely restrictive and discriminatory legislation – withdrawing rights, drastically limiting choice, and rigidly and legally defining inequality. The meagre political rights of the Cape Africans and Coloured people, entrenched in the Union constitution of 1910, were removed – those of the Coloured people in the course of a long and bitter constitutional conflict between 1951 and 1956, and those of the Africans finally in 1959.

Every aspect of the lives of Africans, Coloured people and Indians was affected by the torrent of legislation. A list of even some of these Acts of the white parliament indicates their range and scope. The Prohibition of Mixed Marriages Act 1949 and the Immorality Act 1950 prohibited members of different races from having any intimate relations. The Population Registration Act 1950 which made race a legal as well as a biological concept, was particularly insulting in defining a Coloured person in purely negative terms – 'a person who is not a white person or a native'. The Abolition of Passes and Co-Ordination of Documents Act 1952 made it compulsory for all African men (and later women) to carry a 'reference book', a new term for the old 'pass', and established a country-wide system of influx control to regulate the movements of Africans and to restrict their entry into urban areas. The Group Areas Act 1950 and its amendments and the Separate Amenities Act 1953 attempted complete social and physical separation of the races – the removal of Coloured people, Indians and Africans to the outskirts of cities and towns, rigid segregation in sport and other recreations, use of separate (and inferior) facilities on trains and buses, the use of separate seats in parks, all of which led to a rash of 'Whites Only' signs appearing across the length and breadth of the land. The Native Laws Amendment Act 1957 consolidated the control over Africans in urban areas which had first been attempted in the 1923 Urban Areas Act. The amended Industrial Conciliation Act 1965 legalised job reservation for whites and precluded Africans from the process of industrial conciliation over wages. The Suppression of Communism Act 1950, the Criminal Law Amendment Act 1953 and the Unlawful Organisations Act 1960 aimed at the total suppression of all but the most tame opposition, and were almost unequalled for their harshness in the democratic countries of the western world. Only a few legislative measures of the National Party governments in the 1950s were overtly ideological; the most important of these were the Bantu Education Act 1953 and the Extension of University Education Act 1959, which took African primary and secondary education out of missionary control and created separate (and inferior) university-type institutions for all non-whites; these made education an instrument of government policy in attempting to reshape and control men's minds. Dr Verwoerd, then minister of native affairs, said of the 1953 Act,

Racial relations cannot improve if the wrong type of education is given to the Natives. They cannot improve if the result of Native education is the creation of frustrated people who as a result of the education they receive have expectations in life which circumstances in South Africa do not allow to be fulfilled immediately, when it creates people who are trained for professions not open to them.

Africans, therefore, were to be given an inferior kind of education, to fit them for their main function in South Africa, that of labourers.

As early as 1951 tentative steps were taken along the road of propping up, and then greatly enhancing, the run-down authority of the traditional chiefs in the rural reserves; the Bantu Authorities Act of 1951 was elaborated by the Promotion of Bantu Self-Government Act of 1959. But by and large the mass of legislation enacted by National Party governments before the 1960s differed only in its harshness from that of the previous administrations of Smuts and Hertzog.

Between 1948 and 1979 South Africa had five prime ministers – D. F. Malan, 1948–54, who resigned office an old man; J. G. Strydom, 1954–8, who died in office; H. Verwoerd, 1958–65, who was assassinated by a lunatic; and B. J. Vorster, who had been a member of a fascist movement in the 1930s and had been interned by Smuts during the war. In 1948 the National Party would not have him as a candidate in the election. In 1978 Vorster retired because of ill health and was succeeded by P. W. Botha. Vorster for a time became state president, but he had to resign from that office because of the repercussions of a massive financial scandal involving the unauthorised expenditure of public funds on propaganda activities overseas. The long succession of NP governments has not tampered with the basically 'Westminster' type of parliamentary democracy. Elections have been held regularly, and opposition parties allowed to function within the 'safe' confines of the all-white electorate. Its steadily growing electoral successes have been an indication both of the support the NP built up among some English-speaking electors as well as among the great majority of Afrikaners. In every election held between 1948 and the late 1970s the NP increased its number of seats; in 1974 the NP representation in the House of Assembly was 82 per cent of the seats – the highest proportion ever gained by any one party in South African history. The official opposition, the United Party, failed to find an alternative policy to that of the government and slowly broke up. The Liberal Party was much more outspoken in its criticism of the regime, and individual members were prosecuted under the government's repressive laws. In 1965 the government introduced the Prohibition of Political Interference Act, which made it illegal for anyone to belong to a racially mixed political party; thereupon, the Liberals decided to disband. Another liberally inclined movement, the Progressive Party, was founded in 1959, and this slowly captured the liberal wing of the United Party. By 1975 it had become the Progressive Reform Party, which in the elections won seventeen seats; the rump of UP members formed two smaller parties.

The United and Progressive Parties were not the only opposition to the ruling NP among the whites. Right-wing Afrikaners considered that the NP governments were not sufficiently resolute and extreme in their racial policies. In the 1960s the ruling party was split internally between the so-called enlightened group, *verligtes*, and the hardliners, *verkramptes*. The *verligtes* were in favour of what was called 'positive' apartheid and a policy of detente and dialogue with black African states, while the *verkramptes* were concerned basically to uphold *baaskap*. In 1969 the extreme *verkramptes* formed a new party, the Herstigte Nasionale (Reconstituted National) Party. The HNP never won any seats in parliamentary elections, but their political activities, and those of the *verkramptes* within the NP, acted as a powerful brake on the government in adopting what among South African whites would be considered extremist *verligte* policies.

AFRICAN RESPONSES TO WHITE DOMINATION

The sheer mass, and in some cases the brutality of government policies and legislation, was in part a response to the greatly increased scale of opposition, as was this opposition itself a result of the avalanche of discrimination. The 1950s saw non-white political activity on an unprecedented scale. Early on there were widespread multiracial demonstrations against the government's determination to do away with the Coloured people's franchise – demonstrations which were joined by white groups such as the short-lived ex-servicemen's Torch Commando and the more durable women's Black Sash movement. Then, in 1952, the African National Congress, led by Albert Luthuli, Oliver Tambo, Nelson Mandela and Walter Sisulu, swung into a concerted campaign of passive resistance to various discriminatory rules and regulations, including the carrying of passes. Already in 1951 the government had armed itself with the Suppression of Communism Act, leaving the minister of justice to decide which person or what organisation was 'communist'. In 1953 it enacted further repressive legislation, enabling it to declare a state of emergency, to arrest people for supporting passive resistance and hold them without trial, and to ban people to specific rural areas. This repressive legislation inspired many white radicals (not by any means all communists) to side with the African opposition, as did the main Coloured and Indian groups. They formed a Congress Alliance which in 1953 held a Congress of the People at Kliptown near Johannesburg, which adopted the Freedom Charter, opening with the words 'We, the people of South Africa, declare for all our country and the world to know . . . that South Africa belongs to all who live in it, and that no Government can justly claim authority unless it is based on the will of all the people.' The government's reaction was to charge 156 Congress Alliance leaders with high treason. However, the government bungled the trial, and after four years of legal wrangling all the accused were acquitted.

In the meantime, important changes were taking place within the main, African, opposition. The ANC split between those who supported the multiracial ideal enshrined in the Freedom Charter and those who pursued more specifically African nationalist aims. The latter group, led by Robert Sobukwe, formed the Pan-Africanist Congress in 1959. In spite of the arrest of most of the leadership, mass demonstrations continued, the most successful being a bus boycott at Alexandria in the Transvaal. In 1960 the PAC launched a further campaign of passive resistance to the pass laws, and this led to the 297 most tragic confrontation between the white regime and the African people opposed to it. In the course of the campaign, on 21 March 1960, police fired on a peaceful and unarmed crowd at Sharpeville in the southern Transvaal, killing 72 people and wounding some 186, including women and children. A few days later, 30,000 Africans marched into the centre of Cape Town from their 'location' at Langa miles away; some were killed by police shooting at Langa.

Sharpeville immediately became the signal for worldwide condemnation of the South African regime. The government paid little heed to this, although it was clearly shaken by the strength of African opposition and by the international repercussions of the Sharpeville killings. A state of emergency was declared, most of the leading opposition leaders were arrested and the ANC and PAC were proclaimed unlawful organisations. The ANC attempted yet another peaceful demonstration, a three-day 'stay at home' to coincide with the foundation of the Republic in May 1961, but massive government counteraction (including an increasingly effective spy and informer system set up by the highly effective Bureau of State Security, BOSS), broke this up. Both the ANC and the PAC realised that they had come to the end of a road – a road of peaceful, non-violent demonstrations of resistance to white domination. Both organisations turned, reluctantly, to violent resistance in the face of violent government repression. The ANC mounted the Umkonto we Sizwe (Spear of the Nation) to sabotage government installations, while the PAC was involved in Poqo, which aimed to terrorise whites.

The decade of peaceful demonstration against discrimination and racial domination was characterised by the leadership of the ANC by Albert Luthuli, who was elected president of the movement in 1952 and who was banned to a rural area of Zululand in 1959 for launching the defiance campaign. Luthuli was honoured internationally by being awarded the Nobel Peace Prize, and was grudgingly suspended from his banning order to travel to Norway to receive it. He died in 1967, but before this he wrote,

Who will deny that thirty years of my life have been spent knocking in vain, patiently, moderately, and modestly at a closed and barred door? What have been the fruits of moderation? The past thirty years have seen the greatest number of laws restricting our rights and progress, until today we have reached a stage where we have almost no rights at all.

The non-violent defiance campaigns and demonstrations were largely urban-based and organised by a middle-class African elite. Given the

increasingly tight control exercised by the South African security forces, a major problem for the ANC and PAC leaders was the mobilisation of mass support for their calls for political activity; it is remarkable that they achieved the successes which they did. In rural African areas, however, different kinds of resistance movements emerged, which were more difficult for the government to deal with and which were largely independent of the ANC and PAC elites. The most widespread and prolonged of these were in various parts of the Transvaal and, in particular, in the Transkei, among the Pondo people. Here, after three years of bitter conflict the government declared a state of emergency and launched a full-scale war against the Pondo. Many people were killed and more were injured before open resistance came to an end. The state of emergency remained in force through the setting up of the Transkei Bantustan, and indeed was continued by the Matanzima government of quasi-independent Transkei.

The crushing of open resistance in Pondoland and at Sharpeville marked a turning-point in the history of South Africa, both for the whites of the country and their government and for the black majority. There was an epilogue to Sharpeville. With some members of the outlawed ANC and PAC turning to violent resistance, the government had the occasion to operate even more draconian repression. In 1962 the security police captured Nelson Mandela, who had been operating underground – known as the 'Black Pimpernel' – for over a year and a half; and in July 1963 the police rounded up the rest of the ANC Umkonto leadership at their supposedly secret headquarters at Rivonia (near Johannesburg). The ensuing trial ended in Mandela and eight others receiving life sentences; the six blacks joined Robert Sobukwe, leader of the PAC, who was already serving a life sentence, on Robben Island, a bleak island in the rough seas off Cape Town. A veritable reign of terror destroyed the underground African opposition, as well as less dangerous organisations such as the radical Indian, Coloured and white movements, and created such an atmosphere of repression that even the respectable Liberal Party, as we have seen, gave up the struggle.

THE SOUTH AFRICAN ECONOMY, 1940S TO 1970S

During most of the thirty years of National Party rule, the South African economy expanded rapidly and brought great prosperity to the state and to the white population who dominate it. The bases for what can almost be termed an economic miracle are the immense natural resources of the country, the ability of the skilled whites to support a fast-growing manufacturing sector, and the availability of a   299 large, cheap and strictly controlled labour force. By 1948 South Africa had recovered from the post-war slump. The unexpected election victory of the NP frightened overseas investors in South African industry, but the solid economic and monetary policies of the new government soon overcame the doubts, and capital flowed into the country. The crisis of 1960–1 again caused a short-lived loss of overseas confidence, but thereafter the 1960s and the early 1970s were years of boom conditions. South African economic growth between 1948 and the early 1970s was one of the highest in the world, rivalled only by Japan and certainly peculiarly fortunate mini-economies such as Singapore. Because of the wide disparity in wages between white and black, and the discriminatory measures under which blacks lived their lives, the great prosperity was not equally shared. Whites enjoyed one of the highest standards of living in the world; and it was this high standard of living that most of them were prepared to defend by force if necessary. Other features of this period were the entry of Afrikaner capitalists into an economy previously dominated by English-speaking whites and the growth of large state-controlled sectors of the economy.

Since the mid-1970s, partly as a result of the great increase in the price of oil, South Africa's economy has been in the doldrums, with high inflation. The lowest growth year during the post-war period was 1976–7. Foreign investors and foreign companies operating in South Africa – British, American, French, West German, Italian, Japanese – were under pressure from the international community at least to pay equal wages to all their employees in South Africa, if not to pull out altogether. The question of sanctions against South Africa was frequently discussed. During this inflationary period, African wages increased considerably, but the gap between African and white wages actually increased: in 1975 average white earnings were R182 a month, while African wages averaged R12.50. Inflation affected Africans more severely than it did whites, and many African households, in both urban and rural areas, lived below a theoretical poverty datum line. A further result both of the downturn in the economy, and of changes from labour- to capital-intensive industrial processes, has been the growth of unemployment, especially among Africans. As a direct consequence of the implementation of separate development, which was designed to keep African labour in the urban areas non-permanent and migrant, unemployed urban Africans are 'repatriated' to the 'homelands'. It has been estimated that there were 2 million unemployed Africans in South Africa in 1979 (out of a total African labour force of 8 million).

Towards the end of the 1970s the South African economy obtained sudden stimulus from the greatly increased world price of gold. This was the result of the very shaky performance of the western economies and of the US dollar as an international currency. The high price of gold (gold-mining is still South Africa's single most important industry) is yet a further indication of how dependent the South African economy is on the world economic situation, how responsive it is to international demands and pressures. The western powers, however, have such a huge economic stake in South Africa that they are unlikely deliberately to undermine its economic well-being. The crucial position of South Africa in international politics is another reason why the West is unwilling to help to destabilise a region which might all too easily pass into the control of a rival hegemony. We shall return to the international aspects of the racial confrontation in southern Africa at the end of this chapter.

SOUTH AFRICA, 1960–79: SEPARATE DEVELOPMENT

The news of the shooting of Africans at Sharpeville in March 1960 reverberated around the world. There was universal condemnation of South African policy, but little could be done to change this. African states, and some Asian and western countries, boycotted South African goods. Only in the late 1960s and 1970s did the question of an arms embargo become a serious international issue. Although the South African regime was shaken by the force of African opposition that led up to Sharpeville, it soon recovered its firm grasp of the internal situation. Indeed, Verwoerd felt confident enough to withdraw South Africa from the Commonwealth in March 1961 and to proclaim the country a Republic in May of the same year.

Nevertheless, the crisis of 1960 and its repercussions persuaded the National Party government to take seriously for the first time its own theoretical or ideological policy of apartheid and to put it into practice. The predominant feature of National Party governments from 1948 had been *baaskap*; this continued very largely to be the practice from 1960 onwards, but it was overlaid with specific steps in the implementation of 'separate development'. As late as 1959 Verwoerd was luke-warm towards a policy which was supposed to be largely his creation:

The Bantu will be able to develop into separate states. That is not what we would have liked to see. It is a form of fragmentation that we would have liked if we were able to avoid. In the light of the pressure being exerted on South Africa, there is however no doubt that eventually this will have to be done, 301 thereby buying for the White man his freedom and the right to retain his domination in what is his country.[2]

The fundamental step in the implementation of separate development was the turning of the African reserves – those lands left to the natives after the massive European expropriation of land in the nineteenth century – into Bantustans or Homelands, which would ultimately become constitutionally independent states. The first move in this direction came with the Promotion of Bantu Self-Government Act of 1959, which provided for the setting up of 'territorial authorities' in 'national units', based on the lands occupied by the main African tribal or language groups. The premise of the whole apparatus of separate development was set forth in the preamble of the Act: 'the Bantu peoples . . . do not constitute a homogeneous people, but form separate national units on the basis of language and culture'. After over two centuries of conflict, interaction and close integration into South Africa's urban economy, this premise was of doubtful validity. Nevertheless, it has been firmly held to by the advocates of separate development.

The fact that the 13 per cent of the country's total area which constituted the African reserves could not accommodate the 1960 African population (only about half of this actually lived in the reserves), and were even less likely to do so with the expected numbers by the end of the century (anything up to 50 million Africans), did not deter the regime, which set about its apparently impossible and contradictory task with verve. The ten Homelands were Transkei (Xhosa people), Ciskei (Xhosa), Kwazulu (Zulu), Qwaqwa (South Sotho), Bophuthatswana (Tswana), South Ndebele, Lebowa (North Sotho), Gazankula (Shangaan and Tsonga), Venda and Swazi. None of these Homelands occupied contiguous territory; even the largest, the Transkei, had 'white' lands jutting right into it. The territory received a measure of internal self-government in 1963. Elections were held, the voters including not only those Africans resident in the Transkei but all people of Xhosa origin, many of whom had lived in the urban areas for generations and who had no ties with their so-called homeland. A minority of the 'popular' vote plus the support of the appointed chiefs in the new Transkei parliament enabled Chief Kaiser Matanzima to form an administration. He was one of the number of traditional Homeland leaders who were prepared to support the policy of separate development.

[2] Quoted in H. Wolpe, 'Capitalism and Cheap-Labour Power in South Africa: from segregation to apartheid', *Economy and Society*, 14 (1972), 449.

37   South Africa: Homelands and the 'Common Area'

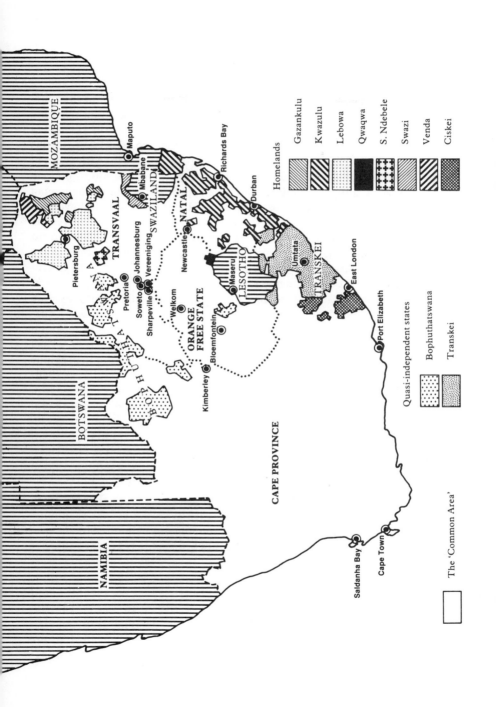

MOZAMBIQUE

Maputo

TRANSVAAL

Mbabane

SWAZILAND

Pietersburg

Pretoria

Johannesburg

Soweto

Vereeniging

Sharpeville

Welkom

NATAL

Newcastle

Richards Bay

Durban

ORANGE FREE STATE

Bloemfontein

Maseru

LESOTHO

Umtata

TRANSKEI

East London

BOTSWANA

Kimberley

Port Elizabeth

NAMIBIA

CAPE PROVINCE

Saldanha Bay

Cape Town

Homelands

Gazankulu

Kwazulu

Lebowa

Qwaqwa

S. Ndebele

Swazi

Venda

Ciskei

Quasi-independent states

Bophuthatswana

Transkei

The 'Common Area'

This became a most divisive factor for Africans in South Africa. There is little doubt that the majority, in the Homelands as well as in the urban areas, were opposed to separate development. Even the Homeland leaders were not unanimous in their support of the policy. One of the most controversial figures to emerge in the 1970s in South Africa was Chief Gatsha Buthelezi of Kwazulu. He used his position not only within the political set-up of Kwazulu, but also on the wider South African, and indeed international, stage, to criticise the racial inequalities perpetuated and reinforced by the South African government. He was not willing to allow Kwazulu to go beyond a limited degree of autonomy and continued to oppose the political fragmentation explicit in separate development. His example was followed by the leaders of seven more of the ten Homelands. Transkei received its formal grant of independence in October 1976, and was followed by Bophuthatswana in 1977. Neither state was recognised by any other country, and both were refused membership of the UN and the OAU. In Transkei the Emergency Laws, which had been in operation since 1960, were incorporated into a new Transkei Public Security Act passed by the Matanzima government in 1977; the territory also set up a Transkei Intelligence Service to take over the functions of the South African BOSS. The offspring was becoming a mirror-image of its parent. However, good relations did not last long. The Vorster regime decided that all Xhosa throughout South Africa would lose their South African citizenship and become citizens of the unrecognised Transkei. This issue probed the core of the separate development policy: that 'white' South Africa would be able to offload its unwanted blacks – unemployed, politically undesirable etc. – on to the Homelands and accept no further responsibility for them. The Transkei refused to accept this situation as far as the nearly 3 million Xhosa living outside the Transkei (out of a total of nearly 5 million) were concerned. The result was an impasse. So bitter was the Transkei quarrel with South Africa that in 1978 it broke off all relations, abrogating a defence agreement and renouncing all South African aid. The consequences of this dramatic move are yet to become manifest.

THE URBAN DILEMMA: THE SOWETO REVOLT AND ITS AFTERMATH

In 1979 more than 9 million Africans, double the total white population, lived outside the reserves/Homelands, in the so-called white areas. Four million of these lived and worked on the white-owned farms; 5 million lived in the urban areas. These urban Africans had been subject to the greatest pressure of the discriminatory policies under which they had to live out their daily lives. Inflation, rampant poverty, social disruption, employment insecurity – and the threat of being 'repatriated' to distant and unknown 'homelands' – lack of urban facilities, lack of hope for their own and their children's future, an increasing crime rate, a high level of violence – these and other factors combined to make people desperate and humiliated.

The largest African urban area was Soweto, the huge African city to the south-west of Johannesburg (Soweto is one of the five or six biggest cities in Africa south of the Sahara). A high proportion of the population of Soweto consisted of children and teenagers. Compared with Africans in the rural areas, these had received a modicum of education, enough to raise their expectations and to make them aware of their situation. The vexed issue of Homeland citizenship compounded the uncertainties of urban life, because from early 1975 Africans could only own their little homes in Soweto (all built on land held on thirty-year leaseholds) on condition that they accepted Homeland citizenship and therefore ceased to be South Africans. This few Soweto residents were prepared to do.

The immediate cause of the outbreak of violent resistance in Soweto in June 1976 was the decision of the white authorities to impose Afrikaans as the medium of teaching subjects such as mathematics in secondary schools. Behind this lay the basic discontent of youngsters with Bantu education. Contrasted with the excellent educational facilities provided for white children, Africans had every reason to feel educationally deprived: in 1975–6 an average of R644 was spent on every white school pupil, whereas only R42 was spent on every African pupil. The reaction of African youngsters was frustration, rage and hatred. But the mood amongst urban Africans was not only negative. The achievement of independence by Mozambique under the radical Frelimo government in 1975 and the failure of the South African military foray into Angola gave many Africans in South Africa a pride, a new-found strength and determination, and a belief that in the long run they would emerge triumphant.

African university students had broken away from the white liberal National Union of South African Students to form the South African Students' Organisation (SASO) in 1969, which was soon followed by the emergence of a new political party, the Black People's Convention (BPC). Although both SASO and BPC encouraged other non-white groups to participate, they played a leading role in the development of a specific Black Consciousness or Black Power movement. The two organisations staged pro-Frelimo rallies in 1975. Less well organised, 305 but equally significant, were African worker activities in the 1970s: a strike of Ovambo workers in South-West Africa (Namibia) in 1971, a massive strike of workers in the Durban area in 1973, and much agitation amongst gold-mine workers in the later 1970s. But it was the school-children of Soweto who made the greatest impact. In May 1976 they went on strike over the language issue. The school strikes spread rapidly and by June had become more general demonstrations, which turned into violent disturbances. Most of the many other African urban areas in the Transvaal (the 'townships') were affected. The police responded to the disturbances both inefficiently and brutally. By August the unrest had spread to Port Elizabeth and the Ciskei and to the western Cape, where Coloured school-children joined Africans in their strikes and demonstrations. These continued through the rest of 1976; there was something of a lull during the first half of 1977, but renewed violence broke out later that year. By that time, several hundred persons had been killed in the Transvaal and in the Cape. Among a few minor concessions, the government quietly dropped its Afrikaans language scheme.

Vorster and his ministers, however, did not confine their action to making minor concessions. All leading Africans, and many other non-whites and some whites, were rounded up and detained under the various security laws. One of those held in custody was Steve Biko, who had founded SASO and who, at the early age of thirty-one, had become one of the most respected and influential of the new generation of African leaders. Biko was arrested in Grahamstown on 18 August 1977 and held and interrogated at Port Elizabeth prison; he was transferred to Pretoria jail for further interrogation and died there on 12 September. Although the magistrate at the inquest found that 'no one was criminally responsible' for Biko's death, the evidence suggests that he died as a result of injuries received while being interrogated by the police. From 1976 to 1979 fifty or more persons were known to have died while in detention under South Africa's security legislation.

During 1977 and 1978 the Vorster regime considered a number of alterations to the system of white domination, while leaving the basic structure intact. It continued to press ahead with the policy of separate development of the Homelands, in spite of the slap in the face received from the Transkei. Two important proposals were put forward. One was for a limited form of local self-government for the African residents of Soweto – almost the creation of a kind of 'urban homeland' there. The other was a constitutional reform which planned to set up in 1980 Coloured and Indian parliaments, as well as the existing white one, in the 'common area', and a tripartite Council of Cabinets. Ultimate power would be with an elected executive state president (who, given the relative voting strength of the three communities, would always be white). Neither of these proposals was received with great enthusiasm. The creation of quasi-independent Homelands, the granting of municipal control to Africans in the urban areas, and the attempt to fit the minority Coloured and Indian groups into the white power structure – all were examples of the ever-more-complex manoeuvres of the NP government to maintain white power in South Africa. The ultimate success or failure of these manipulations will no doubt be determined in South Africa by South Africans, but what happens in neighbouring countries, and how the outside world reacts to events in South Africa, cannot but have a profound effect upon that much-divided land. The post-war histories of the Central African countries were examined in Chapter 21; we must now turn to those other lands in southern Africa whose histories have been so closely interwoven with that of the Republic.

LESOTHO, BOTSWANA AND SWAZILAND: BLACK STATES IN THE MIDST OF THE WHITE SOUTH

From the 1880s Basutoland and Bechuanaland, and from the end of the Anglo-Boer war, Swaziland, were ruled as protectorates by Britain. They were administered by a British high commissioner, who was also governor-general of the Union of South Africa, a divided authority which reflected the peculiar situation of the three countries. Basutoland was completely surrounded by South Africa and was very poor. Its economy had become, by the 1930s if not earlier, wholly reliant upon the wages brought back by migrant Sotho working in the gold-mines and other industries of South Africa. Bechuanaland, although large in size, was mainly a very dry country (much of it covered by the Kalahari desert) and had a small population. It was bordered by South Africa, South-West Africa (including, in the north, the long, narrow Caprivi Strip) and Southern Rhodesia. Many Tswana people worked in South Africa. Swaziland was the smallest of the three but was the richest, in agricultural produce and minerals. It was bordered by Mozambique and by South Africa.

The constitution of the Union of South Africa (1910) provided for the eventual incorporation of these 'High Commission Territories', and South African governments periodically demanded that this should take place, the last occasion being as late as 1963. Britain resisted these demands on the grounds that transfer required the consent of the people concerned. Instead, the protectorates were gradually developed along constitutional lines towards self-government in spite of their poverty and small populations. A number of political parties grew up in each country, representing different class or tribal affiliations as well as differences about the attitudes which should be adopted to their powerful white neighbour.

In Bechuanaland, the Bechuanaland Democratic Party, led by Sir Seretse Khama, who was chief of the Bamangwato people, won the pre-independence election of 1965 and carried the country through to independence in 1966, when its name was changed to Botswana. Seretse Khama became president and soon emerged as one of Africa's foremost statesmen. Botswana was one of the few African states to have retained a multiparty system; in elections held in 1969, the BDP lost seats to its rivals, although popular support was regained in the 1974 elections. The exploitation of big diamond, cupro-nickel and other mineral resources enabled Botswana to become less dependent economically upon South Africa, although the country greatly relied on its neighbour for communications and other services. In 1977 an all-weather road was constructed to the northern tip of Botswana, where at Kazungulu on the Zambezi it shared a short common frontier with Zambia; a ferry crossed the river and provided a slender link between Botswana and the black African states to the north. During the late 1970s Botswana was one of the 'Front Line' states in the struggle over Zimbabwe Rhodesia. Seretse Khama and his ministers showed themselves aware of the economic constraints and political dangers that arose from Botswana's vulnerable position in southern Africa, but were equally determined that their country should remain a well-governed and quietly prosperous land in which black and white could live and work together harmoniously.

Basutoland became an independent kingdom in 1966 and changed its name to Lesotho. It was governed by the conservative Basutoland National Party, under the leadership of Chief Leabua Jonathan, which rather surprisingly won the elections in 1965. Chief Jonathan not only retained close economic links with South Africa – he had no choice in this, as he told people during the election: 'think of your stomachs' – but for a time also played along with that country's policy of 'detente' with black African states, by participating in meetings with Mr Vorster. But Chief Jonathan's support within Lesotho waned. The BNP lost the 1970 election to its main rival, the Basutoland Congress Party led by Ntsu Mokhetle. As the results became known, Chief Jonathan staged a coup, with the acquiescence of the South Africans and with the help of a small paramilitary police force, which employed South African and British mercenaries. The king, Moshweshwe II, was banished for a time, and after his return took little part in politics. Lesotho became in effect a one-party state. Since then, Chief Jonathan has moved away from his subservient position towards South Africa. Although still very dependent on that country, a wide range of international aid has been procured, and Lesotho has increasingly refused to be a pawn in the 'separate development' game being played out by South Africa.

Swaziland was the last of the High Commission Territories to regain independence (in 1968), because of the complexity of its internal politics. The Swazi king, Sobhuza II, a traditionalist of the old order, played a much larger role in politics than did his counterpart in Lesotho. Before independence there were a number of political parties, but Sobhuza organised his own, the Mbokodvu Party, and manipulated the 1964 elections so as to bring about its victory. The Mbokodvu Party was proudly nationalist, and many younger and more radical Swazi joined its ranks. The British imposed a Westminster-model constitution on the Swazi in 1968, making Sobhuza constitutional head of state. He put up with this limited position until 1973, when he took over the government and withdrew the constitution. Sobhuza established or reinstated a variety of so-called traditional institutions and forms of political interchange between the monarch and his subjects. He saw himself as the embodiment of the spirit and unity of the Swazi nation; his was one of the most overtly old-fashioned and aristocratic forms of government in Africa. The system became more difficult to maintain as economic and social changes gathered momentum. The king had to keep a wary eye upon his own subjects and upon his potentially hostile neighbours – white South Africa (individual whites still own nearly 40 per cent of the land of the kingdom) and Marxist black Mozambique. Sobhuza was at the time of writing the oldest reigning monarch in the world, and it was difficult to see that the aristocratic nationalist system which he had personally largely created could long survive his death; but while he lives, Swaziland is unique.

SOUTH-WEST AFRICA/NAMIBIA

South-West Africa is one of the largest African countries in size but has one of the sparsest populations on the continent. A great deal of the territory is desert and arid land. By the 1970s it had a population of under 1,000,000, of whom fewer than 100,000 were whites: perhaps a quarter of these were the descendants of the pre-1914 German

309

colonists, while the rest were mainly Afrikaners. The largest group of African people were the Ovambo, who lived in the more fertile northern areas astride the Angolan frontier. There were several other, smaller African peoples, such as the Herero, who suffered so badly at the hands of the Germans (see p. 145), and Khoi people such as the Nama. The modern name of the country, Namibia, comes from a Nama word meaning 'shelter'.

We have noted (see p. 211) that at the end of the Second World War the South African government refused to accept the authority of the Trusteeship Council of the United Nations over the old mandated territory of South-West Africa. South Africa treated South-West Africa as if it were a fifth province of the Union. The all-white electorate voted its representatives to the South African parliament, and the greater part of the immense structure of Pretoria-based *baaskap* apparatus was applied to South-West Africa, including the pass laws, labour legislation and petty apartheid. In 1960 Ethiopia and Liberia, the only black African states which had been members of the League of Nations, brought a suit in the International Court of Justice at The Hague to test South Africa's right to rule South-West Africa. In July 1966, after six years of proceedings, the court decided by one vote that Ethiopia and Liberia had no legal right to bring the case. The basic questions remained, however: whether South Africa had any right to be in South-West Africa at all, and whether it was maladministrating the territory in a way contrary to the terms of the original mandate. In the same year the UN revoked South Africa's mandate and resolved to take over the territory and guide it towards independence. The South African response to this was to implement the Odendaal Plan, published in 1964, which bound South-West Africa even more closely to the Republic and which imposed on the territory its own form of separate development, planning the creation of nine 'ethnic homelands'. The rest of the country (some 60 per cent) was to be the 'white area'.

Meanwhile, a number of African political movements had developed, of which the South-West Africa People's Organisation (SWAPO) was the largest and best organised. Faced with the Odendaal Plan, SWAPO turned to armed resistance, which started as small-scale guerrilla actions. In 1971 the International Court ruled that South Africa should end its occupation of Namibia (since about that time, most of the outside world used this name), and informed the Security Council that other states should refrain from assisting South Africa to remain in Namibia. Also in 1971 the Ovambo and other African groups mounted a general strike. The South African administration declared a state of emergency in Ovamboland and forcibly broke up the strike. In 1973 the Owambo (Ovambo) and Kavango Homelands were granted a limited form of self-government. The scale of violence in the territory mounted as the security forces used harsh methods in attempting to deal with the disruptive actions of SWAPO, which were mainly directed against the Homeland leaders.

The decisive event in the confrontation over Namibia was the Portuguese coup of 1974 and the consequent civil war and victory of MPLA in Angola. SWAPO was now able to launch more substantial military actions in Namibia from bases in Angola (against which South African forces retaliated from their big military base constructed at Grootfontein, and from others in the Caprivi Strip). Politically, South Africa decided to hold a constitutional conference of 'representatives' of all the 'peoples' of Namibia, to determine the future of the country – without reference to SWAPO or to the UN. This conference began its meetings in September 1975 in a converted gymnasium in the capital, Windhoek; the German name for the hall, Turnhalle, became the popular name of the conference. Goaded by the South African military withdrawal from Angola, the Turnhalle conference issued a statement to the effect that Namibia should obtain independence from South Africa at the end of 1978 as a unitary state; but explicit in the statement was that this state should consist of the existing 'homelands' plus the 'white area', and implicit was that ultimate South African control over Namibia should continue. Neither SWAPO nor the UN accepted the Turnhalle proposals. The Western Security Council members – the United States, Britain, France, West Germany and Canada – took the lead in trying to bring about a peaceful solution. The economic stakes for the West were high: over the years, Namibia was found to be rich in valuable minerals, including uranium. The western countries drew up their own plan for the independence of Namibia, under the supervision of the UN, and attempted to persuade the various parties – the South African government, the Turnhalle Alliance and SWAPO – to agree. South Africa wanted its own troops to maintain law and order until after the crucial elections, and in 1977 declared that Walvis Bay, the country's only large harbour, which had been occupied by the Cape Colony in 1878 before the German annexation of the rest of South-West Africa, should revert to South African sovereignty.

In 1978 the western proposals were accepted in a somewhat modified form (including the stationing of a UN peace-keeping force in Namibia during the transitional period) by the UN secretary-general, 311

Kurt Waldheim. But in September of that year the South African government rejected the Waldheim proposals by announcing its decision to hold elections in the territory under the Turnhalle scheme. It would then unilaterally grant independence to Namibia.

SOUTHERN AFRICA AND THE OUTSIDE WORLD

Since the Second World War, the developing situation in southern Africa has become a major concern to the outside world. This is not only, or mainly, on account of what has already happened there, but much more because of what might happen in the future. There are many states in the world where governments representing a minority of the population tyrannise over the majority, controlling the internal and external movements of their people, using secret police and informers to sniff out the slightest manifestations of dissidence, practising torture in their interrogation chambers and assassination outside. There are many governments in the world, many even in Africa, which have killed far more of their own citizens than the government of South Africa has done so far. What is peculiar about the situation in southern Africa is that, there, these crimes and injustices are compounded by the explosive factors of race and colour. When a Steve Biko dies in the hands of white policemen, every black man in the world feels personally involved. The one last shooting flame in the fire of pan-Africanism is the desire of every self-governing black nation to free its brothers in the south. Even Idi Amin sought to pose as a hero in this crusade, knowing that other African states would find it harder to criticise his internal regime if this item of his external policy was aligned with theirs.

Faced with this situation, the white government of South Africa has in recent years made some efforts to break out of its growing isolation at the tip of the African continent. While continuing to cultivate its economic links with the western countries and Japan, it has also tried hard to launch the notion that South Africa could be both a valuable trading partner and a source of development aid to many countries within Africa. During the 1960s and 1970s Verwoerd and Vorster established close relations with Lesotho and Malawi and held 'dialogues' with countries as far afield as Ivory Coast, Liberia, Ghana and the Malagasy Republic. It is well known that South African goods are on sale in many African countries which do not, officially, admit South African visitors. Botswana, Zambia, Zaïre and Zimbabwe are all to some degree dependent upon South African railways for their access to the sea. And even Mozambique must, for the time being, balance its budget by continuing to send labour migrants to South Africa in exchange for government-to-government payments in gold bullion. What South African diplomacy would particularly like to achieve would be a ring of African-ruled neighbour states dependent enough on South African aid to be obliged to observe correct relations, especially in the matter of harbouring guerrilla forces. But such an outcome does not today seem very likely. In 1969 a fourteen-nation conference of African states issued the Lusaka Manifesto, which reflected above all the thoughts of Presidents Kaunda and Nyerere. The manifesto laid down guide-lines for future dialogue between South Africa and other African states, suggesting that this could be fruitful only after South Africa had shown itself ready to change substantially the policy of separate development or apartheid. Given such a readiness, other African states would recognise that there might be a considerable interval before majority rule was achieved: 'If the commitment to these principles existed among the States holding power in southern Africa, any disagreement we might have about the rate of implementation, or about isolated acts of policy, would be matters affecting only our individual relationship with the States concerned.' But although Vorster and other members of his government occasionally spoke favourably of this approach, the words and deeds of white South Africans since 1969 have in general implied a firm rejection of what could have been a unique opportunity to escape from their self-imposed impasse. By the time of the Soweto uprising in 1976, dialogue was a dead duck.

At the time of writing, Zimbabwe had gained its independence, and the transfer of power to a black government in Namibia appeared likely to occur in the not too distant future, although perhaps only after a violent transition. But in South Africa itself, the stalemate seems total. As the frontiers of independent Africa close in upon those of the white-dominated south, it becomes easier for black South African militants to leave their country for training in insurgency. The industrialised countries of the Soviet bloc, having no investments to defend in South Africa and every motive to promote disruption in a region from which the West draws so many much-needed minerals, stand ready to supply the hardware for destruction. The oppressed people of South Africa, knowing that they can at present expect little more than sympathetic noises from the western countries, have no choice but to look, at least initially, to the East. In terms of conventional weapons and internal policing, the white regime is too powerful to be overthrown within the foreseeable future by means of internal revolution or guerrilla incursions, even if strengthened by arms and 313 'advisers' from outside countries. Such attempts are likely to be made, however, and it is certain that they will be repressed with extreme violence. It is possible that a really savage repression might create a wholly new scenario in which the eastern and western super-powers might combine to issue an ultimatum demanding radical constitutional reforms within a specified short period. By whatever method it comes about, it seems likely that only by the application of great external heat will the contents of the South African crucible be made to melt and fuse.

23 Middle Africa since independence (1): A synoptic view

There is a loose, general sense in which the history of Africa in the 180 years from 1800 to the 1980s has come full circle. In 1800, very few parts of Africa were under European or other foreign control: a number of tiny coastal enclaves in West, West-Central and East Africa; a small colony of white settlement in South Africa. Ottoman suzerainty over North Africa was entirely nominal. Between 1880 and 1940, a mere sixty years, less than the biblical life-span of three-score years and ten, the whole of the continent (with the dubious exception of Liberia) came, for a longer or shorter time, under alien rule. By the late 1970s nearly all the continent was once again ruled by governments representing, in some way or another, the indigenous peoples of Africa. The only remaining exceptions to this are in the extreme south, but even there, as we have seen, changes appear to be on the way. It would seem that it is only a matter of time before a black government rules Namibia (South-West Africa). The future of the Republic of South Africa remains more imponderable.

The black Africa which regained independence in the two decades from 1957 to 1977 is, however, an immensely different Africa from what it was in 1800. The years of European influence, interference, invasion and rule may have been a fairly brief episode in the long course of African history, but during this short time Africa had undergone changes probably more profound, and certainly more rapid, than it had experienced previously. It is with the consequences of these changes that independent African states and their rulers have had to grapple. The lives of individual Africans and of the states of which they are citizens are rooted in the manners and customs and in the political and religious ideas of the pre-colonial past. But even the continuities which have survived from this past have been greatly affected by the colonial era. The myriad small states of pre-colonial Africa have been amalgamated into forty-six countries. The great distances of the past have been drastically reduced by mechanical transport. The mineral resources of the continent have been opened up. The very landscape of Africa, the physical environment in which men live, has been altered, in some cases beyond recognition. Huge man-made lakes have been created in constructing hydro-electric plants, such as Lake Akasombo in Ghana and Lake Kariba on the Zambezi river between Zambia and Zimbabwe. Mountain-sides have been denuded of their tree cover. The area of dense tropical rain-forest has been much reduced. The desert has encroached upon savanna country. Great cities have sprung up, in some cases (such as Nairobi) where not even a village existed before.

The fundamental beliefs of men in Africa have in many instances undergone great change. Many Africans have become Christians or Muslims, while some profess the philosophy of Marxism. Where ancient African beliefs survive, it is either in rather isolated communities or as peculiarly African ways of expressing the more recent universal faiths introduced to the continent. These universal faiths have become partially 'Africanised' – Islam over the course of many centuries, Christianity (except in Ethiopia and a few other tiny areas) over the past two centuries. The languages in which men express their innermost thoughts as well as their everyday communications have changed. For some purposes many people now speak English, French, Portuguese, Arabic or Swahili. In so far as they continue to speak their native tongues, these African languages have been much altered in the process of being transmitted from one generation to the next in written as well as oral form.

People in Africa, as in every other part of the world, have a number of loyalties: towards their family, their employment, their town or village, their local football team, their country. Most Africans also still feel a sense of loyalty towards, an identity with, fellow members of their tribe or ethnic group. Members of a tribe speak the same language, share a common history, have many peculiar customs and habits. Tribal loyalties persisted through the colonial period, but tribes, as political and cultural entities, like so much else in Africa, were imprinted deeply with alien influences. In some instances, as occurred in many French colonies, the political or religious leadership of tribes was demoted by the colonial rulers. In other instances, such as the Fulbe and Hausa emirs of northern Nigeria, the political authority of tribal leaders was strengthened. Some tribes which previously had no centralised system of government had this enforced on them (see the section on indirect rule, pp. 161–2). There are some examples of tribes actually being invented by educated Africans in order to meet the requirements of the colonial authorities: one such is the Tumbuka in Malawi. Some tribes were amalgamated, others split up; some greatly increased in numbers, others declined and indeed even ceased to exist. All tribes were much affected by changes in religious belief, in education, in life-style (wearing European-type clothes, listening to transistor radios), in health standards. Nevertheless, in spite of such transformations, tribal affinities – ethnicity – continue. As we shall see, both political assent and dissent are often expressed in a tribal way. In the last analysis, most people only really trust those who speak the same mother tongue.

Although there are these tangible and intangible continuities with Africa's pre-colonial past, it is the innovations introduced in the colonial era which have so dramatically affected the course of African history. The very states into which Africa is now divided – the stage upon which much of recent history has been enacted – are the old colonies which the European imperialists established during their partition of the continent in the 1880s and 1890s. The most revolutionary change has been very broadly economic. Before 1800 the economies of nearly all African states and peoples were on a small scale and were mainly concerned with local and immediate consumption. In most states only a small part of the economy was concerned with export markets in other communities and beyond the seas. Now, Africa and its people are linked indissolubly to an international economic system, which in origin was capitalist and which remains largely dominated by large-scale capitalist enterprises but also comprises the international economic activities of the non-capitalist, communist countries of the world. Becoming part and parcel of this economic system has its advantages and disadvantages, its privileges and its responsibilities. It enables African states and their rulers to adopt a 'modern' pose, to have splendid government and commercial buildings in their capitals, to have their own airline (or a share in one), their own television network. It enables a privileged few – the elite – to receive excellent education in modern and even luxurious colleges and universities. It enables this elite to be thoroughly international and to play a role in world affairs.

But this affluence, style and importance of a few forms only a thin veneer on the surface of most African economies. Most African economies are still overwhelmingly rural and subsistence-based. The main part that Africa is able to play in international trade is still as the producer of raw materials, mineral and vegetable. The revenues derived from these exports are subject to great world-wide fluctuations of commodity prices, and as many African countries depend on the export of only one or two such commodities, they remain some of the poorest countries in the world. Some cannot produce enough food to feed their growing urban populations. In 1978 the World Food Council identified forty-three 'Food Priority Countries'; twenty-six of these are in Africa. Of the twenty-nine countries defined by UNCTAD as 'Least Developed Countries' (LDCs), eighteen are in Africa. With much-improved health and medical facilities, the population of Africa is increasing rapidly. As a result of western education and of access to newspapers and radio, as well as through the example of the elites, expectations are also rising. Unfortunately, the wealth of most African countries can neither keep up with the increased population nor with the rising expectations. This is the critical dilemma facing responsible people in nearly every country in black Africa.

The colonial era has been credited by some writers – including Africans – as a beneficial and even beneficent period in the history of Africa, one which brought the blessings of modern, international civilisation. In a book written early in his career, the Zimbabwean nationalist leader Ndabaningi Sithole generously acknowledged this aspect of colonialism:

It has given to Africa a new vigorous industrial pattern, a new social consciousness, new insights and visions. It has created a new environment. It has annihilated many tribal and linguistic barriers and divisions. The European colonial powers are to be praised for the work they have done in helping the emergence of African nationalism. It is only a blind man who will not appreciate the fact that colonialism has stimulated and shaped African nationalism. The twentieth-century African nationalism is indeed a child of European colonialism.[1]

To other writers, white and black, the colonialist adventure was an unmitigated disaster for Africa, a period of alien occupation and exploitation upon which all the current ills which beset the continent can be blamed. What imperialism and colonialism did do, over the 180 years from 1800, or, more intensively, from 1880 to 1960, was to wrench black Africa from courses of history which were very largely determined within Africa by Africans into an historical process which was determined for Africans by foreigners, either outside or inside the continent. The regaining of independence has so far only partially returned the initiative for determining the course of their history to African hands. The rulers of independent African states are the products of colonialism, even when they are most critical of it. As the colonial period recedes into the past, their children are the products of the post-colonial (or neo-colonial, in the terminology of some radical and Marxist writers) world, which in many respects is harsher, more dangerous, less sheltered than the insulated area of alien rule, or

[1] *African Nationalism* (London, 1959), p. 74.

trusteeship, as the colonial powers latterly came to call what they were doing in Africa and in other parts of the world.

Among the more obvious of the legacies bequeathed to independent Africa are the political boundaries created by the colonial powers. Some African leaders have spoken critically of this as the 'balkanisation' of Africa. Because of the colonial partition of Africa, however, most of the modern African countries are much larger than the pre-colonial units. A few, like Gambia, Guiné Bissau, Togo, Equatorial Guinea, Lesotho and Dijbouti, are still inconveniently small. Some fairly small states, such as Upper Volta, Rwanda and Burundi, are inconveniently land-locked. Some African states are both large in size and small in population – Botswana, Tchad, Niger and Mali are examples. But countries like Nigeria, Zaïre, Sudan or Tanzania, to name only a few, have far greater potentialities – political, social, economic – than even the largest of the old African kingdoms. Certainly, it would have been better for post-colonial Africa if the colonial partition of Africa had been carried out in fewer and larger slices, but there can be no doubt that the colonial frontiers represent a very great improvement over the pre-colonial situation.

The grave practical disadvantages of the colonial heritage arise less from frontiers than from the closed economic relationship formerly existing between colonies and the metropolitan powers. These were expressed by Sylvanus Olympio, the first president of the Togo Republic:

The effect of the policy of the colonial powers has been the economic isolation of peoples who live side by side, in some instances within a few miles of each other, while directing the flow of resources to the metropolitan countries. For example, although I can call Paris from my office telephone here in Lomé, I cannot place a call to Lagos in Nigeria only 250 miles away. Again, while it takes a short time to send an air-mail letter to Paris, it takes several days for the same letter to reach Accra, a mere 132 miles away. Railways rarely connect at international boundaries. Roads have been constructed from the coast inland but very few join economic centres of trade. The productive central regions of Togo, Dahomey and Ghana are as remote from each other as if they were separate continents.[2]

According to this line of thought, what was needed was not a grand political union of African states as advocated by Nkrumah, but rather the establishment of closer communications between neighbouring African states on a regional basis. President Houphouet-Boigny of the Ivory Coast was even more outspoken. He maintained that a political

[2] 'African Problems and the Cold War', in Philip W. Quigg (ed.), *Africa: a foreign affairs reader* (New York, 1964), p. 296.

union of African states would do nothing to solve Africa's economic poverty. A union between poor countries would not make any of them richer and might actually impede their relations with the richer countries which could help them. Referring to the neutralist position adopted by the countries attending the Afro-Asian Conferences at Bandung and Cairo (1958), he warned his audience against

a spirit of hate which severs the under-developed countries from the powers to which they were attached and finally dooms them, on the one hand to a regrouping in misery and mediocrity, on the other to a kind of perpetual auction, in which a majority of the non-committed countries live, which gives them some short-lived successes but which cannot guarantee them the satisfaction of their constant needs.[3]

Although few African leaders then agreed with Houphouet-Boigny, the years from 1959 through the 1970s in fact saw a strengthening rather than a weakening of the frontiers between African countries. The reasons for this were partly fiscal. African countries found it easiest to tax their small farmers by buying their cash crops at one price and selling them on the world market at another; the consequence was a vast increase in smuggling. More important, however, was the danger of irredentism felt in some measure by all the newly independent states in respect of their border communities whose ethnic territories were so often divided by the ex-colonial frontiers. To these communities the end of colonial rule appeared to offer the opportunity for frontier changes on a scale which could all too easily have thrown every African frontier into jeopardy. In these circumstances most African governments have clubbed together to resist even the slightest changes in what have been sardonically termed 'the holy colonial frontiers', and only a very few of the most outstanding cases, such as those in the Horn of Africa, have led to armed conflict. More serious have been cases of attempted secession by parts of existing countries, such as have occurred in Nigeria and Zaïre, but even these have so far been successfully contained. The disputed cases are, however, only the tip of an iceberg which could threaten the security of nearly all African countries unless frontier issues continue to be handled with the greatest circumspection and restraint.

POLITICAL DEVELOPMENTS IN AFRICAN STATES SINCE INDEPENDENCE

The problems which faced the citizens of the independent African

[3] Félix Houphouet-Boigny, *Afrique Nouvelle*, 22 March 1961.

states and their governments after the safe but stifling cosseting of colonial overrule had been removed were immense. These were not widely appreciated either by the inheritors of political power or by their former masters, or by commentators in the world at large. Africans entered upon their independence full of hope for the future, an optimism which was shared by outside well-wishers, particularly the former colonial powers. The victories of the African nationalist movements were envisaged as, and once achieved, hailed as, ends in themselves. 'Seek ye first the political kingdom', exclaimed Nkrumah, parodying the bible. The achievement of political independence was heralded by some people as the African Revolution.

In effect, as the colonial flags were hauled down and the new African flags were raised, the changes proved largely superficial, and the impressive unity with which African peoples had faced their colonial rulers was seen to be largely a deceptive façade. It had been a unity of anti-colonialism rather than a unity of real nationalism. Black men now sat in the seats of power formerly occupied by white men (many of whom stayed on for a time as senior civil servants, army officers, secondary-school and university teachers). The mechanisms of government were inherited unchanged. Parliaments and assemblies in the new African states had generally been established in some haste several years before independence and were based on the home parliaments of the colonial powers, the Westminster and Paris models. In the circumstances of rapid decolonisation, the colonial authorities, during the transitional period, could hardly have done otherwise; nor would African politicians have accepted anything less than what appeared to be the best of democratic parliamentary institutions (see Chapter 17). Nevertheless, the constitutional systems which suited Britain, France and Belgium, and which had taken centuries to develop national characteristics, were not necessarily ideal institutions for the very different societies of tropical Africa.

In many newly independent African states, tribalism, as we have seen, was still potentially a force stronger than nationalism. Throughout the continent, local or regional interests, based mainly on tribal or language groups, threatened the security and stability of the new states. Governments had to take strong measures to meet these crises (as indeed, the preceding colonial administrations had sometimes had to act in very authoritarian ways), and in so doing they incurred the criticism of using non-democratic methods. Some countries were successful in controlling or curbing these dangerous forces; others were less so, and some suffered a breakdown of law and order. The first to do so on a large scale was Zaïre.

Africa since 1800

African governments not only had to cope with open manifestations of surviving tribalism, but also they had somehow to satisfy the demands of the mass of the people for rapid change, for immediate betterment or improvement, following independence. People were not prepared merely to exchange a set of white rulers for a set of black rulers, who might become just as remote from their daily lives as their predecessors; in the event, however, after two decades of independence, unfortunately for ordinary African people, this is just what has taken place. But in the early days, popular aspirations were reflected among the younger supporters of the nationalist parties, who pressed for radical policies to eradicate poverty and ignorance. In order to survive in power, political leaders had to attempt to satisfy these demands as well as to control tribalism and separatism. During the early years of independence the main solution to these problems was thought to lie in a rapid extension of the western-type educational systems instituted in colonial times. This was also highly popular electorally, and in some newly independent countries the costs of education rose to as much as half the national revenue. While there was probably some pay-off in the growth of national consciousness among the younger citizens, the spread of education also bred dissatisfaction with the conditions of rural life. Huge numbers of young people drifted to the towns and, failing to find employment, sank into abject poverty and often into petty crime.

Meanwhile, with the removal, after independence, of the anti-colonial plank in their platforms, party politics on the western model suffered a severe decline in most African countries. Politicians had few solutions to offer, and those in power turned increasingly to the business of feathering their own nests. Opposition parties, being viewed not merely as political rivals but also as divisive, even subversive and therefore dangerous, elements within the state, were threatened, harried and finally suppressed. To the opposition parties, governments appeared to be, and often were, dictatorial, tyrannical and corrupt. Those in power lived well, often using their positions to extort bribes and to borrow money for profitable investments in housing and business ventures. The great majority of people lived as poorly as they had ever done, and governing parties did not want opposition parties to be free to emphasise these facts.

During the 1960s the constitutional systems of the new African states underwent radical changes. The main features of the move away from colonial models were the setting up of one-party regimes and the involvement in politics of the armed forces. The French-speaking West African states were the first to establish one-party rule. Some

322

states, such as Guinea under Sékou Touré and Ivory Coast under Houphouet-Boigny, had virtually only one political party at independence, and most other French-speaking states in West and Central Africa soon followed suit. Within a very few years many of the former British colonies in West and East Africa had likewise become one-party states. The history of some countries, such as Nigeria and Zaïre, was, as we shall see, very complex. But even in Nigeria, where initially a multiparty system seemed to be a condition of the federation's survival, by the mid-1960s it was acknowledged to be an important ingredient in the collapse of parliamentary democracy. In the absence of recognised oppositions, the formal meetings of parliaments and legislative assemblies became much less important than they had been. More and more powers passed into the hands of presidents and ministers. More and more of the making of policy went on behind the scenes in cabinets and party committees. Decisions were concentrated in too few hands. The result was often stagnation.

Side by side with the elimination of parliamentary opposition went the strengthening of the government and the organisation of the dominant party. The district and provincial commissioners of colonial times were succeeded, not by politically neutral African civil servants, but by party officials. Recruits from party youth organisations were sent for training as army and police officers. Trade unions were brought under government control. So were broadcasting and the press. Presidential powers were extended to include the imprisonment (or even death) without trial of persons suspected of political subversion, and the removal of judges who returned politically unacceptable verdicts. Nkrumah, at least, had forecast developments of this kind. In his autobiography, published on the eve of independence, he had written, 'Even a system based on social justice and a democratic constitution may need backing up, during the period following independence, by emergency measures of a totalitarian kind. Without discipline, freedom cannot survive.' 'Once a free Government is formed,' wrote Nyerere, 'its supreme task lies ahead – the building up of the country's economy. This, no less than the struggle against colonialism, calls for the maximum united effort by the whole country if it is to succeed. There can be no room for difference or division.'

In their speeches and writings both Nyerere and Nkrumah presented the struggle against poverty as similar to a state of war, when, even in western countries, 'national' governments chosen from all parties were held to represent the will of the people. The one-party state was a kind of 'national' government, and Nyerere and others have claimed that it followed the tradition of African life, in which 'the elders sit under the big tree and talk until they agree'. In Tanzania the system of elections adopted in 1965, when voters were asked to choose between rival candidates both representing the single party, went far to meet the main objection to single-party rule, which is that governments can be changed only by plots or violence. Eight ministers lost their seats in this election. Few other African states, however, have been bold enough to follow this flexible attitude towards the political process. In many, the establishment of single-party states has rather represented the determination of those in power to cling to the fruits of office for as long as possible, regardless of the wishes of the electorate.

Most African politicians have described themselves as 'socialists', but this term has proved to have many meanings. Nyerere's concept of African socialism was summed up in his search for the ideal society, or *ujamaa* (a Swahili word which is difficult to translate; it means, roughly, 'brotherhood', 'friendship'). In its ideology, Nyerere's *ujamaa* looked back to a pre-colonial African past, to a traditional society in which 'nobody starved, whether of food or human dignity, because he lacked personal wealth; he could depend on the wealth possessed by the community of which he was a member. That was socialism. That *is* socialism.' In practice, *ujamaa* has meant a more or less forceful resettlement of most of the rural population of Tanzania into villages of a standard pattern designed to facilitate collective farming. Though highly authoritarian, it has at least the merit of addressing itself to the problems of improving African rural life, which have been given little priority in most other African states. While Nyerere was writing about *ujamaa*, Nkrumah warned against a too-simplistic view of Africa's past:

Today the phrase 'African socialism' seems to espouse the view that the traditional African society was a classless society imbued with the spirit of humanism and to express a nostalgia for the spirit. Such a conception of socialism makes a fetish of the communal African society. Colonialism deserves to be blamed for many evils in Africa, but surely it was not preceded by an African Golden Age or paradise. A return to pre-colonial African society is evidently not worthy of the ingenuity and efforts of our people.[4]

Nkrumah was a socialist in the sense that he believed in economic modernisation through the action of state-controlled corporations for industry and marketing. Apart from controlling the prices paid for agricultural produce, however, Nkrumah did little to disturb the

[4] Cited by Ahmed Mohiddin, 'Ujamaa: a commentary on President Nyerere's vision of Tanzanian society', *African Affairs*, 67 (1968), 136.

pattern of peasant proprietorship prevalent over most of Ghana. The main faults of his government were extravagance and corruption, and what caught him out was the collapse in the world price of cocoa, which deprived him of the revenue derived from the difference between the buying and the selling price of the country's main cash crop. In 1957 the world price of cocoa stood at £247 a ton. By 1961 it had fallen to £177. In 1965 it dropped well below £100. This turned the credit economy inherited from the colonial government into one of serious indebtedness. As the external and internal pressures mounted, Nkrumah became increasingly isolated, dictatorial and suspicious. There was a general relief in the country when his regime was at last toppled by a military coup during his absence on a state visit to Peking in February 1966.

THE MILITARY FACTOR IN AFRICAN POLITICS

The fall of Nkrumah marked a turning-point in the political development of independent black Africa. Nkrumah had been perhaps the most typical African leader of the independence period – the lonely student abroad, nurturing himself on the literature of pan-Negro aspirations and Marxist–Leninist revolutionary techniques; the charismatic young politician who built a mass party to challenge the colonial regime; the responsible minister who guided his country to a negotiated independence; the patron of political movements in other African countries; and finally the dictator whose continent-wide ambitions proved too great a burden for his own people to bear. Though it had an undeniably quality of greatness, the inevitable end of such a career was military rule in Ghana. And within a year or two the example of Ghana was followed in many other African countries. The year 1966 especially is remembered as the year of military revolutions in black Africa, and although the circumstances varied greatly from country to country, the root cause was in every case the failure of the civilian governments set up at independence either to sustain widespread popular support for their own policies or to allow alternative policies to be canvassed among their electorates. As we shall see, 1966 was a turning-point even in those countries which avoided military take-overs. The leaders of these countries read the message and reacted. Party organisation was revitalised and a wide variety of remedial measures set in train. The transitional stage to independent rule was over.

The spate of military take-overs around 1966 took even the most experienced observers of the African scene completely by surprise. 325

During the second half of the colonial period, at least, military affairs had been the least-conspicuous aspect of colonial rule. The ultimate sanction behind colonial authority had consisted in the ability of colonial powers to move forces rapidly from one part to another of their empires. Local garrisons stationed within any particular territory were incredibly small. In the British colonies in Africa there was only one soldier for about every 5,000 inhabitants. In French and Belgian Africa the proportion was approximately double this figure. Save in rare emergencies, colonial garrisons stayed in their barracks, out of sight and out of mind. Soldiers, and also policemen, were recruited from the least politically conscious elements in colonial society – typically from the tough tribesmen of the frontier regions, 'unspoiled' by western influence and respected for their martial qualities. They obeyed orders. They were as 'unpolitical' as most of their European officers. No one suspected that they would give any 'trouble', and in all the planning connected with decolonisation scarcely a thought was given to their possible significance in the changed conditions of independence. Above all, and as a direct consequence of their recruitment from the least-westernised elements, the armies of black Africa were still at the time of independence officered overwhelmingly by whites. During the 1950s some senior NCOs were promoted, and a few younger, educated cadets were sent for training, mostly to Britain or France. But, until their return, and until they had then made some progress in seniority, the political leaders of black Africa enjoyed, perhaps unconsciously, the protection of expatriate commanders and police chiefs.

It is significant that Egypt and the Sudan were the first two ex-colonial states whose armies were officered by their own nationals: Egypt since 1936, when native Egyptians rather than the Turkish–Mamluk elite were allowed into the officer corps; and the Sudan as early as the aftermath of the 1924 mutiny (see p. 180), when sons of aristocratic collaborationist families were trained as officers at Gordon College, Khartoum. As we have seen, the army ousted the monarchy from Egypt in 1952 and intervened, under General Abboud, for the first time in the politics of the Sudan in 1958, only two years after the independence of that country. In Middle Africa the pressure for Africanisation, in the army and in the police, as in other areas of government, was surprisingly quick to emerge. In Zaïre it led rapidly to a complete breakdown of law and order. In Tanzania, a few days after the revolution in Zanzibar early in 1964, the army, led by some of the very few junior African officers, mutinied, and rioters looted the streets of Dar es Salaam. The army mutinies – basically over the pace

of Africanisation – spread to Kenya and Uganda. All three governments took the necessary yet humiliating step of recalling British
troops to disarm the mutineers and restore order. Before the British
soldiers actually entered Uganda (from Kenya) the mutiny there had
been dealt with by the offer of a rise in pay – the person who conveyed
this offer to the Ugandan soldiers was a certain Major Idi Amin, the
first experience for him of involvement in politics. Many of the
African troops who formed the United Nations forces in the Congo in
the early 1960s were led by white officers (Ghana was a particular
instance; dissatisfaction with their role in the Congo emergency
caused Ghanaian officers to become increasingly critical of the government of Nkrumah). By the middle of the 1960s, however, most
African armies were under the control of their own officers. Their
appearance coincided in time with the failure of so many of the first
generation of civilian political leaders.

The politicians of former British colonies, it has been said, had been
taught their politics mainly at the London School of Economics, and
the French-speaking leaders at the École Normale William Ponty at
Dakar; the officers had been trained mainly at Sandhurst and St Cyr.
Both their training and their everyday army life, centred upon the
officers' mess (or club), fostered strong personal attachments to their
regiments – a feeling which is called *esprit de corps* – and perhaps
deluded them into thinking that they were superior to, and could
achieve greater things than, the civilian politicians, whom they tended
to despise. Many of the French-speaking officers had served as NCOs
and junior officers in the French army on various overseas campaigns,
including Vietnam and Algeria. In the early 1960s these African
soldiers were demobilised. It was these young officers who planned
the first series of coups, and it was unemployed soldiers who supported them. In Ghana and Nigeria, British officers were gradually
replaced by senior Africans, many of them promoted from the ranks,
who had served with the African contingents used by Britain in the
Second World War. The impetus for change, however, came from
younger officers, who grew impatient both with the civilians and with
their seniors. In a country like Uganda, Africanisation, once it got
under way, was rapid, and long-serving NCOs from the former
King's African Rifles quickly rose to senior positions: Field Marshal
Amin is an example of this accelerated promotion. Whatever the
differences between the military in African states, the temptation to
intervene in politics, to stage a coup, was contagious. In many cases –
Ghana for instance – there were specific as well as more general
reasons for coups. Economy drives by governments threatened not

only the pay but also the jobs of army officers, who responded dramatically to such threats. Often, however, there have been no serious reasons for military intervention: it has taken place because soldiers have had nothing better to do, or because of the example of brother officers in neighbouring states.

Once they had toppled the civilian governments, the problems facing the army officers remained the same as for their predecessors: poverty, inequality and underdevelopment, the forging of national unity, political instability. The officers were mostly far less equipped to cope with these than civilians: consequently military rule often did little more than validate the decisions of the civil service. In the worst cases, however, military dictators proved far more ruthless and tyrannical than even the most corrupt of civilian governments, and many of the older citizens sighed for the relative freedom and justice of colonial days. More generally, although the military officers actually charged with political responsibility were few and senior, one practical result of military government was that all soldiers of all ranks were tempted to batten on the civilian public through the knowledge that they were unlikely to be brought to justice. At one end of the scale gifts could be solicited and property bought cheaply; at the other end women on their way to market could be held at check-points until they paid passage-money. Military rule, though often popular at the outset as an alternative to what had gone before, seldom remained acceptable for any length of time. Faced by the loss of popularity, some military governments favoured a return to the barracks. Others turned increasingly to repression and terrorism. Most of the worst excesses have been committed in the smallest and poorest countries with the most tenuous connections with the outside world, like Burundi and Equatorial Guinea; but Amin's Uganda provides at least one example of a large and previously prosperous country which was reduced to a state of poverty and terror through the ruthless exercise of naked military force. It is remarkable that even the grimmest tyrannies have been able to find some outside source of arms and military technology – usually, though not always, from communist countries; and that the United Nations, with its large majority of Third World members, has been far less ready to condemn abuses of human rights in black Africa than in the white-ruled south.

NEW DIRECTIONS

We have suggested that 1966 was a turning-point not only for those Middle African countries which passed under military rule, but also for those which did not. If so, this fact was by no means apparent at the time. Between 1966 and 1970 black Africa passed through its nadir in world esteem. Its leading country, Nigeria, was torn by civil war. In Zaïre, Mobutu was establishing himself at the centre but was by no means in control of the provinces. In Angola and Mozambique the Portuguese appeared to be winning wars of repression against the liberation movements. In Zimbabwe (Rhodesia) the white government of Ian Smith had declared its independence of Britain and was successfully defying the economic sanctions of the outside world. In Uganda, Obote, with the help of Amin, had driven out the Kabaka and broken up the traditional kingdoms in the most progressive and stable part of the country. In the Sudan there was still an active civil war between the black peoples of the south and their northern rulers. In the Central African Republic a particularly nasty dictatorship had been established by Colonel Bokassa, who spent the equivalent of one-quarter of the country's revenue on a coronation ceremony at which he crowned himself emperor. Amid these unpromising developments in nearby countries, Nyerere, the last shining light among liberal optimists for the future of Africa, abandoned the presidency of Tanzania to reorganise his party. It seemed doubtful whether he would ever return.

And then slowly, very slowly, the tide began to turn. The most obvious sign of it was the end of the Nigerian civil war. The most important country of Africa had survived in one piece and in a spirit of reconciliation between victors and vanquished. In Ghana there had already been a return from military to civilian rule under the civilised leadership of Kofi Busia. His reign was to be a short one, but at least it proved that military government need not be permanent. In Dar es Salaam, Nyerere had returned to the State House with the mandate from a revitalised TANU to proceed with the definitive stage of his *ujamaa* resettlement programme. The Chinese had begun to build a railway to connect Tanzania with Zambia, which it was hoped would free Kaunda from his embarrassing dependence on Rhodesian and South African communications. In Kenya, freed at last from Somali irredentism, it was becoming clear that the Kikuyu-based KANU government would enjoy stability at least during the lifetime of Kenyatta, though few probably imagined how long he would live. Next, the southern Sudan, by the mediation of Haile Selassie, at last came to terms with the north, and this great area, so long a battleground, could look forward to a peaceful future. Taken together with the continued steadiness of Senegal and Ivory Coast, Cameroun and Gabon, the general situation looked altogether more hopeful than in 1966.

Of course, there were not wanting the leftist prophets of doom, who maintained that only in Guinea, Tanzania and the Congo Republic had the real African revolution begun to happen. To these the independence, under Russian and Cuban auspices, of the ex-Portuguese territories of Angola, Mozambique and Guiné Bissau brought further rays of hope. However, the distinction between socialist and capitalist states in Africa has often proved to be more one of rhetoric than reality. Even in countries with a free-enterprise, capitalist philosophy, the degree of state intervention in, and regulation of, the economy is very considerable. The most stalwart defenders of a 'liberal economy', such as Houphouet-Boigny of Ivory Coast, Mobutu of Zaïre and Kenyatta of Kenya, have used the extensive propaganda powers of a one-party state, with large bureaucracies and tough security forces, in attempts to enforce schemes of economic development. In this respect they operate little differently from the leaders of socialist countries. Again, in most nominally socialist states, as in the capitalist ones, there is a small class of salaried people who have the security on which to borrow and therefore to invest in property or business enterprises. These are 'the rich' in the tropical African societies of today, but their wealth is often spread over the needs of a numerous extended family. In the last resort, the socialist or capitalist jargon employed in any individual state is often a reflection of where external aid was mainly coming from at a particular time. This again is a highly variable factor. The external alliances of African countries are no more permanent than are any others.

24 Middle Africa since independence (2): A closer look

An outstanding feature of the histories of the French-speaking states of West Africa after independence was the marked and increasing disparity in their economic performance. Only two countries, Senegal and Ivory Coast, maintained from the colonial period a degree of economic momentum which placed them in the 'better off' category of African states. In certain sectors of its economy, Ivory Coast did indeed become comparatively wealthy, and to this extent it became the dominant Francophone state in West Africa. Three other maritime countries, Guinea, Togo and Bénin (Dahomey), had varying economic fortunes, depending on the world commodity prices for their agricultural or mineral products. The Sahelian countries, Niger (and Tchad, which geographically falls within the old Equatorial African region), Upper Volta, Mali and Mauritania – all, except the last, deeply landlocked countries – remained amongst the poorest in the world. This poverty was exacerbated by the great Sahelian drought of 1972–5. The loss and suffering of people and their animals, and the damage to crops, were severe and will take many years of normal rainfall to make good. Neither the governments of these poor countries nor the outside world coped with this critical situation very efficiently or effectively.

Politically, the richer Francophone states remained fairly stable, while the poor countries experienced stormy times. President Senghor, an experienced and astute politician, retained his hold over Senegal. Senegal not only successfully exploited its agricultural resources, but also possessed in Dakar a city of great international importance for airlines and shipping. There have been a number of unsuccessful attempts to overthrow the president, notably in 1962, but in 1976 Senghor felt secure enough to introduce constitutional changes which legally sanctioned opposition parties. President Houphouet-Boigny likewise survived a few rather half-hearted plots, but he strengthened rather than relaxed his iron grip over the Ivory Coast. The prosperity of the rich and diversified economy was spread widely enough to satisfy most potential contenders for political power. Both Senegal and Ivory Coast have kept close economic, political and military links with France, and considerable numbers of French people continue to work (for high wages) in Dakar, Abidjan and elsewhere. Both presidents manipulated this French presence to their own benefit and maintained personal ties with French leaders such as de Gaulle and President Giscard d'Estaing. In the formal terms of political rhetoric Guinea presented a stark contrast to Senegal and the Ivory Coast; while these evolved a kind of state-directed capitalist development, President Sékou Touré followed a more classically socialist road. His government could be categorised as moderate Marxist, but Sékou Touré dealt harshly with more radical Guineans, as well as with other people opposed to him. France's withdrawal in 1958 forced Guinea to rely on aid from the Soviet bloc, but after the mid-1960s Sékou Touré steered the country away from this dependence, towards a *rapprochement* with France and agreements with the United States and Canada, the main importers of Guinea's bauxite. The practical result, therefore, of these different economic systems, was similar; the limited wealth of each country has been concentrated largely in the hands of a small elite, the majority of the population remained poor, and government has been strongly presidential in character.

The other Francophone West African states have not even achieved autocratic stability. The civilian one-party governments which were established just before or after independence gave way to a succession of military regimes. Mauritania did not have its military coup till 1978, when President Moktar Ould Daddah, who had got his country deeply involved in the Saharan conflict (see Chapter 19), was ousted from power. Mali had two coups, in 1968 and 1969, the first overthrowing the socialist government of Modiba Keita, the second installing Colonel Traore as head of state. In Upper Volta Lieutenant-Colonel Laminsana took over from President Yameogo in 1966, while the long rule of President Diori's single-party government of Niger came to an end in 1974, at the height of the Sahelian drought, when Lieutenant-Colonel Kountche declared himself head of state. In contrast to this fairly simple pattern of transfer from civilian to military rule experienced by the Sahelian countries, the politics of Togo and Bénin have been anything but straightforward. In the early 1960s the tiny Togo army intervened constantly in the troubled affairs of the country. This resulted in the murder of President Olympio in 1963 and the removal of another civilian leader in 1966, when General Eyadema came to power. Togo's problems have not been made easier by its relations with neighbouring Ghana, which have sometimes been bad, because of the agitation of some Ewe people in Ghana to be reunited with Togo. Perhaps the most politically unstable country in the whole of Africa has been Dahomey, which changed its name to Bénin in 1975, and which had no fewer than six military coups or interventions. The basic problem facing the small, elongated country has been an ethnic split between the poorer northerners and the somewhat more prosperous southern Fon and Aja people. In 1972 Lieutenant-Colonel Kerekou took over and set up a government which proclaimed 'Marxist–Leninist scientific socialism' to be Bénin's future guiding principle.

The main contrasting themes of Francophone West African post-independence history have been the twin developments of material wealth and autocracy in the better-off states, typified by Houphouet-Boigny's Ivory Coast, and the low, if not negative, rate of economic growth coupled with political instability of the poorer countries. Recently the countries in the western part of the region have come increasingly under the influence of Nigeria's economically dominant position.

ANGLOPHONE WEST AFRICA

The post-independence history of the three smaller ex-British colonies, Gambia, Sierra Leone and Ghana, and of English-speaking Liberia, has followed much the same course as that of the maritime Francophone countries, but the slow and painful emergence of Nigeria to a position of dominance as a giant not only amongst West African states but throughout much of the continent has been an historical process of altogether greater complexity.

Gambia has been one of the few African countries to retain a two-party parliamentary system, although the president, Sir Dauda Jawara, has been in office since 1962. Attempts to bring about a union between little Gambia and surrounding Senegal have not been successful, partly because such a step has been resisted by those engaged in smuggling, which was rampant (indeed, trans-border smuggling was a feature of most West African states). A miniature Nigeria-like situation developed in Sierra Leone, with the Margai brothers, Milton and Albert, representing the pre-colonial or colonial tribal structure of the old colony, and the trade unionist Siaka Stevens and the junior army officers voicing the dissatisfaction of the small modernising elite. Milton Margai, a Mende from the south, was profoundly traditional, and did his best to delay the ending of colonial rule; he used his   333 membership of a *poro* society (one of the so-called secret societies) to further his political ends. Since independence, politics in Sierra Leone have oscillated between the ethnically based parties led by the Margais and Stevens, and senior and junior officers of the army.

Liberia continued to be dominated by the leading ex-freed-slave families; these American-Liberians number some 50,000 out of a total population of well over 1,000,000. In 1969 William Tubman celebrated the twenty-fifth anniversary of his presidency; he died in 1971 and was succeeded by William Tolbert, who had been vice-president for nineteen years. It is instructive to compare the four territories in Upper Guinea which had old creole-type settlements. Senegal has continued to be dominated by the four *communes* (Dakar, Saint Louis, Rufisque and Gorée – see Chapter 13), and although Senghor was not by origin a 'citizen' – he is a Serer, born at Joal – he has identified himself culturally and politically with the *communes*. In Gambia, the more prosperous rice- and peanut-growing banks of the middle and upper river – the old protectorate – are more important than the infertile swamps around the old colony of Bathurst (Banjul). The Freetown creoles of the 'colony' of Sierra Leone had been overtaken by the diverse groups of the 'protectorate' well before independence; Margai and Stevens did not fight their political battles over the status of the creoles. And in Liberia, the position of the American-Liberians, led by Tubman and Tolbert, would appear to have been undermined by the coup led by Sergeant Doe in 1980.

Turning from these small Upper Guinea countries to Ghana and Nigeria, one immediate if superficial feature has been the rapid decline in the importance in pan-African affairs of Ghana and the subsequent rise of Nigeria. Ghana under Nkrumah achieved a unique position. It was the first colony in black Africa to gain independence, and it led the way for others to follow. Nkrumah, as we have seen (Chapter 18), was the chief exponent of Pan-Africanism. Great hopes were pinned on the new state and its dynamic leader by nationalists throughout Africa and by their supporters overseas. Ghana inherited a buoyant economy from the colonial Gold Coast administration, and upon this basis Nkrumah started to build his version of African socialism. Internally, he moved rapidly and ruthlessly to quell opposition (a Preventive Detention Act was promulgated as early as 1958). By the end of 1957 Ghana had become virtually a one-party state, and in 1960 it was proclaimed a republic with Nkrumah its president. In 1962 an attempt was made on his life, which led to a wide-scale purge, but which was followed by other attempts. The impact of Nkrumah and the CPP upon Ghana was wide-ranging. Young recruits to the party were sent for training to the Winneba Ideological Institute. Construction was begun of the hydro-electric dam on the lower Volta, which was to create the largest man-made lake in the world with modern fishing and agricultural industries around its shores. But from 1964 Ghana's economy was seriously undermined by the dramatic fall in the world price of cocoa (see p. 325). Nkrumah continued to push ahead with his grandiose schemes and attempted to dictate the course of events of much of the rest of Africa with his policy of Pan-Africanism. He committed the Ghanaian army, still under the command of a British general, to service with the UN peace-keeping force in Zaïre from 1960 to 1963, and involved it in political as well as normal military actions. This experience alienated many of the soldiers: Colonel Afrifa, one of the leaders of the 1966 coup, pointedly asked, 'could it be that we had been sent to the Congo to foster the ambitions of Kwame Nkrumah?' At home, the activities of the Workers' Brigade disturbed the regular soldiers.

Early in 1966, while Nkrumah was absent in Peking, the army took over the government, under the leadership of two officers – Kotoka and Afrifa – together with the police commissioner, J. Harlley. They set up a National Liberation Council with a senior officer, General Ankrah, as head of state. The NLC quickly dismantled most of the outward signs of Nkrumah's rule and switched from a pro-communist to a pro-western foreign policy. But it did not provide a particularly stable or efficient government. The NLC only just survived a junior officers' coup in 1967, when Kotoka was killed. Afrifa took over from Ankrah as head of state in 1968 and started the process of return to civilian rule. In September 1969 the army marched back to its barracks, and the veteran conservative politician Kofi Busia took over the reins of power. But Busia's government was no more successful than previous regimes in coping with Ghana's economic and social ills, and in January 1972 the army again intervened under Colonel Ignatius Acheampong. Ghana was ruled by a National Redemption Council until 1975, when this was downgraded and a new legislative and administrative institution, the Supreme Military Council, was set up. Both councils were headed by Colonel Acheampong. In the early 1970s the economic position of Ghana improved, with the world price of cocoa reaching a record of £975 a ton in 1974. But Ghana was already feeling the effects of the immense increase in the price of oil in 1973–4, and its modest boom rapidly evaporated in the face of the collapse in commodity prices, including cocoa. Fluctuating prices, 150 per cent inflation and shortages led to renewed discontent. In 1978 Acheampong was persuaded to resign and hand over power to

335

another officer, General Akuffo. In 1979 the military establishment, which had been in power since 1972, was overthrown in a coup of young officers, led by the airforce officer Jerry Rawlings. The new regime promised to return Ghana to civilian rule, but in the meantime accused many members of the former government of corrupt practices. A number of leading figures in Ghanaian politics were executed.

For Nigeria, the transition from colonial rule to independence had been long and arduous. Independence, when it finally came to the huge country in 1960, seemed to unleash a multitude of problems. The government of the federal prime minister, Sir Abubakar Tafawa Balewa, could not cope effectively with these problems and was sitting on a veritable powder-keg. The first of a series of major explosions came in January 1966, when army officers staged a simultaneous coup in all four regions, murdering, among others, Tafawa Balewa and the premiers of the Western and Northern regions.

The political situation in Nigeria had been dangerous for some three years previously, especially in Western Nigeria, where the federal government had been keeping in power a political party which had not been elected by the people of the region. Nevertheless, the coup did not originate in the West, but among a group of young officers, mainly Easterners. They feared that the prime minister of the Northern region, the Sardauna of Sokoto, was plotting with the Western politicians a northernisation of the Nigerian army. A military government was established under the leadership of General Ironsi, which appointed army governors in the regions. Lieutenant-Colonel Ojukwu held this position in the Eastern region. The young Eastern army officers, mostly Igbo, wanted to unify the country and to reform the corruption of Nigerian politics in general. In May the regions were officially abolished, political parties were dissolved and the public service was unified.

These well-meaning but heavy-handed actions of Ironsi's government caused much fear among many people and produced a vehement reaction. Anti-federal government demonstrations broke out in the North, resulting for the first time in large-scale violence against the Igbo living there. In July 1966 there was a second army revolt in the North and in Yorubaland. Ironsi was captured and later murdered, and Lieutenant-Colonel Gowon, a Northerner from a minority tribe, became head of a new military government. The Easterners had failed to impose their own form of unified structure upon the whole of Nigeria and became increasingly alarmed at the violence of the feelings of other groups against them. In September and October there were serious massacres of some 20,000 Easterners in the North,

causing some hundreds of thousands of survivors to flee into the
Eastern region. Ojukwu refused to attend the constitutional conference set up by Gowon, which initiated the idea for the creation of
twelve 'states' within the federation in place of the four former
regions. The object of this was to transfer the decisive power from the
three large ethnic groups – Hausa, Yoruba and Igbo – into the hands
of the minority groups in all three regions.

Early in 1967 General Ankrah attempted to bring the two sides
together by inviting Gowon and Ojukwu to meet on neutral ground in
Ghana. Although they made a declaration rejecting the use of force in
settling the crisis, none of the big issues was solved. By March
Ojukwu was issuing edicts from Enugu, the capital of the Eastern
region, preventing the transference of revenue from that region to
Gowon's government. As most of the oil resources of Nigeria had been
found in the East (though not in Igboland), this meant a very serious
loss of revenue for the central authorities. On 27 May 1967 Gowon
announced the creation of twelve states (three of them in the East) in
place of the four regions. Ojukwu immediately reacted to this by
declaring the independence of the East as the republic of Biafra, on 30
May. The central government could not accept this secession, and
fighting between the two sides broke out. Ironically, perhaps, this
coincided with the great June war between Israel and the Arab states
and, like these, the Nigerians and Biafrans inevitably became
involved in international politics. Overseas countries, especially Britain, had large amounts of money invested in both parts of Nigeria.
Britain and Russia supplied military material to the federal forces,
while various other countries supplied them to the Biafrans. Unlike
the Arab–Israeli war, however, the conflict between Nigeria and
Biafra was not over in one week. At first the Biafran forces achieved
considerable successes; they crossed the Niger and induced the
Mid-Western region to declare itself independent of the federation.
But the federal forces' superiority in numbers and in armaments
began to tell. They recaptured Benin city in the Mid-West, and in
October took Enugu, the Biafran capital. In spite of these reverses the
Biafrans fought on, the conflict becoming monthly more bitter and
involving larger numbers of the civilian population. The war dragged
on until January 1970. Ojukwu fled the country, leaving what
remained of his government and country in the hands of Major-
General Effiong. Speaking in the final broadcast of Radio Biafra on
12 January 1970, Effiong addressed his 'fellow countrymen':

Throughout history, injured people have had to resort to arms in their
self-defence where peaceful negotiations failed. We are no exception. We took 337

up arms because of the sense of insecurity generated in our people by the events of 1966. We have fought in the defence of that cause. I take this opportunity to congratulate officers and men of our armed forces for their gallantry and bravery which have earned for them the admiration of the whole world . . . I am convinced now that a stop must be put to the bloodshed which is going on as a result of the war. I am also convinced that the suffering of our people must be brought to an immediate end . . . I appeal to all governments to give urgent help of relief and to prevail on the Federal Military Government to order their troops to stop all military operations. May God help us all.

On the same day Gowon told Nigerians,

Thirty months ago, we were obliged to take up arms against our brothers who were deceived and misled into armed rebellion against their fatherland. Our objective was to crush the rebellion, to maintain the territorial integrity of our nation, to assert the ability of the Black man to build a strong, progressive and prosperous modern nation, and to ensure respect, dignity and equality in the community of nations for our prosperity. We welcome with open arms . . . all those who were led into futile attempts to disintegrate the country. Long live one united Nigeria. We thank God for his mercy.

The cost of human and material resources of the civil war was enormous. The task of reconciliation, the restoration of a sense of national unity and economic revival were undertaken by the military federal and state governments under Gowon with considerable initial success. But many of Nigeria's serious problems remained unresolved: inequalities of wealth, urban and rural unemployment or underemployment, industrial, agricultural and governmental ineffectiveness, a waste of the revenues from Nigeria's oil. Above all there was a weak central leadership. In July 1975 Gowon, who was absent at an OAU summit meeting in Kampala, was overthrown by a coup organised by a northerner, General Murtala Muhammed. 'Never', wrote a reporter, 'can a change of this kind have been introduced with such skill and civility . . . and it must not be forgotten that in Nigeria anything short of perfection would have had disastrous consequences.'[1]

General Muhammed set in motion a more energetic and effective government. Seven new states were created (making a total of nineteen). But within a few months, in February 1976, Muhammed was murdered in yet another, but this time abortive, coup. He was succeeded by Lieutenant-General Olusegun Obasanjo, a Yoruba, who initiated further moves to achieve the still-elusive national unity. But to a considerable extent the ancient ethnic divisions were becoming overshadowed by class tensions in the industrial sectors and in the

[1] *West Africa*, London, 11 August 1975.

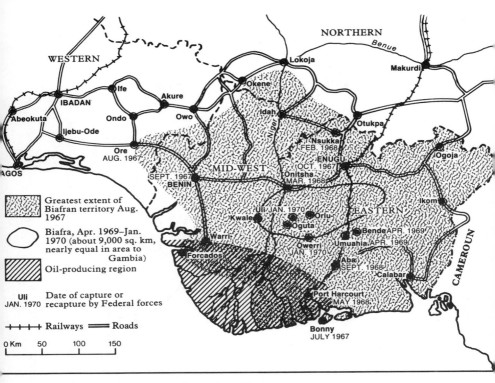

38 The Nigerian civil war: May 1967 to January 1970

Within the map:

NORTHERN
WESTERN
Benue
Lokoja
Makurdi
Ife
Akure
Okene
IBADAN
Owo
Idah
Otukpa
Abeokuta
Ondo
Ijebu-Ode
Nsukka
FEB. 1968
Ogoja
Ore
AUG. 1967
ENUGU
OCT. 1967
AGOS
MID-WEST
Onitsha
MAR. 1968
SEPT. 1967
BENIN
Ikom
EASTERN
Kwale
Uli JAN. 1970
Orlu
Oguta
Bende APR. 1969
Warri
Owerri
JAN. 1970
Umuahia APR. 1969
Forcados
Aba
SEPT. 1968
Calabar
CAMEROUN
Port Harcourt
MAY 1968
Bonny
JULY 1967

Legend:

Greatest extent of Biafran territory Aug. 1967

Biafra, Apr. 1969–Jan. 1970 (about 9,000 sq. km, nearly equal in area to Gambia)

Oil-producing region

Uli JAN. 1970 — Date of capture or recapture by Federal forces

+++++ Railways === Roads

0 Km   50   100   150

urban slums. The year 1978 was one of great tensions, with Obasanjo's regime committed to a return to civilian rule.

Nigeria was the most powerful state economically and militarily in West Africa; it had the largest population of all African countries and was able to play an increasingly dominant role in organisations such as the Economic Community of West African States (ECOWAS). The civil war had undoubtedly done much to weld the country into a single nation, and after that the military government provided an umbrella of security under which a mainly civilian bureaucracy functioned with considerable efficiency. The real test of Nigeria's stability would, however, come with the return to civilian politics in October 1979.

THE CONGO BASIN: ZAÏRE AND ITS NEIGHBOURS

The strife in Zaïre became chronic. It showed no sign of abating even

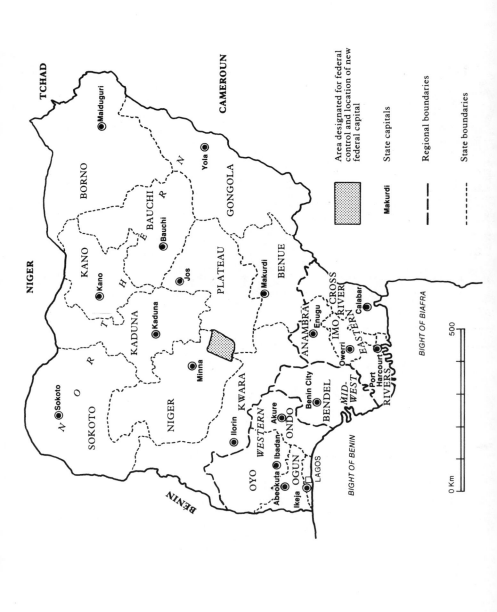

NIGER

TCHAD

CAMEROUN

BENIN

BIGHT OF BENIN

BIGHT OF BIAFRA

SOKOTO

KANO

BORNO

KADUNA

BAUCHI

NIGER

PLATEAU

GONGOLA

BENUE

KWARA

OYO

WESTERN

ONDO

OGUN

LAGOS

BENDEL

MID-WEST

ANAMBRA

IMO

CROSS RIVER

EASTERN

RIVERS

●Sokoto

●Kano

●Maiduguri

●Kaduna

●Bauchi

Yola ●

●Jos

●Makurdi

●Minna

●Ilorin

Akure
●

Abeokuta● ●Ibadan

●Ikeja

Benin City
●

Enugu
●

●Owerri

Calabar
●

Port
Harcourt

N I G E R   R.

B E N U E   R.

Area designated for federal
control and location of new
federal capital

▨ Makurdi

Regional boundaries

State capitals

State boundaries

0 Km   500

after the forced reincorporation of Katanga in 1963 (see Chapter 20). The UN forces withdrew, but the Congolese army could not keep the peace throughout the vast territory. The first of a new series of disturbances began in Kwilu province late in 1963. This was led by the Marxist-trained Pierre Mulele, who organised guerrilla bands known as the Jeunesse, on the model of the Vietcong and other groups in South-East Asia. Another revolt broke out in central Kivu in 1964. The governments appointed by President Kasavubu depended heavily upon American military and economic aid. The Communist countries, and several African states, supported the followers of the murdered Lumumba, who were responsible for the insurrections in the eastern half of Zaïre. Tshombe reappeared upon the political scene and formed an administration in July 1964. He employed white mercenary soldiers from Europe, Rhodesia and South Africa to stiffen the Congolese army, which, although well armed, showed little inclination to fight. Rebel forces under Gbenye controlled Stanleyville and set up a People's Republic of the Congo there. To rescue Europeans in the city, Belgian paratroopers were flown in by US planes. Stanleyville was recaptured only after bitter fighting, in which many people were killed, including Europeans. Once again, the internal conflict in the Congo threatened to become an international issue.

In 1965 elections under a new constitution were held; in a confused political situation, Tshombe's party received the most votes but did not have a majority in the new National Assembly. Kasavubu dismissed Tshombe as prime minister, but relations between the two politicians and their factions were so bitter that in November 1965 the army under General Mobutu again intervened – on this occasion, apparently permanently. A Government of National Unity was set up, headed by one of Mobutu's officers, with one minister for each of the twenty-one provinces into which Zaïre was divided – later reduced to eleven and then increased to nineteen, in efforts (similar to those in Nigeria) to come to terms with the country's ethnic diversity by bureaucratic and administrative means.

The main focus of national unity has been President Mobutu himself. He ceased to be yet another army commander involved in yet another coup, and quickly became the dictator of his country. Amin of Uganda and Bokassa of the Central African Empire assumed similar roles. Mobutu identified himself, and had himself identified by use of most persuasive propaganda, with the emerging nationhood of Zaïre. The old colonial names were changed to African ones – Congo to Zaïre, Leopoldville to Kinshasa. The first few years of Mobutu's   341

39   Nigeria: old regions, new states

rule coincided with a boom in the world price of copper, as did those of President Kaunda in Zambia. Zaïre's agricultural economy recovered, and large-scale development projects were commenced, including a huge hydro-electric scheme on the lower Congo (Zaïre) river and a large steel-mill near Kinshasa. Zaïre continued to rely largely on American aid, although close ties were being made with Belgium (the old colonial ruler), France and West Germany. As the more optimistic times of the late 1960s and early 1970s moved into the difficult economic period of the mid-1970s (the crisis for Zaïre as for the rest of the world came from the 1973 increase in oil prices), so Mobutu's hold over Zaïre became more uncertain. The victory of the MPLA in the Angolan revolt and civil war (see Chapter 21) not only produced an ideologically hostile neighbour but also, as a result of the fighting, caused the cutting of the Benguela railway, the life-line between the mineral wealth of Shaba (Katanga) and the outside world. In a worsening economic situation, Mobutu became even more dependent upon American aid – Zaïre's burden of overseas debt was colossal. In a continent which, within the space of a few years, had become a battleground between Marxist and anti-Marxist protagonists, Zaïre became one of the main bastions of the American position in Africa. It was also seen to be a country of vital economic and strategic importance by the more western-inclined African states and by the two main continental European ex-colonial countries, France and Belgium.

When, in 1977 and 1978, Katangese dissidents (the survivors of Tshombe's old forces) invaded Shaba from Angola, and in the latter year occupied Kolwezi, important for its chrome as well as its copper-mines, it was French and Belgian paratroopers, and an African force made up of Moroccan, Senegalese, Togolese and Gabonese contingents, who saved the day for Mobutu. Even before the Shaba invasions, Mobutu's government was being accused of corruption and brutality. In 1976 the president announced a radical overhaul of the machinery of government, instituting the Mouvement Populaire de la Révolution, which was to introduce more democratic structures into the dictatorial regime; but in 1979 there were further signs of unrest and discontent. Beset as it has been during the two decades of independence by political unrest and economic dislocation almost unprecedented elsewhere in Africa, Zaïre was nevertheless potentially one of the richest and most powerful of African countries. Its greatest economic problem was the slow and antiquated system of river communications linking its capital and its only seaport with the productive regions around the peripheries of the river basin.

To the south of Zaïre, Zambia gained its independence after the break-up of the Central African Federation (see Chapter 21). Its relations with Zaïre were close, as the two countries shared the great Copperbelt. After it became independent in 1964, Zambia was dominated politically by the personality of President Kaunda and by two issues over which it has had little direct control: the fortunes of the huge copper-mining industry and Rhodesia's UDI. Kaunda formulated the particular kind of nationalist development, called Zambian Humanism, which became the official policy of his country. This stressed the need for self-sacrifice and community spirit in the building of a new nation, composed as it was of different tribal/ethnic groups, and with a most unbalanced economy – on the one hand a very poor and long-neglected rural sector and on the other the foreign-owned copper-mining industry. In 1968 a number of smaller foreign companies were partly nationalised, under the control of an Industrial Development Corporation, and the following year the Zambian government acquired a majority holding in the copper companies. But Zambia could not control the price of copper. This had been high throughout most of the 1960s, and independent Zambia was able to get off to a fairly prosperous start. By the late 1960s, however, the world price of copper began to fall, and it continued to do so during most of the 1970s, with a disastrous effect upon the Zambian economy.

The Rhodesian UDI, the imposition of sanctions, and the closing of the border (and therefore of transport links) between the two countries all brought further severe strains to the economy. The opening of the Tanzam railway in 1975 relieved pressure on the transport system to some extent. The railway, which linked Zambia with the Tanzanian port of Dar es Salaam, had been constructed with Chinese money and partly by Chinese labour. It was the largest overseas venture undertaken by the People's Republic of China, and was viewed with concern by western countries and with some alarm by South Africa. The difficult economic situation and the strain of playing host to Zimbabwean nationalist parties and armed forces put the Zambian political system under acute stress. In 1971 Simon Kapwepwe, formerly vice-president and Kaunda's right-hand man, formed a party opposing Kaunda's United National Independence Party (UNIP). Early the following year Kapwepwe was put in detention, and at the end of 1972 Kaunda declared Zambia to be a one-party state. In 1978 the constitutional rules were changed to prevent Kapwepwe standing against Kaunda in the president's fourth re-election to office. Kapwepwe was a Bemba, the largest ethnic group in Zambia, 343 and, as so often happens in black Africa, political and economic dissatisfaction in the country took the form of ethnic or tribal unrest. Increasingly, Zambia's chances of economic recovery and Kaunda's chances of political survival came to depend upon a speedy settlement of the Rhodesian conflict and the emergence of a strong and sympathetic government in Zimbabwe. The presence of Nkomo's forces in Zambia increased tension but also enabled Kaunda to encourage a settlement of the conflict.

Rwanda and Burundi, the tiny states in the highlands to the east of Zaïre, were heavily dependent upon the fortunes and good will of their neighbours. For the transportation of all goods they relied upon the networks of Zaïre to the west and of Uganda, Kenya and Tanzania to the east, and these have not always proved reliable. People have had to leave these overpopulated countries to seek work and money elsewhere, travelling as immigrant labourers to the plantations and towns of Uganda and to the mines of Shaba. The troubles in Shaba (Katanga), especially in the early 1960s, seriously affected Rwanda and Burundi and aggravated their basic ethnic tensions (see pp. 265–6). The massacre of the Batutsi by the Bahutu in Rwanda in the 1960s was paralleled tragically by a similar massacre of Bahutu by Batutsi in Burundi in the 1970s. Both countries experienced numerous constitutional and governmental changes; both suffered a decline in their agricultural potential, largely as a result of the pressure of population.

To the north of Zaïre an arc of states which formerly composed the territories of French Equatorial Africa have experienced materially different political fortunes. Gabon remained within the western orbit and, following the example of Ivory Coast, set about the exploitation of its potentially rich mineral and agricultural resources, using mainly French capital and expertise. French troops intervened in 1964 to rescue President M'Ba from a military coup, a French minister remarking, 'It is not possible to leave a few machine-gun carriers free to seize at any time a Presidential Palace, and it is precisely because such a threat was foreseen and foreseeable that the new-born states signed agreements with France to guard against such risks' (Alain Peyrefitte, minister of the interior). Albert Bongo succeeded to the presidency in 1967 following the death of Léon M'Ba.

A military coup in the Congo Republic (that is, the country to the north of the lower Congo) in 1964 brought a pro-communist government into power, and the state remained a staunchly Marxist People's Republic. A counter-coup in 1966 was foiled with the help of Cuban military advisers – the first intervention by the Cubans in African affairs. The Dacko government of the Central

African Republic also had Marxist, pro-Chinese tendencies until it was overthrown in 1966 by Colonel Jean-Bedel Bokassa. Bokassa, who was strongly pro-French when it suited him, sometimes acted with brutality against opposition. He attempted to consolidate his position by proclaiming himself emperor of the Central African Empire. It was ironic that early in 1979 Bokassa had to call upon Zaïrean soldiers to quell riots in Bangui at the same time as Belgian paratroops flew in to Kinshasa to strengthen Mobutu's army. Later in 1979 Bokassa was overthrown in a coup staged by Dacko.

Tchad was beset by strife not dissimilar to that which erupted in many of the Sahel countries, as well as experiencing the dreadful drought of the 1970s. This strife has been between southern black people, who are Christians or animists and who practise agriculture, and the lighter-skinned desert people, who are Muslims and pastoralists. Tchad has been rent by the ethnic civil war since independence, with France supporting the southern-dominated government and Libya (and other countries) the northern rebels, called Frolinat (the National Liberation Front). This strife abated in 1979 when the opposing forces came together to form a rather shaky coalition government, but many of the basic problems remain unresolved.

In the transitional period to independence, Cameroun was the only African country to attempt the difficult task of uniting territories which had had many years of French and British (and, before the First World War, German) administrations. In many respects, this experiment has been successful, and Cameroun has maintained a fair measure of economic progress. Politically, the price for this stability (which in the French-speaking part of the country has been in marked contrast to the violence of the decade before independence – see Chapter 18) has been an institutionalised, non-military kind of dictatorial regime under Ahmadou Ahidjo, which has dealt harshly with its opponents. But in this respect the record of Cameroun, or of the Central African Empire, pales into insignificance when compared with that of Equatorial Guinea, the former Spanish territories of Rio Muni and Fernando Poo, which became an independent republic in 1968. Between 1968 and 1979 President Macias Nguema terrorised the inhabitants of this unhappy little state.

EAST AFRICA

No single East African country overshadows the region as Nigeria does 345

West Africa and Zaïre does Central Africa, and their histories since independence have shown great diversity. Kenya, with strong presidential institutions, has followed a capitalist road toward economic development. Nyerere's Tanzania, as we saw in the preceding chapter (p. 324), has been the leading exponent of African socialism. Uganda under Obote made some moves in the direction of socialism, but under Amin it pursued a uniquely idiosyncratic course which defies any easy definition. Malawi, like Kenya, has been western-capitalist (and indeed, South African-capitalist) in orientation. All states shared one feature: the rise to dominance of the leader figure – Kenyatta, Nyerere, Amin, Banda.

In many respects, Kenya was the Ivory Coast of East Africa, with Jomo Kenyatta, until his death in 1978, playing the role of Houphouet-Boigny. Foreign investment and participation in the economy were encouraged, with quite a number of the old white settlers of colonial times remaining in farming and in commerce. The political unity achieved by Kenyatta shortly after independence was severely shaken in 1966 when the vice-president, Oginga Odinga, resigned his position and formed a party to rival KANU. The government banned this party in 1969, and Odinga was placed in detention for a time. The assassination of Tom Mboya in 1969 was a further indication of political insecurity. But Kenyatta, his ministers and advisers were busy mending the fences and building up a position of great strength. Although Kenya's parliament continued to sit, and elections were held, political and economic power has come to reside in the office of the president. The old antagonisms of Kenya's ethnic groups have become absorbed to some extent by this office, which operates an elaborate spoils system and effectively controls the country. The regime has adopted a flexible policy in dealing with opposition: a mixture of toughness and liberality, where a vocal press is free to criticise and to unveil corruption. Kenyatta was succeeded in 1978 by the vice-president, Daniel arap Moi, and the unity forged by the Kenyatta regime appears to have survived his death (arap Moi is a member of the Tugen, a small ethnic group). But Kenya has in particularly sharply defined forms the problems of Africa – inequalities of wealth, productive 'luxury' farming areas and a poor peasantry, urban unemployment, a high population growth, and the difficulty, if not impossibility, for the government of meeting rising expectations.

In Tanzania, Nyerere's government similarly survived plots in the late 1960s allegedly aimed at its overthrow, but an electoral system had been devised which absorbed much criticism and discontent within the overall framework of TANU. For a time, Nyerere took time off from being president to build up the local and central apparatus of TANU, to the extent that the party has become the effective government of Tanzania. In 1976 Tanzania and the turbulent island of Zanzibar formally completed the union to which they had committed themselves in 1964, when a communist-inspired revolution overthrew the four-week-old government of Zanzibar (the first important revolution to shake the newly woven fabric of independent Africa). As we have seen (p. 324) Nyerere's ideas on African socialism found concrete expression in the Arusha Declaration of 1967 and operation of the *ujamaa* schemes. Doubts have been expressed about the effectiveness of the Tanzanian experiment and of the parts played by some of the president's advisers, both Tanzanian and foreign, but nevertheless, Nyerere's achievement, in difficult circumstances, has been of great significance for independent Africa.

In Uganda the army was used in 1966 – the year of the military coups – to effect a revolution. The prime minister, Milton Obote, facing dissension within his cabinet, arrested five of his colleagues, including those nearest to the Kabaka Yekka element in the ruling alliance. He next introduced and unconstitutionally drove through parliament a new and unitary constitution, doing away with the privileged position of Buganda within the country, and, on meeting with defiance from the Kabaka and his council, the Lukiiko, sent in the army to attack the Kabaka's palace and the Buganda government headquarters. The Kabaka fled the country and was deposed and succeeded in the presidency by Obote. In September 1967 a new constitution came into operation, which formally declared that Uganda was a republic. The old kingdoms were abolished and even the name of Buganda disappeared: it was divided into four separate districts. These changes represented the victory of the formerly underprivileged, mainly non-Bantu-speaking northern peoples over the once powerful Bantu kingdoms, whose authority had been protected by British colonial rule. But Obote in Uganda faced the disruptive effects of what has been termed 'the politics of poverty', so familiar to most African rulers. Opposition to his rule developed, not only among Baganda; and the army officers, although largely non-Bantu like Obote himself, mistrusted the president and some of his more extravagant schemes. While Obote was attending the Commonwealth Conference of 1971 in Singapore (which was primarily concerned with the Arms for South Africa issue) General Amin took over the government.

The initial period of Idi Amin's rule in Uganda gave little indication of the radical changes to come. Members of Obote's Lango tribe had made themselves unpopular, especially in the army, and Amin, a Muslim from the small Kakwa tribe in the north-western corner of the country, was able to pose as a restorer of unity. He appeased the Baganda by bringing back the body of Kabaka Mutesa, who had died in exile in London in 1969, for reinterment in Buganda. He promised a quick return to civilian government. But once in power, Amin soon made himself absolute master of Uganda. He whipped up popular feeling against the Ugandan Asian community, who numbered some 50,000, and eventually in 1972 expelled them all, whether they held Ugandan passports or not. Most of these expelled Asians settled in Britain, Canada, India and Pakistan. The Ugandan economy suffered considerably because of this expulsion of an important element in the commercial life of the country.

By 1973 Amin had to face opposition within Uganda, and this he dealt with by sometimes extremely brutal methods: public executions and assassinations, including persons of high public standing, and the mass murder of whole sections of the army and police from the tribes thought most likely to oppose him. In 1973 the International Commission of Jurists accused his government of maintaining a reign of terror; Amin retaliated against foreigners in Uganda, especially Britons. By the mid-1970s, Amin had assumed dictatorial powers in Uganda and had further antagonised Ugandans, many of whom were Christians, by his promotion of Islam and his close ties with the Muslim world, especially with Colonel Gaddafy of Libya. Amin survived a number of plots on his life. Furthermore, there was almost continual border friction with Tanzania (where Obote had taken refuge), which sometimes – in 1973 and 1978 for instance – flared up into open conflict. In 1979 a Tanzanian invasion overthrew Amin's regime and installed a provisional government composed of Ugandan civilians.

Given the ideological differences between Kenya and Tanzania, and the conflicts between Tanzania and Uganda, it is not surprising that the East African Community, which had been established in 1965 (as the successor of the colonial East African High Commission and the later East African Common Services Organisation), came under much strain and broke down completely in 1976, in spite of the proposals for regional economic development and co-operation envisaged by the Arusha Declaration (1967). The completion of the Tanzam railway in 1976 strengthened the ties between Nyerere and Kaunda of Zambia, and Tanzania became one of the Front Line states

348

in the black–white conflict over southern Africa (see p. 285). Amin generally maintained cordial relations with President Mobutu of Zaïre, while Kenya has been friendly with Ethiopia, whether under Haile Selassie or under the later Marxist regime, as a result of the two countries' hostility to Somali expansionist aims. Thus the two decades of independence have seen the three main East African countries drift apart, rather than retain even the measure of integration and common services of the colonial period.

Malawi, the third member (with Northern and Southern Rhodesia – see p. 270) of the erstwhile Central African Federation, has been affected greatly by the conflicts in the white-ruled countries to the south. Hastings Banda, who has been president since independence in 1964, has, however, elected to follow a very different road from the 'siege' conditions of Kaunda's Zambia. Soon after independence, Banda quarrelled with some of his younger ministers, had them dismissed and arrested those who did not flee the country. After some months of disturbances, Banda imposed his will with the aid of loyal and sometimes brutal detachments of Young Pioneers. Since 1965 Banda has ruled as a dictator, allowing no opposition to his policies. As Malawi was almost wholly an agricultural land, Banda argued that close economic ties with the richer white-dominated countries to the south were essential for its development. He therefore maintained friendly relations with Portuguese Mozambique, with Rhodesia to some extent and in particular with South Africa.

Malawi became the only black African state in which South African money and expertise played a significant part in economic development. With South African finance and material aid, Banda had a new capital built at Lilongwe. In 1970 Vorster visited Malawi to witness the good works being performed by his fellow countrymen, and the following year Banda returned the compliment by going to South Africa on a ceremonial state visit. This ostentatious exchange of state visits was the high-water mark of South Africa's policy of 'dialogue'. By the end of the 1970s Banda had survived a number of internal crises, had moved warily out of the embrace of South Africa and had started to build up more acceptable relations with his black African neighbours.

The Malagasy Republic, the state which occupies the large island of Madagascar off the south-east coast of Africa, has experienced problems similar to those of many countries of mainland Africa. The decade of the 1960s was comparatively peaceful for the islanders (of mixed Indonesian, African and Arab descent – see pp. 266–7), under the benign rule of President Philibert Tsiranana, who was pro-French 349 and almost obsessively anti-communist. Tsiranana responded to South Africa's 'detente' policy, and links were formed with the Pretoria regime. By the early 1970s, however, economic difficulties and shortcomings intensified class and ethnic differences, and what has been called 'a profound political malaise' developed. Throughout the 1970s, there was much social unrest, often breaking out into serious rioting. In 1972 Tsiranana handed over power to the army, in the person of General Ramanantsoa.

Many of Tsiranana's policies were reversed. Relations with South Africa were broken off, while links with Russia and other communist countries were made for the first time. But the army regime did not itself become Marxist – indeed, a referendum was held at the end of 1972 to beat off threats from Marxist groups by showing apparent popular support for Ramanantsoa. The army adopted strongly nationalist policies, which were inevitably anti-French. French forces withdrew from the military base of Diego Suarez, and many formal ties with France were broken: the considerable number of French people who lived on Madagascar were declared foreigners. Indeed, 1973 has been called the first real year of Malagasy independence.

The army also attempted social reforms. There was a rural reorganisation scheme, which was to set up local *communes* to manage their own affairs, and these were to sell their produce to state agencies. Malagasy (the language of those of Indonesian descent) was declared the sole medium of instruction. These changes led to even greater unrest, with a large-scale rural uprising in the south of the island. A left-wing group, led by Didier Ratsiraka, won the elections in 1976. Ethnic conflict and social unrest continued, although by the end of the 1970s the Ratsiraka regime had succeeded in bringing more stability to the island. With the advent of a left-wing government, the republic aligned itself more closely with communist countries and completed the break with France. The position of Madagascar in the Indian Ocean makes the island of great importance in international politics.

THE INTERNATIONAL RELATIONS OF AFRICAN STATES

As they became independent, the leaders of most African states announced their allegiance to the ideals of Pan-Africanism, which had found a leading advocate in Kwame Nkrumah. In practice, however, the internal problems which faced these young states led most politicians to see Pan-African unity as a long-term goal rather than as something that could be realised in the near future. A few countries – mainly Ghana, Guinea and Algeria – which tended to be more radical politically, clung to the former ideal and came together as the Casablanca group. These were opposed by the Brazzaville–Monrovia group of states, which were much more cautious. Attempts to form local unions or regional organisations in the early 1960s failed, and the differences between the two 'groups' were seen to be more a matter of rhetoric than substance. In May 1963 the leaders of all the then independent states came together in Addis Ababa to form the Organisation of African Unity (OAU). It was a triumph for the political skill and experience of Emperor Haile Selassie and of the high esteem in which he was held at that time that the headquarters of the organisation was stationed in the Ethiopian capital.

The charter of the OAU fell short of the political union demanded by Nkrumah and the older generation of Pan-Africanists. Nyerere in a speech at the end of 1963 stated,

One of the hard facts we have to face in the way to African unity is that this unity means on the part of countries the surrender of sovereignty and on the part of individual leaders the surrender of high positions. We must face quite squarely the fact that so far there has been no such surrender in the name of African unity.

But the specialised agencies or commissions set up by the OAU, especially in the economic and social fields, have come to play an important part in African affairs. On the economic front, the OAU and its specialist agencies have worked closely with the powerful UN Economic Commission for Africa (ECA). In particular, these two organisations were highly successful in bringing together forty-six African, Caribbean and Pacific countries (ACP) and the European Economic Community to sign the Lomé Convention of 1975. The agreement gave the ACP countries privileged access to the European market, economic development and other benefits. A number of regional economic groupings were set up in the 1970s, of which the most significant is the fifteen-nation Economic Community of West African States (ECOWAS), set up in 1976. This West African common market should enable the wealth of Nigeria to fertilise the economies of its poorer neighbours. But from 1973–4 (the international oil crisis year), in spite of the work of the OAU and the ECA and growing international concern, the overall economic prospects of Africa have deteriorated. The executive secretary of the ECA, Adebayo Adedeji, stated in 1976 that 'it can be truthfully said that   351 each time the industrialised market economies sneeze, the African economies catch pneumonia!'

The second main preoccupation of the OAU has been with the racial conflict in southern Africa. For this purpose an African Liberation Committee was established with its headquarters in Dar es Salaam, of which the most active members have naturally been those situated closest to the frontiers of black and white rule. From the earliest days of Tanzanian independence, Nyerere declared his solidarity with the liberation movement in Mozambique and soon turned the southern province of his country into a closed area where guerrillas could be trained and supplies built up. In due course Zambia followed suit, harbouring exiles from Zimbabwe (Rhodesia), South-West Africa (Namibia) and Angola. With the independence of Mozambique and Angola, these countries joined the circle of Front Line states, to which Botswana gradually acceded, serving in the role of a corridor through which exiles from western Zimbabwe and South Africa could pass in safety to training-grounds further north. After years of military and political struggle, an independent black-governed Zimbabwe emerged in 1980. Thereafter, the frontiers between black and white rule moved even further south, to the Limpopo and Kunene rivers. South Africa tried to buy time by giving support to the Smith regime in Rhodesia, and then, briefly, to the 'internal settlement' government of Muzorewa. But even South Africa's more determined policy to maintain its presence in Namibia would appear to be untenable in the face of universal opposition.

If events follow approximately the course which we have suggested, the coming years in the southern states of middle Africa are unlikely to be altogether peaceful. There will be fighting and sabotage, coups and counter-coups, all made more savage by the flow of foreign arms and explosives. The already feeble economies of the region will be threatened still further. The living standards of most people will fall. There is no necessary reason, however, to anticipate a general cataclysm that would involve the continent as a whole or the outside world. Thus far, at least, the forces of anti-colonial 'liberation' have mostly been generated within or near the territories of the states in question. Black Africa as a whole may be ideologically aligned with the process of 'liberation', but most states have too many problems of their own to commit their regular forces far beyond their borders. And wars of conquest undertaken by powers outside Africa seem unlikely to be repeated in the near future. The 'liberation' of southern Africa will come, when it does, mainly from the inside. Only if the greatest powers in the world should see it as in their interests to combine to shake the grip of the last white minority government in the continent could a slow, mainly internal process be greatly accelerated. And probably this could only happen as a sudden reaction to the outbreak of internal violence on a catastrophic scale.

Suggestions for further reading

GENERAL

General histories
Philip Curtin, Steven Feierman, Leonard Thompson and Jan Vansina, *African History* (New York and London, 1978)
Catherine Coquery-Vidrovitch and Henri Moniot, *L'Afrique noire de 1800 à nos jours* (Paris, 1974)
Basil Davidson, *Africa: history of a continent* (London, 1966)
Hubert Deschamps, *Histoire générale de l'Afrique noire* (2 vols., Paris, 1970–1)
J. D. Fage and Roland Oliver (eds.), *The Cambridge History of Africa*, vol. 5, *c. 1790–c. 1870*, ed. John E. Flint (Cambridge, 1976); vols. 6–8 (forthcoming)
J. D. Fage and Roland Oliver, *A Short History of Africa*, 5th edn (Harmondsworth, 1975)
J. D. Fage, *A History of Africa* (London, 1978)

Background works
David B. Barrett, *Schism and Renewal in Africa* (Nairobi, 1968)
J. D. Fage, *An Atlas of African History* 2nd edn. (London, 1978)
Richard Gray and David Birmingham (eds.), *Pre-Colonial African Trade* (London, 1970)
Jean Hiernaux, *The People of Africa* (London, 1974)
N. Q. King, *Religions of Africa: a pilgrimage into traditional religion* (New York, 1976)
I. M. Lewis (ed.), *Islam in Tropical Africa* (London, 1966)
J. Forbes Monroe, *African and the International Economy, 1800–1960* (London, 1976)
A. B. Mountjoy and Clifford Embleton, *Africa: a geographical survey* (London, 1965)

Partition
Henri Brunschwig, *L'avènement de l'Afrique noire* (Paris, 1963)
Ronald Robinson and John Gallagher, *Africa and the Victorians: the official mind of imperialism* (London, 1961)

Colonial period
Raymond Leslie Buell, *The Native Problem in Africa* (2 vols., New York, 1928)

S. Herbert Frankel, *Capital Investment in Africa* (London, 1938)
L. H. Gann and Peter Duignan (eds.), *Colonialism in Africa, 1870–1960* (5 vols., Cambridge, 1969–75)
Lord Hailey, *An African Survey: revised* (London, 1957)
P. Robson and D. A. Dury (eds.), *The Economies of Africa* (London, 1969)

Nationalism and independence
Giovanni Arrighi and John Saul (eds.), *Essays on the Political Economy of Africa* (London, 1973)
James Coleman and Carl G. Rosberg (eds.), *Political Parties and National Integration in Africa* (Berkeley, Calif., 1964)
Franz Fanon, *The Wretched of the Earth* (Harmondsworth, 1965)
Peter Gutkind and Immanuel Wallerstein, *The Political Economy of Contemporary Africa* (Beverly Hills, Calif., 1976)
Thomas Hodgkin, *Nationalism in Colonial Africa* (London, 1956)
Guy Hunter, *The New Societies of Tropical Africa* (London, 1962)
Peter Lloyd (ed.), *The New Elites of Tropical Africa* (London, 1966)
Robert I. Rotberg and Ali A. Mazrui (eds.), *Protest and Power in Black Africa* (New York, 1970)

BY REGION

North Africa
J. M. Abun-Nasr, *A History of the Maghrib* (Cambridge, 1971)
Samir Amin, *The Maghreb in the Modern World* (Harmondsworth, 1970)
Gabriel Baer, *Studies in the Social History of Modern Egypt* (Chicago, 1969)
Jacques Berques, *French North Africa: the Maghreb between two world wars* (London, 1967)
Robert Collins and Robert Tignor, *Egypt and the Sudan* (Englewood Cliffs, N.J., 1967)
P. M. Holt, *A Modern History of the Sudan* (Oxford, 1961)
Wilfred Knapp, *North West Africa: a political and economic survey*, 3rd edn (Oxford, 1977)
Tom Little, *Egypt* (London, 1958)
Henri Terrasse, *Histoire du Maroc*, vol. 2 (Casablanca, 1950)
P. J. Vatikiotis, *The Modern History of Egypt* (London, 1969)

West Africa
J. F. Ade Ajayi and Michael Crowder (eds.), *History of West Africa*, vol. 2 (London, 1974)
Dennis Austin, *Politics in Ghana, 1946–1960* (London, 1964)
James S. Coleman, *Nigeria: a background to nationalism* (Berkeley, Calif., 1958)
Michael Crowder, *West Africa under Colonial Rule*, new edn (London, forthcoming)

Philip Foster, *Education and Social Change in Ghana* (Chicago, 1965)

A. G. Hopkins, *An Economic History of West Africa* (London, 1973)

Martin Kilson, *Political Change in a West African State: a study of the moderni-zation process in Sierra Leone* (Cambridge, Mass., 1966)

David Kimble, *A Political History of Ghana: the rise of Gold Coast nationalism, 1850–1928* (Oxford, 1963)

K. W. J. Post, *The New States of West Africa* (Harmondsworth, 1964)

Virginia Thompson and Richard Adloff, *The Emerging States of French Equatorial Africa* (Stanford, Calif., 1960)

Ivor Wilks, *Asante in the Nineteenth Century* (Cambridge, 1975)

Aristide Zolberg, *Creating Political Order: the party states of West Africa* (Chicago, 1965)

Central and eastern Africa

Roger Anstey, *King Leopold's Legacy: the Congo under Belgian rule, 1908–1960* (London, 1966)

R. Greenfield, *Ethiopia: a new political history* (London, 1965)

Vincent Harlow, E. M. Chilver and Alison Smith (eds.), *History of East Africa*, vol. 2 (Oxford, 1965)

John Iliffe, *A Modern History of Tanganyika* (London, 1979)

A. H. M. Jones and E. Monroe, *The History of Ethiopia* (London, 1955)

René Lemarchand, *Political Awakening in the Belgian Congo* (Berkeley, Calif., 1964)

Colin Leys, *Underdevelopment in Kenya: the political economy of neo-colonialism* (London, 1975)

D. A. Low, *Buganda in Modern History* (London, 1971)

D. A. Low and Alison Smith, *History of East Africa*, vol. 3 (Oxford, 1976)

Harold G. Marcus, *The Life and Times of Menelik II of Ethiopia, 1844–1913* (Oxford, 1974)

C. G. Rosberg and John Nottingham, *The Myth of the Mau-Mau: nationalism in Kenya* (London, 1967)

Harry R. Rudin, *The Congo* (Englewood Cliffs, N.J., 1967)

Ruth Slade, *King Leopold's Congo* (London, 1962)

Crawford Young, *Politics in the Congo: decolonization and independence* (Princeton, N.J., 1965)

Southern Africa

James P. Barber, *Rhodesia: the road to rebellion* (London, 1967)

Helmut Bley, *South West Africa under German Rule* (London, 1971)

Ronald H. Chilcote, *Portuguese Africa* (Englewood Cliffs, N.J., 1967)

Hubert Deschamps, *Histoire de Madagascar* (Paris, 1960)

John Flint, *Cecil Rhodes* (London, 1976)

Richard Gray, *The Two Nations: aspects of the development of race relations in the Rhodesias and Nyasaland* (London, 1960)

C. W. Kiewiet, *A History of South Africa, Social and Economic* (Oxford, 1941)

O. Mannoni, *Prospero and Caliban* (London, 1956)

Shula Marks, *Reluctant Rebellion* (Oxford, 1970)

M. D. D. Newitt, *Portuguese Settlement on the Zambezi* (London, 1973)

Charles van Onselen, *Chibaro: African mine labour in Southern Rhodesia 1900–1933* (London, 1976)

T. O. Ranger, *Revolt in Southern Rhodesia, 1896–7* (London, 1967)

Andrew Roberts, *A History of Zambia* (London, 1976)

G. Shepperson and T. Price, *Independent African: John Chilembwe* (Edinburgh, 1958)

H. J. Simons and R. E. Simons, *Class and Colour in South Africa, 1850–1950* (Harmondsworth, 1969)

Peter Walshe, *The Rise of Nationalism in South Africa: the African National Congress, 1912–1952* (London, 1970)

Douglas L. Wheeler and René Pelissier, *Angola* (London, 1971)

Francis Wilson, *Labour in the South African Gold Mines, 1911–1969* (Cambridge, 1972)

Monica Wilson and L. M. Thompson (eds.), *The Oxford History of South Africa* (2 vols., Oxford, 1969–71)

Index

Index

Index

Guinea (*cont.*)
115, 132–3, 215; independent,
232–3, 323, 330–2, 350
Guiné Bissau, 276–7, 279, 319, 330

Habe rulers, 30–1
Haile Selassie, of Ethiopia, 185, 204,
246, 251–2, 329, 351
Hamadu Bari (Ahmadu Lobo), 32
Harrar, 86, 91–2
Hassan, of Morocco, 236–7
Haud, 184
Hausa, 5, 10, 12, 29–32, 230, 316, 337;
Britain and, 115, 118, 136
Hayford, J. E. Casely, 168, 203
head taxes, 130
Hehe, 71, 148
Heligoland, 112
Hemedi bin Abdullah, 142
Herero, 64, 141, 143, 310
Hertzog, General, 191, 196, 198, 291,
293, 295
Hijaz, 80, 100
Hinde, Sidney, 48
Hitler, Adolf, 185, 204, 206
Ho Chi Minh, 211
Hofmeyr, J. H., 196, 292
Holland, 33, 205, 211; in South Africa,
14, 24–5, 27; in West Africa, 33, 38,
42, 103
Homelands (Bantustans), South Africa,
293–4, 301–2, 304–6, 309
Hottentots, *see* Khoi
Houphouet-Boigny, Felix, 226, 232,
319–20, 323, 331–3, 346
Hova, 28, 76–7, 123, 143, 266–7
Huggins, Godfrey (Lord Malvern),
270, 272
Humanism, Zambian, 343
Husain, Dey of Algiers, 95
Hussainid dynasty, Tunis, 5
hydroelectric power, 215, 241, 271,
278–9, 316

Ibadan, 37, 217
Ibrahim Pasha, 83–5
Idris, of Libya, 182–3, 241–2
Ifni, 236
Igbo, 37, 142, 230, 336–7
Ijaw, 37, 142
Ijebu, 36–7
Ilorin emirate, 31, 37, 118
Imbangala, 43, 46
Imperial British East Africa Company,
139

Independent Schools Association,
Kenya, 170
India, 30, 205, 209–10, 212, 289, 348;
routes to, 14, 80, 93
Indian Ocean, trade of, 78, 350
Indians in East Africa, 66, 69, 140, 348
indirect rule, 97, 161–2, 174, 180, 203,
218, 316
Indo-China, 87, 205, 211
Indonesia, 211, 349
Industrial and Commercial Union,
South Africa, 197–8
industrialisation, 197, 215, 221, 241,
249, 271, 299–301, 306, 338
interlacustrine region, 16, 18, 20, 22–3,
71–2, 92
Internal Settlement (Zimbabwe), 285
International Court of Justice (The
Hague), 236, 310
Ironsi, General, 336
Isandhlwana, battle of (1879), 64
Islam (*also* Muslims), 4, 171, 173, 316;
in East Africa, 25, 27, 348; in Egypt
and Sudan, 4, 78–9, 88, 90, 182,
243–5; in North Africa, 1, 2, 9, 100,
235, 238, 242–3; in West Africa, 11,
19, 29–33, 130, 149, 164, 345
Ismail, Khedive of Egypt, 72, 85–7, 92
Ismail, son of Mohammad Ali, 81
Israel, 182, 241–2, 244, 246–50, 255,
337
Istiqlal party, Morocco, 177, 235–6
Italy, 101, 103, 200; and Eritrea, 119,
122, 183, 185, 204, 252–3; and
Ethiopia, 92, 114, 122, 169, 183–5,
251–3; and North Africa, 94, 119,
182–3, 251, 253; and Somalia,
183–5, 204, 253–4
ivory, 21, 27
Ivory Coast, 12; France and, 103, 115,
132–3, 232; independent, 233, 312,
319–20, 323, 329–30, 331–2, 344,
346
ivory-trade: East Africa, 22, 47, 50–2,
66–7, 69, 70–1, 74, 138; Egypt, 9,
81, 83, 87; Ethiopia, 92; Portuguese
government monopoly of, 47, 51–2

Jabavu, J. T., 188–9, 190, 203
Jaja of Opobo, 118
Jameson, L. S., 128
Janssens, General, 264
Japan, 205–6, 300, 310
Jawara, Sir Dauda, 333
Jesus II, of Ethiopia, 7
Jidda, 80

Index

Libya, 5, 136; Italy and, 182–3, 184–5; independent, 212, 237, 241–3, 246, 249–50, 253, 345, 348; *see also* Cyrenaica, Fezzan
Lilongwe, 349
Livingstone, David, 60, 65, 70
Lobengula, 123, 126
local government, democratic, 218–22
Loi Cadre, 232, 267
Lomé Convention, 351
London Missionary Society, 60, 76–7
Lourenço Marques (Maputo), 281–3
Lovale, 45
Lozi (Barotse), 45, 57, 141
Luanda, 22, 26–7, 42–4, 46, 65, 136, 275–7, 279–80
Luba, 16, 43, 47, 263–4
Lugard, Lord, 118, 135, 159, 161–3, 170, 174
Luhya, 74
Lumumba, Patrice, 256, 262, 264–5, 275, 290, 341
Lunda, 16, 43–4, 47, 50, 148
Luo, 74, 259
Lusaka Manifesto (1969), 313
Luthuli, Albert, 297–8
Lyautey, Marshal, 123, 174–5

Macaulay, Herbert, 203
Machel, Samora, 279, 281–2, 285, 287
Mackay, Alexander, 73
Macleod, Iain, 261, 273
Macmillan, Harold, 269, 273, 290
Madagascar, 27–8, 76–7; France and, 77, 111–12, 114, 122, 140, 143, 220, 236; in Second World War, 205, 208; independent as Malagasy Republic, 233, 266–7, 312, 349–50
Maghrib, 5, 173–5, 177–8, 235–8, 240–3; *see also* Algeria, Libya, Morocco, Tunisia
Mahdi, *see* Muhammad Ahmad
maize, introduction of, 24
Majid, of Zanzibar, 69, 75
Maji-Maji rebellion, 266
Majuba Hill, battle of (1881), 65
Makerere University College, 217
Makoko, ruler of Bateke, 20, 27, 107
Makololo (Bafokeng), 56
Malagasy Republic, *see under* Madagascar
Malan, D. F., 195, 292–3, 295
malaria, 38
Malawi, 66, 270–4, 278, 290, 312, 316, 346, 349; *see also* Nyasaland
Mali, 233, 319, 331–2

Mali Federation, 233
mamluks, 4, 14, 79–80, 181, 326
mandates, 160–1, 211, 310
Mande, 10, 12, 33, 115, 333
Mandela, Nelson, 297, 299
manioc (cassava), introduction of, 23
Mantatisi, 56, 59
marabouts, 6, 11, 96, 99, 171
Margai, Albert, 333–4
Margai, Sir Milton, 333–4
Marx, Karl, 224–5
Masai, 23, 74, 141, 143
Mashona, *see* Shona
Mashonaland, 126
Masina, 11, 32
Massawa, 79, 86, 91, 183, 185, 251
Matabele, *see* Ndebele
Matanzima, Kaiser, 302, 304
Mau-Mau, 257–8
Mauritania, 4, 7, 11, 29, 99, 132, 236, 241, 331–2
Mauritius, 28, 67, 76
Mawlay Sulaiman, of Morocco, 95
M'ba, Léon, President, 344
Mbokodvu Party, Swaziland, 309
Mboya, Tom, 256–7, 290, 346
Mbundu, 22
Menelik, of Ethiopia, 91–2, 122, 183
Mengistu, Haile Mariam, 252–3
Merina kingdom, Madagascar, 28, 76–7, 111, 123
Merriman, John X., 187–8
metal-working, 10, 16, 18, 23, 101
Mfecane, *see* Difaqane
military rule, 325–8; *see also individual countries*
Milner, Lord, 128, 188, 191
Mirambo, 71
missionaries, *see* Christian missions
'missionary road', 65
Mobutu, General, 237, 265, 281, 329–30, 341, 342, 345, 349
Moffat, Robert, 65
Mogadishu, 183–4, 253–4
Moi, Daniel arap, 346
Mokhetle, Ntsu, 308
Mombasa, 26, 69, 74, 86, 112, 121, 139
Monckton Commission, on Central African Federation, 273, 290
Mondlane, Eduardo, 277–9
Monrovia group of states, 351
Morocco, 4–7, 10, 93–4, 205; France and, 97, 114, 119, 121, 173–5; Spain and, 97, 99, 121, 174–5, 236; nationalist movement in, 175, 177–8,

Index

Urabi Pasha, 87, 110
Usuman dan Fodio, 29–32, 94

van Bilsen, Dr A. A. J., 262
Venda, 302
Vereeniging, Peace of (1902), 186
verkrampte, 296
verligte, 296
Verwoerd, Dr Hendrik, 295, 301–2, 312
Vichy regime, France, 204–5, 208, 211
Vietnam, 211, 341
Volta dam (Lake Akasombo, Ghana), 215, 316, 335
Vorster, John, 285, 295–6, 306, 308, 312–13, 349

Wadai, 9, 16, 99, 119
Wafd party, Egypt, 181
Wagadugu, 132
Wahhabi movement, 29, 79
Waldheim, Kurt, 312
Walvis Bay, 311
Watson Commission, on riots in Gold Coast, 207
Welensky, Roy, 270, 272–3
welfare states, 213–14
Wesley, John, 13
West African Students' Union, 169
Western Sahara, 236, 241, 243, 332
wheat production, Tunisia, 5
Wichale, Treaty of (1889), 77, 92, 122
Wilson, Harold, 283
Wilson, President Woodrow, 160–1
Windhoek, 311
Wingate, General F. R., 179
Winneba Ideological Institute, Ghana, 335
Witwatersrand, 111, 128, 186, 291

Xhosa, 24, 61, 188, 293, 302, 304

Yameogo, President, 332
Yao, 67, 70
Yatenga, 132
Yeke (Bayeke), 47
Yom Kippur war, 248
Yoruba, 31, 118, 142, 149, 336, 338
Yoruba language, 12, 230

Zaghlul Pasha, 181
Zaïre (Congo), 16, 18, 21–2, 42, 48–52, 71, 106, 107, 110–11, 121–2, 126, 136–8, 167, 215, 218, 221, 237, 245, 261–5, 269, 275–7, 281, 312, 319–21, 323, 326–7, 329–30, 335, 339–46, 349; *see also* Congo (Belgian)
Zambia (Northern Rhodesia), 16, 42, 45, 123, 268, 270–4, 278, 284–6, 290, 308, 312–13, 316, 342–3, 352; railway between Tanzania and, 329, 343, 349
Zanzibar, 48–9, 66, 69–70, 75–6, 92, 111–12, 121–2; Britain and, 75–6, 86, 112, 121; independent, 261, 326, 347; united with Tanganyika, 347; *see also* Tanzania
Zanzibar coast, 23, 46–7, 69, 136
Zaria, 10
zawiya (religious centres), 100, 182
Zeila, 86, 91
Zimbabwe, 22, 59, 65, 140, 209, 272, 282, 284–5, 308, 312, 316, 318, 343–4, 351; independent, 285–7, 312–13, 329, 352; *see also* Rhodesia, Southern
Zimbabwe African National Union (ZANU), 272, 284–6
Zimbabwe African People's Union (ZAPU), 272, 284–6
Zulu, 24, 55–7, 59–64, 71, 298; as Kwazulu Homeland, 293, 302, 304
Zwangendaba, 59

372